CONTENTS

SOCIAL ANXIETY DISORDER

RECOGNITION, ASSESSMENT AND TREATMENT

National Clinical Guideline Number 159

National Collaborating Centre for Mental Health

commissioned by the

**National Institute for Health
and Care Excellence**

published by
The British Psychological Society and The Royal College of Psychiatrists

British Library Cataloguing-in-Publication Data

A catalogue record for this book is available from the British Library.

ISBN-: 978-1-909726-03-1

Printed in Great Britain by Stanley L. Hunt (Printers) Ltd.

Additional material: data CD-Rom created by Pix18 (www.pix18.co.uk)

developed by	National Collaborating Centre for Mental Health
	The Royal College of Psychiatrists
	3rd Floor
	21 Prescot Street
	London
	E1 8BB
	www.nccmh.org.uk

commissioned by	National Institute for Health and Care Excellence
	1st Floor
	10 Spring Gardens
	London
	SW1X 8PG
	www.nice.org.uk

published by	The British Psychological Society
	St Andrews House
	48 Princess Road East
	Leicester
	LE1 7DR
	www.bps.org.uk

The British
Psychological Society
Promoting excellence in psychology

and

The Royal College of Psychiatrists
21 Prescot Street
London
E1 8BB
www.rcpsych.ac.uk

RC
PSYCH
ROYAL COLLEGE OF
PSYCHIATRISTS

GUIDELINE DEVELOPMENT GROUP MEMBERS

Professor David Clark (Chair, Guideline Development Group)
Professor of Experimental Psychology, University of Oxford

Professor Stephen Pilling (Facilitator, Guideline Development Group)
Director, National Collaborating Centre for Mental Health
Professor of Clinical Psychology and Clinical Effectiveness
Director, Centre for Outcomes Research and Effectiveness, University College London

Dr Evan Mayo-Wilson
Senior Systematic Reviewer and Senior Research Associate, National Collaborating Centre for Mental Health

Dr Ifigeneia Mavranezouli
Senior Health Economist, National Collaborating Centre for Mental Health

Dr Safi Afghan
Consultant Psychiatrist, Dorothy Pattison Hospital, Dudley and Walsall Mental Health Partnership NHS Trust, Walsall

Mr Benedict Anigbogu
Health Economist, National Collaborating Centre for Mental Health (until September 2012)

Mr Peter Armstrong
Director of Training, Newcastle Cognitive and Behavioural Therapies Centre, Northumberland, Tyne and Wear NHS Foundation Trust

Dr Madeleine Bennett
GP and NSPCR Fellow, University College London

Dr Sam Cartwright-Hatton
Clinical Psychologist, National Institute for Health Research Career Development Fellow, University of Sussex

Dr Cathy Creswell
Principal Research Fellow, School of Psychology and Clinical Language Sciences, University of Reading
Honorary Consultant Clinical Psychologist, Berkshire Child Anxiety Clinic, Berkshire Healthcare NHS Foundation Trust

Dr Melanie Dix
Consultant Child and Adolescent Psychiatrist, Cumbria Partnership Foundation Trust

Mr Nick Hanlon
Service User Representative and Chairman, Social Anxiety West, Bristol

Ms Kayleigh Kew
Research Assistant, National Collaborating Centre for Mental Health (until November 2012)

Ms Katherine Leggett
Senior Project Manager, National Collaborating Centre for Mental Health (from October 2012)

Dr Andrea Malizia
Consultant Psychiatrist and Clinical Psychopharmacologist, Clinical Partners and North Bristol NHS Trust

Dr Jane Roberts
Clinical Senior Lecturer and General Practitioner, University of Sunderland and GP

Mrs Kate Satrettin
Project Manager, National Collaborating Centre for Mental Health (until October 2012)

Ms Melinda Smith
Research Assistant, National Collaborating Centre for Mental Health

Mr Gareth Stephens
Service User Representative

Dr Lusia Stopa
Director of CBT Programmes and Senior Lecturer, Psychology Academic Unit, University of Southampton and Honorary Consultant Clinical Psychologist, Southern Health NHS Foundation Trust

Ms Sarah Stockton
Senior Information Scientist, National Collaborating Centre for Mental Health

Dr Clare Taylor
Senior Editor, National Collaborating Centre for Mental Health

Dr Craig Whittington
Associate Director (Clinical Effectiveness), National Collaborating Centre for Mental Health

ACKNOWLEDGEMENTS

The Guideline Development Group and the National Collaborating Centre for Mental Health review team would like to thank the **Clinical Guidelines Technical Support Unit** and specifically the following people:

Professor Tony Ades (PhD)
Professor of Public Health Science, University of Bristol

Dr Sofia Dias (PhD)
Research Fellow (Statistician), University of Bristol

Copy-editing
Ms Nuala Ernest
Assistant Editor, National Collaborating Centre for Mental Health

1   PREFACE

This guideline is concerned with the recognition, assessment and treatment of social anxiety disorder in adults (aged 18 years or older) and children and young people (from school age to 17 years) in primary and secondary care, and educational and other settings where healthcare or related interventions may be delivered. This guideline also updates and replaces the section of *Computerised Cognitive Behaviour Therapy for Depression and Anxiety* (National Institute of Health and Care Excellence [NICE] Technology Appraisal [TA] 97; NICE, 2006) that deals with phobia.

The guideline recommendations have been developed by a multidisciplinary team of healthcare professionals, people with personal experience of social anxiety disorder and guideline methodologists after careful consideration of the best available evidence. It is intended that the guideline will be useful to clinicians and service commissioners in providing and planning high-quality care for people with social anxiety disorder while also emphasising the importance of the experience of care for people with social anxiety disorder and their carers (see Appendix 1 for more details on the scope of the guideline).

Although the evidence base is rapidly expanding there are major gaps, and future revisions of this guideline will incorporate new scientific evidence as it develops. The guideline makes a number of research recommendations specifically to address gaps in the evidence base. In the meantime, it is hoped that the guideline will assist clinicians, people with social anxiety disorder and their carers by identifying the merits of particular treatments and treatment approaches where the evidence from research and clinical experience exists.

1.1   NATIONAL GUIDELINE

1.1.1   What are clinical guidelines?

Clinical practice guidelines are 'systematically developed statements that assist clinicians and patients in making decisions about appropriate treatment for specific conditions' (Mann, 1996). They are derived from the best available research evidence, using predetermined and systematic methods to identify and evaluate the evidence relating to the specific condition in question. Where evidence is lacking, the guidelines incorporate statements and recommendations based upon the consensus statements developed by the Guideline Development Group (GDG).

Clinical guidelines are intended to improve the process and outcomes of healthcare in a number of different ways. They can:
● provide up-to-date evidence-based recommendations for the management of conditions and disorders by healthcare professionals

- be used as the basis to set standards to assess the practice of healthcare professionals
- form the basis for education and training of healthcare professionals
- assist service users and their carers in making informed decisions about their treatment and care
- improve communication between healthcare professionals, service users and their carers
- help identify priority areas for further research.

1.1.2   Uses and limitation of clinical guidelines

Guidelines are not a substitute for professional knowledge and clinical judgement. They can be limited in their usefulness and applicability by a number of different factors: the availability of high-quality research evidence, the quality of the methodology used in the development of the guideline, the generalisability of research findings and the uniqueness of individuals.

Although the quality of research in this field is variable, the methodology used here reflects current international understanding on the appropriate practice for guideline development (AGREE Collaboration, 2003), ensuring the collection and selection of the best research evidence available and the systematic generation of treatment recommendations applicable to the majority of people with social anxiety disorder. However, there will always be some people for whom and situations for which clinical guideline recommendations are not readily applicable. This guideline does not, therefore, override the individual responsibility of healthcare professionals to make appropriate decisions in the circumstances of the individual, in consultation with the person with social anxiety disorder or their carer.

In addition to the clinical evidence, cost-effectiveness information, where available, is taken into account in the generation of statements and recommendations of the clinical guidelines. While national guidelines are concerned with clinical and cost effectiveness, issues of affordability and implementation costs are to be determined by the National Health Service (NHS).

In using guidelines, it is important to remember that the absence of empirical evidence for the effectiveness of a particular intervention is not the same as evidence for ineffectiveness. In addition, and of particular relevance in mental health, evidence-based treatments are often delivered within the context of an overall treatment programme including a range of activities, the purpose of which may be to help engage the child, young person or adult and provide an appropriate context for the delivery of specific interventions. It is important to maintain and enhance the service context in which these interventions are delivered, otherwise the specific benefits of effective interventions will be lost. Indeed, the importance of organising care in order to support and encourage a good therapeutic relationship is at times as important as the specific treatments offered.

1.1.3   Why develop national guidelines?

NICE was established as a Special Health Authority for England and Wales in 1999, with a remit to provide a single source of authoritative and reliable guidance for service users, professionals and the public. NICE guidance aims to improve standards of care, diminish unacceptable variations in the provision and quality of care across the NHS, and ensure that the health service is person-centred. All guidance is developed in a transparent and collaborative manner, using the best available evidence and involving all relevant stakeholders.

NICE generates guidance in a number of different ways, three of which are relevant here. First, national guidance is produced by the Technology Appraisal Committee to give robust advice about a particular treatment, intervention, procedure or other health technology. Second, NICE commissions public health intervention guidance focused on types of activity (interventions) that help to reduce people's risk of developing a disease or condition, or help to promote or maintain a healthy lifestyle. Third, NICE commissions the production of national clinical guidelines focused upon the overall treatment and management of a specific condition. To enable this latter development, NICE has established four National Collaborating Centres in conjunction with a range of professional organisations involved in healthcare.

1.1.4   From national clinical guidelines to local protocols

Once a national guideline has been published and disseminated, local healthcare groups will be expected to produce a plan and identify resources for implementation, along with appropriate timetables. Subsequently, a multidisciplinary group involving commissioners of healthcare, primary care and specialist mental health professionals, service users and carers should undertake the translation of the implementation plan into local protocols, taking into account both the recommendations set out in this guideline and the priorities set in the National Service Framework for Mental Health (Department of Health, 1999) and related documentation. The nature and pace of the local plan will reflect local healthcare needs and the nature of existing services; full implementation may take considerable time, especially where substantial training needs are identified.

1.1.5   Auditing the implementation of clinical guidelines

This guideline identifies key areas of clinical practice and service delivery for local and national audit. Although the generation of audit standards is an important and necessary step in the implementation of this guidance, a more broadly-based implementation strategy will be developed. Nevertheless, it should be noted that the Care Quality Commission in England, and the Healthcare Inspectorate Wales, will monitor the extent to which commissioners and providers of health and social care have implemented these guidelines.

1.2 THE NATIONAL SOCIAL ANXIETY DISORDER GUIDELINE

1.2.1 Who has developed this guideline?

This guideline has been commissioned by NICE and developed within the National Collaborating Centre for Mental Health (NCCMH). The NCCMH is a collaboration of the professional organisations involved in the field of mental health, national service user and carer organisations, a number of academic institutions and NICE. The NCCMH is funded by NICE and is led by a partnership between the Royal College of Psychiatrists and the British Psychological Society's Centre for Outcomes Research and Effectiveness, based at University College London.

The GDG was convened by the NCCMH and supported by funding from NICE. The GDG included people with personal experience of social anxiety disorder, and professionals in psychiatry, clinical psychology, general practice, nursing and psychiatric pharmacy.

Staff from the NCCMH provided leadership and support throughout the process of guideline development, undertaking systematic searches, information retrieval, appraisal and systematic review of the evidence. Members of the GDG received training in the process of guideline development from NCCMH staff, and the service users and carers received training and support from the NICE Public Involvement Programme. The NICE Guidelines Technical Adviser provided advice and assistance regarding aspects of the guideline development process.

All GDG members made formal declarations of interest at the outset, which were updated at every GDG meeting (see Appendix 2). The GDG met a total of 13 times throughout the process of guideline development. It met as a whole, but key topics were led by a national expert in the relevant topic. The GDG was supported by the NCCMH technical team, with additional expert advice from special advisers where needed (see Appendix 3). The group oversaw the production and synthesis of research evidence before presentation. All statements and recommendations in this guideline have been generated and agreed by the whole GDG.

1.2.2 For whom is this guideline intended?

This guideline will be relevant for children, young people and adults with social anxiety disorder and covers the care provided by primary, community, secondary, tertiary and other healthcare professionals who have direct contact with, and make decisions concerning the care of, children, young people and adults with social anxiety disorder.

The guideline will also be relevant to the work, but will not cover the practice, of those in:
● occupational health services
● social services
● the independent sector.

1.2.3   Specific aims of this guideline

The guideline makes recommendations for the recognition, assessment and treatment of social anxiety disorder. It aims to:

- improve access and engagement with treatment and services for people with social anxiety disorder
- evaluate the role of specific psychological and psychosocial interventions in the treatment of social anxiety disorder
- evaluate the role of specific pharmacological interventions in the treatment of social anxiety disorder
- integrate the above to provide best-practice advice on the care of people throughout the course of their social anxiety disorder
- promote the implementation of best clinical practice through the development of recommendations tailored to the requirements of the NHS in England and Wales.

1.2.4   The structure of this guideline

The guideline is divided into chapters, each covering a set of related topics. The first three chapters provide a general introduction to guidelines, an overview of the disorder and clinical practice, and a summary of the methods used to develop the guideline. Chapters 4 to 8 provide the evidence that underpins the recommendations about the recognition, assessment and treatment of social anxiety disorder.

Each evidence chapter begins with a general introduction to the topic that sets the recommendations in context. Depending on the nature of the evidence, narrative reviews or meta-analyses were conducted, and the structure of the chapters varies accordingly. Where appropriate, details about current practice, the evidence base and any research limitations are provided. Where meta-analyses were conducted, information is given about both the interventions included and the studies considered for review. Clinical evidence summaries are then used to summarise the evidence presented. Finally, recommendations related to each topic are presented at the end of each chapter. On the CD-ROM, full details about the included studies can be found in Appendices 12, 13, 16, 18 and 22. Where meta-analyses were conducted, the data are presented using forest plots in Appendices 14, 17 and 26 (see Text Box 1 for details).

Text Box 1: Appendices on CD-ROM

Search strategies for the identification of clinical evidence	Appendix 6
Search strategies for the identification of health economic studies	Appendix 7
Completed methodology checklists for case identification and assessment	Appendix 10
Network meta-analysis diagrams and WinBUGS code	Appendix 11

Interventions for adults (network meta-analysis): study characteristics	Appendix 12
Interventions for adults (pairwise analyses): study characteristics	Appendix 13
Interventions for adults: forest plots	Appendix 14
Interventions for adults: GRADE profiles	Appendix 15
Interventions for children and young people – study characteristics	Appendix 16
Interventions for children and young people – forest plots	Appendix 17
Interventions for adults (relapse prevention): study characteristics	Appendix 18
Interventions for children and young people: GRADE profiles	Appendix 19
Risk of bias summaries	Appendix 20
Completed methodology checklists: economic evaluations	Appendix 21
Health economic evidence tables	Appendix 22
Detailed results of guideline economic analysis	Appendix 23
Economic evidence profile	Appendix 24
Excluded studies	Appendix 25
Interventions for adults (relapse prevention): forest plots	Appendix 26

In the event that amendments or minor updates need to be made to the guideline, please check the NCCMH website (nccmh.org.uk) where these will be listed and a corrected PDF file available to download.

2   SOCIAL ANXIETY DISORDER

2.1   THE DISORDER

2.1.1   What is social anxiety disorder?

Social anxiety disorder (previously termed 'social phobia') was formally recognised as a separate phobic disorder in the mid-1960s (Marks & Gelder, 1965). The term 'social anxiety disorder' reflects current understanding, including in diagnostic manuals, and is used throughout the guideline. As set out in the *International Classification of Diseases*, 10th Revision (ICD-10) (World Health Organization, 1992) and in the *Diagnostic and Statistical Manual of Mental Disorders*, 4th Edition Text Revision (DSM-IV-TR) (American Psychiatric Association, 2000) social anxiety disorder is a persistent fear of one or more social situations where embarrassment may occur and the fear or anxiety is out of proportion to the actual threat posed by the social situation as determined by the person's cultural norms. Typical social situations can be grouped into those that involve interaction, observation and performance. These include meeting people including strangers, talking in meetings or in groups, starting conversations, talking to authority figures, working, eating or drinking while being observed, going to school, shopping, being seen in public, using public toilets and public performance including speaking. While anxiety about some of the above is common in the general population, people with social anxiety disorder can worry excessively about them and can do so for weeks in advance of an anticipated social situation. People with social anxiety disorder fear that they will say or do (involuntarily or otherwise) something that they think will be humiliating or embarrassing (such as blushing, sweating, shaking, looking anxious, or appearing boring, stupid or incompetent). Whenever possible, people with social anxiety disorder will attempt to avoid their most feared situations. However, this is not always feasible, and they will then endure the situation, often with feelings of intense distress. Usually the condition will cause significant impairment in social, occupational or other areas of functioning.

Children may manifest their anxiety somewhat differently from adults. As well as shrinking from interactions, they may be more likely to cry or 'freeze' or have behavioural outbursts such as tantrums. They may also be less likely to acknowledge that their fears are irrational when they are away from a social situation. Particular situations that can cause difficulty for socially anxious children and young people include participating in classroom activities, asking for help in class, activities with peers (such as team sports or attending parties and clubs), participating in school performances and negotiating social challenges.

2.1.2   How common is social anxiety disorder?

There are no UK epidemiological surveys that specifically report data on social anxiety disorder in adults; however, the prevalence of social anxiety disorder has been included in large general population surveys in other western European countries, the US and Australia. Prevalence estimates vary, with much of the variability probably being due to differences in the instruments used to ascertain diagnosis. However, it is clear that social anxiety disorder is one of the most common of all the anxiety disorders. Lifetime prevalence rates of up to 12% have been reported (Kessler et al., 2005a) compared with lifetime prevalence estimates for other anxiety disorders of 6% for generalised anxiety disorder, 5% for panic disorder, 7% for post-traumatic stress disorder (PTSD) and 2% for obsessive-compulsive disorder (OCD). Twelve-month prevalence rates as high as 7% have been reported for social anxiety disorder (Kessler et al., 2005b). Using strict criteria and face-to-face interviews in the US, the lifetime and yearly prevalence figures are halved to 5% and 3%, respectively (Grant et al., 2005b), but it is still more common than the major autoimmune conditions (rheumatoid arthritis, ulcerative colitis, Crohn's disease, systemic lupus erythematosus, diabetes mellitus type I, multiple sclerosis, uveitis, hypothyroidism and hyperthyroidism) put together (American Autoimmune Related Diseases Association, 2011). Data from the National Comorbidity Survey reveals that social anxiety disorder is the third most common psychiatric condition after major depression and alcohol dependence (Kessler et al., 2005a).

Women and men are equally likely to seek treatment for social anxiety disorder, but community surveys indicate that women are somewhat more likely to have the condition (Kessler et al., 2005a). Turk and colleagues (Turk et al., 1998) reported that in a clinical sample women feared more social situations and scored higher on a range of social anxiety measures. It therefore seems that although women are more likely to experience social anxiety, men may be more likely to seek treatment and to do so with less severe symptoms.

Population rates of social anxiety disorder in children and young people have been investigated in several countries. As in adult studies, a range of methods have been used for diagnosis, which probably explains the wide variability in prevalence estimates. A large New Zealand study reported that 11.1% of 18-year-olds met criteria for social anxiety disorder (Feehan et al., 1994). However, a large, British epidemiological survey (Ford et al., 2003) reported that just 0.32% of 5- to 15-year-olds had the disorder, a rate that was higher than that for PTSD, OCD and panic disorder, but lower than separation anxiety disorder, specific phobia and generalised anxiety disorder. Rates of diagnosis in this British study were higher in males than females, and increased slightly with age. A large US-based study reported very similar rates in 9- to 11-year-olds (Costello et al., 2003), while a German study estimated rates of 4% for 14- to 17-year-olds (Wittchen et al., 1999b).

2.1.3   When does social anxiety disorder start and how long does it last?

Social anxiety disorder typically starts in childhood or adolescence. Among individuals who seek treatment as adults the median age of onset is in the early to mid-teens with most people having developed the condition before they reach their 20s. However, there is a small subgroup of people who develop the condition in later life. Some people can identify a particular time when their social anxiety disorder started and may associate it with a particular event (for example, moving to a new school or being bullied or teased). Others may describe themselves as having always been shy and seeing their social anxiety disorder as a gradual, but marked, exacerbation of their apprehension when approaching or being approached by other people. Others may never be able to recall a time when they were free from social anxiety.

Several studies (Bruce et al., 2005; Reich et al., 1994a; Reich et al., 1994b) have followed-up adults with social anxiety disorder for extended periods of time. These studies have generally found that it is a naturally unremitting condition in the absence of treatment. For example, Bruce and colleagues (2005) reported a community study in which adults with various anxiety disorders were followed up for 12 years. At the start of the study, individuals had had social anxiety disorder for an average of 19 years. During the next 12 years 37% recovered, compared with 58% for GAD and 82% for panic disorder without agoraphobia.

Prospective longitudinal studies with children, although more sparse than those with adults, have confirmed that anxiety disorders are very likely to start by adolescence, and that this is particularly the case for social anxiety disorder. However, there is also evidence that some socially anxious young people will outgrow the condition (albeit still maintaining a high risk for other anxiety disorders) (Pine et al., 1998). Putting the adult and child prospective studies together, it appears that a significant number of people who develop social anxiety disorder in adolescence may recover before reaching adulthood. However, if social anxiety disorder has persisted into adulthood, the chance of recovery in the absence of treatment is modest when compared with other common mental disorders.

2.1.4   What other mental disorders tend to be associated with social anxiety disorder?

Four-fifths of adults with a primary diagnosis of social anxiety disorder will experience at least one other psychiatric disorder at sometime during their life (Magee et al., 1996). Among adults, social anxiety disorder is particularly likely to occur alongside other anxiety disorders (up to 70%), followed by any affective disorder (up to 65%), nicotine dependence (27%) and substance-use disorder (about 20%) (Fehm et al., 2008; Grant et al., 2005b). As social anxiety disorder has a particularly early age of onset, many of these comorbid conditions develop subsequently. It is of interest that comorbid anxiety predicts poorer treatment outcomes for people with bipolar affective disorder and major depressive disorder (Fava et al., 2008; Simon et al., 2004) and also that 25% of people presenting with first episode psychosis have social anxiety disorder (Michail & Birchwood, 2009), yet the relevance of this to clinical practice has been somewhat neglected. When people meet criteria for social anxiety disorder and another anxiety disorder, social anxiety comes first in 32% of people; in people with social anxiety and affective disorders or substance misuse, social anxiety precedes these comorbid conditions in 71% and 80%, respectively (Chartier et al., 2003); and in individuals who present with major depressive and social anxiety disorder, the depressive episode may be secondary. This may reflect a common aetiology or a despondency about the way in which social anxiety disorder prevents the person from realising their full potential, or it may be an indication of different peak incidence. One study of adult outpatients presenting for treatment for social anxiety disorder found that 53% had had a previous episode of a depressive disorder, with the average number of episodes being 2.2 in a cohort that had a mean age of 33 years. Similarly, substance misuse problems can develop out of individuals' initial attempts to manage their social anxiety with alcohol and drugs. Of course, the relationship between social anxiety disorder and other clinical conditions can also work the other way. For example, some individuals with scars and/or other physical problems in the context of PTSD may subsequently develop social anxiety disorder when they become concerned about how they will appear to other people. Some individuals who are usually socially confident may develop social anxiety during a depressive episode and recover once the depression lifts. The picture is similar in adolescence: comorbidity is 40% for anxiety disorders, 40% for affective disorders and 16% for substance misuse (Ranta et al., 2009); in one large German study of young people (aged up to 24 years) social anxiety preceded the additional anxiety diagnosis in 64.4% of people, the mood disorder diagnosis in 81.6% and the substance misuse diagnosis in 85.2% (Wittchen et al., 1999b).

There is also a significant degree of comorbidity between social anxiety disorder and some personality disorders. The most common is avoidant personality disorder (APD), with as much as 61% of adults who seek treatment for social anxiety also meeting criteria for a personality disorder (Sanderson et al., 1994). However, there is some controversy about the significance of this finding. There is a marked overlap between the criteria for social anxiety disorder and APD, and some experts consider APD a severe variant of social anxiety disorder. As many people develop their social anxiety disorder in childhood, some researchers have argued that much of the association with APD is simply due to the chronicity of the anxiety disorder. However, research studies have succeeded in identifying a few characteristics that tend to distinguish people with social anxiety disorder alone from those with social anxiety disorder plus APD. These include interpersonal problems, in particular problems with intimacy, increased functional impairment and lower levels of social support (Marques et al., 2012), although the differences have not always been replicated. Whatever the relationship between social anxiety disorder and APD, there is some evidence that successful psychological treatment of social anxiety also reduces the incidence of APD (Clark et al., 2006; McManus et al., 2009a). Similarly, Fahlen (1995) reported that abnormal personality traits wane with successful pharmacological treatment. Besides APD, comorbidity rates with other personality disorders are low and not higher than with other anxiety disorders or depression.

Among children and young people, comorbidity of anxiety disorders is also very high, as is comorbidity between anxiety and mood and behavioural disorders (Ford et al., 2003). The specific comorbidities of social anxiety in this age group are less well explored, but in a large sample of young people (aged 14 to 24 years) Wittchen and colleagues (1999b) found that 41.3% of those with a diagnosis of social anxiety disorder also had a diagnosis of substance misuse (including nicotine), 31.1% a mood disorder and 49.9% another anxiety disorder (compared with 27.9%, 12.1% and 20.8% of participants without a diagnosis of social anxiety disorder, respectively). Social anxiety is a substantial predictor of nicotine use in adolescence (Sonntag et al., 2000). In some people, social anxiety may be expressed as selective mutism (Viana et al., 2009).

2.1.5   How does social anxiety disorder interfere with people's lives?

Social anxiety disorder should not be confused with normal shyness, which is not associated with disability and interference with most areas of life. Educational achievement can be undermined, with individuals having a heightened risk of leaving school early and obtaining poorer qualifications (Van Ameringen et al., 2003). One study (Katzelnick et al., 2001) found that people with generalised social anxiety disorder had wages that were 10% lower than the non-clinical population. Naturally, social life is impaired. On average, individuals with social anxiety disorder have fewer friends and have more difficulty getting on with friends (Whisman et al., 2000). They are less likely to marry, are more likely to divorce and are less likely to have children (Wittchen et al., 1999a). Social fears can also interfere with a broad range of everyday activities, such as visiting shops, buying clothes, having a haircut and using the telephone. The majority of people with social anxiety disorder are employed; however, they report taking more days off work and being less productive because of their symptoms (Stein et al., 1999b). People may avoid or leave jobs that involve giving presentations or performances. The proportion of people who are in receipt of state benefits is 2.5 times higher than the rate for the general adult population. Katzelnick and colleagues (2001) also report that social anxiety disorder is associated with out-patient medical visits.

2.1.6   Are there different types of social anxiety disorder?

Individuals with social anxiety disorder vary considerably in the number and type of social situations that they fear and in the number and range of their feared outcomes. These two features (feared situations and feared outcomes) can vary independently. For example, some people fear just one or two situations but have multiple feared outcomes (such as, 'I'll sound boring', 'I'll sweat', 'I'll appear incompetent', 'I'll blush', 'I'll sound stupid' or 'I'll look anxious'). Others can fear many situations but have only one feared outcome (such as 'I'll blush'). Because of this variability, researchers have considered whether it might be useful to divide social anxiety disorder into subtypes. Several subtypes have been suggested, some of which are defined by specific feared outcomes (fear of blushing, fear of sweating and so on). The most common distinction is between generalised social anxiety disorder, where individuals fear most social situations, and non-generalised social anxiety disorder, where individuals fear a more limited range of situations (which often, but not always, involve performance tasks such a public speaking); however, some authors have suggested that the difference between these subtypes is a difference in degree. The generalised subtype is associated with greater impairment and higher rates of comorbidity with other mental disorders (Kessler et al., 1998). The generalised subtype also has a stronger familial aggregation, an earlier age of onset and a more chronic course. While most psychological therapies are applied to both subtypes, evaluations of drug treatments have mainly focused on generalised social anxiety disorder.

2.2   AETIOLOGY

2.2.1   What do we know about the causes of social anxiety disorder?

As with many disorders of mental health, the development of social anxiety disorder is probably best understood as an interaction between several different biopsychosocial factors (Tillfors, 2004).

Genetic factors seem to play a part, but genes may influence the probability of developing any anxiety or depressive disorder rather than developing social anxiety in particular. Higher rates of social anxiety disorder are reported in relatives of people with the condition than in relatives of people without the condition, and this effect is stronger for the generalised subtype (Stein et al., 1998a). Further evidence for a genetic component comes from twin studies. Kendler and colleagues (1992; 1999) found that if one twin is affected, the chance of the other twin being affected is higher if the twins are genetically identical (monozygotic) than if they only share 50% of their genes (dizygotic). However, heritability estimates are only 25 to 50%, indicating that environmental factors also have an important role in the development of the condition for many people.

Stressful social events in early life (for example, being bullied, familial abuse, public embarrassment or one's mind going blank during a public performance) are commonly reported by people with social anxiety disorder (Erwin et al., 2006). Parental modelling of fear and avoidance in social situations plus an overprotective parenting style have both been linked to the development of the condition in some studies (Lieb et al., 2000).

The success of selective serotonin reuptake inhibitors (SSRIs), serotonin and noradrenaline reuptake inhibitors (SNRI) and monoamine oxidase inhibitors (MAOIs) in treating social anxiety disorder suggests that dysregulation of the serotonin and dopamine neurotransmitter system may also play a role, but studies that establish a causal relationship for such dysregulation in the development of the condition have not yet been reported.

Neuroimaging studies so far suggest different activation of specific parts of the brain (the amygdalae, the insulae and the dorsal anterior cingulate – all structures that are involved in the regulation of anxiety) when threatening stimuli are presented compared with healthy volunteers.

2.3   TREATMENT AND MANAGEMENT IN THE NHS

2.3.1   How well is social anxiety disorder recognised?

Recognition of social anxiety disorder in adults, children and young people by general practitioners (GPs) is often poor. The problem of under-recognition for anxiety disorders in general has recently been highlighted by evidence that the prevalence of PTSD is significantly under-recognised in primary care (Ehlers et al., 2009). In part this may stem from GPs not identifying the disorder, a general lack of understanding about its severity and complexity, and a lack of clearly defined care pathways. But it may also stem from service users' lack of knowledge of its existence, their avoidance of talking about the problem and stigma.

The early age of onset and effects on educational achievement mean that recognition of social anxiety disorders in educational settings is also an issue. As well as underachieving, children with social anxiety disorder may be particularly likely to be the targets of bullying and teasing. Teachers and other educational professionals may have limited knowledge of how to recognise and oversee the management of the condition.

In primary care many service users report being misdiagnosed as having 'pure' major depression. Missing the diagnosis may also occur in secondary care if an adequate history has not been taken. This is a serious omission because having a comorbidity has treatment and outcome implications.

2.3.2   How many people seek treatment?

Despite the extent of suffering and impairment, only about half of adults with the disorder ever seek treatment, and those who do generally only seek treatment after 15 to 20 years of symptoms (Grant et al., 2005a). Likely explanations for low rates and delays include individuals thinking that social anxiety is part of their personality and cannot be changed (or in the case of children, that they will grow out of it), lack of recognition of the condition by healthcare professionals, stigmatisation of mental health services, fear of being negatively evaluated by a healthcare professional, general lack of information about the availability of effective treatments and limited availability of services in many areas.

2.3.3   How can we know whether a treatment is effective?

Randomised controlled trials (RCTs) are the main way of determining whether a treatment is effective. Individuals who are diagnosed with social anxiety disorder are randomly allocated to the treatments under investigation or a control condition. Assessments are conducted at pre-treatment/control and post-treatment/control. The treatment is considered to be effective if significantly greater improvement is observed in the treatment condition than the control condition. In order to determine whether the improvements obtained by treatment are sustained, ideally participants should be systematically followed up for an extended period after the end of treatment.

RCTs are the best way of dealing with threats to internal validity (for example, 'are the improvements that are observed due to the treatment or would they have happened in any case?'). However, they do not necessarily deal well with threats to external validity (for example, 'would the results that are obtained with the rather selective group of participants that were studied in the RCT generalise to most people with social anxiety disorder?'). For this reason, it is helpful if data from RCTs are supplemented by data from large cohorts of relatively unselected people who receive the same treatment.

Researchers have traditionally distinguished between *specific* and *non-specific* treatment effects. The *specific* treatment effect refers to the amount of improvement that is attributable to the unique features of a particular treatment. The *non-specific* treatment effect refers to the amount of improvement that is attributable to features that are common to all (or most) well-conducted therapies.

In RCTs of pharmacological interventions the main contrast is always between the active drug and a placebo. The placebo controls for the non-specific effects of seeing a competent clinician, having one's symptoms consistently monitored, receiving a plausible treatment rationale and taking a tablet. The comparison between active drug and placebo is therefore only an index of the specific treatment effect attributable to a particular chemical. As most chemicals have side effects, some of which are severe, it is generally accepted that a drug must show a specific effect in order to warrant its use. However, it is important to note that service users are likely to show substantially greater improvements than implied by the active drug versus placebo effect size because giving a placebo also produces a further non-specific benefit.

In RCTs of psychological interventions the focus is less exclusively on establishing specific treatment effects. Commonly the control condition is a waitlist. In this case, the observed difference between the treatment and the control condition will be the sum of the relevant non-specific and specific effects. As psychological interventions are generally thought to have few side effects, it seems reasonable for researchers to have a primary interest in determining whether the treatment has any beneficial effects compared with no treatment. However, it is also important that evaluations of psychological interventions attempt to determine whether the treatment has specific effects as this gives us greater confidence in knowing exactly which procedures therapists should be taught in order to replicate the results that the treatment has obtained in RCTs. If a psychological intervention is known to have a specific effect, it is clear that therapists need to be trained to deliver the procedures that characterise that treatment. If a treatment has only been shown to have a non-specific effect people should be informed and it should not usually be offered in a publicly funded system.

In social anxiety disorder it seems highly plausible that part of the improvement that is observed in treatment is simply due to the non-specific effect of meeting someone who is (initially) a stranger while talking about one's emotions and numerous embarrassing topics. In other words, almost all interventions for social anxiety disorder involve a substantial amount of potentially beneficial exposure to feared social situations.

How does one determine whether a psychological intervention has a specific effect? Essentially one needs to demonstrate that the treatment is superior to an alternative treatment that includes most of the features that are common to various psychological interventions (such as seeing a warm and empathic therapist on a regular basis, having an opportunity to talk about one's problems, receiving encouragement to overcome the problems, receiving a treatment that seems to be based on a sensible rationale and having one's symptoms measured regularly). RCTs approach this requirement in one of three ways, each of which has strengths and weaknesses. In the first approach the alternative/control condition is a treatment that was specifically designed for the study and is intended to include non-specific features only, a good example of which is the education-support condition used by Heimberg and colleagues (1990; 1998). In the second approach, the alternative treatment might be something that is used routinely in clinical practice and is considered by some to be an active intervention but it turns out to be less effective than the psychological intervention under investigation, despite involving a similar amount of therapist contact. In the third approach, the psychological intervention is compared with pill placebo, which controls the many non-specific factors but often fails to fully control for therapist contact time because this is usually less in a medication-based treatment.

The fact that RCTs of medications almost always only focus on assessing specific treatment effects, whereas RCTs of psychological intervention may focus on assessing specific, non-specific or both types of effect, means that caution needs to be exercised when comparing the findings of such evaluations. In an ideal world, it should be possible to obtain an estimate of the effectiveness of each type of treatment against controls for specific effects as well as the overall benefit of treatment (compared with no treatment). The network meta-analysis (NMA) that underpins this guideline attempts to provide such information by inferring how medications would fair against no treatment even though most RCTs of medication use placebo controls and do not include a waitlist (no treatment) control (see Chapter 3 for further information about the NMA).

The next section outlines the different psychological and pharmacological interventions that have been tested for efficacy in social anxiety disorder.

2.3.4   Psychological interventions

In the mid 1960s, when social anxiety disorder was formally recognised as a separate phobic disorder (Marks & Gelder, 1965), the dominant evidence-based psychological interventions for anxiety disorders involved repeated exposure to the phobic stimulus in imagination. The first RCTs of psychological interventions for social anxiety disorder used two variants of this approach (systematic desensitisation and flooding) and obtained modest improvements. However, in anxiety disorders in general imaginal exposure treatment soon became superseded by treatments that involved confronting the feared stimulus in real life. Marks (1975) published a seminal review arguing that real life ('*in vivo*') exposure was more efficacious than imaginal exposure. This review had a substantial effect on treatment development work in all anxiety disorders. Subsequent behavioural and cognitive behavioural interventions for social anxiety disorder have therefore focused on techniques that involve real life confrontation with social situations, to a greater or lesser extent.

Exposure in vivo is based on the assumption that avoidance of feared situations is one of the primary maintaining factors for social anxiety. The treatment involves constructing a hierarchy of feared situations (from least to most feared) and encouraging the person to repeatedly expose themselves to the situations, starting with less fear-provoking situations and moving up to more difficult situations as confidence develops. Exposure exercises involve confrontation with real-life social situations through role plays and out of office exercises within therapy sessions and through systematic homework assignments. Many people with social anxiety disorder find that they cannot completely avoid feared social situations and they tend to try to cope by holding back (for example, by not talking about themselves, staying quiet or being on the edge of a group) or otherwise avoiding within the situation. For this reason, exposure therapists devote a considerable amount of time to identifying subtle, within-situation patterns of avoidance (safety-seeking behaviours) and encouraging the person to do the opposite during therapy.

Applied relaxation is a specialised form of relaxation training that aims to teach people how to be able to relax in common social situations. Starting with training in traditional progressive muscle relaxation, the treatment takes individuals through a series of steps that enables them to relax on cue in everyday situations. The final stage of the treatment involves intensive practice in using the relaxation techniques in real life social situations.

Social skills training is based on the assumption that people are anxious in social situations partly because they are deficient in their social behavioural repertoires and need to enhance these repertoires in order to behave successfully and realise positive outcomes in their interactions with others. The treatment involves systematic training in non-verbal social skills (for example, increased eye contact, friendly attentive posture, and so on) and verbal social skills (for example, how to start a conversation, how to give others positive feedback, how to ask questions that promote conversation, and so on). The skills that are identified with the therapist are usually repeatedly practiced through role plays in therapy sessions as well as in homework assignments. Research has generally failed to support the assumption that people with social anxiety disorder do not know how to behave in social situations. In particular, there is very little evidence that they show social skills deficits when they are not anxious. Any deficits in performance seem to be largely restricted to situations in which they are anxious, which suggests that they are an anxiety response rather than an indication of a lack of knowledge. Nevertheless, social skills therapists argue that practising relevant skills when anxious is a useful technique for promoting confidence in social situations.

Cognitive restructuring is a technique that is included in a variety of multicomponent therapies and has also occasionally been used on its own, although this has usually been as part of a research evaluation assessing the value of different components of a more complex intervention. The therapist works with the person to identify the key fearful thoughts that they experience in anxiety-provoking social situations, as well as some of the general beliefs about social interactions that might trigger those thoughts. The person is then taught largely verbal techniques for generating alternative, less anxiety-provoking thoughts ('rational responses'), which they are encouraged to rehearse in anticipation of, and during, social interactions. To facilitate this process, they regularly complete thought records, which are discussed with therapists in the treatment sessions. Some practitioners argue that it is not essential that they fully believe a rational response before they start rehearsing it in fear-provoking situations (Marks, 1981).

Cognitive behavioural interventions encompass various well-recognised and manualised approaches including *cognitive behavioural therapy (CBT)*. However, most cognitive behavioural interventions involve exposure *in vivo* and cognitive restructuring. Some programmes also include some training in relaxation techniques and/or social and conversational skills training. In recent years, research studies have identified several processes that appear to maintain social anxiety in addition to avoidance behaviour. These include self-focused attention, distorted self-imagery and the adverse effects of safety-seeking behaviours, including the way they change other people's behaviour. Some cognitive behavioural interventions have included techniques that aim to address these additional maintaining factors, for example, training in externally focused and/or task-focused attention, the use of video feedback to correct distorted self-imagery and demonstrations of the unhelpful consequences of safety-seeking behaviours. CBT can be delivered in either an individual or group format. When it is delivered in a group format, other members of the group are often recruited for role plays and exposure exercises. Sessions tend to last 2 to 2.5 hours with six to eight people in a group and two therapists. When CBT is delivered in an individual format, therapists may need to identify other individuals who can sometimes join therapy sessions for role plays.

Cognitive therapy (CT) developed by Clark and Wells (1995) is based on a model of the maintenance of social anxiety disorder that places particular emphasis on: (a) the negative beliefs that individuals with social anxiety hold about themselves and social interactions; (b) negative self-imagery; and (c) the problematic cognitive and behavioural processes that occur in social situations (self-focused attention, safety-seeking behaviours). A distinctive form of CT that specifically targets the maintenance factors specified in the model has developed. The procedures used in the treatment overlap with some of the procedures used in more recent CBT programmes, therefore CT can validly be considered to be a variant of CBT. However, it is distinguished from many CBT programmes for social anxiety disorder by the fact that it takes a somewhat different approach to exposure (with less emphasis on repetition and more on maximising disconfirmatory evidence) and it does not use thought records. Instead, the key components of treatment are: developing an individual version of Clark and Wells' (1995) model using the service user's own thoughts, images and behaviours; an experiential exercise in which self-focused attention and safety behaviours are manipulated in order to demonstrate their adverse effects; video and still photography feedback to correct distorted negative self-images; training in externally focused non-evaluative attention; behavioural experiments in which the person tests specific predictions about what will happen in social situations when they drop their safety behaviours; discrimination training and memory rescripting for dealing with memories of past social trauma.

The treatment is usually delivered on an individual basis. However, there is a need for the therapist to be able to call on other people to participate in within-session role plays. It is common for the therapist and the person with social anxiety disorder to also leave the office to conduct behavioural experiments in the real world during therapy sessions. This is easier to do if sessions are for 90 minutes, rather than the usual 50 minutes.

Interpersonal psychotherapy (IPT) was originally developed as a treatment for depression but was modified by Lipsitz and colleagues (1997) for use in social anxiety disorder. Treatment is framed within a broad biopsychosocial perspective in which temperamental predisposition interacts with early and later life experiences to initiate and maintain social anxiety disorder. There are three phases to the treatment. In the first phase, the person is encouraged to see social anxiety disorder as an illness that has to be coped with, rather than as a sign of weakness or deficiency. In the second phase, the therapist works with the person to address specific interpersonal problems particularly in the areas of role transition and role disputes, but sometimes also grief. Role plays encouraging the expression of feelings and accurate communication are emphasised. People are also encouraged to build a social network comprising close and trusting relationships. In the last phase, the therapist and the person review progress, address ending of the therapeutic relationship, and prepare for challenging situations and experiences in the future. Sessions are typically 50 to 60 minutes of individual treatment.

Psychodynamic psychotherapy sees the symptoms of social anxiety disorder as the result of core relationship conflicts predominately based on early experience. Therapy aims to help the person become aware of the link between conflicts and symptoms. The therapeutic relationship is a central vehicle for insight and change. Expressive interventions relate the symptoms of social anxiety disorder to the person's underlying core conflictual relationship theme. Leichsenring and colleagues (2009a) consider that in social anxiety disorder the core conflictual relationship theme consists of three components: (1) a wish (for example, 'I wish to be affirmed by others'); (2) an anticipated response from others (for example, 'others will humiliate me'); and (3) a response from the self (for example, 'I am afraid of exposing myself'). Supportive interventions include suggestion, reassurance and encouragement. Clients are encouraged to expose themselves to feared social situations outside therapy sessions. Self-affirming inner dialogues are also encouraged.

Mindfulness training is a psychological intervention that has developed out of the Buddhist tradition and encourages individuals to gain psychological distance from their worries and negative emotions, seeing them as an observer, rather than being engrossed with them. Treatment starts with general education about stress and social anxiety. Participants then attend weekly groups in which they are taught meditation techniques. Formal meditation practice for at least 30 minutes per day using audiotapes for guidance is also encouraged.

2.3.5 Pharmacological interventions

Several different pharmacological interventions have been used in the treatment of social anxiety, many of which were originally developed as antidepressants.

Antidepressants used in the treatment of social anxiety disorder come from four different classes: SSRIs, SNRIs, noradrenaline and selective serotonin antagonists and MAOIs. A fifth class, tricyclic antidepressants (TCAs), have also been used in the past but this is no longer the case.

SSRIs were initially marketed in the 1980s, having been developed as more selective agents following work on the TCAs and MAOIs. They are thought to act by increasing serotonin concentration in the brain and, after obtaining licences for major depression, many pharmaceutical companies carried out additional studies that indicated their efficacy in social anxiety disorder as well as in other anxiety disorders. The only SNRI that has been studied extensively is venlafaxine and it is possible that its effects in social anxiety disorder are mediated solely through changes in serotonin at usually prescribed doses.

MAOIs inhibit the breakdown of noradrenaline, dopamine, serotonin, melatonin, tyramine and phenylethylamine. This effect is not limited to the brain and affects other parts of the body rich in monoamine oxidase (MAO), for example, the gut. Therapeutic effects in social anxiety disorder are again thought to be related to increased levels of serotonin and dopamine in the brain. However, inhibition of MAO may result in a potentially dangerous interaction with foods containing tyramine which may lead to episodes of dangerously high blood pressure. This risk is much reduced with moclobemide as it is 'reversible' – this means that in the presence of other relevant substances, moclobemide 'comes off the enzyme'. Because of this, moclobemide prescription comes with far fewer dietary restrictions than the older MAOIs, such as phenelzine. MAOIs are now rarely prescribed because of their perceived risks.

Benzodiazepines are restricted by the fact that it is preferable not to administer them for prolonged periods of time because of potential tolerance and dependence. In addition they may complicate some of the more prevalent comorbidities such as PTSD and depression.

Finally, alpha2delta calcium gated channel blockers, such as pregabalin, reduce neuronal excitability but it is not at all clear why these should work when other anticonvulsants have no known therapeutic effects in social anxiety disorder.

2.4   THE ECONOMIC COST OF SOCIAL ANXIETY DISORDER

Social anxiety disorder imposes substantial economic costs on individuals, their families and carers and society, as a result of functional disability, poor educational achievement, loss of work productivity, social impairment, greater financial dependency and impairment in quality of life. These costs are substantially higher in those with comorbid conditions, which are very common in people with social anxiety: 50 to 80% of people with social anxiety disorder presenting to health services have at least one other psychiatric condition, typically another anxiety disorder, depression or a substance-use disorder (Wittchen & Fehm, 2003).

A UK study by Patel and colleagues (2002) assessed the economic consequences of social anxiety disorder for individuals, health services and the wider society using information from the Adult Psychiatric Morbidity Survey conducted in England in

2000 (Singleton et al., 2001). People with social anxiety disorder were less likely to be in the highest socioeconomic group and had lower employment rates and household income compared with those with no psychiatric morbidity. In terms of health service resource use and associated costs, people with social anxiety were estimated to incur a mean annual health service cost per person of £609, attributed to GP visits, inpatient and outpatient care, home visits and counselling. Annual productivity losses due to ill health reached £441 per employed person with social anxiety, while the annual social security benefit per person with social anxiety reached £1,479. Health service costs and social benefits were higher in people with social anxiety when a comorbidity condition was present compared with those with pure social anxiety disorder.

For comparison, people without a mental disorder incurred a mean annual cost per person of £379 for health services, £595 associated with productivity losses, and £794 relating to social security benefits (1997/98 prices).

By extrapolating the data to a population of 100,000 people attending primary care services, Patel and colleagues (2002) estimated that the total healthcare cost of social anxiety disorder would amount to over £195,000 per annum, with primary care costs alone approximating £49,000. Wider costs, such as social security benefit claims, were expected to reach £474,000.

Another study from the Netherlands (Acarturk et al., 2009) estimated the resource use and costs incurred by people with both clinical and subthreshold social anxiety disorder using data from a national mental health survey. Costs assessed included direct medical costs related to mental healthcare services (for example, GP visits, sessions with psychiatrists, hospital days), direct non-medical costs (for example, service users' transportation, parking, and waiting and treatment time) and productivity losses. The annual mean cost per person with social anxiety disorder was €11,952 (2003 prices), significantly higher than the respective cost per person with no mental disorder of €2,957. However, when the cost was adjusted for comorbid conditions, the mean annual cost of social anxiety disorder was reduced to €6,100. For those with subthreshold social anxiety disorder, the annual mean cost was estimated at €4,687. Other costs falling on other sectors like education and social services were not considered in the study.

Despite the debilitating nature of the condition, social anxiety disorder is often unrecognised and under-treated with little information existing on the resource implications of the disorder on the individual, healthcare sector or society (den Boer, 1997; Jackson, 1992; Ross, 1991). Also, given its early onset and chronic nature, the lifetime cost of an untreated individual is quite significant because of the negative impact on productivity (Lipsitz & Schneier, 2000).

A more detailed review of the cost of social anxiety disorder indicated that the economic cost relating to poor educational attainment, social impairment, functional disability and poor quality of life may be greater than the direct healthcare costs. For every 10-point increase on the Liebowitz Social Anxiety Scale (LSAS), wages were found to decrease by 1.5 to 2.9% and college graduation to decrease by 1.8%. However, most of these economic costs have not yet been quantified in monetary values (Lipsitz & Schneier, 2000).

In contrast to the studies summarised above, some evidence indicates that social anxiety disorder alone is not associated with greater use of mental and other health services, with only 5.4% of those with non-comorbid social anxiety disorder seeking treatment from a mental health provider (Davidson et al., 1993a; Lecrubier, 1998; Magee et al., 1996). In a retrospective study assessing the mean annual healthcare costs of anxiety disorders using a US reimbursement claims database of approximately 600,000 people, social anxiety disorder was noted to have the lowest cost of $3,772 per person, compared with that of GAD ($6,472) and major depressive disorder ($7,170) (François et al., 2010). Similarly, an Australian study (Issakidis et al., 2004), reported that individuals with social anxiety disorder utilised fewer healthcare resources (including GP, psychiatrist and medical specialist visits, and psychological and pharmacological interventions) compared with people with other anxiety disorders. A review of cost-of-illness studies confirmed that social anxiety disorder has been consistently found to cost less than other anxiety disorders. The overall mean annual cost of social anxiety disorder was estimated to range from $1,124 to $3,366 (2005 US$) (Konnopka et al., 2009).

In summary, social anxiety disorder is associated with a range of indirect and intangible costs relating to reduced productivity, social impairment and reduction in quality of life. On the other hand, the often lower healthcare cost incurred by people with social anxiety disorder compared with those with other anxiety disorders reflects the under-utilisation of healthcare services by these individuals. Relatively high costs in some groups are often due to comorbidity with conditions like depression and alcohol dependence. Although the costs due to social anxiety disorder vary significantly across studies, countries and groups, they are nevertheless consistently lower than the costs associated with other anxiety disorders. This is understandable given the underlying primary problem, which is chiefly social avoidance.

3 METHODS USED TO DEVELOP THIS GUIDELINE

3.1 OVERVIEW

The development of this guideline drew upon methods outlined by NICE, and further information is available in *The Guidelines Manual* (NICE, 2009b). A team of health-care professionals, lay representatives and technical experts known as the Guideline Development Group (GDG), with support from the NCCMH staff, undertook the development of a person-centred, evidence-based guideline. There are seven basic steps in the process of developing a guideline:

1. Define the scope, which lays out exactly what will be included in the guidance.
2. Define review questions considered important for practitioners and service users.
3. Develop criteria for evidence searching and search for evidence.
4. Design validated protocols for systematic review and apply to evidence recovered by the search.
5. Synthesise and (meta-) analyse data retrieved, guided by the review questions, and produce Grading of Recommendations Assessment, Development and Evaluation (GRADE) evidence profiles and summaries.
6. Consider the implications of the research findings for clinical practice and reach consensus decisions on areas where evidence is not found.
7. Answer review questions with evidence-based recommendations for clinical practice.

The clinical practice recommendations made by the GDG are therefore derived from the most up-to-date and robust evidence for the clinical and cost effectiveness of the treatments and services used in the treatment and management of social anxiety disorder. Where evidence was not found or was inconclusive, the GDG discussed and attempted to reach consensus on what should be recommended, factoring in any relevant issues. In addition, to ensure a service user and carer focus, the concerns of service users and carers regarding health and social care have been highlighted and addressed by recommendations agreed by the whole GDG.

3.2 THE SCOPE

Topics are referred by the Secretary of State and the letter of referral defines the remit which defines the main areas to be covered; see *The Guidelines Manual* (NICE, 2009b) for further information. The NCCMH developed a scope for the guideline based on the remit. The purpose of the scope is to:

- provide an overview of what the guideline will include and exclude
- identify the key aspects of care that must be included

- set the boundaries of the development work and provide a clear framework to enable work to stay within the priorities agreed by NICE and the National Collaborating Centre, and the remit from the Department of Health/Welsh Assembly Government
- inform the development of the review questions and search strategy
- inform professionals and the public about expected content of the guideline
- keep the guideline to a reasonable size to ensure that its development can be carried out within the allocated period.

An initial draft of the scope was sent to registered stakeholders who had agreed to attend a scoping workshop. The workshop was used to:

- obtain feedback on the selected key clinical issues
- identify which population subgroups should be specified (if any)
- seek views on the composition of the GDG
- encourage applications for GDG membership.

The draft scope was subject to consultation with registered stakeholders over a 4-week period. During the consultation period, the scope was posted on the NICE website (www.nice.org.uk). Comments were invited from stakeholder organisations. The NCCMH and NICE reviewed the scope in light of comments received, and the revised scope was signed off by NICE.

3.3 THE GUIDELINE DEVELOPMENT GROUP

During the consultation phase, members of the GDG were appointed by an open recruitment process. GDG membership consisted of: professionals in psychiatry, clinical psychology, nursing, and general practice; academic experts in psychiatry and psychology; and people with experience of social anxiety disorder. The guideline development process was supported by staff from the NCCMH, who undertook the clinical and health economic literature searches, reviewed and presented the evidence to the GDG, managed the process, and contributed to drafting the guideline.

3.3.1 Guideline Development Group meetings

Thirteen GDG meetings were held between July 2011 and February 2013. During each day-long GDG meeting, in a plenary session, review questions and clinical and economic evidence were reviewed and assessed, and recommendations formulated. At each meeting, all GDG members declared any potential conflicts of interest, and service user and carer concerns were routinely discussed as a standing agenda item.

3.3.2 Topic groups

The GDG divided its workload along clinically relevant lines to simplify the guideline development process, and GDG members formed smaller topic groups to undertake guideline work in that area of clinical practice. Topic group 1 covered questions relating to pharmacology, topic group 2 covered children and young people, topic group 3 covered psychological interventions and topic group 4 covered experience of care. These groups were designed to efficiently manage the large volume of evidence appraisal prior to presenting it to the GDG as a whole. Each topic group was chaired by a GDG member with expert knowledge of the topic area (one of the healthcare professionals). Topic groups refined the review questions and the clinical definitions of treatment interventions, reviewed and prepared the evidence with the systematic reviewer before presenting it to the GDG as a whole, and helped the GDG to identify further expertise in the topic. Topic group leaders reported the status of the group's work as part of the standing agenda. They also introduced and led the GDG's discussion of the evidence review for that topic and assisted the GDG Chair in drafting the section of the guideline relevant to the work of each topic group. Topic groups did not write recommendations – these were all produced by the full GDG. Members of the topic groups included the following:

- Topic group 1 (pharmacology): Andrea Malizia (chair), Safi Afghan, Melanie Dix, Nick Hanlon and Gareth Stephens
- Topic group 2 (children and young people): Cathy Creswell (chair), Madeleine Bennett, Sam Cartwright-Hatton, Melanie Dix and Gareth Stephens
- Topic group 3 (psychological interventions): David Clark (chair), Peter Armstrong, Nick Hanlon and Lusia Stopa
- Topic group 4 (experience of care): Madeleine Bennett, Sam Cartwright-Hatton, Nick Hanlon and Gareth Stephens.

3.3.3 Service users and carers

Individuals with direct experience of services for social anxiety disorder gave an integral service-user focus to the GDG and the guideline. The GDG included two people with experience of social anxiety disorder. As full GDG members they contributed to writing the review questions, providing advice on outcomes most relevant to service users and carers, helping to ensure that the evidence addressed their views and preferences, highlighting sensitive issues and terminology relevant to the guideline, and bringing research to the attention of the GDG. In drafting the guideline, they met with the NCCMH team on several occasions to develop the chapter on experience of care and they contributed to writing the guideline's introduction and identified recommendations from the service user and carer perspective.

3.3.4 National and international experts

National and international experts in the area under review were identified through the literature search and through the experience of the GDG members. These experts were contacted to identify unpublished or soon-to-be published studies to ensure that up-to-date evidence was included in the development of the guideline. They informed the GDG about completed trials at the pre-publication stage, systematic reviews in the process of being published, studies relating to the cost effectiveness of treatment and trial data if the GDG could be provided with full access to the complete trial report. Appendix 5 lists researchers who were contacted.

3.4   REVIEW QUESTIONS

Review (clinical) questions were used to guide the identification and interrogation of the evidence base relevant to the topic of the guideline. Before the first GDG meeting, review protocols were prepared by NCCMH staff based on the scope (and an overview of existing guidelines), and discussed with the guideline Chair. The draft review questions were then discussed by the GDG at the first few meetings and amended as necessary. Where appropriate, the questions were refined once the evidence had been searched and, where necessary, subquestions were generated. The review questions can be found in the relevant evidence chapters.

For questions about interventions, the PICO (Population, Intervention, Comparison and Outcome) framework was used (see Table 1).

Questions relating to diagnosis or case identification do not involve an intervention designed to treat a particular condition, therefore the PICO framework was not used. Rather, the questions were designed to pick up key issues specifically relevant to clinical utility, for example, their accuracy, reliability, safety and acceptability to the service user.

Although service user experience is a component of all review questions, specific questions concerning what the experience of care is like for people with social anxiety disorder, and where appropriate, their families/carers, were developed by the GDG.

To help facilitate the literature review, a note was made of the best study design type to answer each question. There are four main types of review question of relevance to NICE guidelines. These are listed in Table 2. For each type of question, the best primary study design varies, where 'best' is interpreted as 'least likely to give misleading answers to the question'.

Table 1: Features of a well-formulated question on effectiveness intervention – the PICO guide

Population	Which population of service users are we interested in? How can they be best described? Are there subgroups that need to be considered?
Intervention	Which intervention, treatment or approach should be used?
Comparison	What is/are the main alternative/s to compare with the intervention?
Outcome	What is really important for the service user? Which outcomes should be considered: intermediate or short-term measures; mortality; morbidity and treatment complications; rates of relapse; late morbidity and readmission; return to work, physical and social functioning and other measures such as quality of life; general health status?

Table 2: Best study design to answer each type of question

Type of question	Best primary study design
Effectiveness or other impact of an intervention	RCT; other studies that may be considered in the absence of RCTs are the following: internally/ externally controlled before and after trial, interrupted time-series
Accuracy of information (for example, risk factor, test, prediction rule)	Comparing the information against a valid gold standard in a randomised trial or inception cohort study
Rates (of disease, service user experience, rare side effects)	Prospective cohort, registry, cross-sectional study
Experience of care	Qualitative research (for example, grounded theory, ethnographic research)

However, in all cases, a well-conducted systematic review (of the appropriate type of study) is likely to always yield a better answer than a single study.

Deciding on the best design type to answer a specific review question does not mean that studies of different design types addressing the same question were discarded.

3.5   SYSTEMATIC CLINICAL LITERATURE REVIEW

The aim of the clinical literature review was to systematically identify and synthesise relevant evidence from the literature in order to answer the specific review questions developed by the GDG. Thus, clinical practice recommendations are evidence-based, where possible, and, if evidence is not available, informal consensus methods are used to try and reach general agreement (see Section 3.5.8) and the need for future research is specified.

3.5.1   The search process

Scoping searches
A broad preliminary search of the literature was undertaken in December 2010 to obtain an overview of the issues likely to be covered by the scope, and to help define key areas. Searches were restricted to clinical guidelines, Health Technology Assessment (HTA) reports, key systematic reviews and RCTs, and conducted in the following databases and websites:
● *BMJ* Clinical Evidence
● Canadian Medical Association Infobase (Canadian guidelines)
● Clinical Policy and Practice Program of the New South Wales Department of Health (Australia)

- Clinical Practice Guidelines (Australian Guidelines)
- Cochrane Central Register of Controlled Trials (CENTRAL)
- Cochrane Database of Abstracts of Reviews of Effects (DARE)
- Cochrane Database of Systematic Reviews (CDSR)
- Excerpta Medica Database (Embase)
- Guidelines International Network
- Health Evidence Bulletin Wales
- Health Management Information Consortium (HMIC)
- HTA database (technology assessments)
- Medical Literature Analysis and Retrieval System Online (MEDLINE/MEDLINE In-Process)
- National Health and Medical Research Council
- National Library for Health (NLH) Guidelines Finder
- New Zealand Guidelines Group
- NHS Centre for Reviews and Dissemination (CRD)
- Organizing Medical Networked Information Medical Search
- SIGN
- Turning Research Into Practice
- US Agency for Healthcare Research and Quality
- Websites of NICE– including NHS Evidence – and the National Institute for Health Research HTA Programme for guidelines and HTAs in development.

Further information about this process can be found in *The Guidelines Manual* (NICE, 2009b).

Systematic literature searches

After the scope was finalised, a systematic search strategy was developed to locate as much relevant evidence as possible. The balance between sensitivity (the power to identify all studies on a particular topic) and specificity (the ability to exclude irrelevant studies from the results) was carefully considered, and a decision made to utilise a broad approach to searching to maximise retrieval of evidence to all parts of the guideline. The broad search was restricted to systematic reviews and RCTs. Additional question specific searching was conducted for other literature where necessary, and restricted to observational studies and qualitative studies or surveys. The following databases were utilised for the searches:

- Allied and Complementary Medicine Database (AMED)
- Applied Social Services Index and Abstracts (ASSIA)
- Australian Education Index (AEI)
- British Education Index (BEI)
- Cumulative Index to Nursing and Allied Health Literature (CINAHL)
- DARE
- CDSR
- CENTRAL [Cochrane database of RCTs and other controlled trials]
- Education Resources in Curriculum (ERIC)
- Embase
- HMIC

- HTA database (technology assessments)
- International Bibliography of Social Science (IBSS)
- MEDLINE/MEDLINE In-Process
- PsycBOOKS
- PsycEXTRA (A grey literature database, which is a companion to PsycINFO)
- Psychological Information Database (PsycINFO)
- Social Services Abstracts (SSA)
- Social Sciences Citation Index – Web of Science (SSCI).

The search strategies were initially developed for MEDLINE before being translated for use in other databases/interfaces. Strategies were built up through a number of trial searches and discussions of the results of the searches with the review team and GDG to ensure that all possible relevant search terms were covered. In order to assure comprehensive coverage, search terms for social anxiety disorder were kept purposely broad to help counter dissimilarities in database indexing practices and thesaurus terms, and imprecise reporting of study populations by authors in the titles and abstracts of records. The search terms for each search are set out in full in Appendix 6.

EndNote
Citations from each search were downloaded into EndNote, the reference management software, and duplicates removed. Records were then screened against the eligibility criteria of the reviews before being quality appraised (see below). The unfiltered search results were saved and retained for future potential re-analysis to help keep the process both replicable and transparent.

Study design filters
To aid retrieval of relevant and sound studies, study design filters were used to limit the searches to systematic reviews, RCTs, observational studies and qualitative studies. The study design filters for systematic reviews and RCTs are adaptations of filters designed by the CRD and the Health Information Research Unit of McMaster University, Ontario. The study design filters for observational studies and qualitative studies were developed in-house. Each filter comprises index terms relating to the study type(s) and associated textwords for the methodological description of the design(s).

Date and language restrictions
Systematic database searches were initially conducted in August 2011 up to the most recent searchable date. Search updates were generated on a 6-monthly basis, with the final re-runs carried out in October 2012 ahead of the guideline consultation. After this point, studies were only included if they were judged by the GDG to be exceptional (for example, if the evidence was likely to change a recommendation).

Although no language restrictions were applied at the searching stage, foreign language papers were not requested or reviewed, unless they were of particular importance to a review question.

Date restrictions were only applied for searches that updated existing reviews. In addition, searches for systematic reviews were limited to research published from 1997 as older reviews were thought to be less useful.

Other search methods

Other search methods involved: (a) scanning the reference lists of all eligible publications (systematic reviews, stakeholder evidence and included studies) for more published reports and citations of unpublished research; (b) sending lists of studies meeting the inclusion criteria to subject experts (identified through searches and the GDG) and asking them to check the lists for completeness, and to provide information of any published or unpublished research for consideration (see Appendix 6); (c) checking the tables of contents of key journals for studies that might have been missed by the database and reference list searches; (d) tracking key papers in the Science Citation Index (prospectively) over time for further useful references; (e) conducting searches in ClinicalTrials.gov for unpublished trial reports; (f) contacting included study authors for unpublished or incomplete datasets. Searches conducted for existing NICE guidelines were updated where necessary. Other relevant guidelines were assessed for quality using the Appraisal of Guidelines for Research and Evaluation (AGREE) instrument (AGREE Collaboration, 2003). The evidence base underlying high-quality existing guidelines was utilised and updated as appropriate.

Full details of the search strategies and filters used for the systematic review of clinical evidence are provided in Appendix 6.

Study selection and quality assessment

All primary-level studies included after the first scan of citations were acquired in full and re-evaluated for eligibility at the time they were being entered into the study information database. More specific eligibility criteria were developed for each review question and are described in the relevant clinical evidence chapters. Eligible studies were critically appraised for methodological quality (see Appendices 8, 10 and 21). The eligibility of each study was confirmed by at least one member of the appropriate topic group.

For some review questions, it was necessary to prioritise the evidence with respect to the UK context (that is, external validity). To make this process explicit, the topic groups took into account the following factors when assessing the evidence:

● participant factors (for example, gender, age and ethnicity)
● provider factors (for example, model fidelity, the conditions under which the intervention was performed and the availability of experienced staff to undertake the procedure)
● cultural factors (for example, differences in standard care and differences in the welfare system).

It was the responsibility of each topic group to decide which prioritisation factors were relevant to each review question in light of the UK context and then decide how they should modify their recommendations.

Unpublished evidence

Authors and principal investigators were approached for unpublished evidence (see Appendix 5). The GDG used a number of criteria when deciding whether or not to accept unpublished data. First, the evidence must have been accompanied by a trial report containing sufficient detail to properly assess the quality of the data. Second, the evidence must have been submitted with the understanding that data from the study and a summary of the study's characteristics would be published in the full guideline. Therefore, the GDG did not accept evidence submitted as commercial in confidence. However, the GDG recognised that unpublished evidence submitted by investigators might later be retracted by those investigators if the inclusion of such data would jeopardise publication of their research.

3.5.2   Data extraction

Quantitative analysis
Study characteristics, methodological quality and outcome data were extracted from all eligible studies that met the minimum quality criteria using Excel based forms (see appendices).

Where possible, outcome data from an intention-to-treat analysis (that is, a 'once-randomised-always-analyse' basis) were used. When making the calculations, if there was good evidence that those participants who ceased to engage in the study were likely to have an unfavourable outcome, early withdrawals were included in both the numerator and denominator. Adverse effects were entered into Review Manager (Cochrane Collaboration, 2011) as reported by the study authors because it is usually not possible to determine whether early withdrawals had an unfavourable outcome.

Masked assessment (that is, blind to the journal from which the article comes, the authors, the institution and the magnitude of the effect) was not used since it is unclear that doing so reduces bias (Berlin, 1997; Jadad et al., 1996).

3.5.3   Evaluating psychometric data

The psychometric properties of instruments that met inclusion criteria were evaluated according to the following criteria:

Reliability[1]
- ≤ 0.60 = unreliable; >0.60 = marginally reliable; ≥ 0.70 = relatively reliable.
- Inter-rater reliability ($r \geq 0.70$) = relatively reliable.
- Test-retest reliability ($r \geq 0.70$) = relatively reliable.

Validity
- Content validity:
  - Content validity index (where available) of: ≥ 0.78 for three or more experts[2].
  - Does a self-report scale have items that capture the components of the disorder? This is judged by evaluating evidence by referring to: (a) established criteria for a particular construct; (b) other published rating scales; (c) characteristic behaviours reported in the literature[3].

---

[1]Sattler (2001).
[2]Polit (2007).
[3]NICE (2012).

- Criterion validity: minimum 0.50[4] (or some suggest 0.30 to 0.40 is more reasonable[5]).
- Construct validity: ≥0.50.
- Sensitivity/specificity (as previously used): ≥0.80.

Clinical utility

The assessment instrument should be feasible and implementable in routine clinical care across a variety of assessment settings. The time and skills required to administer, score and interpret the instrument were also considered, as well as the cost and any copyright issues.

3.5.4   Synthesising the evidence from comparative effectiveness studies

Pairwise meta-analysis

Where possible, meta-analysis was used to synthesise evidence from comparative effectiveness studies using Review Manager. If necessary, re-analyses of the data or sub-analyses were used to answer review questions not addressed in the original studies or reviews.

Dichotomous outcomes were analysed as relative risks (RRs) with the associated 95% CI (see Figure 1 for an example of a forest plot displaying dichotomous data). A relative risk (also called a risk ratio) is the ratio of the treatment event rate to the control event rate. An RR of 1 indicates no difference between treatment and control. In Figure 1 the overall RR of 0.73 indicates that the event rate (that is, non-remission rate) associated with intervention A is about three-quarters of that of the control intervention or, in other words, the RR reduction is 27%.

The CI shows a range of values within which there is 95% confidence that the true effect will lie. If the effect size has a CI that does not cross the 'line of no effect', then the effect is commonly interpreted as being statistically significant.

Continuous outcomes were analysed using the standardised mean difference (SMD) to estimate the same underlying effect (see Figure 2 for an example of a forest plot displaying continuous data). If reported by study authors, intention-to-treat data, using a valid method for imputation of missing data, were preferred over data only from people who completed the study.

To check for consistency of effects among studies, both the I^2 statistic and the chi-squared test of heterogeneity, as well as a visual inspection of the forest plots were used. The I^2 statistic describes the proportion of total variation in study estimates that is due to heterogeneity (Higgins et al., 2003). For a meta-analysis of comparative effectiveness studies, the I^2 statistic was interpreted in the follow way:

- 0% to 25%: might not be important
- 25% to 50%: may represent moderate heterogeneity

---

[4]Andrews and colleagues (1994), Burlingame and colleagues (1995).
[5]Nunnally (1994).

Figure 1: Example of a forest plot displaying dichotomous data

Review: NCCMH clinical guideline review (Example)
Comparison: 01 Intervention A compared with a control group
Outcome: 01 Number of people who did not show remission

Study or sub-category	Intervention A n/N	Control n/N	RR (fixed) 95% CI	Weight %	RR (fixed) 95% CI
01 Intervention A vs. control					
Griffiths1994	13/23	27/28		38.79	0.59 [0.41, 0.84]
Lee1986	11/15	14/15		22.30	0.79 [0.56, 1.10]
Treasure1994	21/28	24/27		38.92	0.84 [0.66, 1.09]
Subtotal (95% CI)	45/66	65/70		100.00	0.73 [0.61, 0.88]

Test for heterogeneity: Chi² = 2.83, df = 2 (P = 0.24), I² = 29.3%
Test for overall effect: Z = 3.37 (P = 0.0007)

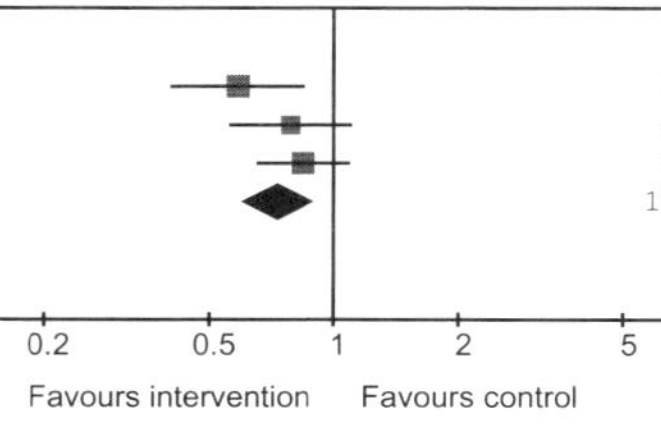

0.2   0.5   1   2   5
Favours intervention   Favours control

Figure 2: Example of a forest plot displaying continuous data

Review: NCCMH clinical guideline review (Example)
Comparison: 01 Intervention A compared with a control group
Outcome: 03 Mean frequency (endpoint)

Study or sub-category	N	Intervention A Mean (SD)	N	Control Mean (SD)	SMD (fixed) 95% CI	Weight %	SMD (fixed) 95% CI
01 Intervention A vs. control							
Freeman1988	32	1.30 (3.40)	20	3.70 (3.60)		25.91	-0.68 [-1.25, -0.10]
Griffiths1994	20	1.25 (1.45)	22	4.14 (2.21)		17.83	-1.50 [-2.20, -0.81]
Lee1986	14	3.70 (4.00)	14	10.10 (17.50)		15.08	-0.49 [-1.24, 0.26]
Treasure1994	28	44.23 (27.04)	24	61.40 (24.97)		27.28	-0.65 [-1.21, -0.09]
Wolf1992	15	5.30 (5.10)	11	7.10 (4.60)		13.90	-0.36 [-1.14, 0.43]
Subtotal (95% CI)	109		91			100.00	-0.74 [-1.04, -0.45]

Test for heterogeneity: Chi² = 6.13, df = 4 (P = 0.19), I² = 34.8%
Test for overall effect: Z = 4.98 (P < 0.00001)

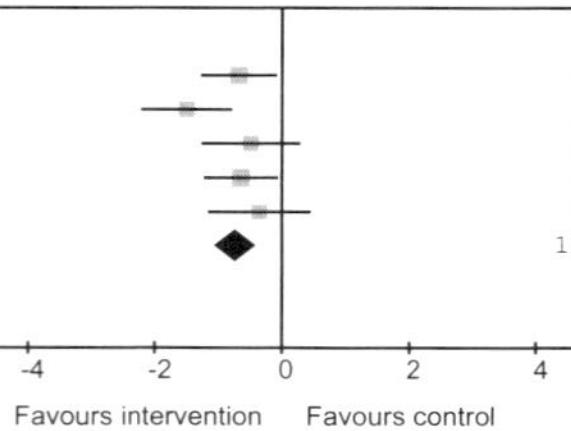

-4   -2   0   2   4
Favours intervention   Favours control

- 50% to 75%: may represent substantial heterogeneity
- 75% to 100%: considerable heterogeneity.

Two factors were used to make a judgement about the importance of the observed value of I^2: (1) the magnitude and direction of effects, and (2) the strength of evidence for heterogeneity (for example, p value from the chi-squared test, or a confidence interval [CI] for I^2).

Where necessary, an estimate of the proportion of eligible data that were missing (because some studies did not include all relevant outcomes) was calculated for each analysis.

Network meta-analysis model

In order to take all trial information into consideration – that is, without ignoring parts of the evidence and without introducing bias by breaking the rules of randomisation (for example, by making 'naïve' additions of data across relevant treatment arms from all RCTs) – mixed treatment comparison meta-analytic techniques, also termed network meta-analysis (NMA), were employed. NMA is a generalisation of standard pairwise meta-analysis for A versus B trials, to data structures that include, for example, A versus B, B versus C, and A versus C trials (Dias et al., 2011; Lu & Ades, 2004). A basic assumption of NMA methods is that direct and indirect evidence estimate the same parameter, that is, the relative effect between A and B measured directly from an A versus B trial, is the same with the relative effect between A and B estimated indirectly from A versus C and B versus C trials. NMA techniques strengthen inference concerning the relative effect of two treatments by including both direct and indirect comparisons between treatments, and, at the same time, allow simultaneous inference on all treatments examined in the pairwise trial comparisons while respecting randomisation (Caldwell et al., 2005; Lu & Ades, 2004). Simultaneous estimation of the relative effect of a number of treatments is possible provided that treatments participate in a single 'network of evidence', that is, every treatment is linked to at least one of the other treatments under assessment through direct or indirect comparisons.

The outcome reported in most trials was mean value at post-treatment on one or more scales with a standard deviation (SD). A few trials reported change from baseline instead of the post-treatment mean for each arm. Some trials reported mean differences with a CI or other summary statistics. In all cases for scale j, measured in arm k of trial i the following was obtained: m_{ijk}, the mean score on Social Anxiety scale j and sd_{ijk} the SD of Social Anxiety scale j; or the difference in means $diff_{ijk} = m_{ijk} - m_{ij1}$ with its SD. The NMA did not consider the size or direction of any differences in pre-treatment scores between intervention conditions within a trial.

There are several options to deal with outcomes reported on different scales, including:

(1) Choose a particular scale to use in the analysis and ignore the information provided by the other scales in the same trial. Crucially, this option will also discard all information from trials not reporting outcomes on the chosen scale.

(2) Define a hierarchy of preferred scales so that the first scale will be used for the analysis if it is reported in the study, otherwise the second, third and so on scales

will be used (in that order). This approach assumes that all scales provide the same information (that is, are equally responsive), but fails to use the information provided by multiple scales reported in the same study.

(3) Pool the data on all scales available within a trial, thereby forming a pooled scale measuring symptoms, which can be used in the analysis. This option also assumes that all scales are equally responsive, but uses all the information provided by multiple scales reported in the same trial. To use this approach the correlation between outcomes measured on different scales in the same trial (that is, on the same patients) must be accounted for.

The second and third options require analysis of outcomes reported on different scales. The SMD is often used as it puts the relative treatment effects on a common, standardised scale on which they can be pooled. This standardisation is usually done by dividing the difference in means by the SD of the measure. Ideally this SD would reflect the true variability of the measure (that is, the scale) in the population, and the same standardising constant would be used for all included studies reporting on that scale. However, this is not usually possible in practice so the SD is estimated from the sample SD in each trial, which is assumed to be the same for all treatment arms and estimated using standard formulae (Higgins & Green, 2011).

Pooling all reported continuous outcomes within a trial

To make full use of the available data, the third option was used, which pools the SMD of the various measures of symptoms within each trial, creating a pooled standardised measure of symptoms for each trial, which is then used in the NMA.

For each trial reporting the mean outcome in each arm, the difference in means on each scale was standardised using the pooled sample SD for that scale in that particular trial. For trials reporting mean change from baseline, the SD at baseline was used to standardise the difference in means, where available. This was to ensure that the standardising constants were comparable across trials because, in general, the SD for the change from baseline is expected to be smaller than the SD of the measure at a particular time point.

Thus, for each trial $diff_{ijk} = m_{ijk} - m_{ijl}$ and SD_{ij}, the SD of the measure in trial i, scale j (assumed common to all arms), were obtained.

The SMD of the treatment in arm k compared with the treatment in arm 1 for each scale in each trial is calculated using Hedges' (adjusted) g, defined as

$$SMD_{ijk} = \frac{m_{ijk} - m_{ij1}}{SD_{ij}} J(df)$$

with

$$J(df) = \frac{\Gamma\left(df/2\right)}{\sqrt{\dfrac{df}{2}}\,\Gamma\left((df-1)/2\right)}$$

and *df* is the degrees of freedom for the SD calculated in that study. The approximate variance for the SMDs is calculated using standard formulae (Higgins & Green, 2011).

Care was taken to ensure a consistent direction of effect. Therefore, some differences had the sign reversed so that for all scales in all trials, a positive SMD favours the treatment being compared (in arm *k*) and a negative SMD favours the 'control' treatment in that trial (the treatment in arm 1).

An examination of the literature and clinical opinion suggested that the correlation between outcomes measured on different scales on the same individuals was approximately 0.65. To pool all SMDs within a trial into a common measure of symptoms, it was assumed that, for a trial with *J* scales, the SMDs on the different scales, X_{ijk}, have a multivariate normal distribution:

$$X_{ik} = \begin{pmatrix} X_{i1k} \\ X_{i2k} \\ \vdots \\ X_{iJk} \end{pmatrix} \sim N_J \left(\begin{pmatrix} SMD_{i1k} \\ SMD_{i2k} \\ \vdots \\ SMD_{iJk} \end{pmatrix}, \Sigma_{ik} \right)$$

where the (symmetric) variance-covariance matrix is defined as:

$$\Sigma_{ik} = \begin{bmatrix} s_{i1k}^2 & \rho s_{i1k} s_{i2k} & \cdots & \rho s_{i1k} s_{iJk} \\ & s_{i2k}^2 & \cdots & \rho s_{i2k} s_{iJk} \\ & & \ddots & \vdots \\ & & & s_{iJk}^2 \end{bmatrix} \qquad (1)$$

That is, the diagonal elements are the variances of the SMDs on each scale and the off-diagonals are given by for row *j*, column *l* with ρ representing the correlation between outcomes measured on different scales for the same individual. These correlations were calculated assuming a between-scale correlation of 0.65 and using the formulae presented in Wei and Higgins (2013).

A pooled scale of symptoms for each arm of each trial compared with arm 1 is defined as a linear combination of all the scales reported in that trial:

$$Y_{ik} = \mathbf{B}^T \mathbf{X}_{ik}$$

Where $\mathbf{B}^T = \dfrac{1}{J}(1,1,\ldots,1)$ is a vector with *J* elements, then, Y_{ik} has a normal distribution with mean:

$$E(Y_{ik}) = \mathbf{B}^T \begin{pmatrix} SMD_{i1k} \\ SMD_{i2k} \\ \vdots \\ SMD_{iJk} \end{pmatrix} = \frac{1}{J} \sum_{J=1}^{J} SMD_{ijk}$$

43

and variance given by:

$$Var(Y_{ik}) = V_{ik} = \mathbf{B}^T \Sigma_{ik} \mathbf{B}$$

Thus for each trial there are data on the relative effect of the treatment in arm k compared with the treatment in arm 1 given as a pooled measure of symptoms, y_{ik}, with variance for $i = 1, \ldots, ns$ and $k = 2, \ldots, na_i$, where na_i represents the number of arms in trial i.

A search for literature on psychometric properties of continuous measures of social anxiety identified a number of papers (Baker et al., 2002; Coles et al., 2001; Connor et al., 2000; Fresco et al., 2001; Heimberg et al., 1999; Marks & Mathews, 1979; Mattick & Clarke, 1998; Osman et al., 1998; Watson & Friend, 1969) with information on between-test correlation and also on test-retest reliability. The populations reported were far from homogeneous, varying from populations of college students with no symptoms of social anxiety to clinical populations with varying degrees and ranges of social anxiety. Correlations that are observed between measurement scales that are subject to measurement error will be highly sensitive to the variation in 'true' patient scores. These same factors vary, of course, between the different trials included in the NMA. The GDG also had access to data collected from consecutive patients attending a social anxiety disorder clinic at the Maudsley Hospital. After examining all this data, it was decided that 0.65 represented a reasonable 'average' correlation between social anxiety tests, and this was the value used for ρ in Equation 1. While it is likely that the true correlations are not entirely uniform, the use of a single average figure appeared to be a reasonable approximation, given the variation in the reported estimates and the clinical heterogeneity of the source studies. It should be noted that if the correlation between the *true* patient scores on each test was 1, then an observed correlation of 0.65 would imply that 19% of the total variance is due to measurement error $(0.806^2 = 0.65)$. This accords with the range of test-retest reliability results, 0.68–0.93, that were reported for these scales.

Then, for all included trials, $i = 1, \ldots, ns$, the continuous measure of symptoms were modelled as:

$$y_{ik} \sim N(\delta_{ik}, V_{ik}) \tag{2}$$

Where δ_{ik} is the relative treatment effect of the treatment in arm k of trial i, relative to the treatment in arm 1 on the pooled SMD scale, thus $\delta_{ik} > 0$ favours the treatment in arm 1 and $\delta_{ik} < 0$ favours the treatment in arm k.

For trials with more than two treatment arms, the normal likelihood for y_{ik} in Equation 2, is replaced with a multivariate normal likelihood for the vector $(y_{i2}, y_{i3}, \ldots, y_{i,na_i})$ where na_i is the number of treatment arms in trial i.

A correlation is induced in the SMDs calculated in a multi-arm trial since these are all taken with respect to the same 'control' treatment (that is, the treatment in arm 1 of that trial). It can be shown that this correlation is equal to the variance of the mean in arm 1, divided by the square of the common standardising constant (Franchini et al., 2012). However, in this case there are no simple SMDs for each arm but a pooled measure on the SMD scale. Conceptually this means that the pooled SMD over all scales for arm k compared with arm 1 in trial i, y_{ik} are formed as:

$$y_{ik} = \frac{\alpha_{ik} - \alpha_{i1}}{\sigma_i}$$

where α_{ik} is the mean outcome in arm k on the pooled scale, and σ_i is the SD of the outcome on the pooled scale (assumed the same for all arms of trial i).

Hence for any $k \neq 1$,

$$Cov(y_{ik}, y_{il}) = \frac{Var(\alpha_{i1})}{\sigma_i^2}$$

with

$$Var(\alpha_{i1}) = \frac{\sigma_i^2}{n_{i1}}$$

Therefore $Cov(y_{ik}, y_{il}) = 1/n_{i1}$, for any $k \neq l$.

Random effects model

A random effects NMA model is used to account for between-trial heterogeneity. The trial-specific treatment effects of the treatment in arm k, relative to the treatment in arm 1, are drawn from a common random effects distribution, under the assumption of consistency:

$$\delta_{ik} \sim N(d_{1,t_{ik}} - d_{1,t_{i1}}, \tau^2)$$

where $d_{1,t_{ik}}$ represents the mean effect of the treatment in arm k in trial i, t_{ik}, relative to treatment 1 (waitlist), and τ^2 represents the between-trial variability in treatment effects (heterogeneity). The between-trials SD, τ, was given a uniform (0, 5) prior. The correlation between the random effects of the trials with more than two arms is taken into account in the analysis.

Due to the sparseness of the network, with most comparisons being informed by only a few trials, a class model was used to borrow strength within treatment classes. However, because of the large number of classes defined in the dataset, the benefits of this class analysis were limited.

Treatments were assigned to classes. For treatments belonging to classes consisting of more than one treatment the pooled relative treatment effects were assumed to be exchangeable within class:

$$d_{1,k} \sim N(m_{D_k}, \tau_{D_k}^2)$$

where D_k indicates the class to which treatment k belongs.

For treatments belonging to a class formed only of themselves in the analysis, the relative treatment effects were assumed to come from normal distribution with a class mean and variance being borrowed from another similar class in the model.

For treatments not believed to belong to a class (that is, forming a class only of themselves) in clinical practice, the relative treatment effects were given non-informative priors $d_{1,k} \sim N(0,100^2)$.

The within-class mean treatment effects were given vague priors $m_j \sim N(0,100^2)$ and the within-class variability had priors $1/\tau_j^2 \sim Gamma(a,b)$ with $a = 3.9$ and $b = 0.35$ chosen so that the mean of the within-class SD is the same as the posterior mean of the between-trial SD (estimated in a previous run of the model without class effects) and the credible interval (CrI) can go from approximately half to double that mean.

However, for treatments not believed to belong to a class, the within-class mean treatment effect was equal to the individual treatment effect, with no added variability.

Relating SMD to probability of recovery

Recovery data were also available for a subset of the included trials. The economic model is driven by the probabilities of recovery on each treatment, but the clinical recommendations rely on both the probabilities of recovery and a continuous measure of improvement in the symptoms (measure by the pooled scale). There are two types of data to inform the relative effects of treatments: the pooled measure of symptoms, y_{ik}, with variance V_{ik} and:

r_{jk} – the number of individuals achieving recovery in arm k of trial j

n_{jk} – the total number of individuals in arm k of trial j

for $j = 1,\ldots, nR$ the trials also reporting recovery.

For trials also reporting recovery ($j = 1,\ldots,nR$) there is the following model

$$r_{jk} \sim \text{Binomial}(p_{jk}, n_{jk})$$

where p_{jk} is the probability of recovery in arm k of trial j. These probabilities are modelled on the log-odds scale as:

$$\text{logit}(p_{jk}) = \mu_j + \lambda_{jk}$$

where λ_{jk} represents the relative treatment effect of the treatment in arm k compared with the treatment in arm 1 in trial j, on the log-odds ratio (LOR) scale and $\lambda_{j1} = 0$. Thus $\lambda_{jk} > 0$ favours the treatment in arm k and $\lambda_{jk} < 0$ favours the treatment in arm 1.

The LOR of recovery can be related to a notional SMD for recovery using the formula (Chinn, 2000):

$$LOR_{\text{Recovery}} = -\frac{\pi}{\sqrt{3}} SMD_{\text{Recovery}} \tag{3}$$

noting the change in sign to retain the interpretation of a positive LOR favouring treatment k.

An empirical examination of the data (see Appendix 11), illustrates the relationship between the LOR of recovery estimated from the recovery data and the LOR obtained from using Equation 3 to convert the pooled SMDs, y_{ik}, in Equation 2. This suggests that a linear regression can be used to estimate the slope of this relationship from the data.

The LOR of recovery is related to the treatment effect on the pooled scale of symptoms using the following relationship:

$$\lambda_{jk} = \beta \times \delta_{jk}^*$$

where δ_{jk}^* is the LOR obtained from transforming the treatment effect on symptoms, δ_{jk}, from the SMD scale using Equation 3. So, the treatment effect on recovery is informed by the corresponding treatment effect in that study on the pooled scale of symptoms as:

$$\lambda_{jk} = \beta \left(-\frac{\pi}{\sqrt{3}} \delta_{jk} \right)$$

for $j = 1, \ldots, nR$, the trials that report both measures.

Information on δ_{jk} will inform estimates of β and λ_{jk}, and information on λ_{jk} (from the studies reporting recovery) will inform the estimates of β and δ_{jk}. In effect this model treats the observed continuous measure on the pooled SMD scale as a surrogate for the probability of recovery, which is of interest to the economic model.

Model properties and assumptions
The model assumes that:
- The populations included in all trials are similar and the treatment effects are exchangeable across all patients (that is, the treatment effects are expected to be similar for all included patients and treatments).
- The treatment effects are exchangeable (that is, similar) within treatment classes.
- The correspondence between the treatment effects on recovery and the pooled continuous scale of symptoms is the same for all treatments.
- The relationship between the LOR of recovery and the pooled continuous scale of symptoms is linear.
- The intercept for regression Equation 3 has been set at zero, meaning that when there is no effect of treatment on the pooled continuous measure of symptoms, there will also be no effect on recovery.
- The underlying distribution of the pooled continuous measure of symptoms is logistic, but can be well approximated by a normal distribution.

The model accounts for:
- The information provided by multiple measures within the same trial and their correlation.
- The uncertainty in the estimated treatment effects on the pooled continuous measure of symptoms on the SMD scale (δ_{jk}).

- The uncertainty in the estimated LOR or recovery (λ_{jk}).
- The correlation between the relative treatment effects in trials with more than two treatments.

Estimation

Model parameters were estimated using Markov chain Monte Carlo simulation methods implemented in WinBUGS 1.4.3 (Lunn et al., 2000; Spiegelhalter, 2001). The first 20,000 iterations were discarded, and 40,000 further iterations were run. In order to test whether prior estimates had an impact on the results, two chains with different initial values were run simultaneously. Convergence was assessed by inspection of the Gelman–Rubin diagnostic plot. Goodness of fit was tested using the posterior mean of the residual deviance, which was compared with the number of data points in the model (Dias et al., 2011).

The WinBUGS code is provided in Appendix 11.

3.5.5 Synthesising the evidence from test accuracy studies

Meta-analysis

Review Manager was used to summarise test accuracy data from each study using forest plots and summary receiver operator characteristics (ROC) plots. Where more than two studies reported appropriate data, a bivariate test accuracy meta-analysis was conducted using Meta-DiSc (Zamora et al., 2006) in order to obtain pooled estimates of sensitivity, specificity, and positive and negative likelihood ratios.

Sensitivity and specificity

The sensitivity of an instrument refers to the probability that it will produce a true positive result when given to a population with the target disorder (compared with a reference or 'gold standard'). An instrument that detects a low percentage of cases will not be very helpful in determining the numbers of service users who should receive further assessment or a known effective intervention, as many individuals who should receive the treatment will not do so. This would lead to an under-estimation of the prevalence of the disorder, contribute to inadequate care and make for poor planning and costing of the need for treatment. As the sensitivity of an instrument increases, the number of false negatives it detects will decrease.

The specificity of an instrument refers to the probability that a test will produce a true negative result when given to a population without the target disorder (as determined by a reference or 'gold standard'). This is important so that people without the disorder are not offered further assessment or interventions they do not need. As the specificity of an instrument increases, the number of false positives will decrease.

This can be illustrated with the following example. From a population in which the point prevalence rate of anxiety is 10% (that is, 10% of the population has anxiety at any one time), 1000 people are given a test that has 90% sensitivity and 85% specificity. It is known that 100 people in this population have anxiety, but the test detects only 90 (true positives), leaving ten undetected (false negatives). It is also known that

900 people do not have anxiety, and the test correctly identifies 765 of these (true negatives), but classifies 135 incorrectly as having anxiety (false positives). The positive predictive value of the test (the number correctly identified as having anxiety as a proportion of positive tests) is 40% (90/90 + 135), and the negative predictive value (the number correctly identified as not having anxiety as a proportion of negative tests) is 98% (765/765 +10). Therefore, in this example, a positive test result is correct in only 40% of cases, while a negative result can be relied upon in 98% of cases.

This example illustrates some of the main differences between positive predictive values and negative predictive values in comparison with sensitivity and specificity. For both positive and negative predictive values, prevalence explicitly forms part of their calculation (Altman & Bland, 1994b). When the prevalence of a disorder is low in a population this is generally associated with a higher negative predictive value and a lower positive predictive value. Therefore although these statistics are concerned with issues probably more directly applicable to clinical practice (for example, the probability that a person with a positive test result actually has anxiety), they are largely dependent on the characteristics of the population sampled and cannot be universally applied (Altman & Bland, 1994a).

On the other hand, sensitivity and specificity do not necessarily depend on prevalence of anxiety (Altman & Bland, 1994a). For example, sensitivity is concerned with the performance of an identification instrument conditional on a person having anxiety. Therefore the higher false positives often associated with samples of low prevalence will not affect such estimates. The advantage of this approach is that sensitivity and specificity can be applied across populations (Altman & Bland, 1994a). However, the main disadvantage is that clinicians tend to find such estimates more difficult to interpret.

When describing the sensitivity and specificity of the different instruments, the GDG defined values above 0.9 as 'excellent', 0.8 to 0.9 as 'good', 0.5 to 0.7 as 'moderate', 0.3 to 0.4 as 'low', and less than 0.3 as 'poor'.

Receiver operator characteristic curves
The qualities of a particular tool are summarised in a ROC curve, which plots sensitivity (expressed as a percent) against (100-specificity) (see Figure 3).

A test with perfect discrimination would have an ROC curve that passed through the top left-hand corner; that is, it would have 100% specificity and pick up all true positives with no false positives. While this is never achieved in practice, the area under the curve (AUC) measures how close the tool gets to the theoretical ideal. A perfect test would have an AUC of 1, and a test with AUC above 0.5 is better than chance. As discussed above, because these measures are based on sensitivity and 100-specificity, theoretically these estimates are not affected by prevalence.

Negative and positive likelihood ratios
Positive (LR+) and negative (LR-) likelihood ratios are thought not to be dependent on prevalence. LR+ is calculated by sensitivity/(1-specificity) and LR- is (1-sensitivity)/specificity. A value of LR + >5 and LR- < 0.3 suggests the test is relatively accurate (Fischer et al., 2003).

Figure 3: Receiver operator characteristic curve

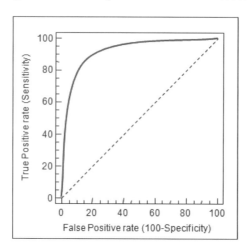

Heterogeneity

Heterogeneity is usually much greater and is to be expected in meta-analyses of test accuracy studies compared with meta-analyses of RCTs (Macaskill et al., 2010). Therefore, a higher threshold for acceptable heterogeneity in such meta-analyses is required. However, when pooling studies resulted in $I^2 > 90\%$, meta-analyses were not conducted.

3.5.6   Grading the quality of evidence

For review questions about interventions, the GRADE approach (Atkins et al., 2004)[6] was used to grade the quality of evidence for critical outcomes assessed in pairwise analyses. The technical team produced GRADE evidence profiles (see below) using GRADEprofiler (GRADEpro) software (Version 3.6), following advice set out in the GRADE handbook (Schünemann et al., 2009).

Evidence profiles

A GRADE evidence profile was used to summarise both the quality of the evidence and the results of the evidence synthesis for each 'critical' and 'important' outcome. The GRADE approach is based on a sequential assessment of the quality of evidence, followed by judgment about the balance between desirable and undesirable effects, and subsequent decision about the strength of a recommendation.

Within the GRADE approach to grading the quality of evidence, the following is used as a starting point:

● randomised trials without important limitations provide high-quality evidence

● observational studies without special strengths or important limitations provide low-quality evidence.

---

[6]For further information about GRADE, see www.gradeworkinggroup.org

For each outcome, quality may be reduced depending on five factors: limitations, inconsistency, indirectness, imprecision and publication bias. For the purposes of the guideline, each factor was evaluated using criteria provided in Table 3.

Table 3: Factors that decrease quality of evidence

Factor	Description	Criteria
Limitations	Methodological quality/ risk of bias.	In the studies that reported a particular outcome, serious risks across most studies. The evaluation of risk of bias was made for each study using NICE methodology checklists.
Inconsistency	Unexplained heterogeneity of results.	Moderate or greater heterogeneity (see Section 3.5.4 for further information about how this was evaluated).
Indirectness	How closely the outcome measures, interventions and participants match those of interest.	If the comparison was indirect, or if the question being addressed by the GDG was substantially different from the available evidence regarding the population, intervention, comparator or outcome.
Imprecision	Results are imprecise when studies include relatively few patients and few events and thus have wide CIs around the estimate of the effect.	If either of the following criteria were met: • the optimal information size (OIS; for dichotomous outcomes, OIS = 300 events; for continuous outcomes, OIS = 400 participants) was not achieved • the 95% CI around the pooled or best estimate of effect included both (1) no effect and (2) appreciable benefit or appreciable harm.
Publication bias	Systematic underestimate or an overestimate of the underlying beneficial or harmful effect because of the selective publication of studies.	If there was evidence of selective publication. This may be detected during the search for evidence or through statistical analysis of the available evidence.

For observational studies without any reasons for downgrading, the quality may be upgraded if there is a large effect, all plausible confounding would reduce the demonstrated effect (or increase the effect if no effect was observed), or there is evidence of a dose-response gradient (details would be provided under the 'other' column).

Each evidence profile also included a summary of the findings: number of participants included in each group, an estimate of the magnitude of the effect, and the overall quality of the evidence for each outcome. Under the GRADE approach, the overall quality for each outcome is categorised into one of four groups, with the following meaning:

- **High quality:** Further research is very unlikely to change our confidence in the estimate of effect.
- **Moderate quality:** Further research is likely to have an important impact on our confidence in the estimate of effect and may change the estimate.
- **Low quality:** Further research is very likely to have an important impact on our confidence in the estimate of effect and is likely to change the estimate.
- **Very low quality:** We are very uncertain about the estimate.

3.5.7   Extrapolation

When answering review questions, it may be necessary to consider extrapolating from another dataset where direct evidence from a primary dataset[7] is not available. In this situation, the following principles were used to determine when to extrapolate:

- a primary dataset is absent, of low quality or is judged to be not relevant to the review question under consideration
- a review question is deemed by the GDG to be important, such that in the absence of direct evidence other data sources should be considered
- a non-primary data source(s) that may inform the review question is, in the view of the GDG, available.

When the decision to extrapolate was made, the following principles were used to inform the choice of the non-primary dataset:

- the populations (usually in relation to the specified diagnosis or problem that characterises the population) under consideration share some common characteristic but differ in other ways, such as age, gender or in the nature of the disorder (for example, acute versus chronic presentations of the same disorder)
- the interventions under consideration have, in the view of the GDG, one or more of the following characteristics:
  - a common mode of action (for example, the pharmacodynamics of drug or a common psychological model of change)
  - the feasibility to deliver the intervention in both populations (for example, in terms of the required skills or the demands of the healthcare system)
  - common side effects/harms in both populations.

---

[7]A primary dataset is defined as a dataset that contains evidence on the population and intervention under review.

- the context or comparator involved in the evaluation of the different datasets shares some common elements that supports extrapolation
- the outcomes involved in the evaluation of the different datasets share some common elements that support extrapolation (for example, improved mood or a reduction in challenging behaviour).

When the choice of the non-primary dataset was made, the following principles were used to guide the application of extrapolation:

- the GDG first considered the need for extrapolation through a review of the relevant primary dataset and was guided in these decisions by the principles for the use of extrapolation
- in all areas of extrapolation datasets were assessed against the four principles (set out above) for determining the choice of datasets
- in deciding on the use of extrapolation, the GDG determined if the extrapolation was reasonable and ensured that:
  - the reasoning behind the decision could be justified by the clinical need for a recommendation to be made
  - the absence of other more direct evidence, and the relevance of the potential dataset to the review question, could be established
  - the reasoning and the method adopted was clearly set out in the relevant section of the guideline.

3.5.8 Method used to answer a review question in the absence of appropriately designed, high-quality research

In the absence of appropriately designed, high-quality research, or where the GDG was of the opinion (on the basis of previous searches or their knowledge of the literature) that there was unlikely to be such evidence, an informal consensus process was adopted. The process involved a group discussion of what is known about the issues. The views of GDG were synthesised narratively, and circulated after the meeting. Feedback was used to revise the text, which was then included in the appropriate evidence review chapter.

Informal consensus
The starting point for the process of informal consensus was that a member of the GDG identified, with help from the systematic reviewer, a narrative review that most directly addressed the review question. Where this was not possible, a brief review of the recent literature was initiated.

This existing narrative review or new review was used as a basis for beginning an iterative process to identify lower levels of evidence relevant to the review question and to lead to written statements for the guideline. The process involved a number of steps:

1. A description of what is known about the issues concerning the clinical question was written by one of the group members.
2. Evidence from the existing review or new review was then presented in narrative form to the GDG and further comments were sought about the evidence and its perceived relevance to the review question.

3. Based on the feedback from the GDG, additional information was sought and added to the information collected. This may include studies that did not directly address the review question but were thought to contain relevant data.
4. If, during the course of preparing the report, a significant body of primary-level studies (of appropriate design to answer the question) were identified, a full systematic review was done.
5. At this time, subject possibly to further reviews of the evidence, a series of statements that directly addressed the review question were developed.
6. Following this, on occasions and as deemed appropriate by the GDG, the report was then sent to appointed experts outside the GDG for peer review and comment. The information from this process was then fed back to the GDG for further discussion of the statements.
7. Recommendations were then developed and could also be sent for further external peer review.
8. After this final stage of comment, the statements and recommendations were again reviewed and agreed upon by the GDG.

3.6   HEALTH ECONOMICS METHODS

The aim of the health economics was to contribute to the guideline's development by providing evidence on the cost effectiveness of interventions for people with social anxiety disorder covered in the guideline. This was achieved by:
● systematic literature review of existing economic evidence
● decision-analytic economic modelling.

Systematic reviews of economic literature were conducted in all areas covered in the guideline. Development of a decision-analytic economic model was considered in areas with likely major resource implications, where the current extent of uncertainty over cost effectiveness was significant and economic analysis was expected to reduce this uncertainty, in accordance with *The Guidelines Manual* (NICE, 2009b). Prioritisation of areas for economic modelling was a joint decision between the guideline health economists and the GDG. The rationale for prioritising review questions for economic modelling was set out in an economic plan agreed by NICE, the GDG, the health economists and the other members of the technical team. The economic question that was identified as a key issue and was subsequently addressed by economic modelling in this guideline was the cost effectiveness of pharmacological and psychological interventions for adults with social anxiety.

In addition, literature on the health-related quality of life (HRQoL) of people with social anxiety was systematically searched to identify studies reporting appropriate utility scores that could be utilised in a cost-utility analysis.

The rest of this section describes the methods adopted in the systematic literature review of economic studies. Methods employed in economic modelling are described in the respective section of the guideline (see Chapter 6, Section 6.10).

3.6.1 Search strategy for economic evidence

Scoping searches

A broad preliminary search of the literature was undertaken in December 2010 to obtain an overview of the issues likely to be covered by the scope, and help define key areas. Searches were restricted to economic studies and HTA reports, and conducted in the following databases:

● Embase
● MEDLINE/MEDLINE In-Process
● HTA database (technology assessments)
● NHS Economic Evaluation Database

Any relevant economic evidence arising from the clinical scoping searches was also made available to the health economist during the same period.

Systematic literature searches

After the scope was finalised, a systematic search strategy was developed to locate all the relevant evidence. The balance between sensitivity (the power to identify all studies on a particular topic) and specificity (the ability to exclude irrelevant studies from the results) was carefully considered, and a decision made to utilise a broad approach to searching to maximise retrieval of evidence to all parts of the guideline. Searches were restricted to economic studies and HTA reports, and conducted in the following databases:

● Embase
● HTA database (technology assessments)
● MEDLINE/MEDLINE In-Process
● NHS Economic Evaluation Database
● PsycINFO.

Any relevant economic evidence arising from the clinical searches was also made available to the health economist during the same period.

The search strategies were initially developed for MEDLINE before being translated for use in other databases/interfaces. Strategies were built up through a number of trial searches and discussions of the results of the searches with the review team and GDG to ensure that all possible relevant search terms were covered. In order to assure comprehensive coverage, search terms for social anxiety disorder were kept purposely broad to help counter dissimilarities in database indexing practices and thesaurus terms, and imprecise reporting of study populations by authors in the titles and abstracts of records.

For standard mainstream bibliographic databases (Embase, MEDLINE and PsycINFO) search terms for social anxiety disorder were combined with a search filter for health economic studies. For searches generated in topic-specific databases (HTA, NHS Economic Evaluation Database) search terms for social anxiety disorder were used without a filter. The sensitivity of this approach was aimed at minimising the risk of overlooking relevant publications, due to potential weaknesses resulting from more focused search strategies. The search terms are set out in full in Appendix 6.

EndNote

Citations from each search were downloaded into EndNote and duplicates removed. Records were then screened against the inclusion criteria of the reviews before being quality appraised. The unfiltered search results were saved and retained for future potential re-analysis to help keep the process both replicable and transparent.

Search filters

The search filter for health economics is an adaptation of a pre-tested strategy designed by the CRD (2007). The search filter is designed to retrieve records of economic evidence (including full and partial economic evaluations) from the vast amount of literature indexed to major medical databases such as MEDLINE. The filter, which comprises a combination of controlled vocabulary and free-text retrieval methods, maximises sensitivity (or recall) to ensure that as many potentially relevant records as possible are retrieved from a search. A full description of the filter is provided in Appendix 7.

Date and language restrictions

Systematic database searches were initially conducted in August 2011 up to the most recent searchable date. Search updates were generated on a 6-monthly basis, with the final re-runs carried out in October 2012 ahead of the guideline consultation. After this point, studies were included only if they were judged by the GDG to be exceptional (for example, the evidence was likely to change a recommendation).

Although no language restrictions were applied at the searching stage, foreign language papers were not requested or reviewed, unless they were of particular importance to an area under review. All the searches were restricted to research published from 1997 onwards in order to obtain data relevant to current healthcare settings and costs.

Other search methods

Other search methods involved scanning the reference lists of all eligible publications (systematic reviews, stakeholder evidence and included studies from the economic and clinical reviews) to identify further studies for consideration.

Full details of the search strategies and filter used for the systematic review of health economic evidence are provided in Appendix 7.

3.6.2   Inclusion criteria for economic studies

The following inclusion criteria were applied to select studies identified by the economic searches for further consideration:

- Only studies from Organisation for Economic Co-operation and Development countries were included because the aim of the review was to identify economic information transferable to the UK context.
- Selection criteria based on types of clinical conditions and study populations, as well as interventions assessed, were identical to the clinical literature review.

- Studies were included provided that sufficient details regarding methods and results were available to enable the methodological quality of the study to be assessed, and provided that the study's data and results were extractable. Poster presentations of abstracts were excluded.
- Full economic evaluations that compared two or more relevant options and considered both costs and consequences, as well as costing analyses that compared only costs between two or more interventions, were included in the review.
- Economic studies were included if they used clinical effectiveness data from an RCT, a cohort study or a systematic review and meta-analysis of clinical studies.

3.6.3 Applicability and quality criteria for economic studies

All economic papers eligible for inclusion were appraised for their applicability and quality using the methodology checklist for economic evaluations recommended by NICE (2009b), which is shown in Appendix 8 of this guideline. The methodology checklist for economic evaluations was also applied to the economic model developed specifically for this guideline. All studies that fully or partially met the applicability and quality criteria described in the methodology checklist were considered during the guideline development process, along with the results of the economic modelling conducted specifically for this guideline. The completed methodology checklists for all economic evaluations considered in the guideline are provided in Appendix 21.

3.6.4 Presentation of economic evidence

The existing economic evidence considered in the guideline is provided in the evidence chapters, following presentation of the relevant clinical evidence. The respective evidence tables that provide an overview of the study characteristics and results are presented in Appendix 22. Methods and results of the economic modelling undertaken alongside the guideline development process are described in detail in Chapter 6 and summarised in an economic evidence profile provided in Appendix 24.

3.6.5 Results of the systematic search of economic literature

The titles of all studies identified by the systematic search of the literature were screened for their relevance to the topic (that is, economic issues and information on HRQoL in people with social anxiety). References that were clearly not relevant were excluded first. The abstracts of all potentially relevant studies (108 references) were then assessed against the inclusion criteria for economic evaluations by the health economist. Full texts of the studies potentially meeting the inclusion criteria (including those for which eligibility was not clear from the abstract) were obtained. Studies that did not meet the inclusion criteria, were duplicates, were secondary publications of one study, or had been updated in more recent publications were subsequently excluded. Economic evaluations eligible for inclusion (four references) were then appraised for their applicability and quality using the methodology checklist for economic evaluations. All four studies met (fully or partially) the applicability and quality criteria set by NICE and were thus considered during guideline development.

3.7 USING NICE EVIDENCE REVIEWS AND RECOMMENDATIONS FROM EXISTING NICE CLINICAL GUIDELINES

When review questions overlap and evidence from another guideline applies to a question in the current guideline, it might be desirable and practical to incorporate or adapt recommendations published in NICE guidelines. Adaptation refers to the process by which an existing recommendation is modified in order to facilitate its placement in a new guideline. Incorporation refers to the placement of a recommendation that was developed for another guideline into a new guideline, with no material changes to wording or structure. Incorporation would be used in relatively rare circumstances, as cross-referring to the other guideline will often be all that is necessary. Incorporation or adaptation is likely to be substantially more complex where health economics were a major part of the decision making. In these circumstances, these methods are only used rarely after full and detailed consideration.

3.7.1 Incorporation

In the current guideline, the following criteria were used to determine when a recommendation could be incorporated:
- a review question in the current guideline was addressed in another NICE guideline
- evidence for the review question and related recommendation(s) has not changed in important ways
- evidence for the previous question is judged by the GDG to support the existing recommendation(s), and be relevant to the current question
- the relevant recommendation can 'stand alone' and does not need other recommendations from the original guideline to be relevant or understood within the current guideline.

3.7.2 Adaptation

The following criteria were used to determine when a recommendation could be adapted:
- a review question in the current guideline is similar to a question addressed in another NICE guideline
- evidence for the review question and related recommendations has not changed in important ways

- evidence for the previous question is judged by the GDG to support the existing recommendation(s), and be relevant to the current question
- the relevant recommendation can 'stand alone' and does not need other recommendations from the original guideline to be relevant
- contextual evidence, such as background information about how an intervention is provided in the healthcare settings that are the focus of the guideline, informs the re-drafting or re-structuring of the recommendation but does not alter its meaning or intent (if meaning or intent were altered, a new recommendation should be developed).

In deciding whether to choose between incorporation or adaptation of existing guideline recommendations, the GDG considered whether the direct evidence obtained from the current guideline dataset was of sufficient quality to allow development of recommendations. It was only where (a) such evidence was not available or insufficient to draw robust conclusions and (b) where methods used in other NICE guidelines were sufficiently robust that the 'incorporate and adapt' method could be used. Recommendations were only incorporated or adapted after the GDG had reviewed evidence supporting previous recommendations and confirmed that they agreed with the original recommendations.

When adaptation is used, the meaning and intent of the original recommendation is preserved but the wording and structure of the recommendation may change. Preservation of the original meaning (that is, that the recommendation faithfully represents the assessment and interpretation of the evidence contained in the original guideline evidence reviews) and intent (that is, the intended action[s] specified in the original recommendation will be achieved) is an essential element of the process of adaptation.

3.7.3   Roles and responsibilities

The guideline review team, in consultation with the guideline Facilitator and Chair, were responsible for identifying overlapping questions and deciding if it would be appropriate to incorporate or to adapt following the principles above. For adapted recommendations, at least two members of the GDG for the original guideline were consulted to ensure the meaning and intent of the original recommendation was preserved. The GDG confirmed the process had been followed, that there was insufficient evidence to make new recommendations, and agreed all adaptations to existing recommendations.

In evidence chapters where incorporation and adaptation have been used, the original review questions are listed with the rationale for the judgement on the similarity of questions. Tables are then provided that set out the original recommendation, a brief summary of the original evidence, the new recommendation, and the reasons for adaptation. For an adapted recommendation, details of any contextual information are provided, along with information about how the GDG ensured that the meaning and intent of the adapted recommendation were preserved.

3.7.4   Drafting of adapted recommendations

The drafting of adapted recommendations conforms to standard NICE procedures for the drafting of guideline recommendations, preserves the original meaning and intent, and aims to minimise the degree or re-writing and re-structuring.

3.8   FROM EVIDENCE TO RECOMMENDATIONS

Once the clinical and health economic evidence was summarised, the GDG drafted the recommendations. In making recommendations, the GDG took into account the trade-off between the benefits and harms of the intervention/instrument, as well as other important factors, such as economic considerations, values of the development group and society, the requirements to prevent discrimination and to promote equality[8], and the GDG's awareness of practical issues (Eccles et al., 1998; NICE, 2009b).

Finally, to show clearly how the GDG moved from the evidence to the recommendations, each chapter has a section called 'from evidence to recommendations'. Underpinning this section is the concept of the 'strength' of a recommendation (NICE, 2009b). This takes into account the quality of the evidence but is conceptually different. Some recommendations are 'strong' in that the GDG believes that the vast majority of healthcare professionals and service users would choose a particular intervention if they considered the evidence in the same way that the GDG has. This is generally the case if the benefits clearly outweigh the harms for most people and the intervention is likely to be cost effective. However, there is often a closer balance between benefits and harms, and some service users would not choose an intervention whereas others would. This may happen, for example, if some service users are particularly averse to some side effect and others are not. In these circumstances the recommendation is generally weaker, although it may be possible to make stronger recommendations about specific groups of service users. The strength of each recommendation is reflected in the wording of the recommendation, rather than by using ratings, labels or symbols.

Where the GDG identified areas in which there are uncertainties or where robust evidence was lacking, they developed research recommendations. Those that were identified as 'high priority' were developed further in the NICE version of the guideline, and presented in Appendix 9.

3.9   STAKEHOLDER CONTRIBUTIONS

Professionals, service users, and companies have contributed to and commented on the guideline at key stages in its development. Stakeholders for this guideline include:
● service user and carer stakeholders: national service user and carer organisations that represent the interests of people whose care will be covered by the guideline

---

[8]See NICE's equality scheme: www.nice.org.uk/aboutnice/howwework/NICEEqualityScheme.jsp

- local service user and carer organisations: but only if there is no relevant national organisation
- professional stakeholders' national organisations: that represent the healthcare professionals who provide the services described in the guideline
- commercial stakeholders: companies that manufacture drugs or devices used in treatment of the condition covered by the guideline and whose interests may be significantly affected by the guideline
- providers and commissioners of health services in England and Wales
- statutory organisations: including the Department of Health, the Welsh Assembly
- Government, NHS Quality Improvement Scotland, the Care Quality Commission and the National Patient Safety Agency
- research organisations: that have carried out nationally recognised research in the area.

NICE clinical guidelines are produced for the NHS in England and Wales, so a 'national' organisation is defined as one that represents England and/or Wales, or has a commercial interest in England and/or Wales.

Stakeholders have been involved in the guideline's development at the following points:

- commenting on the initial scope of the guideline and attending a scoping workshop held by NICE
- contributing possible review questions and lists of evidence to the GDG
- commenting on the draft of the guideline.

3.10   VALIDATION OF THE GUIDELINE

Registered stakeholders had an opportunity to comment on the draft guideline, which was posted on the NICE website during the consultation period. Following the consultation, all comments from stakeholders and experts (see Appendix 4) were responded to, and the guideline updated as appropriate. NICE also reviewed the guideline and checked that stakeholders' comments had been addressed.

Following the consultation period, the GDG finalised the recommendations and the NCCMH produced the final documents. These were then submitted to NICE for a quality assurance check. Any errors were corrected by the NCCMH, then the guideline was formally approved by NICE and issued as guidance to the NHS in England and Wales.

4 IMPROVING ACCESS TO SERVICES AND THE EXPERIENCE OF CARE

4.1 INTRODUCTION

Engaging in any social activity can cause severe distress for someone with a social anxiety disorder, and this is no different when they are seeking help from healthcare services. For some people with social anxiety disorder, accessing care may be even more anxiety provoking than other situations because of its unfamiliarity, its importance to them and the fact that it will involve discussing a number of issues, quite possibly for the first time, which they may find deeply humiliating or embarrassing. Of course, such concerns may be sources of anxiety for anyone accessing healthcare, and particularly mental healthcare, but someone with a social anxiety disorder will be experiencing additional layers of overwhelming and unmanageable anxiety.

People with social anxiety disorder frequently see their anxiety as a personal weakness and are acutely ashamed and embarrassed of it, and of its effect on their life and ability to reach traditional milestones. Accessing treatment will typically involve revealing these perceived inadequacies, and thus the nature of the disorder makes it particularly hard for people to reach out and seek help. Many will not do so, or will do so only when they reach crisis point or have ended up in treatment for other reasons. All these problems will be compounded by the stigma many people associate with seeking help from mental health services.

The GDG decided that these issues should be addressed, because a failure to do so could undermine the primary intention of the guideline in providing effective evidence-based interventions for social anxiety disorder. Related to the issue of access to care is the experience of care itself, because it is only through improving service users' experience that access to care can also be enhanced.

In seeking to improve both access to services and the experience of care the GDG was mindful of other NICE guidelines that had addressed the issues of access to care, such as *Common Mental Health Disorders* (NICE, 2011b), and improving the experience of care, such as *Service User Experience in Adult Mental Health* (NICE, 2011d) and *Patient Experience in Adult NHS Services* (NICE, 2012). The GDG therefore decided to review these guidelines specifically from the perspective of people with social anxiety disorder.

Service User Experience in Adult Mental Health (NCCMH, 2012; NICE, 2011d) sets out the principles for improving the experience of care for people using adult NHS mental health services in seven main areas: (1) access to community care; (2) assessment (non-acute); (3) community care; (4) assessment and referral in crisis; (5) hospital care; (6) discharge and transfer of care; and (7) detention under the Mental Health Act. *Common Mental Health Disorders* (NCCMH, 2011a; NICE, 2011b) provides advice on improving access to services for people with depression and anxiety disorders, and also on developing local care pathways. The GDG judged that the main issues dealt with in *Patient Experience in Adult NHS Services* (NICE, 2012) were covered by *Service User Experience in Adult Mental Health* (NICE, 2011d) and therefore did not review it further.

While various themes relating to access and experience of care covered in *Service User Experience in Adult Mental Health* (NCCMH, 2012; NICE, 2011d) and *Common Mental Health Disorders* (NCCMH, 2011a; NICE, 2011b) may be relevant to people with social anxiety disorder, the GDG judged that there were potentially important areas specific to people with social anxiety that may not have been included or that could require additional detail for this guideline.

An additional challenge faced by the GDG was that the current guideline on social anxiety disorder covers children, young people and adults, which meant that the GDG had to consider issues that were outside the scope of *Service User Experience in Adult Mental Health* (NCCMH, 2012; NICE, 2011d) and *Common Mental Health Disorders* (NCCMH, 2011a; NICE, 2011b), which were developed for adults only. The GDG considered this issue and judged that although the problems associated with social anxiety disorder manifest themselves somewhat differently in children and young people, the mechanisms underlying the disorder (which often has an onset in early adolescence) were sufficiently similar that the principles for improving access and experience of care identified could, with appropriate adaptation, apply to children and young people. This chapter therefore seeks to assess the relevance of these guidelines for people with social anxiety disorder in light of the expert opinion of GDG members and any further evidence specific to social anxiety disorder identified in electronic literature searches and, if necessary, developing new recommendations or adapting existing recommendations for use in the context of this guideline.

4.2   METHOD

In developing the recommendations in this chapter the GDG followed the methods for incorporation and adaptation outlined in Chapter 3. After considering the scope of previous guidelines, the GDG identified two related guidelines:
● *Service User Experience in Adult Mental Health* (NCCMH, 2012; NICE, 2011d)
● *Common Mental Health Disorders* (NCCMH, 2011a; NICE, 2011b).

Additionally, the GDG used the results of a new review of the experience of care for people with social anxiety disorder (see Section 4.3). In undertaking this review, the GDG were concerned to address:
● existing evidence concerning the general areas of access to services and experience of care that applied across all (common) mental health disorders and therefore did not need to be included within this current guideline on social anxiety disorder
● aspects of access to services and experience of care that were specific to social anxiety disorder and which required the generation of new recommendations.

In undertaking these reviews the GDG was guided by the difficulties commonly experienced by people with social anxiety disorder, which the GDG considered needed to be addressed by the guideline if the care of people with social anxiety disorder is to be improved. Drawing on their clinical and service user experience the GDG considered a wide range of potential ways that social anxiety disorder could interact and interfere with the process of accessing and receiving treatment. The issues raised are summarised by the following general themes and points, intended to highlight areas where increased awareness among healthcare professionals is most needed. It is not meant to be comprehensive or representative of all people with social anxiety disorder.

The GDG judged that in the context of accessing and receiving treatment, people with social anxiety disorder may have difficulty with:

- **Communication, including:**
  - initiating discussions and asking for help or information
  - expressing their difficulties and wishes
  - asserting themselves if they are unhappy or do not want something.
- **Performance-related situations, including:**
  - speaking, writing, eating, using the telephone or engaging in other performance-related activities while in the presence of others
  - being the centre of attention or being watched by people
  - concentrating and taking in information, and subsequently processing and remembering it.
- **Being misunderstood, including:**
  - lack of recognition that their hesitancy may be due to fear rather than an inability to understand or a lack of desire to be involved
  - lack of recognition that although they may hide and/or be unable to express it, they may be suffering greatly
  - lack of recognition of the extent of the challenges and limitations that they face
  - a lack of adequate information and support for the people who they need to understand their condition and help them, such as their families or carers.
- **Feeling shame, including:**
  - people noticing that they are anxious or exhibiting symptoms of anxiety or embarrassment
  - people finding out about their anxiety and that they are seeking help for it
  - people knowing they made a mistake or could not do something
  - feeling unworthy of people's time and help.
- **Relationships, including :**
  - fearing that people will get angry at any moment because of their actions or inactions
  - fearing that they will be evaluated negatively and that they are going to let down their healthcare professional or displease them
  - feeling that people do not like them and do not want them around
  - being sensitive to criticism and negative (or ambiguous) verbal and non-verbal feedback
  - being around people who inadvertently heighten their anxiety, for example, authority figures, peers or people of the gender to which they are attracted.

4.3 REVIEW OF THE LITERATURE FOR ACCESS TO SERVICES AND EXPERIENCE OF CARE

4.3.1 Introduction

The GDG decided to focus the literature review on the experience of care because the *Service User Experience in Adult Mental Health* guidance (NCCMH, 2012; NICE, 2011d) was focused in significant part on the experience of secondary care mental health services whereas the vast majority of people with social anxiety disorder are treated in primary care and related services. In contrast, the focus of *Common Mental Health Disorders* (NCCMH, 2011a; NICE, 2011b) was much more on primary care and therefore a review was undertaken to augment the review for *Common Mental Health Disorders* (NCCMH, 2011a; NICE, 2011b), with a specific focus on social anxiety disorder because no clinical guideline was available on social anxiety disorder when *Common Mental Health Disorders* was developed.

4.3.2 Clinical review protocol (access to services and experience of care)

The review protocol, including the review questions, information about the databases searched, and the eligibility criteria used for this section of the guideline, can be found in Table 4 (further information about the search strategy can be found in Appendix 6). A systematic search for published reviews of relevant qualitative studies and other guidance relating to people with social anxiety disorder and their families and carers was undertaken using standard NCCMH procedures as described in Chapter 3.

4.3.3 Studies and reviews identified

No studies that met the inclusion criteria were identified among the 1,105 citations retrieved in the search. After removing duplicates (eight studies), reasons for exclusion were: (a) not relevant to social anxiety disorder (1,044 studies); (b) primary intervention study not relevant to this part of the guideline (21 studies); and (c) not related to improving access to and experience of care (32 studies).

In the absence of any relevant reviews, Healthtalkonline[9] was searched for transcripts relating to the review questions, but no relevant information was found.

4.3.4 Review of existing NICE guidance

All GDG members initially reviewed *Service User Experience in Adult Mental Health* (NCCMH, 2012; NICE, 2011d) and *Common Mental Health Disorders* (NCCMH,

---

[9]http://www.healthtalkonline.org/

Table 4: Clinical review protocol for the review of experience of care

Topic	Access to services and experience of care
Review question(s) (RQs)	**RQ1.1:** What methods increase the proportion and diversity of people with social anxiety disorder initiating and continuing treatment? **RQ1.2:** What dimensions of the experience of care for people with social anxiety disorder require adjustments to the procedures for access to and delivery of interventions for social anxiety disorder over and above those already developed for common mental health disorders?
Subquestion(s)	Do obstacles to access or the effectiveness of interventions differ across the following subgroups: • white people versus black and minority ethnic groups • men versus women • children (5 to 12 years), young people (13 to 18 years), adults (18 to 65 years), older adults (65+ years)?
Objectives	To better characterise the experience of care and identify obstacles to access by updating a previous literature review and by expert consensus.
Criteria for considering studies for the review	
• *Intervention*	Identify methods to overcome obstacles to treatment that are specific to people with social anxiety disorder (that is, included or in addition to those identified in the *Common Mental Health Disorders* and *Service User Experience in Adult Mental Health* NICE guidelines).
• *Types of participants*	Children and young people (5 to 18 years) and adults (18+ years) with social anxiety disorder or suspected social anxiety disorder. Special consideration will be given to the subgroups above.
• *Critical outcomes*	• Initiation of services. • Completion of treatment.
• *Minimum sample size*	None
• *Study setting*	• Primary, secondary, tertiary health and social care. • Children's services and educational settings.

Continued

Table 4: (*Continued*)

Topic	Access to services and experience of care
Search strategy	**General outline:** • Relevant NICE guidelines (including *Common Mental Health Disorders* and *Service User Experience in Adult Mental Health*) will be searched for recommendations and studies about people with social anxiety disorder. • An electronic database search for qualitative systematic reviews, primary qualitative studies and survey literature to update evidence identified by the relevant NICE guidelines. • A broad electronic database search for quantitative systematic reviews and RCTs. **Databases searched:** Qualitative systematic reviews/quantitative reviews/RCTs: Core databases: Embase, MEDLINE, PreMEDLINE, PsycINFO. Topic specific databases: AEI, AMED, ASSIA, BEI, CDSR, CENTRAL, CINAHL, DARE, ERIC, HTA, IBSS, Sociological Abstracts, SSA, SSCI. Primary qualitative studies/survey literature: Embase, MEDLINE, PreMEDLINE, PsycINFO, CINAHL. **Date restrictions:** Quantitative systematic reviews: 1997 onwards. RCTs: inception of databases onwards. Qualitative systematic reviews, primary qualitative studies, survey literature: 2010 onwards.
Study design filter/ limit used	Core databases/topic specific databases*: qualitative reviews, quantitative reviews, RCTs.
Question specific search strategy	Quantitative systematic reviews, RCTs: generic. Qualitative systematic reviews, primary qualitative studies: focused.
Amendments to search strategy/study design filter	None.

Continued

Table 4: (*Continued*)

Topic	Access to services and experience of care
Searching other resources	Hand-reference searching of retrieved literature.
Existing reviews	
• *Updated*	See below ('The review strategy').
• *Not updated*	None
The review strategy	The following sources of information will be used: • If trials of methods to improve access and experience of care for people with social anxiety disorder are found, outcomes will be synthesised using meta-analysis if possible. Otherwise, a narrative review of these studies will be presented. • If qualitative studies are found about improving the experience of care for people with social anxiety disorder specifically, a narrative review of these studies will be presented. • Evidence from existing NICE guidelines will be reviewed by the GDG to determine whether previous recommendations can be incorporated or adapted for adults and for children and young people with social anxiety disorder. • GDG experience will be used to interpret any specific studies, to develop new recommendations, and to incorporate or adapt previous recommendations.

Note. *No filter/limit used for evidence of qualitative primary studies and survey literature.

2011a; NICE, 2011b). The GDG formed a topic group (Experience of Care) to undertake a more detailed review of the guidelines informed by the methods and principles set out in Chapter 3.

The GDG judged that *Service User Experience in Adult Mental Health* applied to the experience of care of children, young people and adults with social anxiety disorder, including: (a) relationships and communication; (b) providing information; (c) avoiding stigma and promoting social inclusion; (d) decisions, capacity and safeguarding; and (e) involving families and carers. The GDG did not consider it necessary to transplant all of the recommendations into the current guideline as they applied to all people with mental disorders and were not specific to people with social anxiety disorder. When considering the recommendations to include in the current guideline, the GDG considered those areas that were concerned with the particular ways in which social anxiety disorder may impact on a person's experience of, or access to, services.

The GDG identified two recommendations from *Service User Experience in Adult Mental Health* that were relevant. In both cases, evidence for the previous recommendation was considered applicable, but the recommendations required some adaptation to be relevant to the experience of, or access to, care for social anxiety disorder (see Table 5). The rationale for why recommendations were adapted is explained in the right-hand column of the table. In the first column the numbers refer to the recommendations in the *Service User Experience in Adult Mental Health* NICE guideline. In the second column the numbers in brackets following the recommendation refer to Section 4.6 in this guideline.

The GDG also reviewed *Common Mental Health Disorders* and decided that the review questions, evidence, and recommendations were applicable to people with social anxiety disorder and would not need to be adapted. It is expected that healthcare professionals will consult *Common Mental Health Disorders* in conjunction with this guideline.

4.4 DEVELOPING PRINCIPLES OF CARE SPECIFICALLY FOR PEOPLE WITH SOCIAL ANXIETY DISORDER

4.4.1 Introduction

The GDG drew on their knowledge and experience to determine whether there were other areas of access to services and experience of care that were not covered by either: (a) the recommendations in *Service User Experience in Adult Mental Health* (NICE, 2011d) and *Common Mental Health Disorders* (NICE, 2011b); or (b) the adapted recommendations included in this chapter, with a view to developing principles of care for people with social anxiety disorder.

4.4.2 Method

In addition to the reviews above, experience of care was considered during topic group discussions related to psychological interventions, pharmacological interventions, and children and young people. Minutes from these meetings were circulated to the whole GDG, which considered experience of care as part of all aspects of this guideline. These discussions are summarised in the section below.

4.4.3 Discussion

As it is a challenging and significant step for those with social anxiety disorder to seek help from others, the GDG discussed the importance of ensuring that their experience is positive, met with care, compassion and understanding, and that as many barriers and triggers as possible are removed from their path to recovery. The GDG felt that if these things do not happen, then there is great risk that people with social anxiety

Table 5: Recommendations from *Service User Experience in Adult Mental Health* for inclusion

Original recommendation from *Service User Experience in Adult Mental Health* (NICE, 2011d)	Review question and evidence base of existing recommendation	Recommendation following adaptation for this guideline	Reasons for adaptation
1.1.4 When working with people using mental health services: • make sure that discussions take place in settings in which confidentiality, privacy and dignity are respected • be clear with service users about limits of confidentiality (that is, which health and social care professionals have access to information about their diagnosis and its treatment and in what circumstances this may be shared with others).	Review question: For people who use adult NHS mental health services, what are the key problems associated with their experience of care? Evidence base: Key problems associated with service user experience (based on a review of 133 qualitative studies or reviews of qualitative studies and three surveys); key requirements for high-quality service user experience (based on GDG expert opinion). See Chapter 9 of *Service User Experience in Adult Mental Health* (NCCMH, 2012).	When working with children and young people and their parents or carers: • make sure that discussions take place in settings in which confidentiality, privacy and dignity are respected • be clear with the child or young person and their parents or carers about limits of confidentiality (that is, which health and social care professionals have access to information about their diagnosis and its treatment and in what circumstances this may be shared with others). [4.6.4.2]	The original recommendation was adapted to refer to children and young people; no further adaptation was required.

1.1.14 Discuss with the person using mental health services if and how they want their family or carers to be involved in their care. Such discussions should take place at intervals to take account of any changes in circumstances, and should not happen only once. As the involvement of families and carers can be quite complex, staff should receive training in the skills needed to negotiate and work with families and carers, and also in managing issues relating to information sharing and confidentiality.	Review question: For people who use adult NHS mental health services, what are the key problems associated with their experience of care? Evidence base: Key problems associated with service user experience (based on a review of 133 qualitative studies or reviews of qualitative studies and three surveys); key requirements for high-quality service user experience (based on GDG expert opinion). See Chapter 7 of *Service User Experience in Adult Mental Health* (NCCMH, 2012).	If parents or carers are involved in the assessment or treatment of a young person with social anxiety disorder, discuss with the young person (taking into account their developmental level, emotional maturity and cognitive capacity) what form they would like this involvement to take. Such discussions should take place at intervals to take account of any changes in circumstances, including developmental level, and should not happen only once. As the involvement of parents and carers can be quite complex, staff should receive training in the skills needed to negotiate and work with parents and carers, and also in managing issues relating to information sharing and confidentiality. [4.6.5.2]	The original recommendation was considered relevant because young people mature enough to make informed decisions might wish to negotiate how their parents or carers are involved with their care. The GDG judged that for younger children parents and carers would almost always be involved. The recommendation was adapted to make it clear that when discussions take place regarding the involvement of parents and carers that the young person's 'developmental level, emotional maturity and cognitive capacity' should be considered. In the first sentence the word 'care' was replaced with 'assessment or treatment' to avoid potential confusion with the routine care provided by a carer.

disorder will not seek treatment, or will disengage from it soon after starting. The GDG was of the view that if people with social anxiety disorder do not seek help then further problems, such as those commonly comorbid with the disorder (see Chapter 2), will develop.

The GDG discussed that although services will recognise that it may be harmful to overly facilitate the avoidance of feared situations, it is important for people with social anxiety disorder that their anxiety is minimised enough for them to access treatment in the first instance. The GDG also discussed that any overt special treatment or 'fuss' will normally heighten anxiety rather than reduce it and should be avoided. The GDG felt therefore that it was important that services offer choice rather than being prescriptive. Elements of the care setting, such as the waiting room and reception area, can provide valuable therapeutic opportunities when the service user feels ready for such a step.

In addition, the GDG considered that while it is difficult for people with social anxiety disorder to access healthcare services in the first place, it may also be difficult for them to maintain contact until they have begun to overcome their fears. It is important, therefore, that at all stages of the care pathway for adults, children and young people are considered carefully and adjustments made where necessary and possible.

Although there will be shared concerns among people with social anxiety disorder, the GDG discussed that it is important to recognise that some fears may be idiosyncratic, and that triggers for and manifestations of those fears can vary considerably. It was the GDG's view that some people struggle to speak at all because they fear saying something wrong or making people angry, whereas others talk excessively to fill uncomfortable silences. Some find group situations easier and feel one-to-one situations are more pressured, yet others feel the reverse. Some are particularly anxious with strangers, while others get more anxious as people get to know them and their personality becomes more open to judgement and criticism. While it is important to be aware of potential unspoken needs, care should be taken to avoid making assumptions about what a person with social anxiety disorder will find comfortable or uncomfortable. Finally, the GDG discussed whether there should be an emphasis on creating an environment where they can open up and share their concerns and where their specific needs could be met in a collaborative way.

4.4.4   Summary

In addition to the discussion summarised in Section 4.4.3, the GDG was guided by the key concerns set out in Section 4.2 and their review of *Service User Experience in Adult Mental Health* and *Common Mental Health Disorders* in Section 4.3 when developing new recommendations specific to people with social anxiety disorder. The considerations that fed into the development of these recommendations are described in the next section.

4.5 FROM EVIDENCE TO RECOMMENDATIONS

With the exception of the two recommendations adapted from *Service User Experience in Adult Mental Health* (NCCMH, 2012; NICE, 2011d), the recommendations in this chapter are based on expert opinion and informal consensus methods. As a consequence the GDG was cautious in making recommendations but after detailed discussion decided that in order to ensure the effective delivery of evidence-based interventions and access to them, specific recommendations to improve access and the experience of care were needed for people with social anxiety disorder. The development of the recommendations was also undertaken in the context of the review of recommendations in *Service User Experience in Adult Mental Health* and *Common Mental Health Disorders*.

The GDG considered that new recommendations were particularly needed in a number of key areas: (1) communication between people with social anxiety disorder and healthcare professionals; (2) accessing services; (3) transfer of care; and (4) inpatient services. In addition, the GDG felt that a number of recommendations needed to be made that were specific to children and young people with social anxiety disorder because the *Service User Experience in Adult Mental Health* and *Common Mental Health Disorders* guidelines covered the care of adults only.

For all people with social anxiety disorder, the GDG was concerned that healthcare professionals lack knowledge and awareness of social anxiety disorder and, in particular, that many people with social anxiety perceive the disorder as a personal failing that is not treatable. As a consequence they often avoid talking about the problem, have difficulty discussing their experience and are vulnerable to shame and stigma if in contact with mental health services. The GDG was very aware of the difficulties many people had with interpersonal communication, particularly when interacting with healthcare professionals in the early stages of a therapeutic intervention. The GDG therefore felt that services and healthcare professionals should offer the option of different modes of communication (for example, text message or letters) at the outset and throughout treatment.

Communicating with children and young people with social anxiety disorder and their parents or carers was regarded by the GDG as especially challenging, which could be exacerbated by the presence of selective mutism, learning disabilities, language delays or sensory problems in some children with social anxiety disorder. In developing recommendations to address these problems, the GDG drew on the review of *Service User Experience in Adult Mental Health* and was also mindful that healthcare professionals should take into account the child or young person's developmental level, emotional maturity and cognitive capacity. The use of plain language and the explanation of any clinical terms were felt to be very important as was the use, where necessary, of communication aids (such as pictures or symbols, braille or sign language).

The GDG also considered access to services and the need to adapt and develop systems for accessing services for people with social anxiety disorder in light of the specific problems highlighted in Section 4.2. This included consideration of variation in appointment times, adjustments to the clinic environment and assistance with issues such as transport, and the manner in which the first appointment is managed, including providing information detailing what the person might be expect. The GDG also felt that particular attention should be paid to changes in the environment, appointment times and therapists. It was judged that people with social anxiety should have a choice of professional where possible because, for example, a professional's gender might in itself provoke anxiety in the service user and be a barrier to engagement and positive outcomes. Relatively few people with social anxiety disorder are treated in inpatient units but many more will spend time in general medical settings and therefore the GDG felt that some specific environmental adjustments should be considered, including to the means of delivery of treatment and the scheduling of meals and other activities. Many of the considerations set out above were, in the view of the GDG, also relevant to children and young people but a number of additional concerns about access to care for children were also identified as important. These included providing childcare support for siblings to support parent and carer involvement (see Chapter 7), offering appointments at times that did not coincide with school activities and offering to provide interventions in a range of non-clinical settings.

Finally, the GDG drew on the review of the *Service User Experience in Adult Mental Health* guidance to make several recommendations about the involvement of parent and carers and the related issues of consent and confidentiality. Two recommendations were adapted from that guideline. Regarding the recommendation on involving parents and carers, the GDG assumed that for younger children, their parents or carers would almost certainly be involved in their treatment and care. However, some older children and young people might be mature enough to make informed decisions about their own care and might therefore wish to discuss and negotiate the extent to which their parents or carers were involved. Related to this, the GDG made further recommendations about ensuring that professionals are trained and skilled in working with parents and carers and managing issues related to confidentiality and the sharing of information.

4.6 RECOMMENDATIONS

4.6.1 Improving access to services

4.6.1.1 Be aware that people with social anxiety disorder may:
- not know that social anxiety disorder is a recognised condition and can be effectively treated
- perceive their social anxiety as a personal flaw or failing
- be vulnerable to stigma and embarrassment
- avoid contact with and find it difficult or distressing to interact with healthcare professionals, staff and other service users

- avoid disclosing information, asking and answering questions and making complaints
- have difficulty concentrating when information is explained to them.

4.6.1.2 Primary and secondary care clinicians, managers and commissioners should consider arranging services flexibly to promote access and avoid exacerbating social anxiety disorder symptoms by offering:
- appointments at times when the service is least crowded or busy
- appointments before or after normal hours, or at home initially
- self-check-in and other ways to reduce distress on arrival
- opportunities to complete forms or paperwork before or after an appointment in a private space
- support with concerns related to social anxiety (for example, using public transport)
- a choice of professional if possible.

4.6.1.3 When a person with social anxiety disorder is first offered an appointment, in particular in specialist services, provide clear information in a letter about:
- where to go on arrival and where they can wait (offer the use of a private waiting area or the option to wait elsewhere, for example outside the service's premises)
- location of facilities available at the service (for example, the car park and toilets)
- what will happen and what will not happen during assessment and treatment.

When the person arrives for the appointment, offer to meet or alert them (for example, by text message) when their appointment is about to begin.

4.6.1.4 Be aware that changing healthcare professionals or services may be particularly stressful for people with social anxiety disorder. Minimise such disruptions, discuss concerns beforehand and provide detailed information about any changes, especially those that were not requested by the service user.

4.6.1.5 For people with social anxiety disorder using inpatient mental health or medical services, arrange meals, activities and accommodation by:
- regularly discussing how such provisions fit into their treatment plan and their preferences
- providing the opportunity for them to eat on their own if they find eating with others too distressing
- providing a choice of activities they can do on their own or with others.

4.6.1.6 Offer to provide treatment in settings where children and young people with social anxiety disorder and their parents or carers feel most comfortable, for example, at home or in schools or community centres.

4.6.1.7 Consider providing childcare (for example, for siblings) to support parent and carer involvement.

4.6.1.8 If possible, organise appointments in a way that does not interfere with school or other peer and social activities.

4.6.2   Communication

4.6.2.1   When assessing a person with social anxiety disorder:
- suggest that they communicate with you in the manner they find most comfortable, including writing (for example, in a letter or questionnaire)
- offer to communicate with them by phone call, text and email
- make sure they have opportunities to ask any questions and encourage them to do so
- provide opportunities for them to make and change appointments by various means, including text, email or phone.

4.6.2.2   When communicating with children and young people and their parents or carers:
- take into account the child or young person's developmental level, emotional maturity and cognitive capacity, including any learning disabilities, sight or hearing problems and delays in language development
- be aware that children who are socially anxious may be reluctant to speak to an unfamiliar person, and that children withal potential diagnosis of selective mutism may be unable to speak at all during assessment or treatment; accept information from parents or carers, but ensure that the child or young person is given the opportunity to answer for themselves, through writing, drawing or speaking through a parent or carer if necessary
- use plain language if possible and clearly explain any clinical terms
- check that the child or young person and their parents or carers understand what is being said
- use communication aids (such as pictures, symbols, large print, braille, different languages or sign language) if needed.

4.6.3   Competence

4.6.3.1   Healthcare, social care and educational professionals working with children and young people should be trained and skilled in:
- negotiating and working with parents and carers, including helping parents with relationship difficulties find support
- managing issues related to information sharing and confidentiality as these apply to children and young people
- referring children with possible social anxiety disorder to appropriate services.

4.6.4   Consent and confidentiality

4.6.4.1   If the young person is 'Gillick competent' seek their consent before speaking to their parents or carers.

4.6.4.2   When working with children and young people and their parents or carers:
- make sure that discussions take place in settings in which confidentiality, privacy and dignity are respected
- be clear with the child or young person and their parents or carers about limits of confidentiality (that is, which health and social care professionals have access to information about their diagnosis and its treatment and in what circumstances this may be shared with others)[10].

4.6.4.3   Ensure that children and young people and their parents or carers understand the purpose of any meetings and the reasons for sharing information. Respect their rights to confidentiality throughout the process and adapt the content and duration of meetings to take into account the impact of the social anxiety disorder on the child or young person's participation.

4.6.5   Working with parents and carers

4.6.5.1   If a parent or carer cannot attend meetings for assessment or treatment, ensure that written information is provided and shared with them.

4.6.5.2   If parents or carers are involved in the assessment or treatment of a young person with social anxiety disorder, discuss with the young person (taking into account their developmental level, emotional maturity and cognitive capacity) what form they would like this involvement to take. Such discussions should take place at intervals to take account of any changes in circumstances, including developmental level, and should not happen only once. As the involvement of parents and carers can be quite complex, staff should receive training in the skills needed to negotiate and work with parents and carers, and also in managing issues relating to information sharing and confidentiality[11].

4.6.5.3   Offer parents and carers an assessment of their own needs including:
- personal, social and emotional support
- support in their caring role, including emergency plans
- advice on and help with obtaining practical support.

4.6.5.4   Maintain links with adult mental health services so that referrals for any mental health needs of parents or carers can be made quickly and smoothly.

4.6.6   Research recommendation

4.6.6.1   What methods are effective in improving uptake of and engagement with interventions for adults with social anxiety disorder? (See Appendix 9 for further details.)

---

[10]This recommendation is adapted from *Service User Experience in Adult Mental Health* (NICE, 2011c).
[11]This recommendation is adapted from *Service User Experience in Adult Mental Health* (NICE, 2011c).

5 CASE IDENTIFICATION AND ASSESSMENT

5.1 INTRODUCTION

Social anxiety disorder is often not detected or recognised in healthcare settings and 50% or more of people go untreated throughout their lives. For those who do engage with treatment they typically have had the disorder for 10 or more years before accessing treatment (Grant et al., 2005a). Efforts to detect anxiety disorders, including social anxiety disorder, have centred on case identification methods in adults. These methods were recently reviewed by NICE in the guideline on *Common Mental Health Disorders* (NICE, 2011b) and form the basis on which the review in this chapter is developed. However, social anxiety disorder has an average age of onset of 13 years (Kessler et al., 2005a) and this argues strongly for shifting the emphasis on case identification from adulthood to childhood and early adolescence.

Despite the potential benefits that could accrue from early identification, there have been few studies of case identification instruments outside clinical trials or epidemiological studies. Specifically there has been little development of age-appropriate brief screening or case identification instruments for young people that might be comparable with, for example, the Generalized Anxiety Disorder scale – 2 items (GAD-2) (Kroenke et al., 2007), which was identified as a useful instrument for adults in *Common Mental Health Disorders*. Identifying such instruments is a key concern in this guideline, and it is a major challenge because children and young people rarely refer themselves to services because of symptoms of social anxiety disorder. More commonly, difficulties are reported by parents or school staff in response to particular areas of functional interference (for example, difficulty attending or participating at school) or because of other comorbid difficulties. The position is further complicated as there are high levels of comorbidity between social anxiety and other anxiety disorders in children and young people. Community studies indicate that about half of young people with social anxiety disorder have another anxiety disorder (Wittchen et al., 1999b), such as GAD, panic disorder with or without agoraphobia, specific phobia, OCD or PTSD. Among treatment-seeking populations the presence of comorbid anxiety disorders is extremely common (for example, 95% among 7 to 12 year olds [Crosby et al., in preparation]). Rates of comorbid mood disorders (for example, major depression) are also significantly inflated among children and young people with social anxiety disorder in comparison with community controls (Wittchen et al., 1999b). Children and young people have also been found to have increased rates of parent-reported behavioural disturbance, including attention deficit hyperactivity disorder (ADHD) (Beidel et al., 2000; Chavira et al., 2004) and oppositional defiant disorder (Crosby et al., in preparation). Eating disorders have also been reported among young people with social anxiety disorder (Wittchen et al., 1999b). Others for whom there should be a higher index of suspicion include children and young people with other anxiety and depressive disorders (see for example, Beidel and colleagues [1999], and Wittchen and colleagues

78

[1999b]), autism spectrum conditions (for example, Simonoff and colleagues [2008]), and the offspring of parents with an anxiety or mood disorder, in particular social anxiety disorder (den Boer, 1997; Lieb et al., 2000).

The under-development of case identification instruments is mirrored by the lack of development of comprehensive systems for the assessment of adult or childhood anxiety disorders except for the diagnostic assessment instruments associated with DSM-IV and ICD-10 (American Psychiatric Association, 2000; World Health Organization, 1992). For example, the *Common Mental Health Disorders* guideline (NCCMH, 2011a; NICE, 2011b) relied largely on previous guidelines and expert consensus to develop its recommendations for the assessment of anxiety disorders and depression in adults. Given the absence of such instruments in adults it was anticipated by the GDG that without robust and well-validated systems in routine practice for children and young people with anxiety disorders, and little development and evaluation work in the area, that they may also be required to draw on other evidence sources and their own expertise to develop recommendations for assessment systems for children and young people.

5.1.1   Clinical review protocol (case identification and assessment)

The review protocol, including the review questions, information about the databases searched and the eligibility criteria used for this section of the guideline, can be found in Table 6 (further information about the search strategies can be found in Appendix 6).

The strategy used for this review included examining recommendations from existing NICE guidelines to determine whether these could be incorporated or adapted for children, young people and adults with social anxiety disorder (using the method described in Chapter 3). In addition, for case identification (RQ2.1), pooled diagnostic accuracy meta-analyses on the sensitivity and specificity of specific case identification instruments for social anxiety disorder were conducted (dependent on available data). In the absence of adequate data, it was agreed by the GDG that a narrative review of case identification instruments would be conducted and guided by a pre-defined list of consensus-based criteria (for example, the clinical utility of the instrument, administrative characteristics, and psychometric data evaluating its sensitivity and specificity). For assessment (RQ2.2), it was decided that a consensus-based approach to identify the key components of an effective assessment would be used.

5.2   CASE IDENTIFICATION

5.2.1   Method

When evaluating case identification instruments, the following criteria were used to decide whether an instrument was eligible for inclusion in the review:

Clinical utility: the instrument should be feasible and implementable in routine clinical care. The instrument should contribute to the identification of further assessment needs and inform decisions about referral to other services.

Table 6: Review protocol for the review of case identification instruments and assessment of social anxiety disorder

Topic	Case identification and assessment
Review question(s) (RQs)	**RQ2.1:** For suspected social anxiety disorder, what identification instruments when compared with a gold standard diagnosis (based on DSM or ICD criteria) have adequate clinical utility (that is, clinically useful with good sensitivity and specificity) and reliability? **RQ2.2:** For people with suspected social anxiety disorder, what are the key components of, and the most effective structure for, a clinical assessment?
Topic group	Case identification and assessment
Objectives	For case identification (RQ2.1): • To identify brief screening instruments to assess need for further assessment of people with a suspected anxiety disorder (as described in the *Common Mental Health Disorders* NICE guideline). • To assess the diagnostic accuracy of brief screening instruments. For assessment (RQ2.2): • To identify the key components of a comprehensive assessment.
Criteria for considering studies for the review	
• *Intervention*	For case identification (RQ2.2): Brief screening questionnaires (<12 items).
• *Comparison*	Gold standard: DSM-IV or ICD-10. Other measures of social anxiety.
• *Types of participants*	Children and young people (5 to 18 years) and adults (18+ years) with suspected social anxiety disorder.
• *Critical outcomes*	• Sensitivity (percentage of true cases identified). • Specificity (percentage of non-cases excluded).
• *Important, but not critical outcomes*	• Positive predictive value: the proportion of patients with positive test results who are correctly diagnosed. • Negative predictive value: the proportion of patients with negative test results who are correctly diagnosed. • Area under the curve (AUC): constructed by plotting the true positive rate as a function of the false positive rate for each threshold.

Continued

Table 6: (*Continued*)

Topic	Case identification and assessment
• *Other outcomes*	• Reliability (for example, inter-rater, test-retest). • Validity (for example, construct, content).
• *Study design*	RCTs, cross-sectional studies.
• *Include unpublished data?*	Unpublished research may be included, but specific searches for grey literature will not be conducted.
• *Restriction by date?*	No
• *Minimum sample size*	No
• *Study setting*	• Primary, secondary, tertiary health and social care. • Children's services and educational settings.
Search strategy	**General outline:** An electronic database search for RCTs and observational studies. **Databases searched:** *RCTs*: Core databases: Embase, MEDLINE, PreMEDLINE, PsycINFO. Topic specific databases: AEI, AMED, ASSIA, BEI, CDSR, CENTRAL, CINAHL, DARE, ERIC, HTA, IBSS, Sociological Abstracts, SSA, SSCI. *Observational studies*: Core databases: Embase, MEDLINE, PreMEDLINE, PsycINFO. **Date restrictions:** None, inception of databases onwards.
Study design filter/ limit used	RCT, observational study.
Question specific search strategy	RCTs: no, generic. Observational studies: yes, focused.
Amendments to search strategy/ study design filter	None.
Searching other resources	Hand-reference searching of retrieved literature.

Instrument characteristics and administrative properties: a case identification instrument should be brief, easy to administer and score, and be able to be interpreted without extensive and specialist training. The GDG agreed that, in order to support its use in a range of non-specialist settings such as primary care, it should contain no more than 12 items and take no more than 5 minutes to administer. Non-experts from a variety of care settings (for example, primary care, general medical services, and educational, residential or criminal justice settings) should be able to complete the instrument with relative ease. The instrument should be available in practice and free to use where possible.

Psychometric data: the instrument should have established reliability and validity (although these data will not be reviewed at this stage). It must have been validated against a gold standard diagnostic instrument such as DSM-IV or ICD-10 and it must have been reported in a paper that described its sensitivity and specificity (see Chapter 3 for a description of diagnostic test accuracy terms).

5.2.2 Case identification instruments for adults[12]

Results of the search

For the purposes of this review, case identification instruments were defined as questionnaires with up to 12 items. Studies were included if they compared a questionnaire with diagnostic interview using DSM or ICD criteria for social phobia or social anxiety disorder. To be included, a study must have reported the sensitivity and specificity of the instrument relative to a diagnostic interview.

The literature search yielded 579 citations. Of those that were potentially relevant, studies with more than 12 items (16 studies) and studies that did not present sensitivity and specificity data that could be used in meta-analysis (two studies) were excluded (Aune et al., 2008; Baldwin et al., 2007; Beard et al., 2011; Birmaher, 1999; Bunevicius et al., 2007; Connor et al., 2000; Katon, 2007; Kroenke, 2010; Kupper et al., 2012; March et al., 1997; Muris et al., 2001; Roberson-Nay et al., 2007; Rodebaugh et al., 2000; Rytwinski et al., 2009; Schwartz et al., 2006; Spence et al., 2003; van Gastel, 2008; Wren et al., 2007). Six studies met all of the eligibility criteria, and two additional studies were identified through correspondence (one was not indexed electronically and one was not identified by a methods filter).

Studies considered

All included studies evaluated case identification instruments for adults and were published in peer-reviewed journals between 2000 and 2012. The eight included studies (N = 5,758) evaluated five instruments and included 135 to 1,017 participants receiving both a screening instrument and a diagnostic interview. Three studies were conducted in primary care, two in psychiatric outpatient clinics, and one study recruited participants in clinical trials (for further information about each study see Table 7; methodologys checklists for each study can be found in Appendix 10).

---

[12]Here and elsewhere in the guideline, included studies are referred to by a study ID in capital letters (primary author and date of study publication, except where a study is in press or only submitted for publication, then a date is not used).

Four studies evaluated the Mini Social Phobia Inventory (Mini-SPIN): CONNOR2001 (Connor et al., 2001), WEEKS2007 (Weeks et al., 2007), SEELEY-WAIT2009 (Seeley-Wait et al., 2009) and OSÓRIO2007 (Osório et al., 2007). In addition, one study each evaluated the following: Anxiety and Depression Detector, MEANS-CHRISTENSEN2006 (Means-Christensen et al., 2006); the Generalized Anxiety Disorder scale (the GAD), KROENKE2007 (Kroenke et al., 2007); the Social Phobia Questionnaire (SPQ), MCQUAID2000 (McQuaid et al., 2000); and the screening questions from the Social Phobia module of the Structured Clinical Interview for DSM-IV (SCID-SP), DALRYMPLE2008 (Dalrymple & Zimmerman, 2008). Case identification instruments included one to ten questions.

Clinical evidence for case identification instruments for adults
Overall, the studies were assessed as having a low risk of bias. The index tests (case identification instruments) were conducted independently of the reference tests (diagnostic interviews) and there was little time between case identification and diagnostic interview. Most instruments were evaluated in one type of setting, except the Mini-SPIN, which was evaluated in several different settings, and therefore, the evidence is more widely applicable (see Table 7).

Review Manager 5 (Cochrane Collaboration, 2011) was used to summarise the test accuracy data reported in each study using forest plots and summary ROC plots.

The five instruments varied in their specificity and sensitivity. As shown in Figure 4, the area under the curve varied reflecting large differences in the effectiveness of the measures (see Chapter 3 for more information about how this was interpreted). The sensitivity and specificity of each measure is included in Table 7.

Clinical evidence summary for case identification instruments for adults
Evidence about the sensitivity and specificity of instruments to identify people with social anxiety disorder comes from only a few studies, and only one instrument has been evaluated in more than one study, so these results should be interpreted with caution.

The Anxiety and Depression Detector has five items in total, but only one question about social anxiety disorder ('Being nervous around people is a problem'). It may be useful for identifying a range of mental disorders, but it may fail to identify many people with social anxiety disorder.

The SCID-SP entry question ('Was there ever anything that you have been afraid to do or felt uncomfortable doing in front of other people, like speaking, eating, or writing?') and the SPQ-Anx (ten items) were somewhat useful in identifying psychiatric outpatients who would meet all criteria for social anxiety disorder. With ten items, the SPQ-Anx takes longer to administer than other questionnaires that appear to be more accurate for detecting social anxiety disorder. The accuracy of the SCID-SP was enhanced when participants were given a list of social situations and asked about their fear of them (DALRYMPLE2008).

Despite its name (suggesting it might be limited to use in generalised anxiety disorder), the GAD scale is a useful instrument for identifying all anxiety disorders (NICE, 2011b). For identifying social anxiety disorder, it was as accurate as the SPQ. There was no important difference in the sensitivity and specificity of the GAD-2 and

Table 7: Study information table for trials comparing a brief identification instrument with 'gold standard' clinical interview

Instrument	Studies	No. of items	Range (cut-off)	Recruitment	N	Percentage female	Age in years	Percentage white	Prevalence	Sensitivity	Specificity
Anxiety and Depression Detector [1]	MEANS-CHRISTENSEN2006	1	Yes/no	Primary care	801	62%	42	65%	25.9%	0.69	0.76
GAD scale	KROENKE2007	2	0–6 (3)	Primary care	965	69%	47	81%	6.2%	0.70	0.81
		7	0–21 (10)							0.72	0.80
Mini-SPIN	CONNOR2001	3	0–15 (6)	Four RCTs (two social phobia, one blood pressure, one other psychiatric problems)	1,017	68%	43	96%	8.2%	0.89	0.90
	WEEKS2007			Seeking treatment for social anxiety or generalised anxiety	135	52%	29	72%	71.9%	0.94	0.63
	SEELEY-WAIT2009			Contacting services for treatment or in response to request for participants	242	52%	34	N/R	76.9%	0.88	0.98
	OSÓRIO2007			Students who had previously participated in a prevalence study	590	73%	21	N/R	71.0%	0.94	0.46
SCID-SP entry[2]	DALRYMPLE2008	1	Yes/no	Psychiatric outpatients	1,797	61%	38	87%	32.1%	0.92	0.69
SPQ-Anx	MCQUAID2000	10	0–30 (10)	Primary care	213	69%	39	61%	13.9%	0.76	0.76

Note. [1]Anxiety and Depression Detector question: 'Being nervous around people is a problem'. [2]SCID-SP entry question: 'Was there ever anything that you have been afraid to do or felt uncomfortable doing in front of other people, like speaking, eating, or writing?'

Figure 4: Summary ROC plot of brief case identification instruments

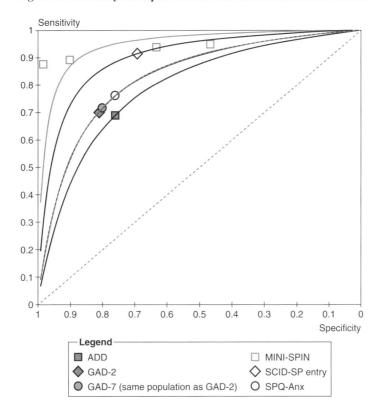

Legend
- ■ ADD
- ◆ GAD-2
- ● GAD-7 (same population as GAD-2)
- □ MINI-SPIN
- ◇ SCID-SP entry
- ○ SPQ-Anx

GAD-7. This confirms the findings of the *Common Mental Health Disorders* guideline (NICE, 2011b), which recommends the GAD-2 for case identification in primary care; 70% sensitivity and 81% specificity for social anxiety disorder suggests that this instrument will identify most cases.

The Mini-SPIN includes only three questions and appears to be the most accurate of the instruments evaluated for identifying people with social anxiety disorder. It has good specificity in primary care and excellent properties in secondary care.

5.2.3   Case identification instruments for children and young people

Results of the search
Systematic searches did not identify any evaluations of instruments for identifying children and young people with social anxiety disorder. The GDG was unaware of other relevant data regarding case identification in this population. In light of this, the GDG drew on their expert knowledge and experience and used informal consensus methods as set out in Chapter 3, a review of related guidance for case identification and a consideration of the evidence on improving access to and experience of care in Chapter 4.

Discussion by informal consensus

More detailed consideration of possible sources of evidence was undertaken, on behalf of the GDG, by an expert topic group (see Section 3.3.2) who met on five occasions between November 2011 and September 2012 to discuss case identification instruments in children and young people with possible social anxiety disorder. The topic group reviewed a list of the measures identified in other literature searches undertaken for the guideline and they were asked to identify other measures that should be considered.

The topic group considered the measures used in clinical trials but did not consider any of them to be appropriate for case identification due to their length. The group identified the screening questions from the Anxiety Disorders Interview Schedule (Silverman & Albano, 1996) as potentially useful, but these could not be reproduced without permission nor did it seem possible to use these questions independently of the full measure, which would have rendered them impractical for use as a case identification instrument.

In reviewing the *Common Mental Health Disorders* guideline (NCCMH, 2011a) no evidence was identified that could have been used to inform the case identification process for children and young people with social anxiety disorder.

As no short, validated scales other than the Anxiety Disorders Interview Schedule entry questions were identified, the GDG decided to draw on their expert knowledge and develop two questions about fear and avoidance because these are two of the central symptoms of social anxiety disorder and commonly found in adult case identification instruments for anxiety disorders. Since the core symptoms of social anxiety disorder are common to both adults and children/young people the GDG felt this was appropriate. These questions were developed initially by the topic group, who based the number and structure of the questions on the adult model but with considerable adaptation to take into account both the developmental stage of the child or young person and the potential role of parents and other informants. The draft questions were then discussed with and refined by the whole GDG.

5.2.4   Health economic evidence

No studies assessing the cost effectiveness of case identification instruments for adults or children and young people with social anxiety disorder were identified by the systematic search of the economic literature. Details on the methods used for the systematic search of the economic literature are described in Chapter 3.

5.2.5   Clinical summary for case identification instruments for adults, children and young people

The review of case identification instruments for adults identified one measure, the Mini-SPIN, which had good sensitivity and specificity and is very brief and easy to administer. The use of this instrument fitted well with the recommendations in the

Common Mental Health Disorders guideline (NICE, 2011b) as the increased sensitivity and specificity of the measure justified its use after an initial screen with the GAD-2, as recommended in *Common Mental Health Disorders*. The GDG was, however, concerned that the GAD-2 did not directly enquire about fear and avoidance of social situations.

No case identification instrument for children and young people was identified so the GDG developed new recommendations based on informal consensus, which was informed by the review of case identification for adults in *Common Mental Health Disorders* and in the review undertaken for adults in this guideline.

5.2.6   From evidence to recommendations

In considering case identification instruments, the primary outcome was the accurate detection of social anxiety disorder.

A number of case identification instruments were identified for which there was good-quality but limited evidence to support their use. In developing recommendations for adults in this area the GDG was concerned not to develop any recommendations that were not compatible with those developed for the *Common Mental Health Disorders* guideline. Furthermore, reviews for this guideline confirmed that the approach in *Common Mental Health Disorders* was appropriate for the identification of social anxiety disorder. The focus in developing any new recommendations was therefore specifically on enhancing case identification for social anxiety disorder. This led to a new recommendation on the use of the Mini-SPIN. The GDG was concerned that this tool might not be practical for some GPs and therefore advised asking specific questions about avoidance of, or fear and embarrassment in, social situations. It was felt that both of these strategies would increase the level of case identification of social anxiety disorder. No economic data were available, but given the very brief nature of the measures and the increase in accurate case identification on a previously cost-effective method this was not seen as a major concern by the GDG.

No evidence to support the use of case identification instruments in children and young people was identified, but given the early onset of social anxiety disorder the GDG decided to develop recommendations about case identification. This was done based on expert opinion, informal consensus, a review of related guidance for case identification and a consideration of the evidence on improving access to, and experience of, care in Chapter 4. One important issue that the GDG wished to stress was the need for staff to be alert to the possible presence of social anxiety disorder given the early onset of the disorder and its poor recognition. The GDG then developed a series of questions that drew on the recommendations for adults but were adjusted to the developmental stage of children and young people and the different ways in which social anxiety disorder may present in this population. The GDG developed the recommendations based on a careful consideration of questions used in routine practice and more comprehensive measures that cannot be used as case identification instruments.

5.3   RECOMMENDATIONS FOR CASE IDENTIFICATION

5.3.1   Identification of adults with possible social anxiety disorder

5.3.1.1   Ask the identification questions for anxiety disorders in line with recommendation 1.3.1.2 in *Common Mental Health Disorders* (NICE clinical guideline 123)[13], and if social anxiety disorder is suspected:
● use the 3-item Mini-Social Phobia Inventory (Mini-SPIN) **or**
● consider asking the following two questions:
   – Do you find yourself avoiding social situations or activities?
   – Are you fearful or embarrassed in social situations?
If the person scores 6 or more on the Mini-SPIN, or answers yes to either of the two questions above, refer for or conduct a comprehensive assessment for social anxiety disorder (see recommendations 5.5.1.4–5.5.1.8).

5.3.2   Identification of children and young people with possible social anxiety disorder

5.3.2.1   Health and social care professionals in primary care and education and community settings should be alert to possible anxiety disorders in children and young people, particularly those who avoid school, social or group activities or talking in social situations, or are irritable, excessively shy or overly reliant on parents or carers. Consider asking the child or young person about their feelings of anxiety, fear, avoidance, distress and associated behaviours (or a parent or carer) to help establish if social anxiety disorder is present, using these questions:
● 'Sometimes people get very scared when they have to do things with other people, especially people they don't know. They might worry about doing things with other people watching. They might get scared that they will do something silly or that people will make fun of them. They might not want to do these things or, if they have to do them, they might get very upset or cross.'
   – 'Do you/does your child get scared about doing things with other people, like talking, eating, going to parties, or other things at school or with friends?'
   – 'Do you/does your child find it difficult to do things when other people are watching, like playing sport, being in plays or concerts, asking or answering questions, reading aloud, or giving talks in class?'
   – 'Do you/does your child ever feel that you/your child can't do these things or try to get out of them?'

---

[13]NICE (2011a).

5.4   ASSESSMENT

5.4.1   Results of the search

In the review of the literature, the GDG was unable to identify any formal evaluations of the structure and content of the overall clinical assessment process for people with possible social anxiety disorder other than the data on the various case identification instruments described above. The GDG therefore decided to consider the evidence and recommendations in the *Common Mental Health Disorders* guideline (NCCMH, 2011a; NICE, 2011b) and where necessary adapt any recommendations from that guideline (in line with the method set out in Chapter 3). This was deemed necessary because no NICE guideline was available on social anxiety disorder when *Common Mental Health Disorders* was developed.

While no formal evaluations of the structure and content of the overall clinical assessment process for people with suspected social anxiety disorder were identified by the literature search, the GDG wanted to be able to identify assessment measures that could be used to augment the clinical assessment process to ensure that the impact of the interventions was properly monitored. This is because there is evidence that routine monitoring improves outcomes (Lambert et al., 2003; NICE, 2011b). The GDG therefore used the literature search undertaken for this guideline to identify such measures.

5.4.2   Clinical evidence for assessment measures to augment the clinical assessment process

The GDG identified several validated measures that are routinely used in the UK (see Table 8). Validation studies for each measure were identified and presented to the GDG, which determined that several measures are likely to be useful for monitoring symptoms during treatment. These data were used by the GDG to inform the recommendation regarding which measures might be used.

From the list of measures identified in Table 8 the GDG selected three that it considered were important based on a consideration of their psychometric properties, their likely value in informing a comprehensive assessment and their feasibility for routine outcome monitoring: (1) the LSAS/the LSAS-Self-Report (LSAS-SR); (2) the Social Phobia Scale/Social Interaction Anxiety Scale (SIAS); and (3) the Social Phobia Inventory (SPIN).

5.4.3   Review of existing NICE guidance

The GDG drew on their expert knowledge and experience regarding the structure and content of a clinical assessment (using informal consensus methods as set out in Chapter 3) to develop recommendations for the assessment of social anxiety disorder where there were no relevant recommendations in the *Common Mental Health Disorders* guideline or the need to develop a new recommendation was identified.

Table 8: Characteristics of assessment instruments

Instrument	Items	Item range	Total range	Validation study	Internal consistency Cronbach's a	Test-retest
Fear of Negative Evaluation scale	30	T/F	0–30	Watson and Friend (1969)	0.94 to 0.96	0.78 to 0.94 (4 weeks)
Social Anxiety and Distress Scale	28	T/F	0–28	Watson and Friend (1969)	0.94	0.68 to 0.79 (4 weeks)
Fear Questionnaire – Social Phobia	5	0–8	0–40	Marks and Mathews (1979), Oei and colleagues (1991)	0.77 to 0.93	None reported
LSAS	24	0–3	144	Heimberg and colleagues (1999), Liebowitz (1987)	0.96	None reported
LSAS-SR	24	0–3	144	Baker and colleagues (2002)	0.95	0.83 (12 weeks)
SIAS	20	0–4	0–80	Mattick and Clarke (1998)	0.86 to 0.94	0.86 to 0.92 (4 to 12 weeks)
Social Phobia Anxiety Inventory- Social Phobia subscale	32	0–6	0–192	Turner and colleagues (1996)	0.94 to 0.96	0.86 (2 weeks)
SPIN	17	0–4	0–68	Connor and colleagues (2000)	0.82 to 0.94	0.78 to 0.89
Social Phobia Scale	20	0–4	0–80	Mattick and Clarke (1998)	0.87 to 0.94	0.66 to 0.93 (4 to 12 weeks)
Brief Social Phobia Scale	18	0–4	72	Davidson and colleagues (1997)	0.81	0.91 (1 week)

This was particularly important for the assessment of children and young people because the *Common Mental Health Disorders* guideline was concerned with adults only. When considering the assessment process, the GDG assumed that any person referred for such an assessment would already have been identified as possibly having social anxiety disorder.

All GDG members initially reviewed the recommendations in *Common Mental Health Disorders* (NCCMH, 2011a; NICE, 2011b), and a topic group was formed to undertake a more detailed review of the guideline informed by the methods and principles set out in Chapter 3 to identify possible recommendations for incorporation or adaptation, and to identify areas where new recommendations may be required and draft them for consideration by the GDG as a whole.

The GDG judged that a number of areas of *Common Mental Health Disorders* applied to children, young people and adults with social anxiety disorder, including: (a) the structure and content of the assessment; (b) the use of formal assessment measures to support the assessment process; (c) the impact of comorbid conditions on the assessment process; (d) communication about the assessment; and (e) the involvement of families and carers.

When developing recommendations to include in the current guideline, the GDG specifically considered those areas that were concerned with the particular ways in which social anxiety disorder might impact on a person during the assessment process.

5.4.4   Discussion by informal consensus

With an absence of evidence on the content of an assessment in adults, the GDG discussed this using informal consensus methods (as set out in Chapter 3) and their expert knowledge and experience. The GDG drew up a list of the following components of an assessment to consider when making recommendations:

- the nature and content of the interview and observation, including personal and development history
- formal diagnostic methods (including their psychometric properties) for the assessment of core features of social anxiety disorder
- the time, competences and resources required
- the assessment of risk
- the assessment of need
- the setting(s) in which the assessment takes place
- the role of the any informants
- the impact on the assessment of any coexisting conditions
- what amendments, if any, need to be made to take into account particular cultural or minority ethnic groups or gender
- how the outcome of the assessment should be communicated.

Decisions on the structure of the recommendations for children and young people took into account the structure of the recommendations developed for adults in this guideline as well as the structure of the assessment in other NICE guidelines that had developed recommendations for the assessment of children and young people.

5.4.5 Health economic evidence

No studies assessing the cost effectiveness of assessment systems or instruments for adults or children and young people with social anxiety disorder were identified by the systematic search of the economic literature. Details on the methods used for the systematic search of the economic literature are described in Chapter 3.

5.4.6 Clinical summary

The GDG was unable to identify any high-quality evidence that related to the process of assessment for people with social anxiety disorder. As a result the GDG drew on their expert knowledge and experience using informal consensus methods. The GDG also reviewed the evidence on the psychometric properties of commonly used assessment scales to inform the choice of measures both to aid the process of assessment and to contribute to routine outcome measurement. A number of measures were identified from the clinical trial data reviewed that met the psychometric criteria and were feasible for routine use. The considerations that fed into the development of these recommendations are described in the next section.

5.4.7 From evidence to recommendations

The recommendations in this chapter are largely based on expert opinion and informal consensus methods. As a consequence the GDG was cautious in making recommendations but after detailed discussion decided that in order to ensure the assessment of people with social anxiety, which is often not recognised or assessed in non-specialist mental health settings, specific recommendations were needed. The development of the recommendations was also undertaken in the context of the review of *Common Mental Health Disorders*. In addition, the GDG took into account the review of the evidence and the recommendations developed in this current guideline on access to, and the experience of, care (see Chapter 4) as they wished to ensure that the particular issues identified in that chapter were also reflected in the recommendations on assessment and that a choice of method for assessment (for example, initial assessment by telephone) should be considered.

The GDG took as their starting point for assessment the need to make an appropriate referral. Following their review of *Common Mental Health Disorders*, they wished to emphasise that if the professional who identified possible social anxiety disorder was not competent to conduct a mental health assessment they should refer the child, young person or adult to an appropriately trained professional.

The GDG also wanted to stress the importance of a full assessment of the fear, avoidance, distress, functional impairment and complex comorbidities that might be associated with social anxiety disorder. The GDG recognised the importance of formal assessment instruments both in augmenting the initial assessment and in routine treatment. A number of such measures with good psychometric properties were identified and the GDG decided to recommend their use.

Finally the GDG was aware of the care that needs to be taken in communicating the outcome of any assessment or proposed treatment if the engagement of people with social anxiety disorder is to be obtained.

As is the case with identification of social anxiety disorder in children and young people, no good evidence was found for assessment instruments or systems for this population. Again the GDG drew on its expert knowledge, a review of other relevant guidance and a consideration of the evidence on access to and experience of care in Chapter 4. The GDG identified that the issues of concern with developing assessment systems for children and young people were broadly similar to those for adults; that is, a full assessment of the fear, avoidance, distress and functional impairment, and the complex comorbidities that may be associated with social anxiety disorder. In addition the GDG also wanted to stress the importance of an assessment of risk and of cognitive abilities as both were likely to be important when planning treatment. The GDG recognised the importance of formal assessment instruments (while accepting the data on psychometric properties were limited) from the review in the NICE guideline on *Antisocial Behaviour and Conduct Disorders in Children and Young People* (NCCMH, 2013), both in augmenting the initial assessment and, along with a number of other quality improvement methods, in improving the outcomes of routine treatment for children and young people.

5.5   RECOMMENDATIONS FOR ASSESSMENT

5.5.1   Assessment of adults with possible social anxiety disorder

5.5.1.1   If the identification questions (see recommendation 5.3.1.1) indicate possible social anxiety disorder, but the practitioner is not competent to perform a mental health assessment, refer the person to an appropriate healthcare professional. If this professional is not the person's GP, inform the GP of the referral.

5.5.1.2   If the identification questions (see recommendation 5.3.1.1) indicate possible social anxiety disorder, a practitioner who is competent to perform a mental health assessment should review the person's mental state and associated functional, interpersonal and social difficulties.

5.5.1.3   If an adult with possible social anxiety disorder finds it difficult or distressing to attend an initial appointment in person, consider making the first contact by phone or internet, but aim to see the person face to face for subsequent assessments and treatment.

5.5.1.4   When assessing an adult with possible social anxiety disorder:
   ● conduct an assessment that considers fear, avoidance, distress and functional impairment
   ● be aware of comorbid disorders, including avoidant personality disorder, alcohol and substance misuse, mood disorders, other anxiety disorders, psychosis and autism.

5.5.1.5 Follow the recommendations in *Common Mental Health Disorders* (NICE clinical guideline 123)[14] for the structure and content of the assessment and adjust them to take into account the need to obtain a more detailed description of the social anxiety disorder (see recommendation 5.5.1.7 in this guideline).

5.5.1.6 Consider using the following to inform the assessment and support the evaluation of any intervention:
- a diagnostic or problem identification tool as recommended in recommendation 1.3.2.3 in *Common Mental Health Disorders* (NICE clinical guideline 123)[15]
- a validated measure for social anxiety, for example, the Social Phobia Inventory (SPIN) or the Liebowitz Social Anxiety Scale (LSAS).

5.5.1.7 Obtain a detailed description of the person's current social anxiety and associated problems and circumstances including:
- feared and avoided social situations
- what they are afraid might happen in social situations (for example, looking anxious, blushing, sweating, trembling or appearing boring)
- anxiety symptoms
- view of self
- content of self-image
- safety-seeking behaviours
- focus of attention in social situations
- anticipatory and post-event processing
- occupational, educational, financial and social circumstances
- medication, alcohol and recreational drug use.

5.5.1.8 If a person with possible social anxiety disorder does not return after an initial assessment, contact them (using their preferred method of communication) to discuss the reason for not returning. Remove any obstacles to further assessment or treatment that the person identifies.

5.5.2 Planning treatment for adults diagnosed with social anxiety disorder

5.5.2.1 After diagnosis of social anxiety disorder in an adult, identify the goals for treatment and provide information about the disorder and its treatment including:
- the nature and course of the disorder and commonly occurring comorbidities
- the impact on social and personal functioning
- commonly held beliefs about the cause of the disorder
- beliefs about what can be changed or treated
- choice and nature of evidence-based treatments.

---

[14]NICE (2011a).
[15]NICE (2011a).

5.5.2.2   If the person also has symptoms of depression, assess their nature and extent and determine their functional link with the social anxiety disorder by asking them which existed first.

- If the person has only experienced significant social anxiety since the start of a depressive episode, treat the depression in line with *Depression* (NICE clinical guideline 90)[16].
- If the social anxiety disorder preceded the onset of depression, ask: 'if I gave you a treatment that ensured you were no longer anxious in social situations, would you still be depressed?'
  - If the person answers 'no', treat the social anxiety (unless the severity of the depression prevents this, then offer initial treatment for the depression).
  - If the person answers 'yes', consider treating both the social anxiety disorder and the depression, taking into account their preference when deciding which to treat first.
- If the depression is treated first, treat the social anxiety disorder when improvement in the depression allows.

5.5.3   Assessment of children and young people with possible social anxiety disorder

5.5.3.1   If the child or young person (or a parent or carer) answers 'yes' to one or more of the questions in recommendation 5.3.2.1 consider a comprehensive assessment for social anxiety disorder (see recommendations 5.5.3.3–5.5.3.10).

5.5.3.2   If the identification questions (see recommendation 5.3.2.1) indicate possible social anxiety disorder, but the practitioner is not competent to perform a mental health assessment, refer the child or young person to an appropriate healthcare professional. If this professional is not the child or young person's GP, inform the GP of the referral.

5.5.3.3   If the identification questions (see recommendation 5.3.2.1) indicate possible social anxiety disorder, a practitioner who is competent to perform a mental health assessment should review the child or young person's mental state and associated functional, interpersonal and social difficulties.

5.5.3.4   A comprehensive assessment of a child or young person with possible social anxiety disorder should:

- provide an opportunity for the child or young person to be interviewed alone at some point during the assessment
- if possible involve a parent, carer or other adult known to the child or young person who can provide information about current and past behaviour
- if necessary involve more than one professional to ensure a comprehensive assessment can be undertaken.

---

[16]NICE (2009a).

5.5.3.5 When assessing a child or young person obtain a detailed description of their current social anxiety and associated problems including:
- feared and avoided social situations
- what they are afraid might happen in social situations (for example, looking anxious, blushing, sweating, trembling or appearing boring)
- anxiety symptoms
- view of self
- content of self-image
- safety-seeking behaviours
- focus of attention in social situations
- anticipatory and post-event processing, particularly for older children
- family circumstances and support
- friendships and peer groups, educational and social circumstances
- medication, alcohol and recreational drug use.

5.5.3.6 As part of a comprehensive assessment, assess for causal and maintaining factors for social anxiety disorder in the child or young person's home, school and social environment, in particular:
- parenting behaviours that promote and support anxious behaviours or do not support positive behaviours
- peer victimisation in school or other settings.

5.5.3.7 As part of a comprehensive assessment, assess for possible coexisting conditions such as:
- other mental health problems (for example, other anxiety disorders and depression)
- neurodevelopmental conditions such as attention deficit hyperactivity disorder, autism and learning disabilities
- drug and alcohol misuse (see recommendation 7.9.1.3)
- speech and language problems.

5.5.3.8 To aid the assessment of social anxiety disorder and other common mental health problems consider using formal instruments (both the child and parent versions if available and indicated), such as:
- the LSAS – child version or the Social Phobia and Anxiety Inventory for Children (SPAI-C) for children, or the SPIN or the LSAS for young people
- the Multidimensional, the Revised Child Anxiety and Depression Scale (RCADS) for children and young people who may have comorbid depression or other anxiety disorders, the Spence Children's Anxiety Scale (SCAS) or the Screen for Child Anxiety Related Emotional Disorders (SCARED) for children.

5.5.3.9 Use formal assessment instruments to aid the diagnosis of other problems, such as:
- a validated measure of cognitive ability for a child or young person with a suspected learning disability
- the Strengths and Difficulties Questionnaire for all children and young people.

5.5.3.10   Assess the risks and harm faced by the child or young person and if needed develop a risk management plan for risk of self-neglect, familial abuse or neglect, exploitation by others, self-harm or harm to others.

5.5.3.11   Develop a profile of the child or young person to identify their needs and any further assessments that may be needed, including the extent and nature of:

- the social anxiety disorder and any associated difficulties (for example, selective mutism)
- any coexisting mental health problems
- neurodevelopmental conditions such as attention deficit hyperactivity disorder, autism and learning disabilities
- experience of bullying or social ostracism
- friendships with peers
- speech, language and communication skills
- physical health problems
- personal and social functioning to indicate any needs (personal, social, housing, educational and occupational)
- educational and occupational goals
- parent or carer needs, including mental health needs.

6   INTERVENTIONS FOR ADULTS

6.1   INTRODUCTION

Social anxiety disorder was formally recognised as a separate phobic disorder in the mid 1960s (Marks & Gelder, 1965), but, as described in Chapter 2, the formal recognition of the disorder has not been widespread, with over half of people with a social anxiety disorder never seeking treatment. Many of those who seek treatment may not have their disorder recognised and, as a consequence, may be offered inappropriate or suboptimal treatment. The past 20 years have seen the development of an evidence base of effective interventions, but these have not always been available (Layard et al., 2006) even when the need for treatment has been recognised. This is a source of real concern because social anxiety disorder can have lifelong and disabling consequences.

This chapter is concerned primarily with the evaluation of psychological and pharmacological interventions, but also considers other physical interventions including botulinum toxin and thoracic sympathectomy.

6.2   CURRENT PRACTICE

6.2.1   Pharmacological interventions

Previous reviews suggest there is evidence that pharmacotherapy may be efficacious for the treatment of social anxiety disorder (Blanco et al., 2012) and several drugs are licensed in the UK for the treatment of the disorder (escitalopram, moclobemide, paroxetine, sertraline, and venlafaxine). Other SSRIs have also been evaluated in the treatment of social anxiety disorder. Monoamine oxidase inhibitors (MAOIs), principally phenelzine and moclobemide, have been used for the treatment of social anxiety disorder as have the anticonvulsants gabapentin and pregabalin. Benzodiazepines have also been used, but their long-term use is actively discouraged. Beta-antagonists such as atenolol or propranolol have often been used to treat specific symptoms such as tremor. However, a number of factors significantly limit the current use of drugs in the treatment of social anxiety disorder. These include: under-recognition or misdiagnosis, which may be related to the masking of the social anxiety disorder by comorbid problems such as depression or alcohol misuse; an unwillingness on the part of many people with social anxiety disorder to take medication for what they perceive to be a personal failing rather than a mental disorder; concerns about side effects; and lack of knowledge on the part of some prescribers about the potential value and the means to provide the necessary support to obtain an optimal outcome from the use of medication. In relation to this latter factor, there is evidence to support the role of prescribers in encouraging graduated exposure in enhancing the efficacy of drugs, and this may occur in good practices. Further issues hampering the effective use of drugs in the treatment of SSRIs include uncertainty about the duration of treatment or their use in combination with psychological interventions (although it should be noted perhaps 20 to 30% of participants in trials of psychological interventions take medication throughout the trials). All this means that current pharmacological treatment for many people with social anxiety disorder is often suboptimal outside a few specialist tertiary treatment centres and for the few people with social anxiety disorder who are offered treatment by specialists in secondary care mental health services.

6.2.2   Psychological interventions

The past 30 years have seen a very significant expansion in the range and availability of psychological interventions for the treatment of social anxiety disorder. Early evidence-based interventions focused on systematic desensitisation and flooding. These were replaced by treatments that involved confronting the feared stimulus in real life (Marks, 1975). Much current evidence-based practice for the treatment of social anxiety disorder has been influenced by this approach. This is most obviously seen in exposure *in vivo* therapy (see Chapter 2) and the development of a range of cognitive and cognitive behavioural interventions, for which there is substantial evidence for the treatment of social anxiety disorder and other anxiety disorders. These interventions can be provided either individually or in groups, although there has been less emphasis on group CBT treatments in the UK when compared with the US or Australia. Other psychological interventions such as IPT, counselling and psychodynamic therapy have also been used for the treatment of social anxiety disorder. Although many service users may prefer psychological interventions, availability in the NHS has been, until recently, very limited. In 2007 the English Department of Health established the Improving Access to Psychological Therapies (IAPT) programme (Clark et al., 2009), which aimed to very significantly increase the availability of evidence-based psychological interventions so that the outcomes obtained in clinical trials could be provided throughout the NHS. There has been impressive progress over the past 5 years (Clark, 2011) with over 4,000 additional therapists trained and by 2015 an additional 900,000 people projected to be receiving treatment.

6.3   DEFINITIONS AND AIMS OF INTERVENTIONS

6.3.1   Pharmacological interventions

There are three main classes of drug that are used in treating social anxiety disorder: (1) antidepressants, (2) benzodiazepines, and (3) anticonvulsants. Other drugs such as beta-antagonists, antipsychotics, St John's wort and cognitive enhancers have also been used in the treatment of social anxiety disorder.

Interventions for adults

Antidepressants
The efficacy of antidepressants is thought to be linked to increases in serotonin and possibly dopamine concentrations in the brain.

Selective serotonin reuptake inhibitors and serotonin and noradrenaline reuptake inhibitors
SSRIs act by increasing serotonin concentration in the brain and have been used in social anxiety disorder as well as other anxiety disorders. The only SNRI that has been studied extensively is venlafaxine and it is possible that its effect in social anxiety disorder is mediated solely through changes in serotonin at usually prescribed doses.

Monoamine oxidase inhibitors
MAOIs inhibit the breakdown of noradrenaline, dopamine, serotonin, melatonin, tyramine and phenylethylamine. This effect is not limited to the brain and affects other parts of the body rich in MAO (for example, the gut). The inhibition of MAO may result in a potentially dangerous interaction with tyramine-containing foods and with some medications leading to episodes of dangerously high blood pressure. This risk is much reduced with moclobemide because it is 'reversible'.

Benzodiazepines
Benzodiazepines augment the effect of *gamma*-Aminobutyric acid, the main inhibitory neurotransmitter in the brain. The use of benzodiazepines is restricted because of potential tolerance and dependence that can develop when administered for prolonged periods of time.

Anticonvulsants
Anticonvulsants, specifically alpha2delta calcium-gated channel blockers, reduce neuronal excitability and are also used in the treatment of neuropathic pain. Their mechanism of action is not currently understood.

Antipsychotics
Antipsychotics are a class of drugs that act on dopamine receptors and are widely used to treat schizophrenia, bipolar disorder and other serious mental illnesses. They have also been used to treat depression and other disorders including anxiety disorders. They have a wide range of side effects including movement disorders, weight gain and sedation.

Cognitive enhancers
The cognitive enhancer D-cycloserine is a partial agonist of the N-methyl-D-aspartate-associated glycine site. It has been tested as an adjunct to psychological interventions in clinical trials.

6.3.2   Psychological interventions

The following section contains definitions of the commonly used psychological interventions included in the review in this chapter. Fuller descriptions can be found in Chapter 2.

Exposure in vivo
Exposure encourages the person to repeatedly confront situations they fear. It is sometimes done following a hierarchy from least to most feared situations. Repeated exposure may lead to habituation. Exposure may also be designed to challenge and to disconfirm unrealistic and maladaptive beliefs. Exposure exercises involve confrontation with real life ('*in vivo*') social situations through role plays and out-of-office exercises in therapy sessions, and through systematic homework assignments.

Applied relaxation
Applied relaxation is a specialised form of relaxation training that aims to teach people how to relax in common social situations. Starting with training in traditional progressive muscle relaxation, the treatment takes individuals through a series of steps that enables them to relax on cue in everyday situations. The final stage of the treatment involves intensive practice in using the relaxation techniques in real life social situations.

Social skills training
Social skills training is based on the assumption that people are anxious in social situations partly because they are uncertain about how to behave. The treatment involves systematic training in non-verbal social skills (for example, increased eye contact, friendly attentive posture, and so on) and verbal social skills (for example, how to start a conversation, how to give others positive feedback, how to ask questions that promote conversation, and so on). The skills that are identified with the therapist are usually repeatedly practiced through role plays in therapy sessions as well as in homework assignments. As with exposure, social skills training may work through habituation or by disconfirming negative beliefs.

Cognitive behavioural therapy
CBT typically involves exposure *in vivo* and cognitive restructuring along with training in relaxation techniques and/or social and conversational skills training. CBT can be delivered in either individual or group format.

Cognitive therapy
CT is a variant of CBT and focuses on: (a) the negative beliefs that individuals with social anxiety disorder hold about themselves and social interactions; (b) negative self-imagery; and (c) the problematic cognitive and behavioural processes that occur in social situations (self-focused attention, safety behaviours, and so on). The treatment is usually delivered on an individual basis. However, there is a need for the therapist to be able to call on other people to participate in within-session

role plays. This is easier to do if sessions are 90 minutes, rather than the usual 50 minutes.

Interpersonal psychotherapy

Interpersonal psychotherapy (IPT) was originally developed as a treatment for depression. There are three phases to the treatment. In the first phase, the person is encouraged to see social anxiety disorder as an illness that has to be coped with rather than as a sign of weakness or deficiency. In the second phase, the therapist works with the person to address specific interpersonal problems particularly in the areas of role transition and role disputes, but sometimes also grief. Role plays encouraging the expression of feelings and accurate communication are emphasised. People are also encouraged to build a social network comprising close and trusting relationships. In the last phase, the therapist and the service user review progress, address ending of the therapeutic relationship, and prepare for challenging situations and experiences in the future.

Short-term psychodynamic psychotherapy

Short-term psychodynamic psychotherapy sees the symptoms of social anxiety disorder as the result of core relationship conflicts predominately based on early experience. Therapy aims to help the person become aware of the link between conflicts and symptoms. The therapeutic relationship is a central vehicle for insight and change.

Mindfulness training

Mindfulness training encourages individuals to gain psychological distance from their worries and negative emotions, seeing them as an observer would see them, rather than being engrossed in them. There are two varieties of mindfulness training considered in this guideline: mindfulness-based stress reduction and mindfulness-based cognitive therapy.

Treatment starts with general education about stress and social anxiety. Participants then attend weekly groups in which they are taught meditation techniques. Formal meditation practice for at least 30 minutes per day using audiotapes for guidance is also encouraged.

Self-help interventions

Self-help interventions are psychological interventions typically based on cognitive behavioural principles that seek to equip people with strategies and techniques to begin to overcome and manage their psychological difficulties. Self-help usually provides information in the form of books or other written materials that include psychoeducation about the problem and describe techniques to overcome it. Although computerised interventions have the potential to be interactive and individualised, those that have been tested in clinical trials for people with social anxiety are, for the most part, relatively fixed programmes. In 'pure', unsupported self-help, only the written materials are used; in supported self-help, a therapist or alternatively a computer-based system (stand alone or web based) assists the service user in using the materials. Supported self-help typically includes 2 to 3 hours of assistance.

Supportive therapy
Supportive therapy uses techniques that aim to enable patients to feel comfortable in discussing their personal experiences in the context of the patient-therapist relationship.

Cognitive bias modification
Cognitive bias modification is a computerised intervention that aims to reduce attention towards threatening stimuli. The most common programs use modified dot-probe tasks in which participants see numerous (sometimes hundreds of) presentations of written or facial stimuli and are asked to make quick decisions based on what has been seen. For example, some tasks present written stimuli with two possible interpretations, one threatening and one benign; participants select one and receive positive reinforcement when they bias towards neutral stimuli. These interventions require limited therapist input and, until recently, these programs were used only to study psychological processes.

Exercise
Exercise is a physical activity that is planned, structured and repetitive, and aims to improve or maintain physical fitness. It may improve anxiety levels and mood generally, provide opportunities to interact with others or function as a form of exposure (for example, for people with a fear of blushing or sweating) and for this reason is classed as a psychological intervention.

6.3.3   Physical interventions

Botulinum toxin
Botulinum toxin is a neurotoxin produced by the bacterium *clostridium botulinum*, which can cause botulism, a serious and life-threatening illness. In the 1960s it was developed as a medical treatment for conditions such as blepharospasm and strabismus. Medical use of the toxin has increased substantially in the past 20 years and has a wide range of uses including the treatment of excessive sweating (hyperhidrosis) in specific parts of the body through localised injections.

Thoracic sympathectomy
Thoracic sympathectomy is used to treat excessive sweating (hyperhidrosis) and has also been used to help treat extreme facial flushing. It involves cutting the sympathetic nerve (through a small incision in the chest), which switches off sweating and blushing in specific parts of the body.

6.4   CLINICAL REVIEW PROTOCOL

The review protocol, including the review questions, information about the databases searched and the eligibility criteria used for this section of the guideline, can be found in Table 9 (further information about the search strategy can be found in

Table 9: Clinical review protocol for the review of interventions in adults with social anxiety disorder

Topic	Interventions
Review question(s) (RQ)	**RQ3.1:** For adults with social anxiety disorder, what are the relative benefits and harms of psychological and pharmacological interventions alone or in combination?
Subquestion(s)	Does the effectiveness of treatment differ across populations: • generalised social anxiety versus performance social anxiety • people with comorbid problems (for example, substance misuse, other anxiety disorders or depression) versus those with only social anxiety disorder.
Chapter	Interventions for adults.
Topic group	• Pharmacological interventions. • Psychosocial interventions.
Objectives	To estimate the efficacy and cost effectiveness of interventions to treat social anxiety disorder.
Criteria for considering studies for the review	
• *Intervention*	• Any psychological intervention. • Any licensed pharmacological intervention. • Combined psychological and pharmacological interventions. • Cognitive enhancers (for example, D-cycloserine). • Surgical interventions (for example, for blushing). • Botulinum toxin injections (for example, for sweating).
• *Comparator*	• Waitlist. • Placebo. • Other interventions.
• *Types of participants*	Adults (18+ years) with social anxiety disorder or APD. Special consideration will be given to the groups above. If some but not all of a study's participants are eligible for review, the study authors will be asked for disaggregated data.

Continued

Table 9: (*Continued*)

Topic	Interventions
• *Outcomes*	• Recovery (no longer meet criteria for diagnosis). • Symptoms of social anxiety (for example, LSAS). • Symptoms of depression (for example, Hamilton Rating Scale for Depression). • Quality of life (for example, Short Form Questionnaire 36 items [SF-36]). • Disability (for example, Sheehan Disability Scale). • Withdrawal. • Side effects (adverse events).
• *Time points*	The main analysis will include outcomes at the end of treatment. Additional analyses will be conducted for controlled effects at follow-up.
• *Study design*	RCTs and cluster RCTs with a parallel group design. Quasi-RCTs, such as trials in which allocation is determined by alternation or date of birth, will be excluded.
• *Include unpublished data?*	Unpublished research may be included.
• *Restriction by date?*	No limit.
• *Dosage*	For pharmacological interventions, all interventions within the British National Formulary (BNF) recommended range will be included. For psychological interventions, all credible interventions will be included; single session treatments will be excluded.
• *Minimum sample size*	No minimum.
• *Study setting*	Primary, secondary, tertiary health and social care.
Search strategy	**General outline:** A broad electronic database search for quantitative systematic reviews and RCTs.

Continued

Table 9: *(Continued)*

Topic	Interventions
	Databases searched: Core databases: Embase, MEDLINE, PreMEDLINE, PsycINFO. Topic specific databases: AEI, AMED, ASSIA, BEI, CDSR, CENTRAL, CINAHL, DARE, ERIC, HTA, IBSS, Sociological Abstracts, SSA, SSCI. Grey literature databases: HMIC, PsycBOOKS, PsycEXTRA. **Date restrictions:** Quantitative systematic reviews: 1997 onwards. RCTs: inception of databases onwards.
Study design filter/ limit used	Core databases/topic specific databases: quantitative systematic reviews, RCT. Grey literature databases: none.
Question specific search strategy	No.
Amendments to search strategy/ study design filter	None.
Searching other resources	All stakeholders, authors of all included studies, and manufacturers of included drugs will be contacted in writing, to request unpublished studies.
Existing reviews	
• *Updated*	None
• *Not updated*	See below ('The review strategy').
The review strategy	**Data management:** *For each study*: year of study, setting, total number of study participants in each included group, age (mean), gender (percent female), inclusion and exclusion criteria, comorbidities, risk of bias. *For each intervention or comparison group of interest*: dose, duration, frequency, co-interventions (if any). *For each outcome of interest*: time points: (i) collected and (ii) reported; missing data (exclusion of participants, attrition).

Continued

Table 9: (*Continued*)

Topic	Interventions
	For cross-over trials, data from the first period only will be extracted and analysed.
	Data synthesis:
	Network meta-analysis: all eligible interventions for adults will be compared using a NMA of continuous measures of social anxiety assessed at post-treatment. Multiple measures of social anxiety will be averaged to obtain a single effect.
	The following will be assessed in pairwise analyses using a random effects model, which is appropriate given differences in the populations and interventions examined:
	• Interventions for adults that are not connected to the main network, including studies with no connected intervention and studies of specific populations (for example, comorbid alcohol misuse).
	• Additional pairwise analyses of secondary outcomes and follow-up results for treatment classes using random effects models (for example, SSRIs, CBT) will be conducted.

Appendix 6). Parts of these questions were addressed in Cochrane reviews (Cabrera et al., 2012; Depping et al., 2010; Norton, 2012; Stein et al., 2000; Wei & Higgins, 2013; Wiltink et al., 2011), but the searches were up to 7 years old and all needed to be updated.

6.5 OVERVIEW OF STUDIES CONSIDERED AND CLINICAL EVIDENCE

A systematic review was conducted to identify RCTs of interventions for adults with social anxiety disorder. The search identified 142 relevant RCTs published between 1988 and 2013. Of these, 100 reported continuous outcomes and compared interventions that the GDG considered could be used as primary treatments for people with social anxiety disorder. Studies of short-term interventions (atenolol) and pharmacological interventions that would not be used in clinical practice (noradrenaline reuptake inhibitors, neurokinin-1 antagonists and St John's wort) were excluded (Furmark et al., 2005; Kobak et al., 2005; Liebowitz et al., 1990; Ravindran et al., 2009). The included trials were used in a NMA comparing symptoms of social anxiety following acute treatment, which included results from approximately 13,097 participants. Of the 100 included trials, 25 reported recovery (loss of diagnosis), which was also included in the model (see Chapter 3 for the method and Appendices 12 and 13 for a list of the studies by intervention and the study characteristics).

Trials of particular subgroups (for example, adults with comorbid substance misuse) and trials of different phases of the disorder (for example, relapse prevention studies) were analysed separately. For interventions that the GDG considered recommending on the basis of the NMA, secondary outcomes (depression, quality of life, anxiety-related disability and withdrawal) and controlled follow-up compared with waitlist and placebo are reported where possible. Analyses of secondary outcomes were not conducted for interventions that the GDG decided not to recommend based on the primary analysis. Uncontrolled follow-up data and other comparisons (for example, between two active interventions) were not analysed. Several comparisons did not connect to the network (that is, neither intervention was included), and these were considered in separate pairwise analyses (see Chapter 3 for the method). Relapse prevention studies (that is, people who responded to acute pharmacotherapy and were randomised to continuation therapy or placebo) were also analysed separately. Studies that were excluded from the analysis and reasons for exclusion can be found in Appendix 25, including trials of drugs that are not available in the UK and were compared with placebo only (that is, would not contribute to estimates of other interventions).

The evidence reviewed in this chapter is organised into five major sections: (1) pharmacological interventions (see Section 6.6), (2) psychological interventions (see Section 6.7), (3) combination interventions (see Section 6.8), (4) specific subgroups (see Section 6.9) and (5) health economic evidence (see Section 6.10). The clinical summary, evidence to recommendations and clinical recommendations appear at the end of the chapter. The chapter includes results from the NMA and from pairwise analyses (see Table 11, Table 12, Table 13, Figure 5 and Figure 6 on pages 112–124).

The GDG had concerns about the comparability of participants in different trials. In particular, participants in pharmacological and psychological trials may differ insofar as users find different interventions more or less tolerable in light of their personal circumstances and preferences. Similarly, self-help trials may recruit participants who would not seek or accept face-to-face interventions. However, large trials have successfully recruited participants who are willing to be randomised to either medication or psychotherapy and to either self-help or face-to-face treatment. Moreover, some participants in psychological intervention trials (typically 25%) were already taking antidepressants and other medication. The NMA assumes that users are willing to accept any of the interventions included; in practice, treatment decisions will be restricted by individual values and goals.

The different results are distinguished by different labels: results labelled 'SMD^N' are taken from the NMA and those labelled 'SMD' are from a pairwise analysis. For all analyses, the number of participants reported is the number receiving treatment who were included in the analysis. For both the NMA and pairwise analyses, the GDG was first interested in the effects for major classes of interventions (for example, SSRIs and individual CBT) and secondly in any differences among members of those classes (for example, between specific drugs). The NMA includes effects for each class and for each member of the class (see Chapter 3 for the method). Pairwise analyses include overall effects for each class, each subgroup and tests for differences among subgroups (for example, different drugs or variations of a therapy). Within each major section, results are organised alphabetically by class and alphabetically by intervention within the class.

In estimating symptoms of social anxiety, all effects are taken from the NMA unless otherwise specified. The structure of the NMA is included in Appendix 11. Effect sizes from the NMA are presented relative to waitlist. As described (see Chapter 3), the relative effects of any two interventions in the NMA can be calculated by subtraction (that is, the choice of baseline comparator for reporting does not affect the results). In addition to estimating active treatments, effects were estimated for pill placebo and for psychological placebo. Results are reported as mean values with 95% credible intervals (CrI), which are analogous to confidence intervals in frequentist statistics (see Table 10).

Table 10: Effects for control groups in the network meta-analysis

Intervention	Number of trials (participants receiving this treatment)	Class effect	Individual effect
Waitlist	28 (802)	SMD = 0	SMD = 0
Pill placebo	42 (3,623)	SMD = −0.47 95% CrI = −0.70 to −0.23	SMD = −0.47 95% CrI = −0.70 to −0.23
Psychological placebo	6 (145)	SMD = −0.63 95% CrI = −0.90 to −0.36	SMD = −0.63 95% CrI = −0.90 to −0.36

Further details about the review are included in the appendices. The complete search strategy and PRISMA[17] chart can be found in Appendix 6. Forest plots for pairwise analyses are included in Appendix 14, and GRADE profiles for pairwise analyses are included in Appendix 15. Study characteristics are included in Appendices 12 and 14.

6.5.1   Network meta-analysis of social anxiety disorder post-treatment

Trials included in the NMA included between 18 and 839 participants at baseline (median 78). Where known, participants were on average (median of means) 36 years old and 80% white. About half of the included participants were female (52%). There were no participants on medication in 44 trials, including most of the pharmacological trials, and it was unclear in 27 trials if participants were taking medication at baseline. In the remaining 27 trials, approximately 27% of participants were taking medication at the start (see Appendix 12).

Quality of the evidence
To rate the quality of evidence, guidelines may use GRADE profiles for critical outcomes. However, GRADE has not yet been adapted for use in NMAs. To evaluate the quality of the evidence from the NMA, information about the factors that would normally be included in a GRADE profile (that is, risk of bias, publication bias, imprecision, inconsistency and indirectness) are reported. Additionally, before conducting the NMA, the results of pairwise comparisons were presented to the GDG and the quality of the included trials and the evidence for each outcome and comparison were discussed. Study quality and risk of bias (see below) were assessed for all studies, irrespective of whether they were included in the NMA or pairwise comparisons.

Risk of bias
All included trials were assessed for risk of bias (see Appendix 20 and Figure 5). Of those in the NMA, 74 were at low risk for sequence generation and 69 of these were at low risk of bias for allocation concealment. Trials of psychological interventions were considered at high risk of bias for participant and provider blinding *per se*, and the rate of side effects may also make it difficult to maintain blinding in pharmacological trials. Most reported outcomes were self-rated, but assessor blinding was considered separately for all trials; 94 were at low risk of bias (no assessor-rated outcomes or assessors blind), one was unclear and assessors were aware of treatment conditions in five trials. For incomplete outcome data, 71 trials were at low risk of bias; it was unclear how missing data were handled in four trials and 25 were at high risk of bias

---

[17] Preferred Reporting Items for Systematic Reviews and Meta-Analyses.

(for example, those that reported per protocol or completer analyses and those with very high amounts of missing data).

Selective outcome reporting and publication bias
Several methods were employed to minimise risk of selective outcome reporting and publication bias. All authors were contacted in writing to request trial registrations and unpublished outcomes, and all authors of included trials, stakeholders and pharmaceutical manufacturers were asked to provide unpublished trials. Nonetheless, most of the included trials were not registered. Only 30 were at low risk of selective outcome reporting bias; 53 were at unclear risk of bias and 18 were at high risk of bias. Trials of psychological and pharmacological interventions were equally likely to be at unclear risk of bias. For interventions developed before the introduction of mandatory trial registration, results may be particularly overestimated as a result of publication bias.

Inconsistency
The random effects model was a good fit with the data, although the between-trials SD (heterogeneity) had a posterior median of 0.19 with 95% credible interval (0.14, 0.25).

Inconsistency was assessed by fitting an unrelated mean effects model (Dias et al., 2012) and comparing the fit with that of the full NMA model using the residual deviance (Dias et al., 2012). There was no evidence of inconsistency in the NMA. The posterior mean of the residual deviance for the NMA model was 164.0 compared with 169.3 in the independent effect mode (lower values are favoured). The results of the NMA were also consistent in magnitude and direction with the results of pairwise comparisons.

Indirectness
All evidence in the NMA is direct insofar as it relates to the population and outcomes of interest. The sections that follow describe the direct comparisons that have been made among the interventions included in the NMA.

The GDG had concerns about the comparability of participants in different trials. In particular, participants in pharmacological and psychological trials may differ insofar as users find different interventions more or less tolerable in light of their personal circumstances and preferences. Similarly, self-help trials may recruit participants who would not seek or accept face-to-face interventions. However, large trials have successfully recruited participants who are willing to be randomised to either medication or psychotherapy and to either self-help or face-to-face treatment. Moreover, some participants in psychological intervention trials (typically 25%) were already taking antidepressants and other medication. The NMA assumes that users are willing to accept any of the interventions included; in practice, treatment decisions will be restricted by individual values and goals.

Table 11: Results from the NMA – summary of treatment and class effects compared with waitlist

Treatment	N	Class effect SMD (CrI)	Individual effect SMD (CrI)	Study ID(s)
Pharmacological interventions				
6.6.1 *Anticonvulsants*		−0.81 (−1.36, −0.28)		
Gabapentin	34		−0.89 (−1.41, −0.37)	PANDE1999 (Pande et al., 1999)
Levetiracetam	9		−0.83 (−1.48, −0.18)	ZHANG2005 (Zhang et al., 2005)
Pregabalin	199		−0.72 (−1.07, −0.37)	FELTNER2011 (Feltner et al., 2011), PANDE2004 (Feltner et al., 2000; Pande et al., 2004), PFIZER2007 (Pfizer, 2007)
6.6.2 *Benzodiazepines*		−0.96 (−1.56, −0.35)		
Alprazolam	12		−0.85 (−1.40, −0.29)	GELERNTER1991 (Gelernter, 1990; Gelernter et al., 1991)
Clonazepam	100		−1.07 (−1.44, −0.70)	DAVIDSON1993 (Davidson et al., 1993b; Sutherland et al., 1996), KNIJNIK2008 (Knijnik et al., 2008), MUNJACK1990 (Munjack et al., 1990), OTTO2000 (Otto et al., 2000)

Continued

	N	Effect size	Studies
6.6.3 *MAOIs*		**−1.01 (−1.56, −0.45)**	
Moclobemide	490	−0.73 (−1.03, −0.44)	BURROWS1997 (Burrows, 1997), OOSTERBAAN2001 (Oosterbaan et al., 2001), PRASKO2003 (Prasko, 2003), SCHNEIER1998 (Schneier et al., 1998), STEIN2002a (Stein et al., 2002a), VERSIANI1992 (Versiani et al., 1992)
Phenelzine	125	−1.28 (−1.57, −0.98)	BLANCO2010 (Blanco et al., 2010), GELERNTER1991 (Gelernter, 1990; Gelernter et al., 1991), HEIMBERG1998 (Heimberg et al., 1998; Liebowitz, 1999; Thyer, 1999), LIEBOWITZ1990 (Liebowitz, 1988; Liebowitz et al., 1990; Liebowitz et al., 1992), VERSIANI1992 (Versiani et al., 1992)
6.6.4 *SSRIs/ SNRIs*		**−0.91 (−1.22, −0.60)**	
Citalopram	18	−0.83 (−1.27, −0.39)	FURMARK2002 (Furmark, 2002), FURMARK2005 (Furmark et al., 2005)
Escitalopram	675	−0.88 (−1.19, −0.56)	KASPER2005 (Kasper et al., 2002; Kasper et al., 2005), LADER2004 (Lader et al., 2004; Stein et al., 2006)
Fluoxetine	107	−0.87 (−1.16, −0.57)	CLARK2003 (Clark, 1998; Clark et al., 2003), DAVIDSON2004b (Davidson et al., 2004b; Ledley, 2005), KOBAK2002 (Kobak et al., 2002)

Table 11: *(Continued)*

Treatment	N	Class effect SMD (CrI)	Individual effect SMD (CrI)	Study ID(s)
Fluvoxamine	500		−0.94 (−1.25, −0.63)	ASAKURA2007 (Asakura et al., 2007), DAVIDSON2004a (Davidson et al., 2000; Davidson et al., 2004a), STEIN1999 (Stein et al., 1999a; Stein et al., 2003), VAN–VLIET1994 (den Boer et al., 1992; Van Vliet et al., 1994), WESTENBERG2004 (Owen, 2008; Stein et al., 2003; Westenberg et al., 2004)
Paroxetine	1,449		−0.99 (−1.26, −0.73)	ALLGULANDER1999 (Allgulander, 1998; Allgulander, 1999; Allgulander, 2001), ALLGULANDER2004 (Allgulander et al., 2004), BALDWIN1999 (Baldwin et al., 1999; Stein et al., 1999; Stein et al., 2001), GSK2006 (GlaxoSmithKline, 2006) (at two doses), LADER2004 (Lader et al., 2004; Stein et al., 2006), LEPOLA2004 (Lepola et al., 2004), LIEBOWITZ2002 (GlaxoSmithKline, 1997; Liebowitz et al., 2002b) (at two doses), LIEBOWITZ2005b (Liebowitz et al., 2005a), PFIZER2007 (Pfizer, 2007), SEEDAT2004 (Seedat & Stein, 2004), STEIN1998 (Stein et al., 1998b; Stein, 2001)
Sertraline	535		−0.91 (−1.22, −0.61)	BLOMHOFF2001 (Blomhoff et al., 2001; Haug, 2003) (at two doses), LIEBOWITZ2003 (Connor et al., 2006; Liebowitz et al., 2002a; Liebowitz et al., 2003), VAN–AMERINGEN2001 (Connor et al., 2006; Van Ameringen et al., 1999; Van Ameringen et al., 2001; Van Ameringen et al., 2004; Walker, 2000)

Venlafaxine	759		−0.96 (−1.25, −0.67)	ALLGULANDER2004 (Allgulander et al., 2004), LIEBOWITZ2005a (Liebowitz, 2002; Liebowitz et al., 2005b), LIEBOWITZ2005b (Liebowitz et al., 2005a), RICKELS2004 (Rickels et al., 2004), STEIN2005 (Stein et al., 2005)
6.6.5 Noradrenaline and selective serotonin antagonists		**−0.80 (−1.62, 0.03)**		
Mirtazapine	30		−0.80 (−1.45, −0.16)	SCHUTTERS2010 (Schutters et al., 2010)
Psychological interventions				
6.7.1 Cognitive behavioural interventions – individual		**−1.19 (−1.57, −0.81)**		
CBT (Heimberg)	53		−1.02 (−1.42, −0.62)	GOLDIN2012 (Goldin et al., 2012), LEDLEY2009 (Ledley et al., 2009) (two groups)
CBT	163		−1.19 (−1.48, −0.89)	COTTRAUX2000 (Cottraux et al., 2000), EMMELKAMP2006 (Emmelkamp et al., 2006), HERBERT2004 (Herbert et al., 2004) (two groups), OOSTERBAAN2001 (Oosterbaan et al., 2001), PRASKO2003 (Prasetyo et al., 2002; Prasko, 2003; Prasko et al., 1999; Prasko et al., 2004; Prasko et al., 2006), ROBILLARD2010 (Robillard et al., 2010) (two groups)

Continued

115

Table 11: *(Continued)*

Treatment	N	Class effect SMD (CrI)	Individual effect SMD (CrI)	Study ID(s)
CT	97		−1.56 (−1.85, −1.27)	CLARK2003 (Clark, 1998; Clark et al., 2003), CLARK2006 (Clark et al., 2006; McManus et al., 2009a), CLARK2012 (Clark et al., 2012)
CT, shortened sessions	249		−0.97 (−1.21, −0.73)	LEICHSENRING2012 (Leichsenring et al., 2009b), MORTBERG2007 (Mortberg, 2007; Mortberg et al., 2007; Mortberg, 2011), STANGIER2003 (Stangier et al., 2003), STANGIER2011 (Stangier et al., 2011)
6.7.2 Cognitive behavioural interventions – group		**−0.92 (−1.34, −0.51)**		
CBT (Heimberg)	338		−0.80 (−1.02, −0.58)	BLANCO2010 (Blanco et al., 2010), GELERNTER1991 (Gelernter et al., 1991), GRUBER2001 (Gruber et al., 2001) (two groups), HEDMAN2011 (Hedman et al., 2011a; Hedman et al., 2011b), HEIMBERG1990 (Heimberg et al., 1990; Heimberg et al., 1993), HEIMBERG1998 (Heimberg et al., 1998; Liebowitz, 1999; Thyer, 1999), HERBERT2005 (Herbert et al., 2005) (two groups), HOPE1995 (Hope et al., 1995), KOSZYCKI2007 (Koszycki et al., 2007), OTTO2000 (Otto et al., 2000), WONG2006 (Wong & Sun, 2007)

	N			
CBT	583		−0.85 (−1.04, −0.67)	ALDEN2011 (Alden & Taylor, 2011), ANDREWS2011 (Andrews et al., 2011), BJORNSSON2011 (Bjornsson et al., 2011), BORGEAT2009 (Borgeat et al., 2009), DAVIDSON2004b (Davidson et al., 2004b; Ledley, 2005) (two groups), FURMARK2002 (Furmark, 2002), MATTICK1988 (Mattick & Peters, 1988), MATTICK1989 (Mattick et al., 1989), MCEVOY2009 (McEvoy et al., 2009) (two groups), MORGAN1999 (Morgan & Raffle, 1999) (two groups), MORTBERG2007 (Mortberg, 2007; Mortberg et al., 2007; Mortberg, 2011), PIET2010 (Piet et al., 2010), RAPEE2007 (Hedman et al., 2011c; Rapee et al., 2007), RAPEE2009 (Rapee et al., 2009), SALABERRIA1998 (Salaberria & Echeburua, 1998), STANGIER2003 (Stangier et al., 2003)
CBT, enhanced	63		−1.10 (−1.49, −0.71)	RAPEE2007 (Hedman et al., 2011c; Rapee et al., 2007)
6.7.4 *Exercise*		**−0.35 (−1.32, 0.62)**		
Exercise promotion	18		−0.34 (−1.06, 0.38)	JAZAIERI2012 (Jazaieri et al., 2012)
6.7.5 *Exposure in vivo and social skills training*		**−0.86 (−1.42, −0.30)**		

Continued

117

Table 11: *(Continued)*

Treatment	N	Class effect SMD (CrI)	Individual effect SMD (CrI)	Study ID(s)
Exposure *in vivo*	199		−0.83 (−1.07, −0.59)	ANDERSSON2006 (Andersson et al., 2006), BORGEAT2009 (Borgeat et al., 2009), CLARK2006 (Clark et al., 2006; McManus et al., 2009a), HOPE1995 (Hope et al., 1995), MATTICK1988 (Mattick & Peters, 1988), MATTICK1989 (Mattick et al., 1989), SALABERRIA1998 (Salaberria & Echeburua, 1998), SMITS2006 (Smits et al., 2006), STRAVYNSKI2000 (Stravynski et al., 2000)
Social skills training	32		−0.88 (−1.38, −0.38)	STRAVYNSKI2000 (Stravynski et al., 2000)
6.7.9 Short-term psychodynamic psychotherapy	**185**	**−0.62 (−0.93, −0.31)**	−0.62 (−0.93, −0.31)	EMMELKAMP2006 (Emmelkamp et al., 2006), KNIJNIK2004 (Knijnik et al., 2004), LEICHSENRING2012 (Leichsenring et al., 2009b)
6.7.11 Self-help without support		**−0.75 (−1.25, −0.25)**		
Book without support	136		−0.84 (−1.08, −0.60)	CHUNG2008 (Chung & Kwon, 2008), FURMARK2009a (Furmark et al., 2009; Hedman et al., 2011c), FURMARK2009b (Furmark et al., 2009; Hedman et al., 2011c), RAPEE2007 (Rapee et al., 2007)
Internet without support	270		−0.66 (−0.94, −0.39)	TITOV2008c (Titov et al., 2008a; Titov et al., 2009d), TITOV2009b (Titov et al., 2009a), TITOV2010b (Titov et al., 2010) (two groups)

Continued

6.7.11 Self-help with support	**-0.86 (-1.36, -0.37)**			
Book with support		52	-0.85 (-1.17, -0.53)	ABRAMOWITZ2009 (Abramowitz et al., 2009), CHUNG2008 (Chung & Kwon, 2008)
Internet with support		696	-0.88 (-1.04, -0.71)	ANDERSSON2012 (Andersson et al., 2012), ANDREWS2011 (Andrews et al., 2011), BERGER2009 (Andersson & Carlbring, 2009; Berger et al., 2009; Berger et al., 2010), CARLBRING2007 (Almlöv et al., 2011; Carlbring et al., 2007; Carlbring, 2009; Nordgreen et al., 2012; FURMARK2009a (Furmark et al., 2009; Hedman et al., 2011c; Nordgreen et al., 2012), FURMARK2009b (Furmark et al., 2009; Hedman et al., 2011c; Nordgreen et al., 2012) (two groups), HEDMAN2011 (Hedman et al., 2011a; Hedman et al., 2011b), TITOV2008a (Titov et al., 2008c; Titov et al., 2009b; Titov et al., 2009d), TITOV2008b (Titov et al., 2008b; Titov et al., 2009b; Titov et al., 2009d), TITOV2008c (Titov et al., 2008a), TITOV2009a (Titov et al., 2009c) (two groups), TITOV2009b (Titov et al., 2009a)
Other psychological interventions	**-0.36 (-0.85, 0.12)**			
6.7.7 Interpersonal psychotherapy		64	-0.43 (-0.83, -0.03)	LIPSITZ2008 (Lipsitz et al., 2008), STANGIER2011 (Stangier et al., 2011)

Table 11: (*Continued*)

Treatment	N	Class effect SMD (CrI)	Individual effect SMD (CrI)	Study ID(s)
6.7.8 Mindfulness training	64		−0.39 (−0.82, 0.04)	JAZAIERI2012 (Jazaieri et al., 2012), KOSZYCKI2007 (Koszycki et al., 2007), PIET2010 (Piet et al., 2010)
6.7.10 Supportive therapy	54		−0.26 (−0.72, 0.21)	COTTRAUX2000 (Cottraux et al., 2000), LIPSITZ2008 (Lipsitz et al., 2008)
Combined psychological and pharmacological interventions		**−1.30 (−1.73, −0.88)**		
6.8 *Group CBT with fluoxetine*	59		−0.95 (−1.33, −0.57)	DAVIDSON2004b (Davidson et al., 2004b; Ledley, 2005)
6.8 *Group CBT with phenelzine*	32		−1.69 (−2.10, −1.27)	BLANCO2010 (Blanco et al., 2010)
6.8 *Group CBT with moclobemide*	22		−1.23 (−1.72, −0.74)	PRASKO2003 (Prasko, 2003)
6.6.5 *Paroxetine with clonazepam*	14		−1.35 (−1.93, −0.78)	SEEDAT2004 (Seedat & Stein, 2004)
6.8 *Psychodynamic psychotherapy with clonazepam*	29		−1.28 (−1.82, −0.75)	KNIJNIK2008 (Knijnik et al., 2008)

Table 12: Results of pairwise comparisons –symptoms of social anxiety at post-treatment

Comparison	SMD (CI)	Heterogeneity	Study ID(s)
6.6.3 Brofaromine versus placebo	−0.71 (95% CI = −1.08 to −0.34)	$I^2 = 36\%$ Chi$^2 = 3.12$ p = 0.21	FAHLEN1995 (Fahlen, 1995), LOTT1997 (Lott et al., 1997), VAN–VLIET1992 (Van Vliet et al., 1992)
6.6.3 Tranylcypromine 60 mg versus 30 mg	−0.85 (95% CI = −1.54 to −0.17)	N/A	NARDI2010 (Nardi et al., 2010)
6.6.4 Duloxetine 120 mg versus 60 mg (following open-label at 60 mg)	−1.22 (95% CI = 0.39 to 2.05)	N/A	SIMON2010 (Simon et al., 2010)
6.6.5 Quetiapine versus placebo	−0.28 (95% CI = −1.36 to 0.81)	N/A	VAISHNAVI2007 (Vaishnavi et al., 2007)
6.6.5 Olanzapine versus placebo	−2.28 (95% CI = −4.00 to −0.55)	N/A	BARNETT2002 (Barnett et al., 2002)
6.7.1 Individual CBT versus applied relaxation	1.13 (95% CI = 0.32 to 1.94)	N/A	RENNER2008 (Renner, 2008)
6.7.2 Group CBT + paroxetine versus paroxetine (for paroxetine non–remitters in open-label)	−0.49 (95% CI = −1.00 to 0.02)	N/A	HEIMBERG2012 (Heimberg, 2012)

Continued

Table 12: *(Continued)*

Comparison	SMD (CI)	Heterogeneity	Study ID(s)
6.7.3 Cognitive bias modification versus sham therapy	−0.30 (95% CI = −0.55 to 0.05)	$I^2 = 27\%$ Chi^2 = 8.26 p = 0.22	AMIR2009 (Amir et al., 2009), AMIR2012 (Amir & Taylor, 2012), BEARD2011 (Beard et al., 2011), BOETTCHER2011 (Boettcher et al., 2011), CARLBRING2012 (Carlbring et al., 2012), HEEREN2012 (Heeren et al., 2012), SCHMIDT2009 (Schmidt et al., 2009)
6.7.6 D–cycloserine versus placebo (both with exposure)	−0.36 (95% CI = −0.61 to −0.11)	$I^2 = 0\%$ Chi^2 = 0.47 p = 0.79	GUASTELLA2008 (Guastella et al., 2008), HOFMANN2006 (Hofmann et al., 2006), HOFMANN2012 (Hofmann et al., 2013)
6.7.6 Oxytocin versus placebo (both with exposure)	0.26 (95% CI = −0.53 to 1.35)	N/A	GUASTELLA2009 (Guastella et al., 2009)
6.8 Preference–based therapy versus treatment as usual	−0.48 (95% CI = −0.83 to −0.14)	N/A	CRASKE2011 (Craske et al., 2011)
6.9.1 Exposure *in vivo* versus waitlist (for fear of public speaking)	−0.60 (95% CI = −1.30 to 0.11)	N/A	NEWMAN1994 (Newman et al., 1994)
6.9.1 Exposure *in vivo* versus self–help (for fear of public speaking)	−0.10 (95% CI = −0.74 to 0.54)	N/A	TILLFORS2008 (Tillfors et al., 2008)

	Effect	Heterogeneity	Study
6.9.1 CBT versus waitlist (for fear of public speaking)	−1.18 (95% CI = −1.72 to −0.65)	N/A	BOTELLA2010 (Botella et al., 2010)
6.9.1 Self-help versus waitlist (for fear of public speaking)	−1.09 (95% CI = −1.56 to −0.63)	N/A	BOTELLA2010 (Botella et al., 2010)
6.9.2 Exposure *in vivo* versus attention training (for fear of blushing)	−0.42 (95% CI = −1.20 to 0.36)	N/A	MULKENS2001 (Mulkens et al., 2001)
6.9.2 Task concentration training versus applied relaxation (for fear of blushing, trembling or sweating)	0.01 (95% CI = −0.48 to 0.50)	N/A	BOGELS2006 (Bögels, 2006)
6.9.2 Social skills training versus group CBT (for fear of blushing, trembling or sweating)	0.19 (95% CI = −0.34 to 0.72)	N/A	BOGELS2008 (Bögels & Voncken, 2008)
6.9.3 Botulinum toxin with paroxetine versus placebo	−0.22 (95% CI = −0.84 to 0.41)	N/A	CONNOR2004 (Connor et al., 2004; Connor, 2006)
6.9.4 CBT versus IPT (residential setting)	−0.07 (95% CI = −0.53 to 0.39)	N/A	BORGE2008 (Borge et al., 2008; Borge et al., 2010; Hoffart, 2009a; Hoffart, 2009b; Hoffart, 2012)
6.9.5 Paroxetine versus placebo (for comorbid alcohol misuse)	−0.91 (95% CI = −1.56 to −0.26)	$I^2 = 15\%$ $Chi^2 = 1.18$ $p = 0.28$	BOOK2008 (Book et al., 2008), RANDALL2001a (Randall et al., 2001a)
6.9.5 CBT + alcohol programme versus CBT alone (for comorbid alcohol misuse)	−0.32 (95% CI = −1.15 to 0.51)	N/A	HAYES2006 (Hayes, 2006)
6.9.6 Atomoxetine versus placebo (for comorbid ADHD)	−0.24 (95% CI = −0.44 to −0.04)	N/A	ADLER2009 (Adler et al., 2009)

Table 13: Results of pairwise comparisons – relapse prevention

Comparison	RR (CI)	Heterogeneity	Study ID(s)
6.6.6 SSRIs versus placebo	0.47 (95% CI = 0.27 to 0.82)	$I^2 = 75\%$ $Chi^2 = 11.96$ $p = 0.008$	KUMAR1999 (Kumar et al., 1999), MONTGOMERY2005 (François et al., 2008; Montgomery et al., 2005; Servant et al., 2003), STEIN2002b (Stein et al., 2002b), VAN-AMERINGEN2001 (Connor et al., 2006; Van Ameringen et al., 2001; Van Ameringen et al., 2004; Walker et al., 2002)
6.6.6 Anticonvulsants versus placebo	0.79 (95% CI = 0.58 to 1.06)	N/A	GREIST2011 (Greist et al., 2011)

Figure 5: Risk of bias summary

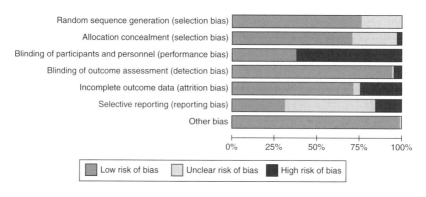

Figure 6: Results of pairwise comparisons – risk of bias summary chart

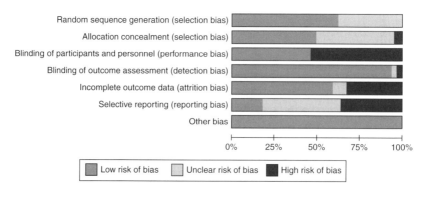

6.6 PHARMACOLOGICAL INTERVENTIONS

6.6.1 Anticonvulsants

Five trials (FELTNER2011, PANDE1999, PANDE2004, PFIZER2007, ZHANG 2005) that evaluated anticonvulsants (gabapentin, levetiracetam and pregabalin) were included in the NMA (242 participants on treatment). Effects for each drug were similar to the medium average effect for the class ($SMD^N = -0.81$, 95% CrI $= -1.36$ to -0.28). All anticonvulsants were significantly different from waitlist.

Gabapentin
One trial (PANDE1999) compared gabapentin (34 participants on treatment) with placebo. While the mean dose at endpoint was not reported, 56% of participants reached the maximum dose of 3,600 mg per day by the end of the 14-week trial. At post-treatment there was a large effect compared with waitlist ($SMD^N = -0.89$, 95% CrI $= -1.41$ to -0.37).

Levetiracetam
One trial (ZHANG2005) compared levetiracetam (nine participants on treatment) with placebo. Participants received a mean dose of 1,140 mg twice a day for 7 weeks. At post-treatment, there was a medium effect compared with waitlist ($SMD^N = -0.83$, 95% CrI $= -1.48$ to -0.18).

Pregabalin
Three trials (FELTNER2011, PANDE2004, PFIZER2007) compared pregabalin (199 participants on treatment) with placebo. Participants in two trials received a fixed daily dose of 600 mg; participants in the other trial received a fixed daily dose of 400 mg. Trials lasted 10 or 11 weeks. At post-treatment, there was a medium effect compared with waitlist ($SMD^N = -0.72$, 95% CrI $= -1.07$ to -0.37).

In two trials (PANDE2004, PFIZER2007), fixed doses at the starting level of the BNF recommended prescription range were excluded from the NMA (150 and 200 mg per day) as the GDG considered these unlikely to be clinically effective and unrepresentative of practice.

6.6.2 Benzodiazepines

Five trials (DAVIDSON1993, GELERNTER1991, KNIJNIK2008, MUNJACK1990, OTTO2000) that evaluated the benzodiazepines alprazolam and clonazepam were included in the NMA (112 participants on treatment). Effects for each drug were similar to the large average effect for the class ($SMD^N = -0.96$, 95% CrI $= -1.56$ to -0.35) and they were significantly different from waitlist.

Alprazolam

One trial (GELERNTER1991) compared alprazolam (12 participants on treatment) with placebo, phenelzine or CBT. Participants received a mean end dose of 4.2 mg per day for 12 weeks. At post-treatment, there was a large effect compared with waitlist (SMD^N = −0.85, 95% CrI = −1.40 to −0.29).

Clonazepam

Four trials (DAVIDSON1993, KNIJNIK2008, MUNJACK1990, OTTO2000) included a group that received clonazepam (100 participants on treatment), compared with placebo, waitlist, psychodynamic psychotherapy plus clonazepam, or group CBT. Participants received 2.4 to 4.0 mg of clonazepam daily for 8 to 12 weeks. At post-treatment, there was a large effect compared with waitlist (SMD^N = −1.07, 95% CrI = −1.44 to −0.70).

6.6.3 Monoamine oxidase inhibitors

Ten trials (BLANCO2010, BURROWS1997, GELERNTER1991, HEIMBERG1998, LIEBOWITZ1990, OOSTERBAAN2001, PRASKO2003, SCHNEIER1998, STEIN2002a, VERSIANI1992) evaluating MAOIs were included in the NMA (615 participants on treatment); the large effect on symptoms of social anxiety for the class (SMD^N = −1.01, 95% CrI = −1.56 to −0.45) was between effects for moclobemide and phenelzine. Both interventions were significantly different from waitlist. One MAOI (brofaromine) was not included in the NMA because it is no longer manufactured, but the GDG considered it might have similar effects and side effects to those that are currently available; it was included in a sensitivity analysis.

In a pairwise analysis of two trials (GELERNTER1991, OOSTERBAAN2001; 37 participants on treatment), there was no evidence of an effect on symptoms of anxiety at follow-up compared with placebo (SMD = −0.27, 95% CI = −1.05 to 0.51) with substantial heterogeneity (I^2 = 67%; Chi^2 = 9.09, p = 0.03).

In seven trials (BLANCO2010, BURROWS1997, HEIMBERG1998, LIEBOWITZ1990, OOSTERBAAN2001, SCHNEIER1998, VERSIANI1992; 393 participants on treatment), there was a small effect on depression at post-treatment (SMD = −0.22, 95% CI = −0.37 to −0.07) with considerable heterogeneity (I^2 = 77%; Chi^2 = 30.02, p = 0.0001). One trial (17 participants on treatment) reported no evidence of an effect on depression at follow-up (SMD = 0.30, 95% CI = −0.39 to 0.99). In the same trials (383 participants on treatment), there was a moderate effect on disability at post-treatment (SMD = −0.54, 95% CI = −0.95 to −0.12) with considerable heterogeneity (I^2 = 82%; Chi^2 = 39.44, p = <0.00001). In two trials (GELERNTER1991, OOSTERBAAN2001; 29 participants on treatment) there was no evidence of an effect on disability at follow-up (SMD = −0.11, 95% CI = −0.66 to 0.43) with no significant heterogeneity (I^2 = 18%; Chi^2 = 1.22, p = 0.27). No trials reported a measure of quality of life.

In two trials (NOYES1997 [Noyes et al., 1997], SCHNEIER1998; 123 participants on treatment), the effect was not statistically significant for withdrawal because of side effects compared with placebo (RR = 1.13, 95% CI = 0.63 to 2.05) with no significant heterogeneity ($I^2 = 0\%$; $Chi^2 = 0.55$, p = 0.46). There was also no evidence of an effect on the total number of people experiencing any adverse event (RR = 1.09, 95% CI = 0.97 to 1.23; 381 participants on treatment) with no heterogeneity.

Moclobemide

Six trials (BURROWS1997, OOSTERBAAN2001, PRASKO2003, SCHNEIER1998, STEIN2002a, VERSIANI1992) included one or more groups who received moclobemide (490 participants on treatment); six were included in the NMA. Participants received 581 to 728 mg daily for 8 to 26 weeks. All included trials included a placebo comparison and one also compared moclobemide with phenelzine. At post-treatment, there was a medium effect compared with waitlist ($SMD^N = -0.73$, 95% CrI = -1.03 to -0.44).

One group in an included trial (BURROWS1997) was below the recommended range in the BNF prescription range and was excluded from the review (300 mg per day).

Other trials were not included in the NMA either because the authors did not report data that could be included in meta-analysis (NOYES1997) or because they included a study population with very severe symptoms (ATMACA2002 [Atmaca et al., 2002]). While many trials included only participants scoring above 70 on the LSAS and had mean values close to the cut-off, participants in ATMACA2002 (36 participants on treatment) scored 122 at baseline; there was a small effect (favouring citalopram) on symptoms of social anxiety at post-treatment (SMD = -0.36, 95% CI = -0.69 to -0.03) and there was no evidence of an effect between the groups on the number of people reporting any adverse event (RR = 1.19, 95% CI = 0.56 to 2.51). No controlled follow-up data were reported.

Phenelzine

Five trials (BLANCO2010, GELERNTER1991, HEIMBERG1998, LIEBOWITZ1990, VERSIANI1992) included one or more groups receiving phenelzine (125 participants on treatment) and were included in the NMA. All included a placebo comparison and one also compared phenelzine with moclobemide, as noted above. Participants received 55 to 76 mg daily for 8 to 12 weeks. At post-treatment, there was a large effect compared with waitlist ($SMD^N = -1.28$, 95% CrI = -1.57 to -0.98).

Tranylcypromine

One trial compared tranylcypromine in fixed daily doses of 30 mg and 60 mg for 12 weeks; it could not be included in the NMA because there was neither a placebo group nor another intervention that was included in the network (NARDI2010;

17 participants on treatment). There was large effect on symptoms of social anxiety disorder at post-treatment favouring the higher dose (SMD = −0.85, 95% CI = −1.54 to −0.17) and the effect was not statistically significant for dose on the number per group reporting at least one adverse event (RR = 0.84, 95% CI = 0.61 to 1.15).

Brofaromine (sensitivity analysis)

Three trials compared brofaromine with placebo (FAHLEN1995, LOTT1997, VAN-VLIET1992) and were not included in the NMA because brofaromine is no longer manufactured. A pairwise analysis was conducted comparing brofaromine (101 participants on treatment) with placebo. Participants received 107 to 150 mg daily for 12 weeks. There was a medium effect compared with placebo at post-treatment (SMD = −0.71; 95% CI = −1.08 to −0.34) with no important heterogeneity (I^2 = 36%; Chi^2 = 3.12%, p = 0.0002). There was no difference in the overall effect of MAOIs versus placebo either with (SMD = −0.58; 95% CI = −0.81 to −0.34) or without (SMD = −0.53; 95% CI = −0.81 to −0.25) the brofaromine trials (see Appendix 14 for the forest plots). One trial reported controlled results at follow-up, but only one participant remained in the placebo group and the data were not analysed.

6.6.4 Selective serotonin reuptake inhibitors (SSRIs) and serotonin and noradrenaline reuptake inhibitors (SNRIs)

Twenty-five trials (ALLGULANDER1999, ALLGULANDER2004, ASAKURA2007, BALDWIN1999, BLOMHOFF2001, DAVIDSON2004a, FURMARK2002, FURMARK2005, GSK2006, KASPER2005, LADER2004, LEPOLA2004, LIEBOWITZ2002, LIEBOWITZ2003, LIEBOWITZ2005a, LIEBOWITZ2005b, PFIZER2007, RICKELS2004, SEEDAT2004, STEIN1998, STEIN1999, STEIN2005, VAN-AMERINGEN2001, VAN-VLIET1994, WESTENBERG2004) evaluating SSRIs (citalopram, escitalopram, fluoxetine, fluvoxamine, paroxetine and sertraline) and SNRIs (venlafaxine) were included in the NMA (4,043 participants on treatment). At post-treatment, effects for each drug were similar to the average effect for the class compared with waitlist (SMD^N = −0.91, 95% CrI = −1.22 to −0.60) and SSRIs/SNRIs were significantly different from waitlist.

SSRIs

In a pairwise analysis of two trials (ALLGULANDER1999, BLOMHOFF2001; 210 participants on treatment), there was no evidence of an effect on symptoms of anxiety at follow-up compared with placebo (SMD = −0.08, 95% CI = −0.32 to 0.16) with moderate heterogeneity between trials (I^2 = 32%; Chi^2 = 2.95, p = 0.23).

One trial (BLOMHOFF2001) reported a medium effect on quality of life at post-treatment (193 participants on treatment) (SMD = −0.41, 95% CI = −0.82 to 0.00) and no evidence of an effect at follow-up (168 participants on treatment (SMD = −0.24, 95% CI = −0.71 to 0.24). In 11 trials (BALDWIN1999, CLARK2003, DAVIDSON2004a, DAVIDSON2004b, GSK2006, KOBAK2002, LADER2004, LEPOLA2004, LIEBOWITZ2003, PFIZER2007, VAN-VLIET1994; 1,736 participants on treatment), there was a small effect on depression at post-treatment (SMD = −0.20, 95% CI = −0.29 to −0.12) with no significant heterogeneity ($I^2 = 8\%$; Chi^2 = 15.17, p = 0.37). In 14 trials (ALLGULANDER1999, ASAKURA2007, BLOMHOFF2001, DAVIDSON2004a, FURMARK2005, KOBAK2002, LADER2004, LEPOLA2004, LIEBOWITZ2003, PFIZER2007, STEIN1998, STEIN1999, VAN-VLIET1994, WESTENBERG2004; 1,987 participants on treatment), there was a medium effect on anxiety-related disability at post-treatment (SMD = −0.57, 95% CI = −0.71 to −0.42) with considerable heterogeneity between trials ($I^2 = 71\%$; Chi^2 = 59.54, p < 0.00001) and between subgroups ($I^2 = 68.8\%$; Chi^2 = 16.04, p = 0.007). In two trials (ALLGULANDER1999, BLOMHOFF2001; 210 participants on treatment), there was a small effect on anxiety-related disability at follow-up (SMD = −0.24, 95% CI = −0.52 to −0.04) with no significant heterogeneity between trials ($I^2 = 49\%$; Chi^2 = 3.91, p = 0.14).

In 17 trials (ALLGULANDER1999, ALLGULANDER2004, ASAKURA2007, BALDWIN1999, CLARK2003, DAVIDSON2004a, FURMARK2005, GSK2006, KASPER2005, LADER2004, LEPOLA2004, LIEBOWITZ2005B, PFIZER2007, STEIN1998, STEIN1999, VAN-AMERINGEN2001, VAN-VLIET1994; 2,488 participants on treatment), there was a large effect on withdrawal because of side effects compared with placebo at post-treatment (RR = 2.35, 95% CI = 1.80 to 3.08) with no significant heterogeneity ($I^2 = 0\%$; Chi^2 = 18.28, p = 0.50). Differences between subgroups were not significant ($I^2 = 25.6\%$; Chi^2 = 5.38, p = 0.25). In 11 trials (ALLGULANDER2004, ASAKURA2007, BALDWIN1999, DAVIDSON2004a, GSK2006, LADER2004, LIEBOWITZ2005b, PFIZER2007, STEIN1999, VAN-VLIET1994, WESTENBERG2004; 1,978 participants on treatment), there was a small effect on the number of participants reporting any adverse event (RR = 1.18, 95% CI = 1.11 to 1.25) with substantial heterogeneity between individual trials ($I^2 = 56\%$; Chi^2 = 32.03, p = 0.004) but not between subgroups ($I^2 = 0\%$; Chi^2 = 0.04, p = 0.98).

Citalopram

Two trials (FURMARK2002, FURMARK2005) included a group receiving citalopram (18 participants on treatment) compared with placebo and were included in the NMA. Participants received 40 mg daily for 6 and 9 weeks. At post-treatment, there was a medium effect compared with waitlist (SMD^N = −0.83, 95% CrI = −1.27 to −0.39).

Escitalopram

Two trials (KASPER2005, LADER2004) included one or more groups receiving escitalopram (675 participants on treatment) compared with placebo. Participants received 5 to 20 mg daily for 12 and 24 weeks. At post-treatment, there was a large effect compared with waitlist ($SMD^N = -0.88$, 95% CrI $= -1.19$ to -0.56).

Fluoxetine

Three trials (CLARK2003, DAVIDSON2004b, KOBAK2002) included a group receiving fluoxetine (107 participants on treatment) compared with placebo, individual CT or group CBT. In one trial (CLARK2003), participants receiving fluoxetine and placebo were instructed to expose themselves to feared situations. Participants received a mean dose of between 44 and 60 mg daily for 12 and 24 weeks. At post-treatment, there was a large effect compared with waitlist ($SMD^N = -0.87$, 95% CrI $= -1.16$ to -0.57).

Fluvoxamine

Five trials (ASAKURA2007, DAVIDSON2004a, STEIN1999, VAN-VLIET1994, WESTENBERG2004) included participants receiving fluoxetine (500 participants on treatment) compared with placebo. Participants received 150 to 225 mg daily for 12 weeks. At post-treatment, there was a large effect compared with waitlist ($SMD^N = -0.94$, 95% CrI $= -1.25$ to -0.63).

Paroxetine

Eleven trials (ALLGULANDER1999, ALLGULANDER2004, BALDWIN1999, GSK2006, LADER2004, LEPOLA2004, LIEBOWITZ2002, LIEBOWITZ2005b, PFIZER2007, SEEDAT2004, STEIN1998) included one or more groups receiving paroxetine (1,449 participants on treatment) compared with placebo, escitalopram or venlafaxine. Participants received a mean dose of between 20 and 46 mg daily. Ten trials lasted between 10 and 12 weeks; one lasted 24 weeks. At post-treatment, there was a large effect compared with waitlist ($SMD^N = -0.99$, 95% CrI $= -1.26$ to -0.73).

One group in an included trial (LIEBOWITZ2002) was outside the recommended BNF prescription range and was excluded from the review (60 mg per day).

Sertraline

Three trials (BLOMHOFF2001, LIEBOWITZ2003, VAN-AMERINGEN2001) included one or more groups receiving sertraline (535 participants on treatment) compared with placebo. Participants received 120 to 159 mg daily for 12 to 24 weeks. Two groups of participants receiving sertraline and placebo were instructed to expose themselves to feared situations in BLOMHOFF2001. At post-treatment, there was a medium effect compared with waitlist (SMD^N = −0.91, 95% CrI = −1.22 to −0.61).

SNRIs
Venlafaxine
In five trials (ALLGULANDER2004, LIEBOWITZ2005a, LIEBOWITZ2005b, RICKELS2004, STEIN2005; 759 participants on treatment) comparing venlafaxine with placebo, a higher dose of venlafaxine or paroxetine, participants received 72 to 213 mg daily for 12 to 28 weeks. At post-treatment, there was a large effect compared with waitlist (SMD^N = −0.96, 95% CrI = −1.25 to −0.67).

In three trials (ALLGULANDER2004, LIEBOWITZ2005b, STEIN2005; 542 participants on treatment), there was a large effect of venlafaxine withdrawal due to side effects at post-treatment (RR = 2.51, 95% CI = 1.57 to 4.02) with no heterogeneity. In three trials (ALLGULANDER2004, LIEBOWITZ2005a, RICKELS2004; 411 participants on treatment), there was a small effect on the number of people reporting any adverse event (RR = 1.10, 95% CI = 1.04 to 1.15) with no heterogeneity. None of the trials reported measures of quality of life, depression or anxiety-related disability.

Duloxetine
One trial (SIMON2010) comparing duloxetine in fixed daily doses of 60 mg and 120 mg for 18 weeks (15 participants on treatment) following a 6-week open-label study of 60 mg of duloxetine could not be included in the NMA because there was neither a placebo group nor another intervention that was included in the network. There was a large effect on symptoms of social anxiety at post-treatment favouring the higher dose (SMD = −1.22, 95% CI = 0.39 to 2.05).

6.6.5   Other pharmacological interventions

Mirtazapine (noradrenaline and selective serotonin antagonist)
Two trials compared mirtazapine with placebo. One was excluded from the NMA because the reported data included improbable figures that the journal and the authors were unable to verify (MUEHLBACHER2005 [Muehlbacher et al., 2005]) despite contacting the study authors directly. In one included trial (SCHUTTERS2010) comparing mirtazapine with placebo, participants (30 participants on treatment) received 40 mg daily for 12 weeks (SCHUTTERS2010). At post-treatment, there was a medium effect compared with waitlist (SMD^N = −0.80, 95% CrI = −1.45 to −0.16).

Antipsychotics

The GDG decided *a priori* not to include trials of antipsychotics in the NMA because they are not used in the primary treatment of social anxiety disorder and the GDG was also concerned that participants in these trials would likely differ from the participants in other trials.

One trial (VAISHNAVI2007) compared quetiapine (ten participants on treatment) with placebo. Participants received 147 mg daily for 8 weeks. There was no evidence of an effect on symptoms of social anxiety disorder at post-treatment (SMD = −0.28; 95% CI = −1.36 to 0.81). In addition to the negative result from this trial, searches identified several completed but unpublished trials of quetiapine for social anxiety disorder.

One trial (BARNETT2002) compared olanzapine (four participants on treatment) with placebo. Participants received a mean daily dose of 9 mg for 8 weeks. There was a large effect on symptoms of social anxiety at post-treatment (SMD = −2.28, 95% CI = −4.00 to −0.55). No controlled follow-up data were reported.

Several completed trials have never been reported and are not included here.

Paroxetine combined with clonazepam

In one trial (SEEDAT2004) comparing combination treatment of paroxetine and clonazepam (14 participants on treatment) with paroxetine alone, participants received combined treatment for 10 weeks. At post-treatment, there was a large effect compared with waitlist (SMD^N = −1.35, 95% CrI = −1.93 to −0.78).

6.6.6 Continued pharmacotherapy for relapse prevention

Selective serotonin reuptake inhibitors

In four trials (KUMAR1999, MONTGOMERY2005, STEIN2002b, VAN-AMERINGEN2001), participants who met criteria for response to a SSRI (paroxetine, escitalopram, or sertraline) were randomly assigned to receive continued treatment (365 participants on treatment) or placebo (see Appendix 18 for the study characteristics). Continued pharmacotherapy was associated with lower relapse (RR = 0.47, 95% CI = 0.27 to 0.82), with approximately 23% of participants on treatment and 54% of participants receiving placebo (unweighted means) relapsing by 16 to 24 weeks after the start of the relapse prevention study (see Table 13 and Appendix 26 for the forest plots and Appendix 15 for the GRADE profiles).

Anticonvulsants

One trial (GREIST2011) randomised participants meeting criteria for response in a 10-week open-label study of pregabalin to receive pregabalin (80 participants on treatment) or placebo (see Appendix 18 for the study characteristics). After 26 weeks of double-blind treatment, the effect was not statistically significant for relapse (RR = 0.79, 95% CI = 0.58 to 1.06) and the majority of people for whom outcomes were known had relapsed in both groups (63% having treatment; 71% taking placebo) (see Table 13 and Appendix 26 for the forest plots and Appendix 15 for the GRADE profiles).

6.6.7 Additional considerations concerning the use of medication for social anxiety disorder

The GDG was aware of the limited evidence available in the trials of the tolerability, side effects and other potential harms (for example, interactions with other prescribed medication) associated with the use of the drugs reviewed. The GDG therefore considered whether additional sources of information could be identified that could inform the development of recommendations for the use of medication in the treatment of people with social anxiety disorder.

The GDG decided, based on an application of the rules for extrapolation and adaptation/incorporation (see Chapter 3), that the guidance developed for the use of the drugs in other anxiety disorders and depression (*Generalised Anxiety Disorder and Panic Disorder (With or Without Agoraphobia) in Adults* [NICE, 2011c] and *Depression* [NICE, 2009a]) could be relevant to social anxiety disorder. Specifically, the GDG considered that there were sufficient commonalities to justify the extrapolation, namely: (a) underlying aetiologies and aspects of presentation in depression and other anxiety disorders and in social anxiety disorder; (b) a high comorbidity between the disorders; and (c) similar modes of action for both the therapeutic and non-therapeutic aspects of drug use. The previous guidelines were considered sufficiently recent for the purpose of this current guideline. Although the previous guidelines considered effects on symptoms of relevant mental disorders, for the purpose of this guideline, the GDG considered only evidence of side effects, which should not differ in people with social anxiety disorder, generalised anxiety disorder or depression (for example, effects on physical health). In addition the GDG also considered those aspects of the presentation of depression and other anxiety disorders and social anxiety disorder that can differ (for example, the impact on social interaction) in reviewing the evidence in *Depression*. Finally, the GDG reviewed the recommendations concerning the safety and tolerability of relevant drugs in *Generalised Anxiety Disorder and Panic Disorder*. A topic group undertook the initial reviews described in this section and presented a summary to the GDG. The GDG used this summary and their own knowledge and expertise to develop the recommendations using an informal consensus method.

Reviews of existing NICE guidelines
The key elements of the reviews of side effects and other harms of medication in *Generalised Anxiety Disorder and Panic Disorder* (NICE, 2011c) and *Depression* (NICE, 2009a) that were identified by the GDG as being relevant to this current guideline are summarised below.

Cardiovascular
Anxiety disorders, including social anxiety disorder, are associated with an increased mortality risk (Mykletun et al., 2009). TCAs are associated with higher risk of developing cardiovascular adverse events and have found to be cardiotoxic in overdose (Taylor, 2008). In contrast to the concerns about the TCAs relatively little concern has

been raised about the potential cardiotoxicity of the SSRIs, although a recent warning about the QTc prolongation and the use of citalopram was raised by the Medicines and Healthcare products Regulatory Agency (MHRA, 2011). Indeed, SSRIs do not appear to be associated with an increase risk in cardiovascular adverse events (for example, Swenson and colleagues [2006], and Taylor [2008]) and are associated with a relatively low fatal toxicity index (number of poisoning deaths per 1,000,000 prescriptions).

Other non-SSRI drugs considered by the GDG in the evidence review, including mirtazapine and moclobemide, were also not identified by *Depression* (NICE, 2009a) as conferring particular risk in overdose. In contrast, phenelzine can cause postural hypotension particularly in the early weeks of treatment and may also be associated with significant bradycardia. However, its fatal toxicity index in overdose appears to be less than most TCAs. Concern has been raised about venlafaxine with some evidence of increased blood pressure in higher doses and concern about a higher fatal toxicity index in overdose than SSRIs (Buckley & McManus, 2002; Taylor, 2008). Duloxetine has been associated with small increases in diastolic blood pressure, tachycardia and cholesterol compared with placebo (Dugan & Fuller, 2004; Wernicke et al., 2007).

Bleeding

Observational studies using data from national prescribing databases have found a relatively strong association (approximately three-fold increase in risk of bleeding) between SSRIs and increased risk of gastrointestinal bleeding (Weinrieb et al., 2003; Yuan et al., 2006). However, it should be noted that the outcome was a rare event, with approximately four to five events per 1000 person years. This effect was stronger (approximately 15-fold increase of bleeding) in people concurrently using non-steroidal anti-inflammatory drugs and SSRIs and the risk may be increased in older people.

Gastrointestinal symptoms

There is evidence both in depression and anxiety disorders of an increased risk of gastrointestinal symptoms such as nausea, vomiting and diarrhoea associated with SSRI use (Beasley et al., 2000; Brambilla et al., 2005). TCAs may be associated with higher risk of constipation when compared with fluoxetine (Beasley et al., 2000). This was supported by the review undertaken by in *Generalised Anxiety Disorder and Panic Disorder* (NICE, 2011c).

Sexual dysfunction

There was consistent evidence of sexual adverse effects in association with SSRIs, duloxetine and venlafaxine in people with depression (Beasley et al., 2000; Gregorian et al., 2002; Keller, 2000; Werneke et al., 2006).

Weight

Fluoxetine appears to be associated with greater weight loss compared with placebo (Beasley et al., 2000), TCAs and other SSRIs (Brambilla et al., 2005). However, it was noted in *Generalised Anxiety Disorder and Panic Disorder* (NICE, 2011c) that there is a possibility that paroxetine and fluoxetine may actually be associated with weight gain, but this needs further research to establish this finding. There is some evidence that duloxetine was associated with weight loss with a mean reduction of 2.2 kg compared with 1 kg for placebo (Dugan & Fuller, 2004). Pregabalin is associated with weight increase (Cabrera et al., 2012).

Cognitive/neurological

Pregabalin was reported in *Generalised Anxiety Disorder and Panic Disorder* to be reasonably well tolerated but could for some people give rise to headaches, dizziness and somnolence. In contrast, benzodiazepines were associated with a number of cognitive side effects including impairment in speech and memory along with sedation, fatigue and ataxia. However, the most commonly reported problem with benzodiazepine use was risk of dependence. This suggests only short-term use of this treatment is appropriate and that particular caution should be exercised for people with comorbid alcohol or drug misuse.

Discontinuation

A specific issue that the GDG considered important, and which supported extrapolation from the evidence reviews in *Depression*, included a focus on 'discontinuation' rather than 'withdrawal' symptoms because the GDG for the current guideline accepted the view set out in *Depression* that drugs commonly used in the treatment of depression (for example, the SSRIs) are not addictive. However, the GDG did accept the view (as with depression) that some discontinuation symptoms may be hard to distinguish from the underlying symptoms of social anxiety disorder. Following *Depression*, the GDG divided discontinuation symptoms into six groups, which by definition are not attributable to other causes: (1) affective (for example, irritability); (2) gastrointestinal (for example, nausea); (3) neuromotor (for example, ataxia); (4) vasomotor (for example, sweating); (5) neurosensory (for example, paraesthesia); and (6) other neurological (for example, dreaming) (Delgado, 2006). They are experienced by at least a third of patients taking SSRIs (Lejoyeux et al., 1996; MHRA, 2004) and are seen to some extent with all antidepressants (Taylor et al., 2006). Of the commonly used antidepressants, the risk of discontinuation symptoms seems to be greatest with paroxetine, venlafaxine and amitriptyline (Taylor et al., 2006). *Depression* considered a number of prospective studies examining the effect of discontinuation in people taking a range of antidepressants. These studies suggest an increase in discontinuation symptoms in those taking paroxetine compared with escitalopram (Baldwin et al., 2006), fluoxetine (Bogetto et al., 2002; Hindmarch et al., 2000; Judge et al., 2002; Michelson et al., 2000; Rosenbaum et al., 1998), sertraline (Hindmarch et al., 2000; Michelson et al., 2000), citalopram (Hindmarch et al., 2000) and venlafaxine when compared with escitalopram (Montgomery et al., 2004) or sertraline (Sir et al., 2005).

The onset of discontinuation symptoms is usually within 5 days of stopping treatment, or occasionally during taper or after missed doses (Michelson et al., 2000; Rosenbaum et al., 1998). This is influenced by a number of factors, which may include a drug's half-life. Symptoms can vary in form and intensity and occur in any combination. They are usually mild and self-limiting, but can be severe and prolonged, particularly if withdrawal is abrupt. Some symptoms are more likely with individual drugs, for example, dizziness and electric shock-like sensations with SSRIs, and sweating and headache with TCAs (Haddad, 2001; Lejoyeux et al., 1996). Although anyone can experience discontinuation symptoms, the risk is increased in those prescribed short half-life drugs (Rosenbaum et al., 1998), such as paroxetine and venlafaxine (Fava et al., 1997; Hindmarch et al., 2000; MHRA, 2004). They can also occur in people who do not take their medication regularly. Two-thirds of people prescribed SSRIs and other related drugs skip a few doses from time to time (Meijer et al., 2001). The risk is also increased in the following people: those who have been taking the drugs for 8 weeks or longer (Haddad, 2001); those who developed anxiety symptoms at the start of antidepressant treatment (particularly with SSRIs); those receiving other centrally acting medications (for example, antihypertensives, antihistamines, antipsychotics); children and young people; and those who have experienced discontinuation symptoms before (Haddad, 2001; Lejoyeux & Ades, 1997).

Although it is generally advised that antidepressants (except fluoxetine) should be discontinued over a period of at least 4 weeks, preliminary data suggest that it may be the half-life of the antidepressant rather than the rate of taper that ultimately influences the risk of discontinuation symptoms (Tint et al., 2008). When switching from one antidepressant to another with a similar pharmacological profile, the risk of discontinuation symptoms may be reduced by completing the switch as quickly as possible (within a few days at most). A different approach may be required at the end of treatment where a slower taper is likely to be beneficial. People taking MAOIs may need the dosage to be tapered over a longer period (Haddad, 2001). Tranylcypromine may be particularly difficult to stop. It is not clear if the need for slow discontinuation of MAOIs, and particularly tranylcypromine, is due to the discontinuation syndrome or the loss of other neurochemical effects of these drugs.

Many people experience discontinuation symptoms despite a slow taper. For these, the option of abrupt withdrawal should be discussed. Some may prefer a short period of intense symptoms rather than a prolonged period of milder symptoms. There are no systematic randomised studies in this area, therefore treatment is pragmatic. Mild symptoms are not uncommon after discontinuing an antidepressant and they will pass in a few days. For severe symptoms the original antidepressant (or another with a longer half-life from the same class) can be reintroduced and tapered gradually while monitoring for symptoms (Haddad, 2001; Lejoyeux & Ades, 1997).

Suicidal ideation and suicidal behaviour

The *Depression* guideline was particularly concerned with suicide because depression is the largest cause of suicide, with two-thirds of people who attempt suicide experiencing depression, and suicide is the main cause of the increased mortality of depression. Suicidal ideation may also be present in anxiety disorders, particularly if comorbid with depression (Nepon et al., 2010). In a systematic review, Stone and colleagues (2009) identified the association between antidepressant use and suicidal ideation and/or suicidal behaviour. For those under 25 years, there were increased odds of suicidal behaviour (odds ratio 2.30; 95% CI = 1.04, 5.09) associated with antidepressants compared with placebo. There was a borderline statistically significant increase in the odds of suicidal ideation and suicidal behaviour (odds ratio 1.62; 95% CI = 0.97, 2.71). Two meta-analyses of RCTs (Fergusson et al., 2005; Gunnell et al., 2005) (k = 702 and k = 477, respectively) and a large nested case-control study comparing new prescriptions of SSRIs and TCAs (Martinez et al., 2005) found no evidence of an increase in completed suicide with SSRIs but possible evidence of increased suicidal/self-harming behaviour with SSRIs compared with placebo (the number needed to harm was 684 and 754 in the two meta-analyses). There was no overall difference between SSRIs and TCAs, but there was some evidence for increased self-harming behaviour with SSRIs compared with TCAs in people under 19 years (Fergusson et al., 2005; Martinez et al., 2005). In a similar vein, a review by Möller and colleagues (2008) concluded that all antidepressants carry a small risk of inducing suicidal thoughts and suicide attempts in those aged below 25 years with the risk reducing at about 30 to 40 years of age.

There may be a delay in noticeable improvement after starting antidepressants, and, just after initiation of treatment, mood remains low with prominent feelings of guilt and hopelessness, but energy and motivation can increase and it has been hypothesised that this may be related to increased suicidal thoughts. A similar situation can arise with people who develop akathisia or increased anxiety due to a direct effect of some SSRIs and related drugs, which may increase the propensity to suicidal ideation and suicidal behaviour (Healey, 2003). Careful monitoring was therefore recommended by the *Depression* guideline when treatment is initiated with an antidepressant. The guideline also recommended that people taking antidepressants should be monitored regardless of the apparent severity of their depression.

A meta-analysis of observational studies (Barbui et al., 2009) found that compared with people with depression who did not take antidepressants, young people taking SSRIs had a significantly higher risk of suicide attempts and completed suicide. In contrast, adults (especially older adults) had a significantly lower risk of suicide attempts and completed suicide.

Risk in overdose

Antidepressants can be toxic in overdose and given elevated levels of suicidality with some anxiety disorders the use of antidepressants is of concern. Antidepressants were involved in 18% of deaths from drug poisoning between 1993 and 2002 (Morgan et al., 2004), with TCAs, which are cardiotoxic in overdose, accounting for 89% of these. This is equivalent to 30.1 deaths per 1,000,000 prescriptions. Dothiepin/dosulepin alone accounted for 48.5 deaths per 1,000,000 prescriptions (Morgan et al., 2004). By contrast, over the same period SSRIs accounted for around 6% of deaths by suicide, and other antidepressants, including venlafaxine, accounted for around 3%. This is equivalent to 1 and 5.2 deaths per 1,000,000 prescriptions, respectively (Morgan et al., 2004). Venlafaxine accounted for 8.5 deaths per 1,000,000 prescriptions. Morgan and colleagues (2004) showed an overall reduction in mortality rates over the time period studied, with a fall in rates related to TCAs, little change for SSRIs, but an increase for other antidepressants largely due to venlafaxine. It should be noted that the MHRA (2006) concluded that the increased rate seen with venlafaxine was partly, but not wholly, attributable to individual characteristics.

Adapting existing NICE guideline recommendations
The GDG considered the evidence concerning side effects and related issues in *Generalised Anxiety Disorder and Panic Disorder (With or Without Agoraphobia) in Adults* (NCCMH, 2011b; NICE, 2011c). After careful consideration they identified two areas of particular importance, but the related recommendations required some adaptation for use in the current guideline (see Chapter 3 for an explanation of the method). These recommendations are set out in Table 14. The rationale for why recommendations were adapted is explained in the right-hand column of the table. In column one the numbers refer to the recommendations in *Generalised Anxiety Disorder and Panic Disorder*. In column two the numbers in brackets following the recommendation refer to Section 6.13 in this guideline.

Clinical summary
Previous NICE guidelines support the view of the GDG that the side-effect profile of the various pharmacological interventions that could potentially be used in social anxiety disorder are common to many disorders. In particular, nausea, insomnia and sexual dysfunction associated with the SSRIs and SNRIs fitted with their experience of the use of such treatments in social anxiety disorder. The GDG saw no reason not to take into account the wide range of side effects concerning the cardiovascular system and the problems with sedation, tolerance, withdrawal and potential dependence associated with the use of benzodiazepines. Similarly, the GDG noted suicidality and discontinuation symptoms as problems associated with antidepressant drug use in general, and the risk of gastrointestinal bleeding associated with the use of SSRIs.

6.7   PSYCHOLOGICAL INTERVENTIONS

6.7.1   Cognitive behavioural interventions – individual

Fifteen trials (CLARK2003, CLARK2006, CLARK2012, COTTRAUX2000, EMMELKAMP2006, GOLDIN2012, HERBERT2004, MORTBERG2007,

Table 14: Recommendations from *Generalised Anxiety Disorder and Panic Disorder (With or Without Agoraphobia) in Adults* for inclusion

Original recommendation from *Generalised Anxiety Disorder and Panic Disorder (With or Without Agoraphobia) in Adults* (NICE, 2011c)	Review question and evidence base of existing recommendation	Recommendation following adaptation for this guideline	Reasons for adaptation
1.2.29 For people aged under 30 who are offered an SSRI or SNRI: • warn them that these drugs are associated with an increased risk of suicidal thinking and self-harm in a minority of people under 30 **and** • see them within 1 week of first prescribing **or** • monitor the risk of suicidal thinking and self-harm weekly for the first month.	Review question: in the treatment of GAD, which drugs improve outcomes compared with other drugs and with placebo? Evidence base: one systematic review published in 2009 and the *Depression* (NCCMH, 2010) guideline.	For people aged under 30 years who are offered an SSRI or SNRI: • warn them that these drugs are associated with an increased risk of suicidal thinking and self-harm in a minority of people under 30 **and** • see them within 1 week of first prescribing **and** • monitor the risk of suicidal thinking and self-harm weekly for the first month. [6.13.5.3]	Based on the reviews undertaken in Section 6.6.4 and 6.6.7, the GDG considered this recommendation relevant to adults with social anxiety disorder with no adaptation required.
1.2.30 For people who develop side effects soon after starting drug treatment, provide information and consider one of the following strategies: • monitoring the person's symptoms closely (if the side effects are mild and acceptable to the person) **or** • reducing the dose of the drug **or** • stopping the drug and, according to the person's preference, offering either – an alternative drug **or** – a high-intensity psychological intervention.	Review question: in the treatment of GAD, which drugs improve outcomes compared with other drugs and with placebo? Evidence base: 20 systematic reviews published between 1999 and 2009, and the *Depression* (NCCMH, 2010) guideline.	For people who develop side effects soon after starting a pharmacological intervention, provide information and consider one of the following strategies: • monitoring the person's symptoms closely (if the side effects are mild and acceptable to the person) • reducing the dose of the drug • stopping the drug and offering either an alternative drug or individual CBT, according to the person's preference. [6.13.5.7]	Based on the reviews undertaken in Section 6.6.7, the GDG considered this recommendation relevant to adults with social anxiety disorder. It was adapted to refer to the treatment choices specified in the current guideline.

139

LEICHSENRING2012, LEDLEY2009, OOSTERBAAN2001, PRASKO2003, ROBILLARD2010, STANGIER2003, STANGIER2011) evaluated individual CBT/CT and were included in the NMA (562 participants on treatment). At post-treatment, there was a large effect for the class compared with waitlist (SMD^N = −1.19, 95% CrI = −1.57 to −0.81); this was the only group of interventions (psychological or pharmacological) that differed significantly from both waitlist and pill placebo. The content, number of sessions and duration of treatment varied across trials; interventions were grouped into categories based on these features.

Compared with waitlist, one trial (STANGIER2003; 18 participants on treatment) reported a non-significant effect on symptoms of social anxiety at follow-up (SMD = −0.60, 95% CI = −1.26 to 0.05). One trial (LEDLEY2009; 15 participants on treatment) reported a non-significant effect on quality of life (SMD = −0.40, 95% CI = −1.08 to 0.29). In six trials (CLARK2006, CLARK2012, LEICHSENRING2012, ROBILLARD2010, STANGIER2003, STANGIER2011; 307 participants on treatment), there was a large effect on symptoms of depression at post-treatment (SMD = −0.86, 95% CI = −1.17 to −0.54) with substantial heterogeneity between trials (I^2 = 52%, Chi^2 = 14.61, p = 0.04) and between subgroups (I^2 = 82%, Chi^2 = 10.94, p = 0.004). In one trial (STANGIER2003; 18 participants on treatment), the effect was not statistically significant for depression at follow-up (SMD = −0.51, 95% CI = −1.15 to 0.14). In three trials (CLARK2012, LEDLEY2009, STANGIER2003; 92 participants on treatment), there was a large effect on anxiety-related disability at post-treatment (SMD = −1.23, 95% CI = −2.08 to −0.37) with considerable heterogeneity (I^2 = 83%, Chi^2 = 17.21, p = 0.0006). In one trial (STANGIER2003; 18 participants on treatment), there was no evidence of an effect on disability at follow-up (SMD = −0.35, 95% CI = −0.99 to 0.29).

Specific forms of individual CBT/CT

Two trials (GOLDIN2012, LEDLEY2009) included CBT (53 participants on treatment) delivered following the Heimberg manual (Hope et al., 2006) compared with waitlist. Participants received approximately 16 hours of therapy over 16 to 20 weeks. At post-treatment, there was a large effect compared with waitlist (SMD^N = −1.02, 95% CrI = −1.42 to −0.62).

Three trials (CLARK2003, CLARK2006, CLARK2012) included CT (97 participants on treatment) delivered following the Clark and Wells (1995) manual compared with waitlist, pill placebo, fluoxetine and exposure. Participants received approximately 21 hours of therapy over 14 weeks. At post-treatment, there was a large effect compared with waitlist (SMD^N = −1.56, 95% CrI = −1.85 to −1.27).

Six trials included one or more groups receiving a form of individual CBT that did not appear to follow one of the manuals above (COTTRAUX2000, EMMELKAMP2006, HERBERT2004, OOSTERBAAN2001, ROBILLARD2010, PRASKO2003; 164 participants on treatment) compared with waitlist, moclobemide, psychodynamic psychotherapy, supportive therapy, and another form of individual CBT. Participants received approximately 10 to 30 hours of therapy over 12 to 26 weeks. At post-treatment, there was a large effect compared with waitlist (SMD^N = −1.19, 95% CrI = −1.48 to −0.89).

Four trials (LEICHSENRING2012, MORTBERG2007, STANGIER2003, STANGIER2011) included CT (shortened sessions) with reduced therapist time for behavioural experiments (249 participants on treatment) compared with waitlist, group CBT, IPT and psychodynamic psychotherapy. Participants received approximately 15 hours of therapy over 15 to 26 weeks. At post-treatment, there was a large effect compared with waitlist ($SMD^N = -0.97$, 95% CrI = -1.21 to -0.73).

One trial (RENNER2008) reported that participants received individual CBT (14 participants on treatment) or applied relaxation (14 participants on treatment), but the intervention was not sufficiently described to determine whether it was similar to other interventions in the analysis, so a separate pairwise analysis was conducted. Comparing two sessions of a poorly described CBT intervention with two sessions of applied relaxation, there was a large effect favouring applied relaxation at post-treatment (SMD = 1.13, 95% CI = 0.32 to 1.94).

6.7.2   Cognitive behavioural interventions – group

Twenty seven trials (ALDEN2011, ANDREWS2011, BLANCO2010, BJORNSSON-2011, BORGEAT2009, DAVIDSON2004b, FURMARK2002, GELERNTER1991, GRUBER2001, HEDMAN2011, HEIMBERG1990, HEIMBERG1998, HERBERT2005, HOPE1995, KOSZYCKI2007, MATTICK1988, MATTICK1989, MCEVOY2009, MORGAN1999, MORTBERG2007, OTTO2000, PIET2010, RAPEE2007, RAPEE2009, SALABERRIA1998, STANGIER2003, WONG2006) evaluated group CBT and were included in the NMA (984 participants on treatment). At post-treatment, there was a large effect for the class compared with waitlist ($SMD^N = -0.92$, 95% CrI = -1.34 to -0.51). In two trials (SALABERRIA1998, STANGIER2003; 39 participants on treatment), the effect was not statistically significant for symptoms of social anxiety at follow-up (SMD = -0.76, 95% CI = -1.98 to 0.47) compared with waitlist, with substantial heterogeneity between trials ($I^2 = 85\%$; Chi^2 = 6.80, p = 0.009). In one trial (HEIMBERG1990; 15 participants on treatment), there was no evidence of an effect on symptoms of social anxiety disorder at follow-up (SMD = -0.37, 95% CI = -1.14 to 0.39) compared with psychological placebo.

In two trials (GRUBER2001, STANGIER2003; 51 participants on treatment), the effect was not statistically significant for depression compared with waitlist at post-treatment (SMD = -0.58, 95% CI = -1.24 to 0.08) with substantial heterogeneity ($I^2 = 63\%$, Chi^2 = 5.43, p = 0.07). In two trials (SALABERRIA1998, STANGIER2003; 39 participants on treatment) there was a medium effect (SMD = -0.59, 95% CI = -1.04 to -0.14) at follow-up, with no heterogeneity ($I^2 = 0\%$, Chi^2 = 0.78, p = 0.38). In two trials (HEIMBERG1990, HEIMBERG1998; 48 participants on treatment), there was no evidence of an effect on depression compared with psychological placebo at post-treatment (SMD = 0.15, 95% CI = -0.81 to 1.11), with considerable heterogeneity ($I^2 = 81\%$, Chi^2 = 5.31, p = 0.02). In one trial (HEIMBERG1990; 27 participants on treatment), there was no evidence of an effect at follow-up (SMD = -0.23, 95% CI = -0.85 to 0.39), with no significant heterogeneity ($I^2 = 20\%$, Chi^2 = 1.25, p = 0.26). One trial (STANGIER2003) comparing group CBT (22 participants on treatment) with waitlist reported no evidence of an effect on anxiety-related disability at post-treatment (SMD = −0.15, 95% CI = −0.75 to 0.45) or at follow-up (SMD = −0.44, 95% CI = −1.06 to 0.18). A trial with two CBT groups (RAPEE2009; 127 participants on treatment) reported a small effect compared with psychological placebo at post-treatment (SMD = −0.35, 95% CI = −0.67 to −0.03) with no heterogeneity between the groups (I^2 = 0%, Chi^2 = 0.53, p = 0.47). None of the trials reported quality of life outcomes.

In addition to the trials of acute treatment, one trial (HEIMBERG2012) randomised participants to paroxetine alone or CBT plus paroxetine after an open-label phase of the drug for 12 weeks. During the randomised phase, participants in the combination therapy group (32 participants on treatment) received 16 weeks of group CBT alongside paroxetine (unknown dosage). Because of the open-label phase, the GDG chose not to include the trial in the NMA. At post-treatment, there was a small effect in favour of combination therapy on symptoms of social anxiety, which was nearly significant (SMD = −0.49, 95% CI = −1.00 to 0.02).

Specific forms of group CBT
Eleven trials (BLANCO2010, GELERNTER1991, GRUBER2001, HEDMAN2011, HEIMBERG1990, HEIMBERG1998, HERBERT2005, HOPE1995, KOSZYCKI2007, OTTO2000, WONG2006) included group CBT (338 participants on treatment) delivered following Heimberg and colleagues' manual (Heimberg et al., 1995) compared with waitlist, pill placebo, psychological placebo, alprazolam, clonazepam, exposure, group CBT with phenelzine, mindfulness training and phenelzine. Participants received between 20 and 30 hours of therapy in groups of about seven people over 12 weeks. At post-treatment, there was a large effect compared with waitlist (SMD^N = −0.80, 95% CrI = −1.02 to −0.58).

Sixteen trials (ALDEN2011, ANDREWS2011, BJORNSSON2011, BORGEAT2009, DAVIDSON2004b, FURMARK2002, MATTICK1988, MATTICK1989, MCEVOY2009, MORGAN1999, MORTBERG2007, PIET2010, RAPEE2007, RAPEE2009, SALABERRIA1998, STANGIER2003) included one or more groups receiving a form of group CBT that did not appear to follow Heimberg and colleagues' manual (583 participants on treatment) compared with waitlist, pill placebo, psychological placebo, citalopram, exposure, fluoxetine, group CBT with fluoxetine, individual CT, mindfulness training, self-help, treatment as usual, and another form of group CBT. Participants received approximately 6 to 14 hours of therapy over 7 to 15 weeks. At post-treatment, there was a large effect compared with waitlist (SMD^N = −0.85, 95% CrI = −1.04 to −0.67).

One trial (RAPEE2009) also used an enhanced form of group CBT with enhanced exposure (63 participants on treatment) and there was a large effect compared with waitlist (SMD^N = −1.10, 95% CrI = −1.49 to −0.71).

6.7.3   Cognitive bias modification

Seven trials (AMIR2009, AMIR2012, BEARD2011, BOETTCHER2011, CARLBRING2012, HEEREN2012, SCHMIDT2009) compared computerised cognitive bias modification (156 participants on treatment) with a sham intervention. Studies lasted 4 days to 6 weeks, with total time using the programs ranging from 4 to 21 hours. No trials included an intervention connected to the NMA, so pairwise comparisons were performed for all relevant outcomes.

In three trials (AMIR2012, BOETTCHER2011, SCHMIDT2009; 75 participants on treatment), there was no evidence of an effect on recovery at post-treatment (RR = 0.59, 95% CI = 0.25 to 1.42), with considerable heterogeneity (I^2 = 92%, Chi^2 = 23.71, p = 0.00001). One trial (SCHMIDT2009; 19 participants on treatment) reported a moderate effect at follow-up (RR = 0.62, 95% CI = 0.39 to 0.99).

Combining all seven trials (AMIR2009, AMIR2012, BEARD2011, BOETTCHER2011, CARLBRING2012, HEEREN2012, SCHMIDT2009; 156 participants on treatment), there was moderate-quality evidence of a modest effect on continuous measures of social anxiety at post-treatment (SMD = −0.30, 95% CI = −0.55 to −0.05; I^2 = 27%, Chi^2 = 8.26, p = 0.22). At follow-up, there was low-quality evidence and the effect was not statistically significant (SMD = −0.58, 95% CI = −1.20 to 0.04), with considerable heterogeneity (I^2 = 79%, Chi^2 = 14.13, p = 0.003).

One trial (CARLBRING2012; 40 participants on treatment) reported no evidence of an effect on quality of life at post-treatment (SMD = −0.20; 95% CI = −0.64 to 0.24) or at follow-up (SMD = −0.16, 95% CI = −0.60 to 0.28). In four trials (AMIR2009, AMIR2012, BOETTCHER2011, SCHMIDT2009), there was no evidence of an effect on depression at post-treatment (SMD = 0.04, 95% CI = −0.43 to 0.51), with substantial heterogeneity (I^2 = 64%, Chi^2 = 8.44, p = 0.04). In two trials (BOETTCHER2011, SCHMIDT2009; 53 participants on treatment), there was no evidence of an effect on depression at follow-up (SMD = −0.03, 95% CI = −0.64 to 0.59), with no significant heterogeneity (I^2 = 47%, Chi^2 = 1.88, p = 0.17). In two trials (AMIR2009, AMIR2012; 45 participants on treatment), there was a medium effect on anxiety-related disability at post-treatment (SMD = −0.61, 95% CI = −1.03 to −0.19) with no heterogeneity.

6.7.4 Exercise

One trial (JAZAIERI2012) compared an exercise intervention (18 participants on treatment) with mindfulness-based stress reduction. Participants were required to complete at least two individual moderate intensity exercise sessions and one group session per week for 8 weeks. At post-treatment, there was no evidence of an effect compared with waitlist (SMD^N = −0.34, 95% CrI = −1.06 to 0.38).

6.7.5 Exposure *in vivo* and social skills training

Eight trials (ANDERSSON2006, BORGEAT2009, CLARK2006, HOPE1995, MATTICK1988, SALABERRIA1998, SMITS2006, STRAVYNSKI2000) reported a controlled effect for exposure or social skills training. At post-treatment, there was a large effect for the intervention class compared with waitlist (SMD^N = −0.86, 95% CrI = −1.42 to −0.30).

All eight trials included one or more groups receiving exposure (199 participants on treatment) compared with waitlist, psychological placebo, group CBT, individual CT, social skills training and other forms of exposure. Participants received approximately 4 to 21 hours of therapy in groups over 1 to 14 weeks. At post-treatment, there was a large effect compared with waitlist (SMD^N = −0.83, 95% CrI = −1.07 to −0.59).

Three trials included social skills training, but two did not report usable outcomes: SHAW1979 (Shaw, 1979), ALDEN1989 (Alden, 1989). One trial (STRAVYNSKI2000) compared social skills training (32 participants on treatment) with exposure. Participants received 24 hours of therapy over 12 weeks. At post-treatment, there was a large effect compared with waitlist (SMD^N = −0.88, 95% CrI = −1.38 to −0.38).

In a pairwise analysis compared with waitlist, one trial (ANDERSSON2006) reported a medium effect of exposure (30 participants on treatment) on quality of life at post-treatment (SMD = −0.73, 95% CI = −1.25 to −0.22). In two trials (ANDERSSON2006, CLARK2006; 51 participants on treatment) compared with waitlist, there was a large effect of exposure on depression at post-treatment (SMD = −0.50, 95% CI = −0.89 to −0.10) with no heterogeneity (I^2 = 0%, Chi^2 = 0.97, p = 0.32). One trial (SALABERRIA1998) reported a large effect of exposure (18 participants on treatment) on depression at follow-up (SMD = −1.17, 95% CI = −1.87 to −0.48). None of the trials reported anxiety-related disability outcomes at any timepoint.

6.7.6   Exposure with cognitive enhancers

In four trials (GUASTELLA2008, GUASTELLA2009, HOFMANN2006, HOFMANN2012), participants received some exposure therapy and either a cognitive enhancer or pill placebo. The trials were considered to be different from those in the NMA because the exposure was a diminished form of what was provided in the other trials in the network. Pairwise comparisons were therefore performed.

Three trials (GUASTELLA2008, HOFMANN2006, HOFMANN2012) assigned participants to exposure with the cognitive enhancer D-cycloserine (127 participants on treatment) or exposure alone. There was a small effect on symptoms of social anxiety at post-treatment (SMD = −0.36, 95% CI = −0.61 to −0.11) with no heterogeneity (I^2 = 0%, Chi^2 = 0.47, p = 0.79). There was a small but not significant effect at follow-up (SMD = −0.20, 95% CI = −0.45 to 0.05) with no significant heterogeneity (I^2 = 1%, Chi^2 = 2.02, p = 0.36).

In one trial of oxytocin (GUASTELLA2009; 12 participants on treatment), there was no evidence of an effect on symptoms of social anxiety disorder at post-treatment (SMD = 0.26, 95% CI = −0.53 to 1.35) or at 1 month's follow-up (SMD = 0.15, 95% CI = −0.64 to 0.93).

6.7.7   Interpersonal psychotherapy

Two trials (LIPSITZ2008, STANGIER2011) of IPT (64 participants on treatment) compared with waitlist, individual CT and supportive therapy were included in the

NMA. Participants received approximately 14 hours of therapy over 14 to 20 weeks. At post-treatment, there was evidence of a significant medium effect compared with waitlist ($SMD^N = -0.43$, 95% CrI = -0.83 to -0.03).

6.7.8 Mindfulness training

Three trials (JAZAIERI2012, KOSZYCKI2007, PIET2010) included mindfulness training (64 participants on treatment) compared with exercise and group CBT. Participants received about 20 hours of therapy delivered in groups of approximately 12 people over 8 weeks. At post-treatment, there was evidence of a non-significant medium effect compared with waitlist ($SMD^N = -0.39$, 95% CrI = -0.82 to 0.04).

6.7.9 Short-term psychodynamic psychotherapy

Three trials (EMMELKAMP2006, KNIJNIK2004, LEICHSENRING2012) included psychodynamic psychotherapy (185 participants on treatment) compared with waitlist, individual CT, individual CBT and supportive therapy. In the largest study (LEICHSENRING2012), which accounts for most of the reported effects, participants received approximately 1 hour of therapy per week for 26 weeks. At post-treatment, there was a medium effect compared with waitlist ($SMD^N = -0.62$, 95% CrI = -0.93 to -0.31).

In a pairwise analysis compared with waitlist, one trial (LEICHSENRING2012; 132 participants on treatment) reported a small effect on depression at post-treatment ($SMD = -0.39$, 95% CI = -0.72 to -0.06). No trials reported controlled effects for symptoms at follow-up, quality of life or anxiety-related disability.

6.7.10 Supportive therapy

Two trials (COTTRAUX2000, LIPSITZ2008) compared supportive therapy (54 participants on treatment) with individual CBT and IPT. Participants received 3 and 14 hours of therapy over 12 and 14 weeks, respectively. At post-treatment there was no evidence of an effect compared with waitlist ($SMD^N = -0.26$, 95% CrI = -0.72 to 0.21).

6.7.11 Self-help with and without support

Sixteen trials (ABRAMOWITZ2009, ANDERSSON2012, ANDREWS2011, BERGER2009, CARLBRING2007, CHUNG2008, FURMARK2009a, FURMARK2009b, HEDMAN2011, RAPEE2007, TITOV2008a, TITOV2008b, TITOV2008c, TITOV2009a, TITOV2009b, TITOV2010b) evaluated self-help with or without support (1,154 participants on treatment) and were included in the NMA. All trials used a cognitive behavioural approach and included varying levels of contact with researchers and therapists. At post-treatment, there was a medium effect for self-help without support (406 participants on treatment) compared with waitlist ($SMD^N = -0.75$, 95% CrI = -1.25 to -0.25) and a large effect for self-help with support (748 participants on treatment) compared with waitlist ($SMD^N = -0.86$, 95% CrI = -1.36 to -0.37).

In a pairwise analysis compared with waitlist, one trial (FURMARK2009a; 80 participants on treatment) reported no evidence of an effect on recovery at follow-up (RR = 0.77, 95% CI = 0.56 to 1.06). In a pairwise analysis of three trials (ANDERSSON2012, CARLBRING2007, FURMARK2009a; 211 participants on treatment) compared with waitlist, there was a medium effect on quality of life at post-treatment (SMD = -0.51, 95% CI = -0.86 to -0.17) with substantial heterogeneity between trials ($I^2 = 55\%$, Chi^2 = 6.70, p = 0.08) and between subgroups that varied by contact ($I^2 = 84.2\%$, Chi^2 = 6.35, p = 0.01). In one trial (FURMARK2009a; 80 participants on treatment), the effect was not statistically significant for quality of life at follow-up (SMD = -0.32, 95% CI = -0.70 to 0.06) and there was no heterogeneity. In a pairwise analysis of six trials (ABRAMOWITZ2009, ANDERSSON2012, BERGER2009, CARLBRING2007, FURMARK2009a, TITOV2008c; 314 participants on treatment) compared with waitlist, there was a medium effect on depression at post-treatment (SMD = -0.61, 95% CI = -0.78 to -0.43), with no heterogeneity between trials and no significant heterogeneity between subgroups ($I^2 = 20\%$, Chi^2 = 3.74, p = 0.29). In one trial (FURMARK2009a; 80 participants on treatment), the effect was not statistically significant for depression at follow-up (SMD = -0.22, 95% CI = -0.60 to 0.16). In a pairwise analysis of two trials (BERGER2009, TITOV2008c; 92 participants on treatment) compared with waitlist, the effect was not statistically significant for anxiety-related disability (SMD = -0.32, 95% CI = -0.66 to 0.02) with no heterogeneity.

Self-help without support
Three trials (TITOV2008c, TITOV2009b, TITOV2010b) compared internet self-help (270 participants on treatment) with waitlist and self-help with support. At post-treatment, there was a medium effect compared with waitlist ($SMD^N = -0.66$, 95% CrI = -0.94 to -0.39).

Four trials (CHUNG2008, FURMARK2009a, FURMARK2009b, RAPEE2007) compared a self-help book (136 participants on treatment) with waitlist, group CBT, internet self-help without support, and self-help with support. At post-treatment, there was a large effect compared with waitlist ($SMD^N = -0.84$, 95% CrI = -1.08 to -0.60).

Self-help with support
Twelve trials (ANDERSSON2012, ANDREWS2011, BERGER2009, CARLBRING2007, FURMARK2009a, FURMARK2009b, HEDMAN2011, TITOV2008a, TITOV2008b, TITOV2008c, TITOV2009a, TITOV2009b) compared internet self-help with support (696 participants on treatment) with waitlist, group CBT, self-help without support, and another form of internet self-help with support. Contact with a researcher or therapist varied, but usually included 2 to 3 hours of contact during treatment (by email or telephone) in addition to an initial clinical assessment. At post-treatment, there was a large effect compared with waitlist ($SMD^N = -0.88$, 95% CrI = -1.04 to -0.71).

Two trials (ABRAMOWITZ2009, CHUNG2008) compared a self-help book with support (52 participants on treatment) with waitlist and self-help without support. At post-treatment, there was a large effect compared with waitlist ($SMD^N = -0.87$, 95% $CrI = -1.33$ to -0.40). Additionally, one trial compared a self-help book with a moderated discussion group (28 participants) with other forms of self-help. At post-treatment, there was a large effect compared with waitlist ($SMD^N = -0.85$, 95% $CrI = -1.17$ to -0.53).

6.8   COMBINED PSYCHOLOGICAL AND PHARMACOLOGICAL INTERVENTIONS

One trial (DAVIDSON2004b) compared combination therapy (group CBT combined with fluoxetine) with fluoxetine alone, group CBT alone, pill placebo, and group CBT with pill placebo. Participants (59 participants on treatment) received 14 hours of group CBT and 47 mg of fluoxetine daily for 14 weeks. At post-treatment, there was a medium effect for combination therapy compared with waitlist ($SMD^N = -0.95$, 95% $CrI = -1.33$ to -0.57).

One trial (BLANCO2010) compared combination therapy (Heimberg's group CBT combined with phenelzine) with phenelzine alone, group CBT alone, and pill placebo. Participants (32 participants on treatment) received 30 hours of group CBT and 62 mg of phenelzine daily for 12 weeks. At post-treatment, there was a large effect compared with waitlist ($SMD^N = -1.69$, 95% $CrI = -2.10$ to -1.27).

One trial (PRASKO2003) compared combination therapy (group CBT combined with moclobemide) with moclobemide alone and individual CBT with pill placebo. There were 22 participants receiving combination therapy, the dose of which was not reported. At post-treatment there was a large effect compared with waitlist ($SMD^N = -1.23$, 95% $CrI = -1.72$ to -0.74).

One trial (KNIJNIK2008) compared combination therapy (psychodynamic psychotherapy combined with clonazepam) with clonazepam alone. Participants (29 participants on treatment) received 18 hours of psychodynamic psychotherapy and 1 mg of clonazepam daily for 12 weeks. At post-treatment there was a large effect compared with waitlist ($SMD^N = -1.28$, 95% $CrI = -1.82$ to -0.75).

One trial (CRASKE2011) compared preference-based therapy (74 participants on treatment) with treatment as usual. There was a medium effect on symptoms of social anxiety disorder at post-treatment ($SMD = -0.48$, 95% $CI = -0.83$ to -0.14) and at 12-month follow-up ($SMD = 0.39$, 95% $CI = -0.74$ to -0.05), which was no longer significant after 18 months ($SMD = 0.30$, 95% $CI = -0.64$ to 0.05).

6.9   SPECIFIC SUBGROUPS

6.9.1   Interventions for fear of public speaking

One trial (NEWMAN1994) compared exposure (16 participants on treatment) with waitlist for people with social anxiety disorder and a predominant fear of public speaking. Participants received approximately 16 hours of therapy in groups of six people over 8 weeks. At post-treatment, there was a non-significant medium effect on symptoms of social anxiety disorder (SMD = −0.60, 95% CI = −1.30 to 0.11).

In one trial (TILLFORS2008) participants with social anxiety disorder and a predominant fear of public speaking received self-help and either five sessions of exposure (18 participants on treatment) or email support from the therapist over 9 weeks. There was no difference between the groups on symptoms of social anxiety disorder at post-treatment (SMD = −0.10, 95% CI = −0.74 to 0.54) or at follow-up (SMD = 0.15, 95% CI = −0.51 to 0.81).

One trial (BOTELLA2010) compared individual CBT (36 participants on treatment) with self-help and waitlist for participants with a predominant fear of public speaking. At post-treatment, there were large effects compared with waitlist on symptoms of social anxiety disorder for both CBT (SMD = −1.18, 95% CI = −1.72 to −0.65) and self-help (SMD = −1.09, 95% CI = −1.56 to −0.63).

6.9.2 Interventions for fear of blushing, trembling or sweating

One trial (MULKENS2001) compared exposure (12 participants on treatment) with attention training for people with social anxiety disorder and a predominant fear of blushing. Participants received 6 hours of exposure therapy or attention training over 6 weeks. There was no evidence of an effect on symptoms of social anxiety at post-treatment (SMD = −0.42, 95% CI = −1.20 to 0.36) or at follow-up (SMD = −0.15, 95% CI = −1.02 to 0.71).

One trial (BOGELS2006) compared task concentration training (33 participants on treatment) with applied relaxation (32 participants on treatment) for people with social anxiety disorder and a predominant fear of blushing, trembling or sweating. Participants received approximately 13 hours of attention training or applied relaxation therapy over 8 weeks. There was no difference on symptoms of social anxiety disorder at post-treatment (SMD = 0.01, 95% CI = −0.48 to 0.50) or at 3-month (SMD = 0.02, 95% CI = −0.47 to 0.50) or 12-month follow-up (SMD = −0.17, 95% CI = −0.65 to 0.32).

One trial (BOGELS2008) compared social skills training (28 participants on treatment) with group CBT (27 participants on treatment) for people with social anxiety disorder and a predominant fear of blushing, trembling or sweating. Participants received 24 hours of CBT or social skills training in groups of seven people over 12 weeks. There was no evidence of an effect on symptoms of social anxiety disorder at post-treatment (SMD = 0.19, 95% CI = −0.34 to 0.72) or at 12-month follow-up (SMD = 0.11, 95% CI = −0.42 to 0.64).

6.9.3 Physical interventions for fear of blushing or sweating

One trial (CONNOR2004) randomised participants with social anxiety and palmar hyperhidrosis (excessive hand sweating) to paroxetine with botulinum toxin injections

(20 participants on treatment) or paroxetine with placebo injections. There was no evidence of a differential effect on symptoms of social anxiety disorder at post-treatment (SMD = −0.22; 95% CI = −0.84 to 0.41) and the between-group effect for anxiety-related disability was a non-significant medium effect (SMD = −0.63; 95% CI = −1.27 to 0.02).

Systematic searches did not identify any trials of thoracic sympathectomy for the treatment of people with social anxiety disorder.

In the absence of evidence about physical interventions for people with social anxiety disorder, the GDG considered extrapolating from trials that suggested physical interventions may reduce blushing or sweating (for example, in people with hyperhidrosis [Boley et al., 2007]). As social anxiety disorder is characterised by fear and avoidance of situations in which the person believes something embarrassing may happen rather than the actual presence of physical symptoms, the GDG agreed that the results from other populations were not relevant and could not be extrapolated to this guideline.

6.9.4   Residential interventions

One trial (BORGE2008) compared group CBT (35 participants on treatment) with IPT (38 participants on treatment) for people with social anxiety receiving residential treatment. Participants received four group sessions of around 45 minutes and one individual session per week of either IPT or CBT for 10 weeks. There was no difference between groups on symptoms of social anxiety disorder at post-treatment (SMD = −0.07, 95% CI = −0.53 to 0.39) or at follow-up (SMD = −0.02, 95% CI = −0.48 to 0.44).

6.9.5   Interventions for social anxiety disorder and comorbid alcohol misuse

Two trials (BOOK2008, RANDALL2001a) compared paroxetine (26 participants on treatment) with placebo for people with social anxiety disorder and comorbid alcohol misuse or dependence. Participants received 45 mg daily for 8 and 16 weeks. There was a large effect on symptoms of social anxiety disorder at post-treatment (SMD = −0.91, 95% CI = −1.56 to −0.26) with no significant heterogeneity ($I^2 = 15\%$, Chi^2 = 1.18, p = 0.28). There was no significant effect on withdrawal because of side effects (RR = 3.29, 95% CI = 0.14 to 76.33).

Three trials (HAYES2006, HEIDEMAN2008 [Heideman, 2008], RANDALL2001b [Randall et al., 2001b]) included a CBT intervention for people with social anxiety disorder and comorbid alcohol misuse, but two of these did not report usable data for symptoms of social anxiety disorder. In the remaining trial (HAYES2006), all participants received CBT and one group also received an intervention for alcohol misuse (ten participants on treatment). There was no difference between groups on symptoms of social anxiety disorder at post-treatment (SMD = −0.32, 95% CI = −1.15 to 0.51).

6.9.6 Interventions for social anxiety disorder comorbid with attention deficit hyperactivity disorder

One trial (ADLER2009) compared atomoxetine (200 participants on treatment) with placebo for people with comorbid social anxiety disorder and ADHD. Participants received 83 mg daily for 14 weeks. There was a small effect on symptoms of social anxiety disorder at post-treatment (SMD = −0.24, 95% CI = −0.44 to −0.04) and there was a small effect on the number of people reporting any adverse event (RR = 1.09, 95% CI = 1.00 to 1.19).

6.10 HEALTH ECONOMIC EVIDENCE

6.10.1 Systematic literature review

The systematic search of the economic literature undertaken for this guideline identified four eligible studies on interventions for adults with social anxiety (François et al., 2008; Gould et al., 1997; Hedman et al., 2011a; Titov et al., 2009b). One study was conducted in the UK (François et al., 2008), one in the US (Gould et al., 1997), one in Sweden (Hedman et al., 2011a) and one in Australia (Titov et al., 2009b). Details on the methods used for the systematic review of the economic literature are described in Chapter 3; completed methodology checklists of the studies are provided in Appendix 21, and the respective evidence tables are provided in Appendix 22.

François and colleagues (2008) assessed the cost effectiveness of escitalopram versus placebo in maintenance treatment of adults with social anxiety who had previously responded to treatment with escitalopram, from a UK NHS and personal social services (PSS) perspective, as well as from a societal perspective. The economic analysis was conducted alongside a multi-national placebo-controlled trial of escitalopram for relapse prevention (MONTGOMERY2005). The study sample consisted of people with a primary diagnosis of social anxiety disorder who had responded to 12 weeks of open-label treatment with escitalopram. Treatment was continued for 24 weeks unless a person relapsed or was withdrawn for other reasons. Costs considered in the analysis included physician consultations and other healthcare professional visits, hospitalisation and drug acquisition costs; productivity costs were reported separately. The cost year was 2006. The primary outcome of the analysis was the HRQoL of study participants, measured by Short Form Questionnaire Six Dimensional Health State Classification (SF-6D) utility scores (Brazier et al., 2002).

Costs were reported exclusively for people who did not relapse during the trial. The cost per person not relapsing was £111 in the escitalopram arm and £180 in the placebo arm over the first 12 weeks of the trial (p = 0.39), while the respective figures over the period from 12 to 24 weeks of the trial were £124 and £202 (p = 0.44). Escitalopram led to a reduction of relapses compared with placebo. The mean SF-6D scores at the end of the trial (24 weeks) were 0.715 for escitalopram and 0.698 for placebo (p = 0.009). Based on these results, the authors concluded that escitalopram was an effective treatment that led to significant improvement in HRQoL and resulted in cost savings that might potentially offset drug acquisition costs.

The study by François and colleagues (2008) is directly applicable to the guideline context as it is conducted from the NHS and PSS perspective. The measure of outcome was reported in the form of utility scores that were not transformed into quality-adjusted life years (QALYs); nevertheless, this did not affect interpretation of the results given that escitalopram was the dominant option. One of the limitations of the study was that costs were reported exclusively for people not relapsing during the trial; costs incurred by people who relapsed were not included in the analysis. However, given that escitalopram led to a reduction of relapses in the trial, omission of costs for people relapsing, which are expected to be higher than those incurred by 'non-relapsed' participants, is likely to only have underestimated the cost savings associated with escitalopram. The authors acknowledged a number of other limitations in how their study was conducted, such as the fact that in the analysis it was not possible to distinguish between study participants who did not utilise any resource and participants who failed to report resource use; this may have led to an underestimation of costs, irrespective of treatment group or time period of the analysis. Moreover, costs were estimated by applying UK unit prices to resource use reported from study participants in other countries; however, treatment may have a different impact on resource utilisation across countries in terms of type and frequency of resources used, and it was not possible to account for this in the study. Overall, the study findings suggest that escitalopram may be a cost-effective option in the maintenance treatment of adults with social anxiety.

Gould and colleagues (1997) evaluated the cost effectiveness of group CBT relative to pharmacological treatment (comprising phenelzine, fluvoxamine or clonazepam) and to combination therapy (comprising group CBT and pharmacological treatment) for adults with social anxiety disorder in the US. For each therapy considered in the study, the authors estimated its intervention cost over 2 years of treatment, and assessed its effect size for symptoms of social anxiety disorder or avoidance versus a control (mainly a minimal intervention: placebo or waitlist) after conducting a systematic review and meta-analysis of published trials. Intervention costs were estimated from a third-party payer perspective and consisted of CBT sessions including booster sessions, as well as drug acquisition costs, prescription charges and consultations with clinicians for pharmacological interventions.

The total intervention cost was estimated at $760 for group CBT; for pharmacological treatment it ranged from $1,744 (clonazepam) to $5,496 (fluvoxamine); and for combination therapy it ranged from $2,504 to $6,256 (price year not reported, but it was likely to have been 1996). The effect size was found to be 0.74 for group CBT, 0.62 for pharmacological treatment and 0.49 for combination therapy. Based on these findings, the authors concluded that group CBT was the most cost-effective treatment option for adults with social anxiety disorder in the US because it had the highest effect size and the lowest intervention cost.

The study is only partially applicable to the UK setting because it was conducted from a third-party payer perspective in the US, and suffers from a number of serious methodological limitations (including that costs only included intervention costs and other healthcare costs incurred by people with social anxiety disorder were not considered). More importantly, the estimates of effect size for each intervention referred to a different comparator (baseline treatment): this was, for example, waitlist or minimal treatment for group CBT and placebo for pharmacological treatment. Placebo is likely to have a significant relative effect compared with waitlist, which means that the effectiveness of pharmacological treatment is likely to have been underestimated relative to group CBT. The figures for effect sizes reported for each intervention were not comparable and should not be used to assess comparative effectiveness; instead, a (direct or indirect) relative effect size between the treatments considered in the study should have been estimated to assess comparative effectiveness. Finally, the uncertainty around the cost estimates and effect sizes was not reported. The findings of this study should be therefore interpreted with caution.

Hedman and colleagues (2011a) explored the cost effectiveness of computer-based self-help with support relative to group CBT for adults with social anxiety disorder in Sweden. The economic analysis, which was performed alongside an RCT (HEDMAN2011), adopted a societal perspective; nevertheless, medical costs were reported separately. Costs included intervention costs (therapist's time), GP visits, consultations with doctors, counsellors, psychotherapists, medical specialists and physiotherapists, health-related services (for example, alternative and home care, self-help groups), as well as productivity losses including informal care. The primary measure of outcome was the clinician-administered LSAS; in addition, the study estimated the percentage of responders defined using the Jacobson and Truax (1991) criteria. HRQoL was also measured for each participant, using the European Quality of Life – 5 Dimensions (EQ-5D) UK tariff utility scores. Costs and outcomes were measured at post-treatment (15 weeks) and at 6 months' follow-up.

Total mean medical costs over the 15 weeks of treatment reached $1,343 per person for self-help with support and $3,502 per person for group CBT (in 2009 US$); of these, $464 and $2,687 comprised intervention costs of self-help with support and group CBT, respectively. The total mean medical costs over the period from 15 weeks until 6 months' follow-up were $1,067 and $841 per person, for self-help with support and group CBT, respectively. In terms of outcomes, at 15 weeks the mean LSAS score was 39.4 (SD 19.9) for self-help with support and 48.5 (SD 25.0) for group CBT; the percentage of responders was 55% for self-help with support and 34% for group CBT; and the mean EQ-5D utility score was 0.82 (SD 0.14) for self-help with support and 0.80 (SD 0.17) for group CBT. At 6 months, the mean LSAS score was 32.1 (SD 23.1) versus 40.7 (SD 23.7) for self-help with support and group CBT, respectively; the percentage of responders was 64% versus 45%, while the mean EQ-5D utility score was 0.85 (SD 0.14) versus 0.81 (SD 0.17) for self-help with support and group CBT, respectively. Self-help with support showed lower intervention costs, which resulted in lower total medical costs, compared with group CBT, while the effectiveness of the two interventions was similar. Thus the study concluded that self-help with support was more cost effective than group CBT in adults with social anxiety disorder. The authors also performed probabilistic sensitivity analysis and reported that the probability of self-help being cost effective compared with group CBT was 81% at zero willingness to pay (WTP) per extra person responding to treatment, while this probability would rise at 89% at a WTP of $3,000 per extra person responding. The authors also reported that self-help with support had 80% probability of being cost effective at WTP ranging between zero and $40,000 per QALY gained.

The results of probabilistic analysis should be interpreted with caution because it appears that the authors double-counted the intervention costs (that is, they included them both in cost estimates during the 16 weeks of treatment and in cost estimates during the follow-up period). Moreover, although the study reports the probability of cost effectiveness for different levels of WTP per extra QALY gained, no QALYs seem to have been estimated in the study for each intervention; instead, EQ-5D utility scores were measured post-treatment and at 6-month follow-up. The study has not considered the costs associated with provision of computers or other infrastructure required in order to run the computerised self-help program. In any case, the study is only partially applicable to the guideline context because it was conducted in Sweden.

The study by Titov and colleagues (2009b) examined the cost effectiveness of computer-based self-help with support compared with group CBT for adults with social anxiety disorder from the perspective of the Australian health service. Costs included therapists' time only. The primary outcome measure was the number of years lived with disability (YLD) averted. Clinical effectiveness of the interventions assessed and related resource use were based on two RCTs (TITOV2008a, TITOV2008b) and a non-comparative study.

According to the study results, the mean cost of self-help with support was AU$300 per person, while the mean cost of group CBT reached AU$800 per person (2008 prices). The number of YLD averted of self-help with support versus waitlist was estimated at 0.2007; the number of YLD averted of group CBT compared with a 'do nothing' option was estimated at 0.1407. The authors estimated the incremental cost-effectiveness ratio (ICER) of self-help with support versus waitlist at AU$1,495 per YLD averted, and of group CBT versus a 'do nothing' option at AU$5,686 per YLD averted. Based on these findings they concluded that self-help with support was a more cost-effective option because it provided a better outcome at a lower cost.

The study is only partially applicable to the guideline context because it was conducted in Australia. Moreover, it is characterised by a number of important limitations. Cost estimates were limited to those relating to therapists' time. Costs of computers and other infrastructure required in order to run the computerised self-help program, as well as costs associated with further healthcare resource use (for example, visits to other healthcare professionals), were not considered. Also, it was not clear how effect sizes were estimated from different studies with different designs and then converted into number of YLD averted. There was no direct or indirect comparison between the two interventions assessed; rather, results were presented for each intervention in comparison with a given control (waitlist or do nothing).

Overall the existing economic evidence on interventions for adults with social anxiety disorder is sparse, not directly applicable to the guideline context, and characterised by serious methodological limitations. Based on this evidence, no safe conclusion on the cost effectiveness of the range of interventions available for adults with social anxiety disorder in the UK can be made.

6.10.2   Economic modelling

Introduction – objective of economic modelling

The cost effectiveness of interventions for adults with social anxiety disorder was considered by the GDG as an area with likely significant resource implications. Existing economic evidence in this area was very limited and not directly applicable to the UK setting: only one out of the four relevant economic studies identified in the guideline systematic review was conducted in the UK. The economic studies included in the review were characterised by several important limitations; moreover, they assessed only a limited number of interventions available in the UK for adults with social anxiety disorder. However, the clinical evidence was judged to be sufficient and of adequate quality to inform primary economic modelling. Based on the above considerations, this area was prioritised for further economic analysis. An economic model was therefore developed to assess the relative cost effectiveness across different interventions for adults with social anxiety disorder in the UK.

Economic modelling methods

Interventions assessed

The guideline economic analysis assessed those interventions for adults with social anxiety disorder that are available in the UK, and for which there was adequate clinical evidence to indicate their effectiveness along with an acceptable risk-to-benefit ratio. Further to these criteria, pharmacological interventions were included in the economic analysis if they are prescribed in routine UK clinical practice for the management of anxiety disorders. Benzodiazepines were not included in the economic analysis because they are not indicated for use longer than 2 to 4 weeks for the treatment of anxiety (Joint Formulary Committee, 2013). Computerised interventions were included in the economic analysis, despite their current unavailability in UK routine practice, because they are used in other countries and because they are likely to become available in the UK. Moreover, this guideline updates the NICE TA on computerised CBT (CCBT) for depression and anxiety (NICE, 2006), regarding phobias (see Chapter 8). Social skills training was not considered a separate intervention in the analysis because it is an element contained in other psychological interventions that were included in the economic model and the GDG was of the view that it is best provided as part of those therapies rather than as a separate intervention.

Based on the above criteria the following interventions were included in the economic analysis:

Pharmacological interventions: citalopram, escitalopram, fluoxetine, fluvoxamine, mirtazapine, moclobemide, paroxetine, phenelzine, pregabalin, sertraline and venlafaxine; for the latter, extended release formulations were considered, in accordance with the formulations used in the relevant RCTs included in the NMA that informed the economic model.

Psychological interventions: group CBT, individual CBT, group CBT (Heimberg), individual CBT (Heimberg), standard CT (Clark and Wells), CT (Clark and Wells) with shortened sessions, exposure *in vivo*, mindfulness training, IPT, psychodynamic psychotherapy, self-help (book) with and without support, self-help (internet) with and without support, and supportive therapy.

The model also considered treatment with pill placebo, consisting, in terms of resource use, of GP visits only, as well as waitlist as alternative treatment options, in order to assess the cost effectiveness of active interventions versus a non-specific medical management (represented by pill placebo) and a 'do nothing' option (represented by waitlist). Combined interventions (comprising concurrent provision of both pharmacological and psychological interventions) were not considered in the model structure because the GDG judged that the respective evidence was very limited (each combination therapy included in the guideline systematic review was assessed in one single small trial). Moreover, in many trials combined interventions were found to be less effective than their components and were associated with increased side effects and lower tolerability, so they were obviously less cost effective (more intensive and less effective) than single interventions; consequently there was no need for a formal evaluation of their cost effectiveness.

Model structure

A hybrid decision-analytic model consisting of a decision-tree followed by a two-state Markov model was constructed using Microsoft Office Excel 2007. The model estimated the total costs and benefits associated with provision of various interventions to adults with social anxiety disorder. The structure of the model, which aimed to simulate course of illness and relevant clinical practice in the UK, was also driven by the availability of clinical data.

According to the model structure, hypothetical cohorts of adults with social anxiety disorder were initiated on each of the 28 treatment options assessed, including treatment with pill placebo or inclusion in a waitlist. The duration of initial treatment was 12 weeks for drugs and pill placebo; for psychological interventions it varied by intervention (range between 9 and 16 weeks). In order to estimate QALYs it was assumed that psychological interventions lasted 12 weeks as well, which was consistent with the trial data and with clinical practice. Following treatment, people in each cohort either recovered (that is, they did not meet criteria for a diagnosis of social anxiety disorder any longer) or did not recover. Those recovering were given 6 months of maintenance therapy if they had been initiated on pharmacological treatment in order to sustain the treatment effect. No booster sessions were modelled for psychological interventions, as clinical evidence indicated that these are not necessary for sustained treatment effect. People who did not recover were assumed to stop treatment rather than switch to an alternative intervention; according to the expert opinion of the GDG, because of the nature of the disorder people are usually reluctant to keep in contact with health services and try an alternative treatment option.

During the year post-treatment, people who had recovered might experience a relapse, meaning that they again met the criteria for social anxiety disorder. People who had not recovered following treatment were assumed to remain in a state of social anxiety and not to recover spontaneously over this year. From that point on, all people in each cohort – both those who no longer met criteria for social anxiety disorder (that is, those who recovered and did not relapse) and those who met criteria (that is, those who recovered but relapsed as well as those who did not recover following therapy) – were entered into the Markov model. They could remain in the same health state or move between the two states of 'no social anxiety' and 'social anxiety'. The Markov model was run in yearly cycles. A half-cycle correction was applied. Because of lack of long-term comparative clinical data, transitions between the two health states in the Markov model were assumed to be independent of intervention received at the start of the model.

The analysis considered two time horizons in order to explore short and longer-term costs and benefits: (1) intervention time (12 weeks) plus 1 year post-treatment (represented by the decision tree); and (2) intervention time (12 weeks) plus 5 years post-treatment (consisting of the decision tree and four yearly cycles of the Markov model). The GDG was interested in the long-term cost, benefits and cost effectiveness of the interventions assessed in the analysis and focused on the 5-year post-treatment results. However, 1-year post-treatment findings were also reviewed in order to explore the changes in the relative cost effectiveness of interventions over time. A schematic diagram of the economic model structure is presented in Figure 7.

Costs and outcomes considered in the analysis

The economic analysis adopted the perspective of the NHS and PSS, as recommended by NICE (2009b). Costs consisted of intervention costs (healthcare professional time, drug acquisition and equipment/infrastructure required for self-help interventions) and other health and social care costs incurred by people with social anxiety disorder not recovering following treatment or experiencing a relapse

Figure 7: Schematic diagram of the economic model constructed for the assessment of the relative cost effectiveness of interventions for adults with social anxiety disorder

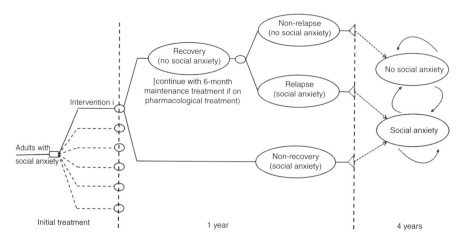

following recovery (including GP consultations, home visits from health and social services, counselling or therapy contacts, and inpatient and outpatient secondary care). A secondary analysis that adopted a wider perspective which, in addition to NHS and PSS costs, considered receipt of social security benefits by people with social anxiety disorder was also undertaken. The measure of outcome was the QALY.

Clinical input parameters and overview of methods employed for evidence synthesis

Clinical model input parameters consisted of the probability of recovery at end of treatment, the probability of relapse following recovery within the first year post-treatment, as well as the probabilities of recovery and relapse in the 4-year Markov model phase.

The probability of recovery at end of treatment for all interventions was derived from the NMA undertaken for this guideline. The clinical effectiveness of all interventions was expressed in the form of SMDs. For the economic analysis, the SMDs were transformed into LORs as described in Chapter 3, and these were further transformed into probabilities of recovery, using as baseline the absolute probability of recovery for waitlist, which was estimated from available recovery data on waitlist arms in RCTs that were included in the guideline systematic review. The 40,000 iterations that were recorded in WinBUGS (as described in Chapter 3) were thinned by 4 so as to obtain 10,000 iterations for use in the economic model. This transformation of SMDs derived from the NMA into LORs and the subsequent indirect estimation of probability of recovery for every intervention assessed in the economic analysis was necessary for three reasons:

1. The recovery data reported in the RCTs included in the guideline systematic review were sparse and not available for all interventions assessed in the economic analysis: of the 101 studies included in the NMA, only 25 reported recovery data; such data were available for 14 out of the 29 interventions considered in the economic analysis. Consequently, available recovery data were not adequate for populating all arms of the economic model.

2. The economic analysis needed to reflect (and thus utilise) the same relative treatment effects that were estimated in the NMA, which determined the comparative clinical effectiveness of the interventions considered in this guideline.

3. The methodology adopted allowed estimation of probability of recovery for every intervention included in the economic analysis while preserving the effect of randomisation, because the probability of recovery of each intervention was 'linked' to the relative treatment effect of the intervention as estimated in the NMA.

The results of the NMA that were used to populate the economic model are provided in Table 15. The table shows the probability of recovery at end of treatment for each intervention considered in the economic analysis. Treatment options have been ranked from most to least efficacious in terms of mean probability of recovery.

The probability of relapse after recovery within the first year following pharmacological intervention was estimated based on relevant data reported in relapse

Table 15: Results of the NMA that were utilised in the economic model – probability of recovery at end of treatment

Intervention	Probability of recovery (95% credible intervals)
CT (Clark and Wells)	0.62 (0.16 to 0.95)
Phenelzine	0.51 (0.10 to 0.91)
Individual CBT	0.47 (0.08 to 0.89)
Individual CBT (Heimberg)	0.41 (0.06 to 0.87)
Paroxetine	0.39 (0.06 to 0.85)
CT (Clark and Wells), shortened sessions	0.38 (0.06 to 0.84)
Venlafaxine	0.38 (0.05 to 0.84)
Fluvoxamine	0.37 (0.05 to 0.83)
Sertraline	0.36 (0.05 to 0.83)
Escitalopram	0.35 (0.04 to 0.82)
Self-help (internet) with support	0.35 (0.05 to 0.80)
Fluoxetine	0.34 (0.04 to 0.81)
Self-help (book) with support	0.34 (0.04 to 0.81)
Group CBT	0.34 (0.04 to 0.80)
Citalopram	0.33 (0.04 to 0.82)
Self-help (book) without support	0.33 (0.04 to 0.80)
Mirtazapine	0.33 (0.03 to 0.84)
Exposure *in vivo*	0.33 (0.04 to 0.79)
Group CBT (Heimberg)	0.32 (0.04 to 0.78)
Moclobemide	0.30 (0.03 to 0.76)
Pregabalin	0.29 (0.03 to 0.76)
Self-help (internet) without support	0.27 (0.03 to 0.74)
Psychodynamic psychotherapy	0.26 (0.03 to 0.72)
Pill placebo	0.21 (0.02 to 0.64)
IPT	0.20 (0.02 to 0.64)
Mindfulness training	0.19 (0.02 to 0.63)
Supportive therapy	0.16 (0.01 to 0.57)
Waitlist	0.10 (0.01 to 0.39)

prevention studies included in the guideline systematic review. Five placebo-controlled trials assessed the efficacy of pharmacological interventions in preventing relapse in people with social anxiety disorder: four of them assessed an SSRI (KUMAR1999 and STEIN2002b assessed paroxetine, MONTGOMERY2005 escitalopram, VAN-AMERINGEN2001 sertraline) and one assessed pregabalin (GREIST2011). All five studies reported a 6-month 'drug' relapse rate for people with social anxiety disorder who had responded to initial drug treatment (12 weeks) and were maintained on drug treatment during the 6 months of the trial (therefore the 6-month 'drug' relapse rate referred to participants who relapsed while taking an active drug as maintenance treatment), as well as a 6-month 'placebo' relapse rate for people with social anxiety disorder who had responded to initial 12-week drug treatment and received placebo during the 6 months of the study (therefore the 6-month 'placebo' relapse rate referred to participants who had responded to 12-weeks of initial drug treatment but then were discontinued from the drug and were given placebo instead). The economic model structure assumed that within the first year following initial drug treatment people who recovered received 6 months of maintenance treatment. Assuming that drug maintenance treatment does provide a benefit and reduces the risk of relapse (compared with discontinuation of the drugs immediately after the initial 12-week treatment), the risk of relapse in the 6 months following maintenance treatment should be lower than the pooled 'placebo' relapse rate from the placebo arms of the relapse prevention studies. Conversely, the risk of relapse after stopping the 6-month maintenance treatment should be higher than the pooled 'drug' relapse rate from the active drug arms of the relapse prevention studies, which was recorded while people were still on a drug. It was therefore assumed that over the first year following pharmacological intervention people who recovered were maintained on their initiated drug for 6 months and experienced relapses at the 'drug' relapse rate, and, after stopping the drug, for the remaining 6 months, they continued to experience some relapses at an overall (annual) rate that was lower than the 6-month 'placebo' relapse rate (it was assumed that the 'placebo' relapse rate did not increase after 6 months following discontinuation, and therefore the annual 'placebo' relapse rate should not be different from the 6-month 'placebo' relapse rate). For the purposes of simplicity and because of a lack of more suitable data, it was assumed that the probability of relapse after recovery within the first year following pharmacological treatment equalled the midpoint between the pooled 'drug' relapse rate and the pooled 'placebo' relapse rate reported in the relapse prevention studies included in the guideline systematic review. This estimate was utilised in all decision nodes of the model that involved drug treatment because relapse data for drugs were sparse and not available for the majority of pharmacological interventions considered in the economic analysis.

The probability of relapse following recovery in the pill placebo arm of the model was assumed to equal that for drug arms. This probability was deliberately not set to equal the 'placebo' relapse rate because people who had recovered in this arm had not been initiated on a drug (so they did not experience drug discontinuation that might potentially lead to an increase in the risk of relapse similar to the relapse rate of the placebo arms of the relapse prevention studies).

The probability of relapse after recovery within the first year following psychological intervention was calculated using the respective probability of relapse for drugs, estimated as described above, and the risk ratio (RR) of relapse between drugs and psychological interventions. The latter was derived from an observational study that evaluated the effects of maintenance treatment with phenelzine and group CBT (Liebowitz et al., 1999). The study followed an RCT that compared phenelzine, group CBT, pill placebo and psychological placebo (HEIMBERG1998). People who were initiated on either phenelzine or group CBT and had responded to 12 weeks of treatment (N = 28) were continued on their initial treatment for 6 months, and followed up for another 6 months during which they received no treatment. The study reported relapse rates over the 6-month maintenance treatment period, the 6-month follow-up period, and the combined 12-month period. A risk ratio of relapse for drugs (represented by phenelzine) versus psychological intervention (represented by group CBT) was estimated using the 12-month combined relapse data reported in the study. The probability of relapse after recovery for the psychological arms of the model was subsequently calculated as:

$$P_{relapse} \text{ (psychological interventions)} = RR_{relapse} / P_{relapse} \text{ (drugs)}$$

This probability was applied to all psychological intervention arms of the economic model, since no differential relapse data for the range of psychological interventions considered in the model are available in the literature.

The probability of relapse after recovery in the waitlist arm of the model was based on data reported in a prospective naturalistic study that followed people with anxiety disorders over 12 years (Bruce et al., 2005). The study followed 176 people with social anxiety disorder and reported a 12-year probability of recurrence, calculated using standard survival analysis methods. This probability allowed estimation of an annual probability of relapse that was applied to the first year after recovery in the waitlist arm.

The annual probabilities of recovery and relapse for all treatments in the 4-year Markov model phase were assumed to be independent of initial treatment and were also based on data reported in Bruce and colleagues (Bruce et al., 2005). In addition to the 12-year probability of recurrence, the authors also calculated a 12-year probability of recovery using survival analysis, which was used to estimate an annual probability of recovery. The estimated annual probabilities of recovery and relapse were applied to all cohorts in the economic model, regardless of initial treatment, in years 2 to 5 post-treatment (that is, in the Markov phase of the model).

Utility data and estimation of quality-adjusted life years
In order to express outcomes in the form of QALYs, the health states of the economic model needed to be linked to appropriate utility scores. Utility scores represent the Health Related Quality of Life (HRQoL) associated with specific health states on a scale from 0 (death) to 1 (perfect health); they are estimated using preference-based measures that capture people's preferences on the HRQoL experienced in the health states under consideration.

The systematic search of the literature identified one study that reported utility scores for specific health states associated with social anxiety (François et al., 2008) and two studies that reported utility data for adults with social anxiety disorder (and adults without a mental disorder), without differentiating between distinct health states of the condition: (1) Alonso and colleagues (2004), with data analysed and reported in Kaltenthaler and colleagues (2006), and (2) Saarni and colleagues (2007).

François and colleagues (2008) generated utility scores using SF-36 data derived from 517 people with social anxiety disorder who participated in 12 weeks of open-label treatment with escitalopram. Those responding to treatment were entered into a double-blind, placebo-controlled, multinational clinical trial of escitalopram for relapse prevention (MONTGOMERY2005). Participants were included in the open-label phase if they had had a primary diagnosis of generalised social anxiety and a score of 70 or more on the LSAS. Response to treatment was defined as a Clinical Global Impression-Improvement (CGI-I) score of 1 or 2; relapse was defined as either an increase in LSAS total score of 10 or more points or withdrawal of the participant from the study because of lack of efficacy as judged by the investigator. SF-36 data were obtained from participants at baseline, the end of the open-label period, and at 12 and 24 weeks after randomisation. Participants who did not complete the study attended an early discontinuation visit, at which the SF-36 was administered. SF-36 scores were converted into utility scores using the SF-6D algorithm (Brazier et al., 2002). The SF-6D algorithm has been generated using the standard gamble (SG) technique in a representative sample of the UK general population.

Alonso and colleagues (2004) reported EQ-5D and SF-36 data of people participating in a large, community-based mental health European survey, the European Study of the Epidemiology of Mental Disorders. Participants were members of the general population that underwent psychiatric assessments and completed various HRQoL instruments. The authors conducted additional analyses to those reported in their publication and generated EQ-5D and SF-36 utility scores for people who had experienced a wide range of mental disorders over the past 12 months (among whom 219 had social anxiety) and 19,334 people without a mental disorder over the past 12 months. Estimated utility scores were subsequently provided to the research team that conducted the economic analysis for the NICE TA on the use of CCBT for depression and anxiety (Kaltenthaler et al., 2006). Thus, EQ-5D and SF-6D utility scores derived from the European Study of the Epidemiology of Mental Disorders are available in Kaltenthaler and colleagues (2006). Utility scores for EQ-5D have been elicited from the UK general population using the time trade-off technique (TTO) (Dolan et al., 1996; Dolan, 1997). The SF-6D algorithm has been generated using SG in a representative sample of the UK general population (Brazier et al., 2002).

Saarni and colleagues (2007) reported EQ-5D data obtained from people aged 30 years or older, participating in a national health survey in Finland. The survey consisted of a health interview, a health examination and self-report questionnaires. The study reported EQ-5D utility scores for people who had experienced a range of mental disorders over the past 12 months (among whom 60 had social anxiety anxiety, with

14 having pure social anxiety) and 5,279 people with no mental disorder over the last 12 months. The authors used the UK TTO tariff (Dolan, 1997) in order to estimate utility scores from EQ-5D data.

Table 16 summarises the methods used to derive and value health states associated with social anxiety disorder in the literature and presents the respective utility scores reported in the three utility studies that were identified by the systematic search of the literature.

According to NICE guidance (NICE, 2013) on the selection of utility values for use in cost-utility analysis, the measurement of changes in HRQoL should be reported directly from people with the condition examined, and the valuation of health states should be based on public preferences elicited using a choice-based method, such as the TTO or SG, in a representative sample of the UK population. NICE recommends the EQ-5D (Brooks, 1996; Dolan, 1997) as the preferred measure of HRQoL in adults for use in cost-utility analysis. When EQ-5D scores are not available or are inappropriate for the condition or effects of treatment, NICE recommends that the valuation methods be fully described and comparable to those used for the EQ-5D (NICE, 2013).

The study by François and colleagues (2008) was the only one that reported utility data for different health states of social anxiety disorder. However, the GDG questioned the quality of the data because of the methodological limitations of MONTGOMERY2005, such as the high attrition rates. Moreover, the GDG felt that the utility data reported in the study represented a rather narrow benefit in HRQoL, as the difference in the utility scores between the states of response and non-response was only 0.031; for comparison, a study with similar design that estimated utility scores in responders and non-responders in generalised anxiety reported a respective difference of 0.13 (Allgulander et al., 2007). In addition, the reduction in utility for those relapsing following response was 0.017 in people with social anxiety disorder according to François and colleagues, and 0.03 in people with generalised anxiety according to Allgulander and colleagues. The GDG therefore judged that utility data reported by François and colleagues might have failed to capture the true benefit in HRQoL once a person with social anxiety disorder responds to treatment, and the true loss in HRQoL once the person relapses following response.

It should be noted that François and colleagues compared their findings with those of Allgulander and colleagues and admitted that 'the effect of escitalopram on HRQoL was somewhat more modest in patients with generalised social anxiety disorder than in those with generalised anxiety disorder'. However, it was not the effect of escitalopram that was responsible for the discrepancies in the utility changes between the two studies and populations because utility changes reflected alterations in HRQoL once a person had/had not experienced response or relapse, with the two states being defined in a similar way in the two studies. Another point for consideration was that the GDG was interested in the utility of the recovery state, whereas the data reported in François and colleagues referred to the state of response. Finally, François and colleagues reported utility values based on the SF-6D, which is not the NICE preferred measure for use in cost-utility analysis. For all the above reasons the GDG decided not to use the utility data reported in François and colleagues, despite

Table 16: Summary of studies reporting utility scores for social anxiety

Study	Definition of health states	Valuation method	Population valuing	Results
François et al., 2008	SF-36 data on 517 people with social anxiety disorder transformed into SF-6D scores. Definition of social anxiety disorder health states: Response: CGI-I score of 1 or 2 Relapse: an increase in LSAS ≥ 10 or withdrawal from study due to lack of efficacy, as judged by the investigator.	SG	UK general population	Baseline (excluding discontinuation): 0.659 Response: 0.708 (95% CI = 0.702 to 0.714) No response (including discontinuation): 0.677 (95% CI = 0.665 to 0.688) Relapse following response: 0.691 (SD 0.071) No relapse following response: 0.718 (SD 0.068)
Alonso et al., 2004	EQ-5D and SF-6D profiles from 219 people with social anxiety disorder over the last 12 months and 19,334 people with no mental disorder over the last 12 months participating in a large community-based mental health European survey.	TTO (EQ-5D) / SG (SF-6D)	UK general population	*EQ-5D scores:* 12-month social anxiety disorder: 0.79 (95% CI = 0.75 to 0.84) No 12-month mental disorder: 0.91 (95% CI = 0.90 to 0.91) *SF-6D scores:* 12-month social anxiety disorder: 0.69 (95% CI = 0.66 to 0.71) No 12-month mental disorder: 0.84 (95% CI = 0.84 to 0.84)
Saarni et al., 2007	EQ-5D profiles from 60 people with social phobia (14 with pure social phobia) over the last 12 months and 5,279 people with no mental disorder over the last 12 months, aged ≥ 30 years, participating in a national survey in Finland.	TTO	UK general population	12-month social anxiety disorder: 0.659 (SE* 0.034) 12-month pure social anxiety disorder: 0.729 (SE 0.052) No 12-month mental disorder: 0.866 (SE 0.002)

Note. *SE = standard error.

163

these being the only utility data capturing HRQoL in different health states of social anxiety disorder that were identified in the literature.

The GDG then assessed the EQ-5D-based utility data reported in Alonso and colleagues (2004) and the utility data from Saarni and colleagues (2007). The two studies were very similar in terms of design and reported utility data for people with social anxiety disorder over the last 12 months and for people without a mental disorder over the last 12 months. It was agreed that the utility data for the former could be used for the state of non-recovery or relapse ('social anxiety') in the guideline economic model; the utility data for people without a mental disorder over the last 12 months could be used as a proxy for the state of recovery ('no social anxiety'). It was acknowledged that this is probably not a very accurate proxy because people recovering from social anxiety disorder may not reach the HRQoL of a person without a mental disorder over the last 12 months. Another limitation of these data is that the diagnosis of social anxiety disorder referred to a period of 12 months prior to the study, so some participants in both studies might have experienced an improvement in their condition over this period (and actually might not have social anxiety disorder at the point of interview). Nevertheless, the GDG accepted these as reasonable limitations and decided to use the data by Saarni and colleagues (2007) in the base-case analysis (which reflect a greater improvement in HRQoL following recovery), and to use the more conservative data by Alonso and colleagues in sensitivity analysis. Utility data from both studies are based on the EQ-5D UK tariff and therefore are in accordance with NICE guidance on the selection of utility data for use in cost-utility analysis (NICE, 2013).

It was assumed that the improvement in utility for people with social anxiety disorder recovering following treatment occurred linearly over the duration of treatment, starting from the utility value of social anxiety disorder and reaching the utility value of no social anxiety disorder. The duration of all treatments considered in the analysis was assumed to be 12 weeks in order to simplify calculation of utilities in people improving following treatment across cohorts. All changes in utility between the two states of 'social anxiety' and 'no social anxiety' were assumed to occur linearly over the time period of the change.

Side effects from medication are expected to result in a reduction in utility scores of people with social anxiety disorder. Disutility because of side effects was not considered in the analysis because the model structure did not incorporate side effects. This was due to inconsistent reporting of specific side effect rates across the studies included in the guideline systematic review. Moreover, no studies on people with social anxiety disorder reporting 'disutility' because of side effects were identified in the literature. However, Revicki and Wood (1998) examined the effect of side effects from antidepressants in the HRQoL of people with depression. According to the study, people with a side effect reported lower utility scores compared with those not experiencing side effects. The observed mean disutility ranged from 0.01 for dry mouth and nausea to 0.12 for nervousness and light-headedness. However, except for light-headedness and dizziness, the reduction in utility caused by side effects did not reach statistical significance. The GDG felt that it may be reasonable to extrapolate this evidence to the population of people with social anxiety disorder; consequently, it is possible that lack of consideration of disutility because of side effects has not had a great impact on the results of the economic analysis. Nevertheless, omission of the negative impact of drugs on HRQoL of adults with social anxiety disorder is acknowledged as a limitation of the analysis because it may have resulted in an over-estimation of the cost effectiveness of pharmacological interventions relative to psychological interventions considered in the model.

Cost data

Costs considered in the economic model consisted of intervention costs and extra health and social care costs incurred by adults with social anxiety disorder not recovering following treatment or relapsing following recovery. In addition, a secondary analysis considered receipt of social security benefits by adults with social anxiety disorder not recovering or relapsing following recovery.

Pharmacological intervention costs consisted of drug acquisition costs and GP visit costs. Intervention costs of placebo related to GP visit costs only. Costs were calculated by combining resource use estimates with respective national unit costs. Drug acquisition costs were taken from the NHS Electronic Drug Tariff, February 2013 (NHS Business Services Authority Prescription Pricing Division, 2013). For each drug the lowest reported price was selected and used in the analysis; where available, costs of generic forms were considered. The average daily dosage of each drug was determined according to optimal clinical practice (according to GDG expert opinion) and was consistent with the respective average daily dosage reported in the RCTs considered in the NMA that informed the economic model. Initial treatment with drugs was estimated to last 12 weeks, while people recovering following drug treatment received another 6 months (26 weeks) of maintenance treatment at the same daily dosage. All people under any pharmacological treatment (or placebo) were assumed to visit their GP four times over the 12 weeks of initial treatment; in addition, those recovering were assumed to pay three extra GP visits during maintenance treatment. The GP unit cost (£43 per patient contact lasting 11.7 minutes) was taken from *Unit Costs of Health and Social Care 2012* (Curtis, 2012). This figure includes direct care staff costs and qualification costs.

Details on the resource use and total intervention costs of pharmacological interventions for adults with social anxiety are presented in Table 17.

Intervention costs of psychological interventions were also calculated by combining resource use estimates with relevant national unit costs. Resource use estimates in terms of therapists' time were based on relevant data reported in RCTs included in the NMA that informed the economic model. For self-help studies the additional cost of a book or a computerised program was considered. All psychological interventions were assumed to be delivered by Band 7 clinical psychologists because this is broadly consistent with the type of therapists who delivered the interventions in the majority of RCTs included in the NMA. The unit cost of a Band 7 clinical psychologist per hour of client contact has been estimated based on the median full-time equivalent basic salary for Agenda for Change Band 7 and includes

Table 17: Average daily dosage, drug acquisition costs and total intervention costs of pharmacological interventions for adults with social anxiety disorder included in the economic model (2012 prices)

Drug	Mean daily dosage	Drug cost – 12 weeks*	Drug cost – 26 weeks*	GP visits	Total cost – 12 + 26 weeks; includes GP cost*
Citalopram	40 mg	£3.15	£6.83	Four visits during 12 weeks of initial treatment and three visits during the 26-week maintenance period	£311
Escitalopram	20 mg	£75.60	£163.80		£540
Fluoxetine	40 mg	£4.70	£10.19		£316
Fluvoxamine	150 mg	£62.64	£135.71		£499
Mirtazapine	30 mg	£4.77	£10.34		£316
Moclobemide	600 mg	£71.96	£155.91		£529
Paroxetine	40 mg	£10.30	£22.33		£334
Phenelzine	60 mg	£75.60	£163.80		£540
Pregabalin	450 mg	£193.20	£418.60		£913
Sertraline	200 mg	£7.32	£15.86		£324
Venlafaxine XL	150 mg	£110.43	£239.27		£651
Placebo	NA	NA	NA		£301

Note. *Drug acquisition costs from NHS Electronic Drug Tariff, February 2013 (NHS Business Services Authority Prescription Pricing Division, 2013); GP unit costs from Curtis (2012).

salary, salary on-costs and overheads, but excludes qualification costs because the latter are not available for clinical psychologists (Curtis, 2010). However, exclusion of qualification costs from the clinical psychologist unit cost would underestimate the total psychological intervention costs and would therefore, in all likelihood, overestimate their cost effectiveness relative to pharmacological interventions. In order to consider the qualification cost for clinical psychologists, a number of mental health professionals with different qualifications and salary bands were selected (for example, consultant psychiatrists and mental health nurses) and the reported unit costs for these professions with and without qualification costs were compared. The rate of unit costs without/with qualification costs was found to be 0.85, and this allowed estimation of a unit cost for Band 7 clinical psychologists at £101 per hour of client contact in 2012 prices, which included qualification costs. This cost was used in the base-case analysis. A one-way sensitivity analysis tested delivery of a self-help intervention by a Band 5 therapist (such as a mental health nurse) and delivery of group therapies by one Band 7 and one Band 6 (for example, trainee in clinical psychology) therapist.

In addition to therapists' time, the intervention costs of all psychological interventions included an initial GP visit for referral to psychological services. Moreover, the intervention costs of self-help programmes included the cost of either a book or a computerised program and related infrastructure/equipment required for the delivery of such a program (licence fee or website hosting, personal computers [PCs] and capital overheads).

The cost of a book for self-help was based on the cost of Rapee's *Overcoming Shyness and Social Phobia: A Step by Step Guide* (Rapee, 1998) available in the market (£22.95). The website hosting cost of computerised self-help was estimated based on information provided by the GDG, relating to a pilot research internet-based self-help program for people with social anxiety disorder currently tested in England. According to this information, the annual cost of secure internet hosting reached £14,000 (including maintenance and software bug fixing of the program), and was paid at an individual service level. Based on IAPT audit of activity data (information provided by the GDG), an average IAPT service sees about 2,500 people every year, of which 1.5% are estimated to have social anxiety disorder. Assuming 80% of these are offered (and accept) internet-based self-help, this means 30 people with social anxiety disorder use the internet-based self-help program, resulting in a website hosting cost of £467 per person. Since the particular internet-based self-help program was developed for research purposes, no licence fee was considered at the estimation of the intervention cost, although this cost component, which may be considerable, needs to be taken into account in the assessment of cost effectiveness of other computerised self-help packages for social anxiety disorder that may be available in the future. The annual costs of hardware and capital overheads (space around the PC) were based on reported estimates made for the economic analysis undertaken to inform the NICE TA on CCBT for depression and anxiety (Kaltenthaler et al., 2006) and equal £161 and £1,070, respectively (in 2012 prices). Kaltenthaler and colleagues (2006) estimated that one PC can serve around 100 people with a mental disorder treated with computerised programs per year. Assuming that a PC is used to full capacity (that is, it serves no fewer than 100 people annually, considering that it is available for use not only by people with social anxiety disorder, but also by people with other mental disorders, such as depression), the annual cost of hardware and capital overheads was divided by 100 users, leading to a hardware and capital overheads cost per user of £13. It must be noted that if users of such programs can access them from home or a public library, then the cost of hardware and capital overheads to the NHS is zero.

No booster (maintenance) sessions were assumed for psychological interventions. The intervention cost of waitlist was zero. Table 18 presents the resource use elements and the estimated intervention costs of all psychological interventions considered in the model.

Costs of treating side effects of drugs were not considered in the economic analysis due to lack of consistency in reporting appropriate side effect data across all drugs. Nevertheless, the GDG estimated that the majority of common side effects, such as nausea, insomnia, sexual problems, dizziness, fatigue, palpitations and tachycardia, would be discussed during GP monitoring, which was considered at the estimation of intervention costs relating to initial and maintenance pharmacological intervention. Regarding less common side effects, such as hypertension (associated with SNRIs) and gastrointestinal bleeding (associated with SSRIs), these were thought to result in higher management costs at an individual level, but given their low frequency they were deemed to entail smaller economic implications at a study population level. Therefore, although the omission of costs associated with management of side effects is acknowledged as a limitation of the analysis, it is not considered to have substantially affected the economic modelling results.

The extra health and social care costs incurred by adults with social anxiety disorder not recovering post-treatment or relapsing following recovery were taken from Patel and colleagues (2002). The authors analysed service use data on 63 people with social anxiety and 8,501 people without psychiatric morbidity derived from the Psychiatric Morbidity Survey conducted in the UK in 1993–1994 (Meltzer et al., 1995). The study combined data on GP consultations, home visits from health and social services, counselling or therapy contacts and inpatient and outpatient secondary care with relevant national unit costs and subsequently estimated an annual total health and social care cost incurred by people with social anxiety disorder and people without psychiatric morbidity. People with social anxiety disorder in the model were estimated to incur the annual total health and social care cost for this population reported in Patel and colleagues, whereas people who recovered and were in the state of 'no social anxiety' were assumed to incur the respective cost incurred by people without psychiatric comorbidity reported in the study. People who relapsed following recovery during the first year post-treatment were assumed to incur the 'social anxiety' health and social care cost for 6 months and the 'no social anxiety' health and social care cost for the remaining 6 months.

Patel and colleagues also reported the mean annual value of social security benefits for people with social anxiety disorder and those without psychiatric comorbidity, and these costs were used in a secondary analysis that adopted a wider perspective in order to capture the broader economic implications of social anxiety disorder.

Table 18: Resource use and estimated intervention costs of psychological interventions (2012 prices)

Intervention	Resource use details	Total cost per person; includes a GP visit*
Self-help (book) no support	75 minutes of contact with therapist plus cost of book (Rapee's *Overcoming Shyness and Social Phobia: A Step by Step Guide* [1998] current cost on Amazon: £22.95).	£193
Self-help (internet) no support	75 minutes of contact with therapist; the annual cost of internet hosting is £14,000 (GDG information) divided by 30 people with social anxiety disorder expected to use the program annually (IAPT audit of activity data provided by the GDG; cost of hardware and capital overheads £12/person (2012 prices, based on Kaltenthaler and colleagues [2006]).	£649
Self-help (book) with support	210 minutes of contact with therapist plus cost of book as above.	£421
Self-help (internet) with support	210 minutes of contact with therapist plus cost of internet hosting, hardware and capital overheads as above.	£877
Exposure *in vivo*	12 group sessions × 2.5 hours each, two therapists and six participants per group = 10 therapist hours per service user.	£1,057
Psychodynamic psychotherapy	25 individual sessions × 50 minutes each = 20.83 therapist hours per service user.	£2,155
IPT	18 individual sessions × 50 minutes each = 15 therapist hours per service user.	£1,563
Supportive therapy	14 individual sessions × 1 hour each = 14 therapist hours per service user.	£1,462

Continued

169

Table 18: (*Continued*)

Intervention	Resource use details	Total cost per person; includes a GP visit*
Mindfulness training	Eight group sessions × 2.5 hours each plus an all-day retreat (7.5 hours), two therapists and 12 participants per group = 4.58 therapist hours per service user.	£508
CBT group	15 group sessions × 2 hours each, two therapists and six participants per group = 10 therapist hours per service user.	£1,057
CBT individual	16 sessions × 1 hour each = 16 therapist hours per service user.	£1,665
CBT (Heimberg), group	12 sessions × 2.5 hours, two therapists and six participants per group = 10 therapist hours per service user.	£1,057
CBT (Heimberg), individual	16 individual sessions × 1 hour each, with the exception of the first in-session exposure session, which lasts 1.5 hours = 16.5 therapist hours per service user.	£1,715
CT (Clark and Wells), standard	14 individual sessions × 90 minutes each = 21 therapist hours per service user.	£2,172
CT (Clark and Wells), shortened sessions	14 individual sessions × 75 minutes each = 17.5 therapist hours per service user.	£1,817
Waitlist	No related resource use.	£0

Note. All interventions assumed to be delivered by Band 7 clinical psychologists. Total cost includes a GP visit for referral to psychological services. Clinical psychologist unit costs from Curtis (2010); GP unit costs from Curtis (2012).

Health and social care costs as well as social security benefits were assumed to be the same across all arms of the economic model during the period of initial (12-week) treatment and therefore were excluded from further consideration.

All costs were expressed in 2012 prices, uplifted, where necessary, using the Hospital and Community Health Services Pay and Prices Index (Curtis, 2012). Costs and QALYs were discounted at an annual rate of 3.5%, according to NICE guidance (NICE, 2009b).

Table 19 reports the values of all input parameters utilised in the economic model and provides information on the distributions assigned to specific parameters in probabilistic analysis, as described in the next section.

Handling uncertainty

Model input parameters were synthesised in a probabilistic analysis. This means that all model input parameters were assigned probability distributions (rather than being expressed as point estimates), to reflect the uncertainty characterising the available clinical and cost data. Subsequently, 10,000 iterations were performed, each drawing random values out of the distributions fitted onto the model input parameters. Results (mean costs and QALYs for each intervention) were averaged across the 10,000 iterations. This exercise provided more accurate estimates than those derived from a deterministic analysis (which utilises the mean value of each input parameter ignoring any uncertainty around the mean), by capturing the non-linearity characterising the economic model structure (Briggs et al., 2006).

The distributions of the probability of recovery following treatment (year 1 of the model), which were obtained from the NMA, were defined directly from values recorded in each of the 10,000 respective iterations performed in WinBUGS and used in the economic analysis, as described earlier. The log-odds of recovery on waitlist was assumed to follow a normal distribution with mean -2.629 and variance 1.235. The LORs of recovery for each treatment relative to waitlist, as estimated by the WinBUGS model (described in Chapter 3), were applied to simulated values of this normal distribution and converted onto the probability scale. This ensured that the full posterior distribution of the relative treatment effects was used to estimate the absolute probabilities of recovery for each treatment.

The distribution of the probability of relapse for drugs was determined by assigning beta distributions to the pooled relapse rates reported for drug arms and placebo arms in the four relapse prevention RCTs included in the guideline systematic review. The risk ratio of relapse of drugs versus psychological interventions was assigned a log-normal distribution. Utility values were assigned beta distributions using the method of moments. The distributions of the annual probabilities of recovery and relapse in years 2–5 of the model were determined by assigning beta distributions to the 12-year respective probabilities that were used to estimate annual probabilities. The estimation of distribution ranges was based on available data in the guideline meta-analysis and the published sources of evidence.

Table 19: Input parameters utilised in the economic model of interventions for adults with social anxiety disorder

Input parameter	Mean value	Probabilistic distribution	Source of data – comments
Annual probability of recovery, all interventions – year 1	See Table 15	Distribution based on NMA	Guideline NMA; distribution formed by 10,000 iterations.
Annual probability of recovery, all interventions – years 2 to 5	0.0377	Beta distribution on 12-year probability: $\alpha = 65$; $\beta = 111$	Bruce et al., 2005.
Annual probability of relapse, drugs – year 1	0.4169	Midpoint between two beta distributions: $\alpha = 107$; $\beta = 293$ $\alpha = 222$; $\beta = 170$	Midpoint between pooled relapse rate from drug arms and pooled relapse rate from placebo arms of four relapse prevention RCTs included in the guideline systematic review
Risk ratio of relapse, drugs versus psychological interventions – year 1	3.00	Log-normal distribution 95% CIs = 0.73 to 12.39	Liebowitz et al., 1999.
Annual probability of relapse, all interventions – years 2 to 5	0.0409	Beta distribution on 12-year probability: $\alpha = 26$; $\beta = 40$	Bruce et al., 2005.
Utilities Recovery (no social anxiety) Non-recovery, relapse (social anxiety)	0.866 0.659	Beta distribution $\alpha = 4572$; $\beta = 707$ $\alpha = 40$; $\beta = 20$	Estimated using method of moments, based on data reported in (Saarni et al., 2007).

Intervention resource use and costs			
Drug acquisition costs and healthcare professional unit costs	See Table 17 and Table 18	No distribution assigned	Curtis, 2012; NHS Business Services Authority Prescription Pricing Division, 2013.
Number of GP visits assigned to pharmacological interventions			Number of visits based on GDG expert opinion; estimated probabilities based on completion rates reported in large pharmacological intervention RCTs included in the NMA (more than 100 participants in each trial) and further assumptions. If number of GP visits in initial treatment equalled 1 or 2, no maintenance treatment followed. If number of GP visits in initial treatment equalled 1, only 50% of the 12-week drug acquisition costs were incurred; if number of GP visits equalled zero in maintenance treatment, no 26-week drug acquisition costs were considered.
Initial treatment (12 weeks)	4	Different probabilities assigned to different numbers of sessions 65%: 4; 10%: 3, 5 or 6; 25%: 1 or 2	
Maintenance treatment (26 weeks)	3	55%: 3; 45%: 0 or 1 or 2 or 4	

Continued

Table 19: *(Continued)*

Input parameter	Mean value	Probabilistic distribution	Source of data – comments
Number of sessions in individual psychological interventions		Different probabilities assigned to different numbers of sessions	Number of sessions and estimated probabilities based on number of sessions and completion rates reported in respective RCTs included in the NMA and further assumptions.
Psychodynamic psychotherapy	25	70%: 25; 15%: 21–24; 15%: 1–20	
IPT	18	70%: 18; 15%: 14–17; 15%: 1–13	
Supportive therapy	14	70%: 14; 15%: 10–13; 15%: 1–9	
CBT, individual	16	70%: 16; 15%: 12–15; 15%: 1–11	
CBT Heimberg, individual	16	70%: 16; 15%: 12–15; 15%: 1–11	
CT (Clark and Wells), standard	14	80%: 14; 20%: 10–13	
CT (Clark and Wells), shortened sessions	14	70%: 14; 15%: 10–13; 15%: 1–9	
Number of sessions in group psychological interventions	As in Table 18	No distribution assigned	Participants missing one or more sessions assumed not to be replaced by others; therefore changes in number of sessions do not affect total intervention cost.
Annual health and social care cost		Gamma distribution	Patel et al., 2002.
Recovery (no social anxiety)	£583	SE: 84	
Non-recovery, relapse (social anxiety)	£937	SE: 188	
Annual social security benefit		Gamma distribution	Patel et al., 2002.
Recovery (no social anxiety)	£1,221	SE: 127	
Non-recovery, relapse (social anxiety)	£2,273	SE: 437	
Annual discount rate	0.035	No distribution assigned	NICE, 2009b.

Uncertainty in intervention costs was taken into account by assigning different probabilities in the number of GP visits (pharmacological interventions) or number of sessions (individual psychological interventions) attended by adults with social anxiety disorder. These probabilities were determined by data reported in the respective RCTs included in the NMA, such as completion rates, average number of sessions attended, and so on. Regarding pharmacological interventions, the same completion rate was applied to all drugs due to lack of relevant data specific to each of the drugs considered in the model. Based on data reported in large pharmacological intervention RCTs included in the NMA (N > 100), the completion rate of the 12-week initial treatment with pharmacological interventions was estimated at 75%. It was therefore assumed that 65% of people in each drug arm of the model attended four GP visits (as described in Table 17) and 10% attended either one less or one or two more visits (which might be occasionally required for the management of side effects). The 25% of people discontinuing the 12-week drug treatment were assumed to pay one or two visits to their GP. People discontinuing treatment were assumed to incur only 50% of the 12-week drug acquisition cost; in addition, if they recovered, they were assumed not to continue with the 26-week maintenance treatment. People who recovered and were thus offered 26 weeks of maintenance treatment were assumed to attend three GP visits (as described in Table 17) at a probability of 55%. The remaining 45% were assumed to pay either fewer visits (0 to 2) or one more visit because of side effects. If the number of GP visits during maintenance treatment equalled zero, no 26-week drug acquisition costs were considered in the model.

Regarding individual psychological interventions, based on relevant reported data, the completion rate was estimated at approximately 85% for all interventions except standard CT (Clark and Wells), which reached a 100% completion rate in the respective RCTs. According to the studies, participants were broadly considered as completers if they had missed no more than four sessions in total. Using this information and the average number of sessions in each arm of a trial or in the subgroup of completers, where reported, the following assumptions were made for all individual psychological interventions with the exception of standard CT (Clark and Wells): 70% of people in each individual psychological intervention arm of the model attended the optimal number of sessions (as described in Table 18); another 15% of people completed treatment but attended one to four fewer sessions; the remaining 15% of people in each cohort discontinued treatment and attended randomly a lower number of sessions (missed five or more sessions and at minimum attended only one session of the intervention).

The cost of group psychological intervention was deemed to be stable and not subject to uncertainty, irrespective of compliance with treatment; this is because participants in a group are not replaced by another person when they occasionally miss one or more sessions or discontinue treatment. Therefore the same resources (in terms of healthcare professional time) are consumed and the full cost of treatment is incurred whether people attend the full course or fewer group sessions. Drug acquisition costs are also not subject to uncertainty. Consequently intervention costs of group psychological interventions and drug acquisition costs were not assigned probabilistic distributions. Extra health and social care costs for people not recovering or relapsing following recovery, as well as social security benefit costs, were assigned a gamma distribution, determined by data reported in the source study.

Table 19 provides details on the types of distributions assigned to each input parameter and the methods employed to define their range.

Extra probabilistic sensitivity analyses were also undertaken to explore the impact on the results of the following alternative scenarios:

● Adoption of a wider perspective which, in addition to NHS and PSS costs, considered receipt of social security benefits by people with social anxiety disorder, as reported in Patel and colleagues (2002).

● A change in the healthcare professional unit cost for self-help and group-based interventions: this scenario assumed delivery of self-help interventions by a Band 5 therapist (for example, a mental health nurse) and delivery of group interventions by one Band 7 and one Band 6 therapist (the latter reflecting the salary of a trainee in clinical psychology). The unit cost of a Band 5 mental health nurse was taken from *Unit Costs of Health and Social Care 2012* (Curtis, 2012). The unit cost of a Band 6 trainee therapist was not available and was therefore assumed to be in the middle between the unit cost of a Band 5 mental health nurse and a Band 7 clinical psychologist.

● Use of utility data from Alonso and colleagues (2004) instead of Saarni and colleagues (2007).

Presentation of the results

Results of the economic analysis are presented as follows:

For each intervention, mean total costs and QALYs are presented, averaged across 10,000 iterations of the model. An incremental analysis is provided, where all options have been ranked from the most to the least effective (in terms of QALYs gained). Options that are dominated by absolute dominance (that is, they are less effective and more costly than one or more other options) or by extended dominance (that is, they are less effective and more costly than a linear combination of two alternative options) are excluded from further analysis. Subsequently, ICERs are calculated for all pairs of consecutive options remaining in the analysis.

ICERs are calculated by the following formula:

$$ICER = \Delta C / \Delta E$$

where ΔC is the difference in total costs between two interventions and ΔE the difference in their effectiveness (QALYs). ICERs express the extra cost per extra unit of benefit (QALY in this analysis) associated with one treatment option relative to its comparator. The treatment option with the highest ICER below the NICE lower cost-effectiveness threshold of £20,000 per QALY (NICE, 2008) is the most cost-effective option.

In addition to ICERs, the mean net monetary benefit (NMB) of each intervention is presented. This is defined by the following formula:

$$NMB = E \cdot \lambda - C$$

where E is the effectiveness (number of QALYs) and C the costs associated with the treatment option, and λ is the level of the willingness-to-pay per unit of effectiveness, set at the NICE lower cost-effectiveness threshold of £20,000 per QALY (NICE, 2008). The intervention with the highest NMB is the most cost-effective option (Fenwick et al., 2001). Moreover, for the most cost-effective intervention, the probability that it is the most cost-effective option is also provided, calculated as the proportion of iterations (out of the 10,000 iterations run) in which the intervention had the highest NMB among all interventions considered in the analysis.

Economic modelling results

The results of the economic analysis for the time horizon of 5 years post-treatment are provided in Table 20. This table provides mean QALYs and mean total costs for each intervention assessed in the economic analysis, as well as the results of incremental analysis, the NMB of each intervention, and its ranking by cost effectiveness (with higher NMBs indicating higher cost effectiveness). Interventions have been ordered from the most to the least effective in terms of number of QALYs gained.

At 5 years post-treatment, standard CT (Clark and Wells) is the most effective intervention because it produces the highest number of QALYs. This result was not unexpected, given that the intervention had the highest probability of recovery among all interventions in the NMA. At the same time, it is the second most costly intervention, following psychodynamic psychotherapy. According to the NMBs provided in Table 20, standard CT (Clark and Wells) produces the highest NMB and therefore appears to be the most cost-effective intervention. Its ICER versus phenelzine (which is the next most effective intervention not dominated by absolute or extended dominance in incremental analysis) equals £8,426 per QALY, which is below the NICE lower cost-effectiveness threshold of £20,000 per QALY. The probability of standard CT (Clark and Wells) being the most cost-effective intervention is 69%, which reflects the proportion of the 10,000 iterations of the economic model in which it had the highest NMB among all interventions. According to the analysis, the second most cost-effective option at 5 years post-treatment is individual CBT. Phenelzine ranks third in terms of cost effectiveness, while book-based self-help without support ranks fourth. Individual CBT (Heimberg) ranks fifth and book-based self-help with support ranks sixth. Of the other individual psychological interventions, CT with shortened sessions ranks ninth, psychodynamic psychotherapy ranks 25th, and IPT ranks 26th, just above waitlist; supportive therapy is the least cost-effective intervention, ranking in 28th place. Group psychological interventions rank in places between 10 and 15, with the exception of mindfulness training, which ranks 23rd. Drugs (with the exception of phenelzine) rank between places 8 and 22, with paroxetine being the most cost-effective drug after phenelzine, followed by venlafaxine, fluvoxamine, sertraline, fluoxetine and escitalopram. Internet-based self-help ranks seventh (with support) and 20th (without support).

Figure 8 provides the cost effectiveness plane of the analysis, 5 years post-treatment. Each intervention is placed on the plane according to its incremental costs and QALYs compared with waitlist (which is placed at the origin).

Table 20: Results of economic modelling, 5 years post-treatment – base-case analysis: NHS and PSS perspective

Intervention	Mean QALYs	Mean total costs (£)	Incremental analysis and ICERs (£/QALY)	Mean NMB per person (£)	Ranking by highest NMB
	Per 1000 people				
CT (Clark and Wells), standard	3,747	5,737,076	8,426	69,194	1
CBT, individual	3,635	5,306,288	Dominated by extended dominance	67,392	2
CBT (Heimberg), individual	3,585	5,447,708	Dominated	66,246	5
Phenelzine	3,571	4,260,025	1,396	67,165	3
CT, shortened sessions	3,568	5,540,834	Dominated	65,821	9
Self-help (internet) with support	3,540	4,870,068	Dominated	65,932	7
CBT group	3,534	5,059,169	Dominated	65,625	10
Self-help (book) with support	3,533	4,425,363	Dominated	66,243	6
Self-help (book) without support	3,530	4,202,609		66,400	4
Exposure	3,528	5,070,369	Dominated	65,480	14
CBT (Heimberg), group	3,520	5,082,853	Dominated	65,319	15
Paroxetine	3,507	4,249,441	Dominated	65,893	8
Venlafaxine	3,499	4,411,964	Dominated	65,571	11
Fluvoxamine	3,494	4,346,825	Dominated	65,540	12

Sertraline	3,490	4,270,481	Dominated	65,524	13
Self-help (internet) without support	3,484	4,738,438	Dominated	64,939	20
Escitalopram	3,481	4,381,574	Dominated	65,243	17
Fluoxetine	3,478	4,283,637	Dominated	65,285	16
Psychodynamic psychotherapy	3,474	6,045,290	Dominated	63,432	25
Citalopram	3,473	4,290,401	Dominated	65,175	18
Mirtazapine	3,467	4,301,367	Dominated	65,046	19
Moclobemide	3,451	4,417,847	Dominated	64,603	21
Pregabalin	3,449	4,587,005	Dominated	64,402	22
IPT	3,432	5,567,309	Dominated	63,074	26
Mindfulness training	3,424	4,699,069	Dominated	63,776	23
Placebo	3,401	4,396,547	Dominated	63,631	24
Supportive therapy	3,400	5,516,623	Dominated	62,480	28
Waitlist	3,366	4,289,254	Dominated	63,038	27

Figure 8: Cost-effectiveness plane of all interventions for adults with social anxiety disorder assessed in the economic analysis plotted against waitlist – incremental costs and QALYs per 1000 adults with social anxiety disorder, 5 years after treatment

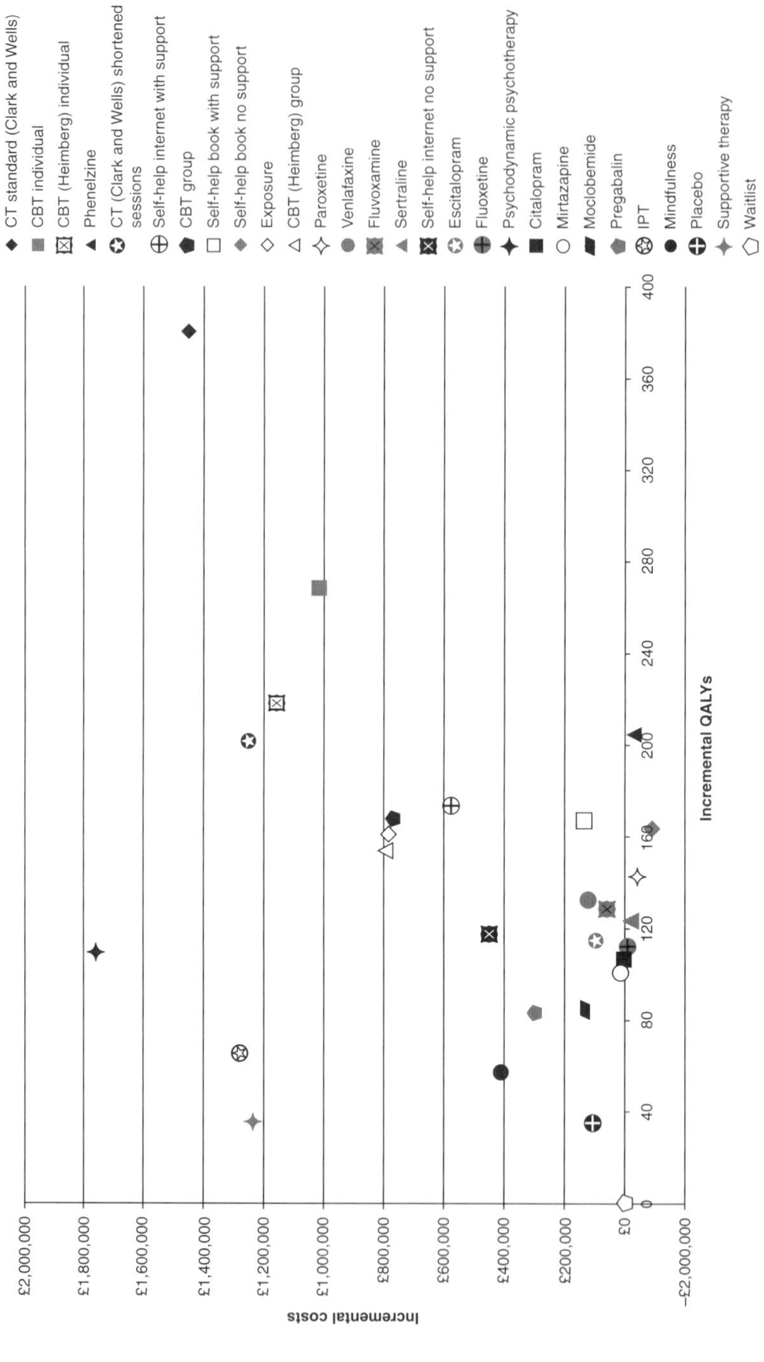

Detailed results of the base-case economic analysis, with 95% CIs of costs and QALYs and disaggregation of costs are provided in Appendix 23.

Regarding 1 year post-treatment, phenelzine was the most cost-effective intervention among those considered in the analysis because it produced the highest NMB. Its ICER to paroxetine, which was the next most effective non-dominated intervention in incremental analysis, was £4,063 per QALY, while the ICER of standard CT (Clark and Wells) versus phenelzine exceeded £47,000 per QALY, which is well above the NICE cost-effectiveness threshold of £20,000 per QALY. The probability of phenelzine being the most cost-effective intervention at 1 year post-treatment was 55%. The second most cost-effective option at 1 year post-treatment was paroxetine, followed by book-based self-help (without support) and sertraline. Overall, results indicated that in the short term, drugs seemed to be more cost effective than psychological interventions for adults with social anxiety disorder: drugs ranked in the first 13 places, with the exception of places 3 (book-based self-help without support) and 11 (book-based self-help with support). The various forms of individual CBT, including CT (Clark and Wells), seemed to follow drugs and book-based self-help in terms of cost effectiveness. Group psychological interventions, internet-based self-help and other individual psychological interventions were less cost effective compared with drugs, book-based self-help, and individual forms of CBT. Results for 1 year post-treatment, including mean QALYs and costs with 95% CIs, disaggregation of costs, incremental analysis, NMBs, ranking of interventions by cost effectiveness and the cost-effectiveness plan are presented in Appendix 23.

Results were robust under all alternative scenarios examined in sensitivity analyses. Standard CT (Clark and Wells) was the most cost-effective intervention at 5 years post-treatment when a wider perspective that included social security benefits was adopted, alternative unit costs for self-help and group psychological interventions were assumed, and alternative utility values were used. Ranking of interventions in terms of cost effectiveness was broadly the same after using a wider perspective, and alternative unit costs and utility values. Results of secondary and sensitivity analyses can be found in Appendix 23. The economic evidence profile of the guideline economic analysis is provided in Appendix 24.

Discussion – limitations of the analysis
The guideline economic analysis assessed the cost effectiveness of a broad range of pharmacological and psychological interventions for adults with social anxiety disorder over 5 years post-treatment. In addition, 1-year post-treatment results were obtained and compared with the 5-year post-treatment results. This is because the GDG was interested in the potential changes in the relative cost effectiveness of interventions over time. The results of the analysis suggest that, although in the short-term pharmacological interventions appear to be, overall, more cost effective than psychological interventions, at 5 years post-treatment the relative cost effectiveness of individual forms of CBT improves significantly, so that standard CT (Clark and Wells), individual CBT, individual CBT (Heimberg) and CT (Clark and Wells) with shortened sessions rank first, second, fifth and ninth, respectively, in terms of cost effectiveness. The probability of standard CT (Clark and Wells) being the most

cost-effective intervention at 5 years is 69%. Phenelzine is the third most cost-effective intervention. Book-based self-help also appears to be cost effective compared with other treatment options, with the two forms of it (with and without support) being among the six most cost-effective interventions of those assessed. Group-based psychological interventions do not appear to be particularly cost effective relative to other available treatments, ranking in places between 10 and 15, with the exception of mindfulness training, which ranks 23rd. Drugs (with the exception of phenelzine) are also not particularly cost effective, ranking between places 8 and 22; following phenelzine, the next most cost-effective drugs are (in order): paroxetine, venlafaxine, fluvoxamine, sertraline, fluoxetine and escitalopram. Internet-based self-help ranks seventh (with support) and 20th (without support). Other individual psychological interventions, such as psychodynamic psychotherapy, IPT and supportive therapy rank 25th, 26th and 28th, respectively.

The emergence of individual psychological interventions in the form of CBT as cost-effective options at 5 years can be attributed to two factors: first, over the 5-year time horizon there is a longer time period to accrue the benefits resulting from the differential relapse rate between psychological and pharmacological interventions, which was applied in the first year of the economic model. Based on the model input parameters, the proportion of people who relapse following post-treatment recovery is substantially lower if they receive a psychological, rather a pharmacological, intervention, and at 5 years post-treatment the benefit of being free from social anxiety has been enjoyed over a longer time period. Second, over a 5-year time horizon the high intervention costs of individual psychological interventions (which are responsible for the relatively low performance of these interventions in terms of cost effectiveness at 1 year post-treatment) are spread over a longer time period and are offset to a greater extent by NHS and PSS cost savings because there are fewer people relapsing and incurring such extra costs.

Results of the economic analysis were overall robust to different scenarios explored through sensitivity analysis. Results were practically unaffected when a wider perspective incorporating social security benefits was adopted, and when self-help and group psychological interventions were assumed to be delivered by less trained therapists. Moreover, using alternative utility data that assumed more conservative utility gains following recovery did not change the overall conclusions.

The clinical effectiveness data utilised in the model were derived from the NMA undertaken for this guideline. This methodology enabled evidence synthesis from both direct and indirect comparisons between interventions, and allowed simultaneous inference on all treatments examined in pairwise trial comparisons while respecting randomisation (Caldwell et al., 2005; Lu & Ades, 2004). The NMA utilised continuous data to estimate the relative treatment effects of interventions, and then transformed the estimated SMDs into probabilities of recovery, using waitlist as baseline, as discussed in Chapter 3. This was necessary in order to populate the economic model, as no comprehensive recovery data were available for the range of interventions assessed in the economic analysis. Moreover, the economic analysis needed to reflect the same relative treatment effects that were estimated in the NMA, which determined the comparative clinical efficacy of the interventions considered in this guideline. Transformation of SMDs into probabilities of recovery is valid as long as the relative treatment effect estimated using continuous data is equal to the treatment effect estimated using recovery data. Such an assumption cannot be checked for all interventions included in the economic analysis (since no recovery data are available for a large number of interventions); however, a comparison between continuous and recovery data indicated a strong relationship between them and therefore this transformation is unlikely to have introduced strong bias in the analysis (more details are provided in Chapter 3).

The assumptions and any limitations of the NMA model, as well as the limitations of individual studies considered in the NMA, have unavoidably impacted on the quality of the economic model clinical input parameters. For example, many of the included studies were not registered and both the clinical and economic results may be vulnerable to reporting and publication bias. The assumptions underlying the NMA model have been described in detail in Chapter 3; the characteristics and any limitations of the individual studies and the NMA model have been described in Section 6.5.2.

Treatment discontinuation because of side effects or other reasons was not considered in the model structure because no relevant data were systematically reported in the trials considered in the guideline systematic literature review. However, the probabilistic model did assume that a percentage of people might have not completed treatment or there might have been less than perfect compliance. In addition, most clinical efficacy data were analysed on an intention-to-treat basis and implicitly accounted for discontinuation.

One limitation of the model is the relapse data used to populate the model. Relapse data for pharmacological interventions are very sparse in the literature. Ideally, the economic model required drug-specific data on the probability of relapse after 6 months of maintenance treatment for adults with social anxiety disorder who have recovered following initial 12-week drug treatment. However, no such data were identified in the literature. Because of the lack of relevant relapse data specific to each drug considered in the analysis, the probability of relapse for all pharmacological interventions was assumed to be the same, and was estimated as the midpoint of the pooled relapse rates reported for drug and placebo arms in the relapse prevention RCTs included in the guideline systematic review. These rates referred to relapse *during* pharmacological maintenance treatment and relapse after discontinuation of initial (12-week) pharmacological treatment *without* maintenance, respectively. Moreover, relapse prevention studies measured relapse following response to treatment rather than recovery, which was the modelled outcome in the economic analysis. It is possible that the probability of relapse following recovery is lower than that following response to treatment and therefore the economic analysis may have potentially overestimated relapse following treatment. Furthermore, in reality, different drugs are likely to be associated with different risks for relapse, and this possibility has not been reflected in the economic model due to lack of drug-specific relapse data in the literature.

The RR of relapse of pharmacological versus psychological interventions was adopted from a small observational study (N = 28) that evaluated the effects of maintenance treatment with phenelzine and group CBT (Liebowitz et al., 1999), due to lack of other relevant data. Subsequently, as with pharmacological interventions, all psychological interventions were assumed to have the same risk of relapse due to lack of intervention-specific data, but, as in the case of drugs, this assumption may not hold. Nevertheless, the mean probabilities of relapse for pharmacological and psychological interventions estimated for the economic model (42% versus 14%, respectively) are very close to respective relapse rates reported for people with OCD (45% versus 12%, respectively) (Simpson & Fallon, 2000) and broadly consistent with respective figures reported for panic disorder (40% versus 5%, respectively) (Clark et al., 1994).

The RR of relapse of pharmacological versus psychological interventions was applied to the first year of the model only. For years 2 to 5 the model conservatively assumed that the same probability of relapse applied to all interventions, both psychological and pharmacological. This assumption may have favoured drugs, if the beneficial effect of psychological interventions relative to drugs in terms of reduced relapse rates, as indicated by Liebowitz and colleagues (1999), persists beyond 1 year.

Utility data used in the economic model were taken from a study that analysed survey data on people who had experienced social anxiety disorder (or other mental disorders) and people without a mental disorder over the 12 months prior to the survey interview. A limitation of these data is that the diagnosis of social anxiety disorder referred to a period of 12 months prior to the survey, so some participants might have experienced an improvement in their condition over this period, and might have actually recovered at the point of interview. Therefore, it is not certain that the HRQoL of this mixed group of people accurately reflects the HRQoL of the study population in the model (that is, people with a current diagnosis of social anxiety disorder). Moreover, the HRQoL of people without a mental disorder over the last 12 months may be higher than the HRQoL of people recovering from social anxiety disorder. However, after reviewing relevant literature, the GDG decided that these utility data were most appropriate to use in the economic model, because compared with other available utility data, they were judged to reflect more closely the HRQoL of adults with social anxiety disorder and those recovering following treatment, and also met the NICE criteria for the selection of utility data for cost-utility analysis.

Owing to the lack of comprehensive overall and specific side effect rates across all interventions, (dis)utility data due to side effects associated with drug treatment, and costs of treating these side effects, the model did not consider these parameters. Nevertheless, probabilistic analysis did take into account that a small proportion of people receiving pharmacological interventions may attend a higher number of GP visits for the management of side effects. In any case, omission of side effects from the model structure may have potentially led to overestimation of the cost effectiveness of drugs relative to psychological interventions, and may have had an impact on the relative cost effectiveness between different drugs.

Extra NHS and PSS costs incurred by people with social anxiety disorder not recovering or relapsing following recovery were taken from a study that utilised service use data from a national survey (Patel et al., 2002). The survey was conducted in

1993–1994 and is therefore outdated. However, it was not possible to identify recent data specific to UK service use of people with social anxiety disorder in the literature. The recent *Adult Psychiatric Morbidity Survey* (McManus et al., 2009b) did not report data specific to people with social anxiety disorder. More recent service use data for people with social anxiety disorder have been reported in a US study (Wang et al., 2005) and a study conducted in the Netherlands (Acarturk et al., 2008) but these refer to different healthcare settings and do not necessarily reflect UK relevant resource use. Therefore, the study by Patel and colleagues (2002) was the best source for obtaining this cost parameter for the economic model.

A secondary analysis that adopted a wider perspective incorporating social security benefits was undertaken. The relative cost effectiveness of interventions was practically unaffected by inclusion of such benefits. However, it must be noted that, because of a lack of more specific data, the model assumed that people recovering from social anxiety disorder received reduced benefits (equalling benefits received by people without a mental disorder), and then returned to receipt of higher social benefits (equalling benefits received by people with social anxiety disorder) if they relapsed. However, receipt of social benefits is a long-term process that is not necessarily directly related to events characterising the clinical course of social anxiety disorder, such as recovery or relapse, within a short period of time, such as the 5 years of the model time horizon. Thus this secondary analysis may have overestimated the reduction in social benefits received by people recovering following treatment.

Overall conclusions from the economic evidence
Existing economic evidence is very sparse in the area of interventions for adults with social anxiety disorder and is characterised by important limitations; therefore, it is difficult to draw conclusions on the cost effectiveness of interventions for adults with social anxiety disorder based on existing evidence.

The economic analysis undertaken for this guideline concluded that, although drugs appear to be, overall, more cost effective in the short-term, various forms of individual CBT such as standard CT (Clark and Wells), individual CBT and individual CBT (Heimberg) are overall more cost effective in the longer term. It is possible that the cost effectiveness of pharmacological interventions has been overestimated because the disutility associated with the presence of side effects from drugs was not taken into account in the analysis. Book-based self-help also appears to be cost effective compared with other treatment options; in contrast, group-based psychological interventions and other individual psychological interventions (such as psychodynamic psychotherapy, IPT and supportive therapy) appear to be less cost effective than individual forms of CBT, book-based self-help and pharmacological interventions. Supported internet-based self-help is a potentially cost-effective option, however it is not available in UK clinical practice yet, and the associated intervention costs used in the analysis were based on a relevant research programme currently being piloted in the UK. Once such an intervention becomes available in UK clinical practice, its cost effectiveness will need to be reassessed after taking into account relevant costs specific to the intervention (including any licence or internet hosting fees).

6.11   OVERALL CLINICAL SUMMARY

6.11.1   Pharmacological interventions

The review of clinical effects suggests that several pharmacological interventions may be efficacious in reducing symptoms of social anxiety disorder and may also improve mood, though the exclusion in some trials of participants with depression make it difficult to demonstrate this conclusively. The strongest evidence was for classes of drugs, which suggests that SSRIs, SNRIs, MAOIs and anticonvulsants may be efficacious. Main effects were large with overlapping CIs, all of which included the CIs for pill placebo; although there may be some differences in efficacy within classes, there was little evidence of this post-treatment. Among the SSRIs and SNRIs, escitalopram, fluvoxamine, fluoxetine, paroxetine, sertraline and venlafaxine were efficacious. The MAOIs phenelzine and moclobemide appear to be efficacious and there is some limited evidence for the anticonvulsants gabapentin and pregabalin. There was little evidence to support the use of other medications, including citalopram and levetiracetam. Among benzodiazepines, there was better evidence for clonazepam than for alprazolam. The health economic model identified phenelzine as the most cost-effective drug, although the GDG had concerns about the side effects (including hypotension), dietary restrictions, potential toxicity, and the quality of the data, which may have overestimated the effects; the GDG also notes that it is not licensed for social anxiety disorder. There was some evidence to support paroxetine, venlafaxine, fluvoxamine, sertraline, fluoxetine and escitalopram, if phenelzine were excluded from the analysis. The evidence reviewed also identified a number of other factors to consider in the use of those drugs thought to be efficacious, including: dietary restrictions associated with the use of MAOIs (in particular phenelzine); increased risk of blood pressure elevation and cardiac effects (for example, for venlafaxine) and hypotension (for example, for phenelzine); discontinuation symptoms with the antidepressants, particularly for paroxetine and venlafaxine; and tolerance and problems with withdrawal associated with the use of benzodiazepines.

In addition, the GDG reviewed existing NICE guidance (*Depression* [NCCMH, 2010; NICE, 2009a] and *Generalised Anxiety Disorder and Panic Disorder [With or Without Agoraphobia] in Adults* [NCCMH, 2011b; NICE, 2011c]) regarding the safe use of the drugs reviewed and the monitoring of side effects.

6.11.2   Psychological interventions

The strongest clinical evidence for large and sustained benefits supports the use of psychological interventions. This was particularly the case for CBT (individual and group), self-help (supported and unsupported), exposure and social skills, with more modest effects for short-term psychodynamic psychotherapy, IPT and mindfulness training, although for the latter two the effect was not significant.

Evidence suggests that psychological interventions also improve secondary outcomes, including depression and disability, and the benefits are sustained at follow-up.

Individual CBT had the largest clinical effect, and it was the only intervention in the NMA that was clearly superior to both waitlist and pill placebo. All manualised forms of individual CBT had very large effects; there was some evidence that the Clark and Wells model may be superior to other forms of CBT, but it should be noted that all trials were conducted by the developer. Manualised forms of group CBT also had large effects, particularly those following the Heimberg manual.

A number of interventions, including cognitive bias modification, exposure (which was efficacious as a stand-alone intervention but has been adapted into more recent and efficacious interventions) and social skills training, contained components of efficacious psychological interventions for social anxiety disorder. The GDG concluded that people with social anxiety disorder should be offered an integrated programme of treatment rather than separate components that, in the main, have not demonstrated clinical efficacy as stand-alone interventions. For example, exposure alone, although clinically efficacious, was found not to be cost effective.

The economic model identified individual standard CT (Clark and Wells) as the most cost-effective psychological intervention and the most cost-effective intervention overall, at 5 years after treatment. Over the same time horizon, individual CBT and individual CBT (Heimberg) were ranked as second and fifth most cost-effective interventions, respectively, whereas book-based self-help without and with support were ranked fourth and sixth most cost-effective interventions, respectively.

6.11.3   Interventions for fear of public speaking, sweating, and other subtypes

The evidence for the treatment of fear of public speaking (task concentration training and social skills) suggests that interventions that have been specifically developed for this fear were not effective in reducing symptoms of social anxiety disorder, but there was limited evidence for individual CBT. Psychological interventions focused specifically on blushing or sweating did not appear to be effective. In a study of inpatient settings no difference was identified between group CBT and group IPT.

The evidence does not suggest there are any benefits of botulinum toxin injections and thoracic sympathectomy on symptoms of social anxiety disorder. The GDG noted that both interventions may have a benefit for some physical symptoms in other populations (for example, people with hyperhidrosis), but there is no evidence of benefit for people with social anxiety disorder and the results of other trials are not applicable to this population.

There was no evidence to suggest that interventions that work for people with generalised social anxiety disorder would not work for people with the performance subtype or with specific primary fears.

6.11.4   Combined psychological and pharmacological interventions

Evidence for combined interventions, including for cognitive enhancers in addition to exposure, was of very low quality. No combination was tested in more than one trial, and the included trials included fewer than 200 participants having treatment. Estimated effects for some combinations were lower than the component therapies.

6.11.5   Interventions for comorbid disorders

There is only very low-quality evidence for the treatment of social anxiety disorder in trials that include only participants with a comorbid disorder including alcohol misuse (paroxetine) and ADHD (atomoxetine), which suggested no additional important benefit on symptoms of social anxiety disorder.

6.12   FROM EVIDENCE TO RECOMMENDATIONS

The GDG determined that the primary outcome was a clinically important reduction in symptoms of social anxiety disorder. The GDG would have preferred to have compared recovery (loss of diagnosis), but less than 25% of trials reported recovery and many trials reported only limited data beyond end-of-treatment scores. Symptoms at endpoint were therefore chosen as the main outcomes for use in the NMA. Effect sizes were adjusted using available recovery data and the clinical model was used to estimate recovery for a health economic model. The quality of the evidence was considered using the GRADE method for all pairwise comparisons; the quality of evidence analysed in the NMA was first examined through pairwise comparisons, then by considering quality (inconsistency, indirectness, imprecision, risk of bias and publication bias) for all interventions in the NMA. The economic model developed for this guideline assessed the cost effectiveness of pharmacological and psychological interventions over 1 and 5 years following treatment. Consideration of a 5-year time horizon was assessed as being the most important as this allowed assessment of the costs, effects and cost effectiveness of interventions in the longer term. The GDG therefore focused on the 5-year economic results in order to make recommendations on interventions for social anxiety disorder. However, long-term clinical data were limited and a number of assumptions were made in the economic analysis. Such assumptions are likely to have underestimated the long-term benefits of psychological interventions, as discussed in Section 6.7.

The clinical and economic analyses identified a number of potentially clinically and cost-effective interventions including individual CBT, CBT-based self-help, and medication including some SSRIs and MAOIs. In developing recommendations, the GDG was mindful of a number of important issues concerning the delivery of interventions for social anxiety disorder. In developing recommendations for pharmacological interventions the GDG took into account the following factors: the very limited long-term follow-up data with drugs and the attrition rates in some continuation studies, the side effects of the medication (for example, possible blood pressure changes with venlafaxine and phenelzine), discontinuation symptoms (with all SSRIs and paroxetine and venlafaxine in particular), potential drug interactions (with fluvoxamine), the small evidence base for fluoxetine relative to other drugs (N = 107), dietary restrictions with the MAOIs, the likelihood of relapse following discontinuation, and withdrawal and tolerance with the benzodiazepines. There was no evidence to support the use of beta-blockers for social anxiety disorder. In addition a number of the drugs that were identified as potentially clinically efficacious are rarely prescribed in primary care (where over 95% of prescriptions for social anxiety disorder are issued). These factors, along with a clear view from clinical and service user members of the GDG that most service users have a strong preference for psychological interventions, led the GDG to conclude that drugs should usually be a second-line treatment for social anxiety disorder. These factors, and the GDG's concerns about the relative seriousness and magnitude of risks of various side effects, also led to the development of a sequence of recommendations for the use of drugs in social anxiety disorder based on a balance of the benefits and disbenefits of treatment. SSRIs (escitalopram or sertraline) were recommended as first-line drug treatments, followed by fluvoxamine, paroxetine and venlafaxine, which although possibly as effective as the other SSRIs, were considered second-line pharmacological options because of concerns about side effects and discontinuation effects (with paroxetine and venlafaxine). The MAOIs were considered third-line pharmacological interventions because of the drug interactions, dietary restrictions and side effects.

The reviews undertaken for the *Depression* (NCCMH, 2010) and the *Generalised Anxiety Disorder and Panic Disorder (With or Without Agoraphobia) in Adults* (NCCMH, 2011b) guidelines proved a strong evidence base on which the GDG could develop, through informal consensus methods and using their expert knowledge of social anxiety disorder, recommendations concerning the safe use of the drugs recommended in this chapter. Given the level of extrapolation from evidence on other disorders, the GDG was cautious in making recommendations but decided that in order to support the effective and safe delivery of pharmacological interventions specific advice was needed for people with social anxiety disorder. The GDG developed these recommendations in light of the recommendations on the clinical and cost-effectiveness of the pharmacological interventions (see Section 6.6).

With regard to specific recommendations the GDG felt it was important to inform service users of any possible side effects and what might be done to better manage them. The GDG was particularly concerned that the increased agitation sometimes seen with the use of SSRIs might present particular problems for people with social anxiety disorder if they were not informed of these risks before taking the drug. Although suicide risk is not as high in social anxiety disorder as in depression, because of the uncertainty about the risk of increased suicidality particularly in younger people the GDG felt it was important to draw prescribers' attention to these risks and ensure that adequate follow-up and monitoring is provided. Additional recommendations were also developed concerning pharmacological and dietary restrictions with the MAOIs, the management of short-term side effects and the requirement to gently taper most medication when stopping it.

The clinical and cost-effectiveness analyses established that individual CT (Clark and Wells model) was the most efficacious intervention but the GDG noted that the class effect for individual CBT was also very large and the different forms were largely overlapping in their likely effects. Even if the Clark and Wells model is excluded from consideration, individual CBT remains the most clinically and cost-effective intervention. The GDG considered a number of factors in developing the recommendation for individual CBT including the demands of training staff to deliver the intervention, the number and variety of trials (other than the model developers) supporting a model and the feasibility for use in the UK healthcare system. In light of this, the GDG decided to recommend two models of individual CBT, both of which are well-established: the Clark and Wells (Clark & Wells, 1995) and Heimberg (Hope et al., 2006) models. To guide practitioners in delivering these interventions, the GDG referred to the manuals used in clinical trials and extracted the key components of each therapy. The GDG was aware, however, that not all participants responded to individual CBT and wished to offer alternative psychological interventions (as is the case for the pharmacological interventions). The GDG did consider suggesting group CBT, but it is less efficacious than individual CBT and the economic model demonstrated that group CBT is also less cost effective than individual CBT. For people who do not want individual CBT, the GDG felt that a group form of the same treatment was not likely to be an acceptable option.

The GDG therefore decided to recommend two other psychological interventions as second-line psychological treatments. For people who do not want individual CBT, the GDG decided to recommend CBT-based supported self-help because the effects were greater than for unsupported self-help. Supported self-help offers a different mode of delivery from individual CBT and there was some evidence to suggest that it might be taken up by some people who would refuse an offer of face-to-face interventions (individual or group). In addition, self-help was identified as a cost-effective psychological intervention in the economic analysis. However, in making this recommendation the GDG was clear that supported self-help was not considered to be a 'low-intensity intervention' that could be offered to people with a milder form of social anxiety disorder or as a 'stepped treatment' to be offered before individual CBT. The GDG was also concerned to offer alternative treatments to individual CBT and CBT-based self-help because, in their expert opinion, people who wanted psychological treatment and had refused or not benefitted from individual CBT would be unlikely to take up or benefit from either group CBT or interventions such as social skills, exposure or cognitive bias modification, which share similar components to some CBT treatments. In developing a recommendation for alternative psychological treatments, the GDG wished to recommend treatments that had evidence of effect compared with waitlist and were established and used in the UK healthcare system. Using these criteria the GDG chose to recommend short-term psychodynamic psychotherapy specifically developed to treat social anxiety disorder (for which the evidence is weaker than for individual CBT and self-help), but with the important qualifier that before this intervention is considered the service user has to have been offered and declined CBT, supported self-help and pharmacological interventions. In this context, the GDG noted that although short-term psychodynamic psychotherapy has demonstrated effects compared with waitlist, the NMA suggests it is no more effective than psychological placebo.

The evidence for combination treatment was limited and of poor quality. However, the GDG, drawing on their expert opinion, did consider that the addition of an SSRI might facilitate the treatment of people receiving CBT who had not fully responded after a course of CBT, had made some progress and wished to continue with CBT.

The GDG was also concerned to limit the use of treatments for which it considered there to be insufficient evidence to support their use (that is, mindfulness training and supportive therapy), or where there was very limited evidence of benefit when the potential harms were considered (that is, TCAs, antipsychotics, anticonvulsants, beta-blockers and St John's wort). The GDG was also of the view that benzodiazepines had no role in the routine treatment of social anxiety disorder.

The use of physical interventions for perceived symptoms (for example, thoracic sympathectomy and botulinum toxin) are not recommended in the treatment of social anxiety disorder as there was no evidence of any benefits, and they may be associated with serious physical side effects and could contribute to a worsening of symptoms. Members of the GDG were keen to develop a 'do not use' recommendation because of their clinical experience of a number of people actively seeking these interventions as treatments for their social anxiety disorder and a concern that treatment for physical problems could reinforce maladaptive beliefs and worsen symptoms.

The evidence for particular subgroups (that is, people with a fear of public speaking, sweating or blushing) suggested that interventions designed specifically for these fears are not effective. The available evidence supports the use of standard treatments for all forms of social anxiety disorder, so the GDG decided to make no specific recommendations about these subtypes. Similarly, no specific treatments for comorbid disorders were identified that would lead to a modification of existing NICE guidance.

6.13   RECOMMENDATIONS

6.13.1   Treatment principles

6.13.1.1   All interventions for adults with social anxiety disorder should be delivered by competent practitioners. Psychological interventions should be based on the relevant treatment manual(s), which should guide the structure and duration of the intervention. Practitioners should consider using competence frameworks developed from the relevant treatment manual(s) and for all interventions should:

- receive regular, high-quality outcome-informed supervision
- use routine sessional outcome measures (for example, the SPIN or LSAS) and ensure that the person with social anxiety is involved in reviewing the efficacy of the treatment
- engage in monitoring and evaluation of treatment adherence and practitioner competence – for example, by using video and audio tapes, and external audit and scrutiny if appropriate.

6.13.1.2   For people (including young people) with social anxiety disorder who misuse substances, be aware that alcohol or drug misuse is often an attempt to reduce anxiety in social situations and should not preclude treatment for social anxiety disorder. Assess the nature of the substance misuse to determine if it is primarily a consequence of social anxiety disorder and:

- offer a brief intervention for hazardous alcohol or drug misuse (see *Alcohol-Use Disorders* [NICE clinical guideline 115][18] or *Drug Misuse* [NICE clinical guideline 51][19])
- for harmful or dependent alcohol or drug misuse consider referral to a specialist alcohol or drug misuse service[20].

6.13.2 Initial treatment options for adults with social anxiety disorder

6.13.2.1 Offer adults with social anxiety disorder individual cognitive behavioural therapy (CBT) that has been specifically developed to treat social anxiety disorder (based on the Clark and Wells model or the Heimberg model; see recommendations 6.13.4.1 and 6.13.4.2).

6.13.2.2 Do not routinely offer group CBT in preference to individual CBT. Although there is evidence that group CBT is more effective than most other interventions, it is less clinically and cost effective than individual CBT.

6.13.2.3 For adults who decline CBT and wish to consider another psychological intervention, offer CBT-based supported self-help (see recommendation 6.13.4.3).

6.13.2.4 For adults who decline cognitive behavioural interventions and express a preference for a pharmacological intervention, discuss their reasons for declining cognitive behavioural interventions and address any concerns.

6.13.2.5 If the person wishes to proceed with a pharmacological intervention, offer a selective serotonin reuptake inhibitor (SSRI) (escitalopram or sertraline). Monitor the person carefully for adverse reactions (see recommendations 6.13.5.1–6.13.5.7).

6.13.2.6 For adults who decline cognitive behavioural and pharmacological interventions, consider short-term psychodynamic psychotherapy that has been specifically developed to treat social anxiety disorder (see recommendation 6.13.4.4). Be aware of the more limited clinical effectiveness and lower cost effectiveness of this intervention compared with CBT, self-help and pharmacological interventions.

6.13.3 Options for adults with no or a partial response to initial treatment

6.13.3.1 For adults whose symptoms of social anxiety disorder have only partially responded to individual CBT after an adequate course of treatment,

---

[18]NICE (2011).

[19]NICE (2007).

[20]This recommendation also appears in Chapter 7 regarding interventions for children and young people.

consider a pharmacological intervention (see recommendation 6.13.2.5) in combination with individual CBT.

6.13.3.2 For adults whose symptoms have only partially responded to an SSRI (escitalopram or sertraline) after 10 to 12 weeks of treatment, offer individual CBT in addition to the SSRI.

6.13.3.3 For adults whose symptoms have not responded to an SSRI (escitalopram or sertraline) or who cannot tolerate the side effects, offer an alternative SSRI (fluvoxamine[21] or paroxetine) or a serotonin noradrenaline reuptake inhibitor (SNRI) (venlafaxine), taking into account:
- the tendency of paroxetine and venlafaxine to produce a discontinuation syndrome (which may be reduced by extended-release preparations).
- the risk of suicide and likelihood of toxicity in overdose.

6.13.3.4 For adults whose symptoms have not responded to an alternative SSRI or an SNRI, offer a monoamine oxidase inhibitor (phenelzine[22] or moclobemide).

6.13.3.5 Discuss the option of individual CBT with adults whose symptoms have not responded to pharmacological interventions.

6.13.4 Delivering psychological interventions for adults

6.13.4.1 Individual CBT (the Clark and Wells model) for social anxiety disorder should consist of up to 14 sessions of 90 minutes' duration over approximately 4 months and include the following:
- education about social anxiety
- experiential exercises to demonstrate the adverse effects of self-focused attention and safety-seeking behaviours
- video feedback to correct distorted negative self-imagery
- systematic training in externally focused attention
- within-session behavioural experiments to test negative beliefs with linked homework assignments
- discrimination training or rescripting to deal with problematic memories of social trauma
- examination and modification of core beliefs
- modification of problematic pre- and post-event processing
- relapse prevention.

---

[21]At the time of publication, fluvoxamine did not have a UK marketing authorisation for use in adults with social anxiety disorder. The prescriber should follow relevant professional guidance, taking full responsibility for the decision. Informed consent should be obtained and documented. See the General Medical Council's *Good Practice in Prescribing and Managing Medicines and Devices* (2013) for further information.

[22]At the time of publication, phenelzine did not have a UK marketing authorisation for use in adults with social anxiety disorder. The prescriber should follow relevant professional guidance, taking full responsibility for the decision. Informed consent should be obtained and documented. See the General Medical Council's *Good Practice in Prescribing and Managing Medicines and Devices* (2013) for further information.

6.13.4.2 Individual CBT (the Heimberg model) for social anxiety disorder should consist of 15 sessions of 60 minutes' duration, and one session of 90 minutes for exposure, over approximately 4 months, and include the following:

- education about social anxiety
- cognitive restructuring
- graduated exposure to feared social situations, both within treatment sessions and as homework
- examination and modification of core beliefs
- relapse prevention.

6.13.4.3 Supported self-help for social anxiety disorder should consist of:

- typically up to nine sessions of supported use of a CBT-based self-help book over 3–4 months
- support to use the materials, either face to face or by telephone, for a total of 3 hours over the course of the treatment.

6.13.4.4 Short-term psychodynamic psychotherapy for social anxiety disorder should consist of typically up to 25–30 sessions of 50 minutes' duration over 6–8 months and include the following:

- education about social anxiety disorder
- establishing a secure positive therapeutic alliance to modify insecure attachments
- a focus on a core conflictual relationship theme associated with social anxiety symptoms
- a focus on shame
- encouraging exposure to feared social situations outside therapy sessions
- support to establish a self-affirming inner dialogue
- help to improve social skills.

6.13.5 Prescribing and monitoring pharmacological interventions in adults

6.13.5.1 Before prescribing a pharmacological intervention for social anxiety disorder, discuss the treatment options and any concerns the person has about taking medication. Explain fully the reasons for prescribing and provide written and verbal information on:

- the likely benefits of different drugs
- the different propensities of each drug for side effects, discontinuation syndromes and drug interactions
- the risk of early activation symptoms with SSRIs and SNRIs, such as increased anxiety, agitation, jitteriness and problems sleeping
- the gradual development, over 2 weeks or more, of the full anxiolytic effect
- the importance of taking medication as prescribed, reporting side effects and discussing any concerns about stopping medication with the prescriber, and the need to continue treatment after remission to avoid relapse.

6.13.5.2 Arrange to see people aged 30 years and older who are not assessed to be at risk of suicide within 1 to 2 weeks of first prescribing SSRIs or SNRIs to:
- discuss any possible side effects and potential interaction with symptoms of social anxiety disorder (for example, increased restlessness or agitation)
- advise and support them to engage in graduated exposure to feared or avoided social situations.

6.13.5.3 After the initial meeting (see recommendation 6.13.5.2), arrange to see the person every 2–4 weeks during the first 3 months of treatment and every month thereafter. Continue to support them to engage in graduated exposure to feared or avoided social situations.

6.13.5.4 For people aged under 30 years who are offered an SSRI or SNRI:
- warn them that these drugs are associated with an increased risk of suicidal thinking and self-harm in a minority of people under 30 **and**
- see them within 1 week of first prescribing **and**
- monitor the risk of suicidal thinking and self-harm weekly for the first month[23].

6.13.5.5 Arrange to see people who are assessed to be at risk of suicide weekly until there is no indication of increased suicide risk, then every 2–4 weeks during the first 3 months of treatment and every month thereafter. Continue to support them to engage in graduated exposure to feared or avoided social situations.

6.13.5.6 Advise people taking a monoamine oxidase inhibitor of the dietary and pharmacological restrictions concerning the use of these drugs as set out in the *British National Formulary* (2013)[24].

6.13.5.7 For people who develop side effects soon after starting a pharmacological intervention, provide information and consider one of the following strategies:
- monitoring the person's symptoms closely (if the side effects are mild and acceptable to the person)
- reducing the dose of the drug
- stopping the drug and offering either an alternative drug or individual CBT, according to the person's preference[25].

6.13.5.8 If the person's symptoms of social anxiety disorder have responded well to a pharmacological intervention in the first 3 months, continue it for at least a further 6 months.

6.13.5.9 When stopping a pharmacological intervention, reduce the dose of the drug gradually. If symptoms reappear after the dose is lowered or the drug is

---

[23]This recommendation is adapted from *Generalised Anxiety Disorder and Panic Disorder (With or Without Agoraphobia) in Adults* (NICE clinical guideline 113; NICE, 2011b).
[24]Joint Formulary Committee, 2013.
[25]This recommendation is adapted from *Generalised Anxiety Disorder and Panic Disorder (With or Without Agoraphobia) in Adults* (NICE clinical guideline 113; NICE, 2011b).

stopped, consider increasing the dose, reintroducing the drug or offering individual CBT.

6.13.6 Interventions that are not recommended to treat social anxiety disorder

6.13.6.1 Do not routinely offer anticonvulsants, tricyclic antidepressants, benzo-diazepines or antipsychotic medication to treat social anxiety disorder in adults.

6.13.6.2 Do not routinely offer mindfulness-based interventions[26] or supportive therapy to treat social anxiety disorder.

6.13.6.3 Do not offer St John's wort or other over-the-counter medications and preparations for anxiety to treat social anxiety disorder. Explain the potential interactions with other prescribed and over-the-counter medications and the lack of evidence to support their safe use.

6.13.6.4 Do not offer botulinum toxin to treat hyperhidrosis (excessive sweating) in people with social anxiety disorder. This is because there is no good-quality evidence showing benefit from botulinum toxin in the treatment of social anxiety disorder and it may be harmful.

6.13.6.5 Do not offer endoscopic thoracic sympathectomy to treat hyperhidrosis or facial blushing in people with social anxiety disorder. This is because there is no good-quality evidence showing benefit from endoscopic thoracic sympathectomy in the treatment of social anxiety disorder and it may be harmful.

6.13.7 Research recommendations

6.13.7.1 What is the clinical and cost effectiveness of combined psychological and pharmacological interventions compared with either intervention alone in the treatment of adults with social anxiety disorder? (See Appendix 9 for further details.)

6.13.7.2 What is the clinical and cost effectiveness of additional psychological and pharmacological interventions in the treatment of adults with social anxiety disorder who have not recovered when treated with individual CBT?

---

[26]This includes mindfulness-based stress reduction and mindfulness-based cognitive therapy.

7 INTERVENTIONS FOR CHILDREN AND YOUNG PEOPLE

7.1 INTRODUCTION

In Chapter 5 the problems of case identification were discussed and the significant under-recognition of social anxiety disorder in children and young people was noted. This is a cause of considerable concern as social anxiety disorder usually starts in late childhood or early adolescence. As a consequence of under-recognition many children and young people with social anxiety disorder often only access treatment years after the onset of symptoms and a referral for early help from child and adolescent mental health services (CAMHS) is relatively rare. In addition, social anxiety disorder may evade identification in children and young people known to specialist CAMHS, its presence being overshadowed by more noticeable comorbid problems. Although effective interventions, in particular psychological interventions, have been identified for the treatment of social anxiety disorder, access to such interventions even for those in the care of CAMHS has been limited. In 2011 the English Department of Health launched an IAPT programme for children and young people[26], which has some similarities to the IAPT adult programme (see Chapter 6) but is focused more on the transformation of the existing services rather than the training of a new cadre of psychological therapists. The initial focus of the child IAPT programme is on CBT interventions for depression and anxiety disorders and social learning-based programmes for parent training.

7.1.1 Pharmacological interventions

Pharmacological interventions to manage social anxiety disorder are used infrequently in CAMHS. In part this is because children and young people with social anxiety disorder are rarely treated in CAMHS (see Chapter 2) and because, as with all other anxiety disorders in children and young people, psychological interventions are accepted as first-line treatment for social anxiety disorder. However, if medication is used then it is usually with SSRIs, which are increasingly being prescribed in the management of other anxiety disorders, after non-response to psychological interventions, particularly where there is comorbid depression. All such prescribing is in the context of the MHRA statement[27] regarding the balance of risks and benefits

---

[26]http://www.iapt.nhs.uk/cyp-iapt

[27]http://www.mhra.gov.uk/Safetyinformation/Generalsafetyinformationandadvice/Product-specificinformationandadvice/Product-specificinformationandadvice-M-T/Selectiveserotoninre-uptakeinhibitors/Patientsummary/index.htm

of using SSRIs in the treatment of depression in children and young people and caution in the prescribing of SSRIs is now widespread, particularly among GPs. Some potential prescribers are deterred by the concerns about the possible effects of SSRIs on the developing brain, some worry that suicidality and impulsivity may be precipitated in those without a previous history of this problem, while others are rather less concerned believing that the risk of precipitating self-harm is reduced if there is no comorbid depression, although the precise mechanism for the increase in suicidality with SSRIs in children and young people is not understood.

Children and young people with social anxiety disorder together with their parents and psychiatrist might decide against the option of an SSRI after reviewing their potential side effects, some of which might be particularly troublesome for people with social anxiety disorder. With respect to licensing considerations, while some SSRIs are licensed in those under 18 years of age (fluvoxamine for the treatment of OCD in children and young people aged over 8 years and sertraline for the treatment of OCD in children and young people aged over 6 years), none of the SSRIs are licensed for the treatment of social anxiety disorder for under 18s. Other SSRIs (for example, paroxetine) are not licensed for use in children in either the UK or USA for any conditions and do not feature in the BNF for children (Paediatric Formulary Committee, 2012–2013) as an unlicensed option.

Beta-adrenoceptor blocking drugs are sometimes considered as an option by psychiatrists in CAMHS and by GPs. In young people, these drugs could be seen as a safer option than SSRIs (once asthma has been excluded), although as can be seen in Chapter 6 the evidence in adults for their efficacy is limited. As in other anxiety disorders in children and young people, the doses of beta-blockers prescribed rarely have a significant impact on the impressive attempts of the body to protect itself in a situation of perceived threat. For this reason the results of beta-blocker use in social anxiety disorder are often disappointing, but nevertheless they continue to be tried periodically especially when a young person's preference is for a pharmacological option to help alleviate or fractionally reduce their symptoms.

Benzodiazepines are not used and, while the BNF for children (Paediatric Formulary Committee, 2012–2013) does indicate that antipsychotics have a possible place in the short term for 'severe anxiety', they do not feature in the current management of social anxiety disorder in CAMHS. Other agents described in Chapter 6 do not have evidence specifically targeted to children and young people.

7.1.2   Psychological interventions

A range of psychological interventions can be offered in CAMHs including CBT, systemic therapy (including family interventions), parenting interventions, counselling and psychodynamic therapy. The past 30 years have seen significant shifts in the provision of psychological interventions with the nature of the therapy moving away from psychodynamic to systemic approaches, to some extent, and more recently to cognitive behavioural interventions. There has been relatively little formal evaluation of these interventions until recent times but the last 20 years have seen a large expansion in RCT-based evidence particularly in the area of conduct disorder and oppositional defiant disorder.

To date various forms of CBT (individual, group or parent-delivered) are the only psychological interventions that have been evaluated within RCTs including children and young people with social anxiety disorder. Because of the high level of comorbidity between different anxiety disorders in children and young people, those with a principal primary social anxiety disorder have most commonly been included among groups of children and young people with other principal diagnoses (such as generalised anxiety disorder and separation anxiety disorder) in programmes that take a general cognitive behavioural approach to the treatment of anxiety disorders. In these programmes children and young people will be assisted in applying general cognitive and behavioural principles to the area that causes them greatest concern or impairment. Typically these studies have not included a sufficient number of participants to compare outcomes for children and young people with different principal anxiety diagnoses. Overall, they find that CBT is efficacious for anxiety disorders in children, but the evidence, reviewed by Cochrane (James et al., 2013), is insufficient to compare it with other therapies. Moreover, recent reports have suggested that children and young people with social anxiety disorder may have poorer outcomes (Hudson et al., 2010) or may not demonstrate equivalent gains beyond the end of treatment (Kerns et al., 2012) from these general interventions, compared with children and young people with other anxiety disorders.

Although there is variability in the particular procedures used in different manualised treatments for children and young people, the content of these interventions are broadly similar to adult CBT programmes, with most programmes (both for general anxiety and specifically for social anxiety disorder) involving exposure *in vivo* and cognitive restructuring. However, many of the programmes that have been developed specifically for children and young people with social anxiety disorder include social skills.

One other key factor that also distinguishes some programmes developed for children and young people from adult-oriented programmes is the involvement of parents to support treatment. The extent and manner of parental involvement varies across different treatments programmes. In some treatments parents are not included at all, at the other end of the scale treatment is delivered entirely via parents. The most common ways in which parents are involved in treatment are as follows:

● Parent-education (for example, Beidel and colleagues [2000; 2007]): the parent is provided with information about the nature of social anxiety disorder and the focus of the programme in which their child is participating.

● Parent-support (for example, March and colleagues [2009], Spence and colleagues [2000; 2011]): the parent attends sessions in parallel with the sessions for the child or young person. The sessions aim to teach parents to model, encourage and prompt the use of new skills, and manage socially anxious behaviour and avoidance, using instruction, discussion, modelling and role play.

- Parent-led CBT (for example, Cartwright-Hatton and colleagues [2011], Lyneham and colleagues [2013], Rapee and colleagues [2006], Thirlwall and colleagues [2012]): this approach has been evaluated with pre-adolescents, either in a parent-group format or as a low-intensity treatment in which the parent is supported in working through a 'self-help' book. The child does not attend the treatment sessions at all, but the parent is taught skills for helping their child manage anxious thoughts and alter avoidant behaviour, given the opportunity to rehearse with a therapist and to problem solve difficulties that arise.
- Therapeutic input for parents in their own right, for example, parent anxiety management (for example, Hudson and colleagues [2013]).

7.2   CLINICAL REVIEW PROTOCOL

A systematic review to identify RCTs of interventions for children and young people with social anxiety disorder was conducted. The review protocol, including the review questions, information about the databases searched, and the eligibility criteria used for this section of the guideline, is presented in Table 21. The first systematic evaluation of a programme to specifically target social anxiety disorder in children and young people was only published as recently as 2000 (Spence et al., 2000). This review therefore considers outcomes for children and young people with social anxiety disorder from both treatments aimed specifically at social anxiety disorder and generic anxiety treatments. From studies randomising people with social anxiety disorder and other mental disorders, only data for children and young people with social anxiety disorder, which were requested from authors when it was not available in published reports, were included in the analysis in this guideline. Only measures of social anxiety or subscales relating to social anxiety were analysed. Parts of these questions were addressed in Cochrane reviews, but the searches were up to 8 years old and all needed to be updated. Further details are included Appendix 6 (the complete search strategy and PRISMA[28] chart), Appendix 16 (study characteristics), Appendix 17 (forest plots) and Appendix 19 (GRADE profiles). In the sections that follow, the number of participants reported is the number receiving treatment included in the analysis. Studies that were excluded from the analysis and reasons for exclusion are included in Appendix 25.

7.2.1   Extrapolation

The GDG took the view that with limited primary data of good quality (for example, RCTs) for children and young people with social anxiety disorder, it might be necessary to extrapolate from other populations.

For psychological interventions, the decision was made to extrapolate from the data for adult interventions for social anxiety disorder to mature adolescents.

---

[28]Preferred Reporting Items for Systematic Reviews and Meta-Analyses.

Table 21: Clinical review protocol for the interventions for children and young people

Component	Description
Review question(s) (RQs)	RQ3.2: For children and young people with social anxiety disorder, what are the relative benefits and harms of psychological and pharmacological interventions?
Objectives	To estimate the efficacy and cost effectiveness of interventions to treat social anxiety disorder.
Population	Children and young people (aged 5 to 18 years) with social anxiety disorder or APD. If some, but not all, of a study's participants are eligible for review, disaggregated data will be requested from the study authors. Where data from child and young person populations were not sufficient, the GDG decided that extrapolating from an adult population was valid.
Intervention	Any psychological intervention, for example: • acceptance and commitment therapy) • attention training • counselling • CBT (individual, group) • cognitive bias modification • exposure • hypnosis • IPT • mindfulness training • psychodynamic psychotherapy • relaxation (for example, progressive muscle relaxation) • self-help (with and without support; CBT and other modalities) • social skills training • support groups • supportive therapy. Additional psychological interventions specifically for children and young people. Any licensed pharmacological intervention, for example: • benzodiazepines • beta-blockers • MAOIs, reversible MAOIs • SNRIs • SSRIs • tricyclic antidepressants • other antidepressants.

Continued

Table 21: (*Continued*)

Component	Description
	Combined psychological and pharmacological treatment. Cognitive enhancers (for example, D-cycloserine). Surgical interventions (for example, for blushing). Botulinum toxin injections (for example, for sweating).
Comparator	• Waitlist. • Placebo. • Other interventions.
Outcomes	• Recovery (no longer met criteria for diagnosis). • Self-rated symptoms of social anxiety disorder. • Parent-rated symptoms of social anxiety disorder.
Dosage	• For pharmacological interventions, all interventions within the BNF recommended range will be included. • For psychological interventions, all credible interventions will be included; single session treatments will be excluded.
Time points	The main analysis will include outcomes at the end of treatment. Additional analyses will be conducted for further follow-up data.
Electronic databases	Core databases: Embase, MEDLINE, PreMEDLINE, PsycINFO Topic specific databases: AEI, AMED, ASSIA, BEI, CDSR, CENTRAL, CINAHL, DARE, ERIC, HTA, IBSS, Sociological Abstracts, SSA, SSCI. Grey literature databases: HMIC, PsycBOOKS, PsycEXTRA.
Date searched	Quantitative systematic reviews: 1997 onwards. RCTs: inception of databases onwards.
Study design	RCTs and cluster RCTs with a parallel group design. Quasi-RCTs, such as trials in which allocation is determined by alternation or date of birth, will be excluded.
Review strategy	**Data management:** For each study: • year of study

Continued

Table 21: *(Continued)*

Component	Description
	• setting • total number of study participants in each group • age (mean) • gender (percent female) • inclusion and exclusion criteria • comorbidities • risk of bias. For each intervention or comparison group of interest: • dose • duration • frequency • co-interventions (if any). For each outcome of interest: • time points (1) collected and (2) reported • missing data (exclusion of participants, attrition). For cross-over trials, data from the first period only will be extracted and analysed.
	Data synthesis: Psychological and pharmacological interventions for children and young people will be assessed in pairwise analyses using random effects models. All stakeholders, authors of all included studies, and manufacturers of included drugs will be contacted to request unpublished studies. Unpublished research may be included.
	No restriction by date.

Extrapolation was performed on the basis that the extrapolated population shared common characteristics with the primary population (for example, some young people who have the cognitive and emotional capacity are able to describe their thoughts and feelings much like adults), where the harms were similar for the extrapolated dataset as for the primary dataset, and where the outcomes were comparable across trials. Extrapolated data were recognised as lower-quality evidence than data from studies on children and young people with social anxiety disorder.

7.3   OVERVIEW OF CLINICAL EVIDENCE

The search identified 23 RCTs that included children and young people with social anxiety disorder, including trials of interventions for all anxiety disorders that provided disaggregated data; four were unpublished and 19 were published in peer-reviewed journals between 1994 and 2012. Of these, 22 RCTs were included in at least one analysis; the remaining trial (BAER2005 [Baer & Garland, 2005]) merged groups for analysis and it was not possible to analyse the results of the trial (see Table 22 for a summary).

Meta-analyses were conducted for classes of interventions. For all classes, subgroup analyses were conducted to explore differences between members of the class (for example, different drugs or variations of a therapy). For each comparison, recovery (clinician-rated) and symptoms of anxiety were analysed. Symptom ratings by the child or young person and the parent were analysed separately. Analyses of secondary outcomes were not conducted to reduce the risk of spurious findings as the review includes many comparisons and very few studies.

The study characteristics can be found in Appendix 16, forest plots in Appendix 17 and GRADE evidence profiles in Appendix 19.

7.3.1   Study characteristics

Trials included between 15 and 322 participants at baseline (median 73), but many of these participants were not eligible for this review; that is, authors of several published studies that included children and young people with mixed anxiety disorders provided data for the subgroup of children with social anxiety disorder. Included trials randomised approximately 2,467 participants but only 1,194 are included in this review. Most of this difference results from the exclusion of participants who did not have social anxiety disorder and therefore were not eligible for inclusion rather than because of missing data.

Participants were on average (median of means) 11 years old, ranging from 4 to 21 years old. Approximately 77% were white. About half of the included participants were female (55%). Some participants were taking medication at baseline in two trials (HERBERT2009, RAPEE2006), and it was unclear in 11 studies if any participants were taking medication at baseline.

7.3.2   Risk of bias

All included trials were assessed for risk of bias (see Figure 9 and Appendix 20). Thirteen were at low risk for sequence generation and 11 of these were at low risk of bias for allocation concealment. Allocation concealment was unclear in ten trials, and one trial was at high risk of bias. Trials of psychological therapies were considered at high risk of bias for participant and provider blinding *per se*; three trials were at low risk of bias for blinding participants and providers, although the rate of side effects may make it difficult to maintain blinding in pharmacological trials. Most reported outcomes were self-rated, but assessor blinding was considered separately for all trials, and all were at low risk of bias (no assessor rated outcomes or assessors blind). For incomplete outcome data, 18 trials were at low risk of bias and four trials were at high risk of bias (for example, those that reported per protocol or completer analyses and those with very large amounts of missing data).

Table 22: Summary of results at post-treatment

Comparison	Clinician-rated recovery	Self-rated symptoms of social anxiety	Parent-rated symptoms of social anxiety	Study ID(s) and reference(s)
Pharmacological interventions: SSRI or SNRI				
versus placebo	RR = 0.85 [0.78, 0.92]	SMD = −0.53 [−0.69, −0.36]	–	BEIDEL2007 (Beidel et al., 2007; De Los Reyes et al., 2010; Scharfstein et al., 2011; Young et al., 2006); DINEEN-WAGNER2004ab (Dineen-Wagner, 2004); MARCH2007 (Albano et al., 2004; Greenhill, 1999; March et al., 2007)
versus CBT	RR = 0.59 [0.44, 0.79]	SMD = 0.15 [−0.27, 0.58]	–	BEIDEL2007 (Beidel et al., 2007; De Los Reyes et al., 2010; Scharfstein et al., 2011; Young et al., 2006)
versus placebo (for selective mutism)	–	–	SMD = −0.74 [−1.81, 0.32]	BLACK1994 (Black & Uhde, 1994)
Psychological interventions: CBT				
CBT (individual and group) versus waitlist	RR = 0.65 [0.50, 0.85]	SMD = −1.20 [−1.97, −0.43]	SMD = −0.29 [−0.96, 0.38]	GALLAGHER2004 (Gallagher et al., 2004); LAU2010 (Lau et al., 2010); LYNEHAM2012 (Lyneham et al., 2013; unpublished data from author); MELFSEN2011 (Melfsen et al., 2011); RAPEE2006 (Rapee et al., 2006; unpublished data from author); SPENCE2000 (Spence et al., 2000); SPENCE2011 (Spence et al., 2011)

Continued

Table 22: *(Continued)*

Comparison	Clinician-rated recovery	Self-rated symptoms of social anxiety	Parent-rated symptoms of social anxiety	Study ID(s) and reference(s)
CBT (individual and group) versus psychological placebo	RR = 0.72 [0.51, 1.02]	SMD = −0.56 [−1.16, 0.04]	SMD = 0.19 [−0.18, 0.56]	BEIDEL2000 (Beidel et al., 2000); HERBERT2009 (Herbert et al., 2009); HUDSON2009 (Hudson et al., 2009; unpublished data from author); MASIA-WARNER2007 (Masia-Warner, 2005; Masia-Warner et al., 2007)
CBT versus pill placebo	RR = 0.51 [0.39, 0.66]	SMD = −0.22 [−0.66, 0.21]	–	BEIDEL2007 (Beidel et al., 2007; De Los Reyes et al., 2010; Scharfstein et al., 2011; Young et al., 2006)
CBT versus CBT + parent anxiety management	RR = 1.31 [0.41, 4.20]	SMD = 0.19 [−0.48, 0.87]	SMD = −0.13 [−0.81, 0.56]	HUDSON2012 (Hudson et al., 2013)
Group CBT versus group CBT + individual CBT (six sessions)	RR = 1.20 [0.76, 1.90]	SMD = 0.18 [−0.46, 0.82]	–	OLIVARES2008 (Olivares-Olivares et al., 2008)
Group CBT versus group CBT + individual CBT (12 sessions)	RR = 1.37 [0.82, 2.29]	SMD = 0.50 [−0.16, 1.16]	–	OLIVARES2008 (Olivares-Olivares et al., 2008)

Other comparisons

CBT delivered via parents versus waitlist	RR = 0.82 [0.64, 1.06]	SMD = −0.15 [−1.03, 0.73]	SMD = −0.38 [−0.96, 0.19]	CARTWRIGHT-HATTON2012 (Cartwright-Hatton et al., 2011; unpublished data from author); LYNEHAM2012 (Lyneham et al., 2013; unpublished data from author); RAPEE2006 (Rapee et al., 2006; unpublished data from author); THIRLWALL 2012 (Thirlwall et al., 2012; unpublished data from author)
Individual CBT versus supported internet self-help	-	SMD = 0.13 [−0.64, 0.90]	SMD = 0.21 [−0.57, 1.00]	SPENCE2011 (Spence et al., 2011)
Group CBT versus CBT delivered via parents	-	SMD = −0.26 [−1.32, 0.79]	SMD = 0.20 [−0.85, 1.25]	LYNEHAM2012 (Lyneham et al., 2013)
Self-help versus waitlist	RR = 0.85 [0.62, 1.15]	SMD = −0.47 [−1.71, 0.78]	SMD = −0.33 [−0.94, 0.27]	MARCH2009 (March et al., 2009); SPENCE2011 (Spence et al., 2011); TILLFORS2011 (Tillfors et al., 2011)

Figure 9: Risk of bias summary

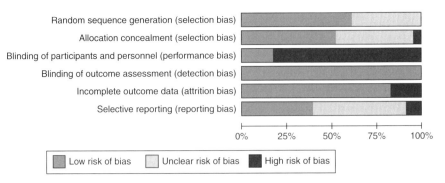

Selective outcome reporting and publication bias

Several methods were employed to minimise risk of selective outcome reporting and publication bias. All authors were contacted to request trial registrations and unpublished outcomes, and all authors of included studies, all stakeholders, and all pharmaceutical manufacturers were asked to provide unpublished trials. Nonetheless, most of the included studies were not registered. Only eight were at low risk of selective outcome reporting bias; 12 were unclear and one at high risk of bias.

7.4 PHARMACOLOGICAL INTERVENTIONS

7.4.1 Selective serotonin reuptake inhibitors (SSRIs) and serotonin and noradrenaline reuptake inhibitors (SNRIs)

Compared with placebo

Three studies compared an antidepressant with placebo in children with primary social anxiety disorder. One study (DINEEN-WAGNER2004) compared paroxetine (165 participants) with placebo; children (8 to 11 years; DINEEN-WAGNER2004a) received 29 mg daily and young people (12 to 17 years; DINEEN-WAGNER2004b) received 36 mg daily for 16 weeks. One study (MARCH2007) compared venlafaxine (137 participants) with placebo; children and young people (8 to 17 years) received 142 mg of venlafaxine daily for 16 weeks. One study (BEIDEL2007) compared fluoxetine (43 participants) with placebo; children and young people (7 to 17 years) received 30 mg daily for 12 weeks. The mean age of participants in the included studies was 12 to 14 years.

In two studies (BEIDEL2007, DINEEN-WAGNER2004) there was a small effect on clinician-rated recovery at post-treatment (RR = 0.85, 95% CI = 0.78 to 0.92) with no significant heterogeneity between drugs ($I^2 = 0\%$, $Chi^2 = 0.00$, p = 0.96). In three studies (BEIDEL2007, DINEEN-WAGNER2004b, MARCH2007), there was a medium effect on self-rated symptoms of social anxiety disorder at post-treatment (SMD = −0.53, 95% CI = −0.69 to −0.36) with no heterogeneity between drugs ($I^2 = 0\%$, $Chi^2 = 1.41$, p = 0.50). No controlled effects at follow-up were reported.

DINEEN-WAGNER2004 reported withdrawal from the study because of side effects with paroxetine, for which there was a difference between groups with very wide CIs (RR = 3.09, 95% CI = 0.19 to 50.43). Consistent with results for paroxetine in children and young people with depression (NCCMH, 2005), a GlaxoSmithKline investigation ([Redacted], 15 May 2003, unpublished) identified four 'suicide-related' events in the paroxetine group and none in the placebo group.

Compared with CBT
One of the SSRI studies also compared fluoxetine with CBT (BEIDEL2007). At post-treatment, there was a medium effect on recovery favouring CBT (RR = 0.59, 95% CI = 0.44 to 0.79), but the effect was not statistically significant for self-rated symptoms of social anxiety disorder (SMD = 0.15, 95% CI = −0.27 to 0.58).

Compared with placebo for selective mutism
One study (BLACK1994) compared fluoxetine with placebo for children (6 to 12 years) with selective mutism, which may be a specific form of social anxiety disorder. Six participants received 21 mg daily for 12 weeks. At post-treatment, there was a moderate effect on parent-rated symptoms of social anxiety (SMD = −0.74, 95% CI = −1.81 to 0.32).

7.5 PSYCHOLOGICAL INTERVENTIONS

7.5.1 Cognitive behavioural therapy

Compared with waitlist
Eight studies compared CBT with waitlist. These included: individual CBT as a specific treatment for social anxiety disorder (MELFSEN2011); individual CBT as a generic anxiety treatment (SPENCE2011); group CBT specifically for social anxiety disorder (GALLAGHER2004, SANCHEZ-GARCIA2009, SPENCE2000); and group CBT for mixed anxiety disorders (LAU2010, LYNEHAM2012, RAPEE2006). For studies of children and young people with multiple diagnoses, data for those with primary social anxiety disorder were included in the main analysis. A sensitivity analysis included participants with social anxiety disorder as either their primary or secondary diagnosis, thus adding social anxiety outcomes for participants whose social anxiety disorder was not their main problem (see Appendix 17). Treatment lasted 3 to 20 weeks and the group treatments had a mean of six to eight participants. The mean age of participants ranged from 9 to 14 years, and variation in participant age within studies was as great as the variation between them.

All studies reported clinician-rated recovery at post-treatment, and there was a medium effect (RR = 0.65, 95% CI = 0.50 to 0.85) with substantial heterogeneity between studies (I^2 = 67%, Chi^2 = 21.13, p = 0.004). The subgroups (specific [RR = 0.48, 95% CI = 0.31 to 0.77] and general CBT [RR = 0.65, 95% CI = 0.50 to 0.85]) were different (I^2 = 80.2%, Chi^2 = 5.04, p = 0.02), but each subgroup contained only four studies with no more than 40 events recorded (see Figure 10). No study reported controlled effects for clinician-rated recovery at follow-up.

In six studies (all but LAU2010 and SANCHEZ-GARCIA2009), there was a large effect on self-rated symptoms of social anxiety disorder at post-treatment (SMD = −1.20, 95% CI = −1.97 to −0.43), with considerable heterogeneity between studies (I^2 = 84%, Chi^2 = 44.38, p = 0.00001) but not between specific and general subgroups (I^2 = 0%, Chi^2 = 0.24, p = 0.62). One study of group CBT specifically for social anxiety disorder (SANCHEZ-GARCIA2009) reported a large effect on self-rated symptoms at follow-up (SMD = −3.08, 95% CI = −3.75 to −2.41).

In two studies (LYNEHAM2012, SPENCE2011), there was a small effect for parent-rated symptoms at post-treatment that was not statistically significant (SMD = −0.29, 95% CI = −0.96 to 0.38) with no heterogeneity. Controlled effects for parent-rated symptoms were not reported at follow-up.

Figure 10: Recovery for CBT compared with waitlist

Study or Subgroup	CBT Events	Total	Waitlist Events	Total	Weight	Risk Ratio (Non-event) M-H, Random, 95% CI	Risk Ratio (Non-event) M-H, Random, 95% CI
3.1.1 CBT, specific							
Spence 2000	15	17	0	7	4.2%	0.15 [0.05, 0.47]	
Gallagher 2004	6	12	1	11	10.4%	0.55 [0.30, 1.00]	
Spence 2000	11	19	0	7	11.4%	0.45 [0.26, 0.78]	
Melfsen 2011	7	21	0	23	16.7%	0.67 [0.50, 0.91]	
Subtotal (95% CI)		69		48	42.7%	0.48 [0.31, 0.77]	
Total events	39		1				
Heterogeneity: Tau² = 0.13; Chi² = 7.89, df = 3 (P = 0.05); I² = 62%							
Test for overall effect: Z = 3.10 (P = 0.002)							
3.1.2 CBT, general							
Lyneham 2012	2	7	1	7	11.1%	0.83 [0.48, 1.46]	
Lau 2010	3	8	0	13	11.6%	0.63 [0.37, 1.08]	
Spence 2011	3	12	0	10	15.6%	0.77 [0.54, 1.09]	
Rapee 2006	4	27	1	16	19.1%	0.91 [0.74, 1.11]	
Subtotal (95% CI)		54		46	57.3%	0.84 [0.72, 0.99]	
Total events	12		2				
Heterogeneity: Tau² = 0.00; Chi² = 2.31, df = 3 (P = 0.51); I² = 0%							
Test for overall effect: Z = 2.09 (P = 0.04)							
Total (95% CI)		123		94	100.0%	0.65 [0.50, 0.85]	
Total events	51		3				
Heterogeneity: Tau² = 0.09; Chi² = 21.13, df = 7 (P = 0.004); I² = 67%							
Test for overall effect: Z = 3.17 (P = 0.002)							
Test for subgroup differences: Chi² = 5.04, df = 1 (P = 0.02), I² = 80.2%							

0.5 0.7 1 1.5 2
Favours CBT   Favours waitlist

Compared with psychological placebo

Four studies compared CBT with psychological placebo, and one of these had two intervention arms. These included: individual CBT as a specific treatment for social anxiety disorder (HERBERT2009); group CBT as a specific treatment for social anxiety disorder (BEIDEL2000, HERBERT2009, MASIA-WARNER2007); and group CBT for mixed anxiety disorders (HUDSON2009). For studies of children and young people with multiple diagnoses, data for those with primary social anxiety disorder were included in the main analysis. A sensitivity analysis included participants with social anxiety disorder as either their primary or secondary diagnosis (see Appendix 17). Treatment lasted 10 to 12 weeks and the group treatments had a mean of five or six participants per group. The mean age of participants in the included studies was 9 to 15 years, and variation in participant age within studies was as great as the variation between them.

Across all studies, there was a medium effect for clinician-rated recovery at post-treatment that was not statistically significant (RR = 0.72, 95% CI = 0.51 to 1.02), with considerable heterogeneity between studies ($I^2 = 79\%$, $Chi^2 = 19.47$, p = 0.0006). A test for subgroup differences was not significant ($I^2 = 0\%$, $Chi^2 = 0.73$, p = 0.39), but, again, the largest effect was for CBT designed specifically for social anxiety disorder (see Figure 11). At follow-up, there was a medium effect for recovery that was not statistically significant (RR = 0.79, 95% CI = 0.57 to 1.10), with substantial heterogeneity ($I^2 = 72\%$, $Chi^2 = 10.86$, p = 0.01) and no significant differences between subgroups ($I^2 = 0\%$, $Chi^2 = 0.21$, p = 0.65).

Across all studies, there was a medium effect for self-rated symptoms of social anxiety at post-treatment that was not statistically significant (SMD = −0.56, 95% CI = −1.16 to 0.04), with substantial heterogeneity between studies ($I^2 = 70\%$, $Chi^2 = 13.47$,

Figure 11: Recovery for CBT compared with psychological placebo

Study or Subgroup	CBT Events	Total	Attention-matched control Events	Total	Weight	Risk Ratio (Non-event) M-H, Random, 95% CI
4.1.1 CBT, specific						
Masia-Warner 2007	10	19	0	17	17.8%	0.49 [0.31, 0.78]
Beidel 2000	20	36	1	31	20.2%	0.46 [0.32, 0.67]
Herbert 2009 (group)	3	23	2	13	22.3%	1.03 [0.78, 1.36]
Herbert 2009 (individual)	5	24	1	13	22.8%	0.86 [0.66, 1.11]
Subtotal (95% CI)		102		74	83.0%	0.68 [0.45, 1.05]
Total events	38		4			
Heterogeneity: Tau² = 0.16; Chi² = 20.01, df = 3 (P = 0.0002); I² = 85%						
Test for overall effect: Z = 1.75 (P = 0.08)						
4.1.2 CBT, general						
Hudson 2009	4	12	4	15	17.0%	0.91 [0.55, 1.50]
Subtotal (95% CI)		12		15	17.0%	0.91 [0.55, 1.50]
Total events	4		4			
Heterogeneity: Not applicable						
Test for overall effect: Z = 0.37 (P = 0.71)						
Total (95% CI)		114		89	100.0%	0.72 [0.51, 1.02]
Total events	42		8			
Heterogeneity: Tau² = 0.12; Chi² = 19.47, df = 4 (P = 0.0006); I² = 79%						
Test for overall effect: Z = 1.84 (P = 0.07)						
Test for subgroup differences: Chi² = 0.73, df = 1 (P = 0.39), I² = 0%						

Risk Ratio (Non-event) M-H, Random, 95% CI
0.5 0.7 1 1.5 2
Favours CBT   Favours Attention-matched

p = 0.009). Subgroups were not significantly different ($I^2 = 0\%$, Chi$^2 = 0.04$, p = 0.85). The effect was similar at follow-up (SMD = −0.54, 95% CI = −1.21 to 0.13), with substantial heterogeneity between studies ($I^2 = 66\%$, Chi$^2 = 8.84$, p = 0.03) and no significant subgroup differences ($I^2 = 0\%$, Chi$^2 = 0.57$, p = 0.45).

In three studies (HERBERT2009, HUDSON2009, MASIA-WARNER2007), the effect was not statistically significant for parent-rated symptoms of social anxiety at post-treatment (SMD = 0.19, 95% CI = −0.18 to 0.56) with no significant heterogeneity between studies or subgroups ($I^2 = 0\%$, Chi$^2 = 0.13$, p = 0.72). At follow-up, the effect was not statistically significant (SMD = 0.13, 95% CI = −0.82 to 1.09) with considerable heterogeneity between individual studies ($I^2 = 83\%$, Chi$^2 = 17.91$, p = 0.0005), but not between subgroups ($I^2 = 0\%$, Chi$^2 = 0.02$, p = 0.90).

Compared with pill placebo
One study (BEIDEL2007) compared CBT with pill placebo. At post-treatment, there was a moderate effect on recovery (RR = 0.51, 95% CI = 0.39 to 0.66) and a small effect for self-rated symptoms of social anxiety disorder that was not statistically significant (SMD = −0.22, 95% CI = −0.66 to 0.21). No controlled effects at follow-up were reported.

Compared with CBT plus parent anxiety management
In one study (HUDSON2012) comparing CBT versus CBT with an intervention to help parents manage their own anxiety, the effect was not statistically significant for recovery at post-treatment (RR = 1.31, 95% CI = 0.41 to 4.20) or at follow-up (RR = 1.23, 95% CI = 0.50 to 3.02). The effect was not statistically significant for self-rated symptoms of social anxiety disorder at post-treatment (SMD = 0.19, 95% CI = −0.48 to 0.87) or at follow-up (SMD = 0.58, 95% CI = −0.16 to 1.31). Similarly, the effect was not statistically significant for parent-rated symptoms of social anxiety disorder at post-treatment (SMD = −0.13, 95% CI = −0.81 to 0.56) or at follow-up (SMD = 0.23, 95% CI = −0.51 to 0.96).

Group CBT compared with group CBT plus individual CBT
One study (OLIVARES2008) compared three groups receiving: (1) group CBT with social skills training; (2) group CBT with 12 individual CBT sessions; and (3) group CBT with six individual sessions. The effect was not statistically significant for recovery at post-treatment comparing group CBT with the addition of 12 individual sessions (RR = 1.37, 95% CI = 0.82 to 2.29) or six individual sessions (RR = 1.20, 95% CI = 0.76 to 1.90). For self-rated symptoms of social anxiety disorder at post-treatment, there was a medium effect compared with the addition of 12 individual sessions that was not statistically significant (SMD = 0.50, 95% CI = −0.16 to 1.16) compared with the addition of six individual sessions (SMD = 0.18, 95% CI = −0.46 to 0.82). The same was true for self-rated symptoms at follow-up compared with the addition of 12 individual sessions (SMD = 0.55, 95% CI = −0.11 to 1.21) and compared with the addition of six individual sessions (SMD = 0.22, 95% CI = −0.42 to 0.86).

7.5.2　Cognitive behavioural therapy delivered via parents

Compared with waitlist

Three studies provided a CBT intervention that parents and carers were instructed to deliver to their children with some therapist support (CARTWRIGHT-HATTON2012, LYNEHAM2012, THIRLWALL2012); one study provided an intervention to be delivered by parents without therapist support (RAPEE2006). For studies of children with multiple diagnoses, data for children and young people with primary social anxiety disorder were included in the main analysis. A sensitivity analysis included participants with social anxiety disorder as either their primary or secondary diagnosis (see Appendix 17). Treatment lasted 10 to 16 weeks. The mean age of participants in the included studies was 7 to 10 years, and variation in participant age within studies was as great as the variation between them. For the supported interventions, parents received approximately 8 to 20 hours of therapist contact.

Across all studies, the effect was small for clinician-rated recovery at post-treatment (RR = 0.82, 95% CI = 0.64 to 1.06) with no significant heterogeneity between studies ($I^2 = 37\%$, $Chi^2 = 6.39$, p = 0.17) nor between subgroups ($I^2 = 0\%$, $Chi^2 = 0.20$, p = 0.65). The CIs increased at follow-up (RR = 0.72, 95% CI = 0.19 to 2.67) with considerable heterogeneity between studies ($I^2 = 80\%$, $Chi^2 = 5.02$, p = 0.03) and no significant difference between subgroups ($I^2 = 50\%$, $Chi^2 = 2.00$, p = 0.16).

In two studies (LYNEHAM2012, THIRLWALL2012), the effect was small for self-rated symptoms of social anxiety disorder at post-treatment, but not significant (SMD = −0.15, 95% CI = −1.03 to 0.73), with no significant heterogeneity ($I^2 = 43\%$, $Chi^2 = 3.52$, p = 0.17).

In the three studies with therapist support (CARTWRIGHT-HATTON2012, LYNEHAM2012, THIRLWALL2012), there was a small effect for parent-rated symptoms of social anxiety disorder at post-treatment that was not significant (SMD = −0.38, 95% CI = −0.96 to 0.19), with no heterogeneity ($I^2 = 0\%$, $Chi^2 = 1.64$,

Figure 12: Recovery for CBT via parents compared with waitlist

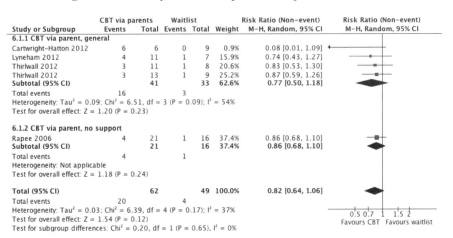

p = 0.65). Only one study reported controlled effects for parent-rated symptoms at follow-up (CARTWRIGHT-HATTON2012), and the effect was larger but not significant with wide CIs (SMD = −0.72, 95% CI = −1.80 to 0.35).

Compared with self-help
One study (LYNEHAM2012) compared a group cognitive behavioural intervention with a self-help book for parents delivered with therapist support over 16 weeks. Participants were 6 to 13 years and received approximately 20 hours of contact in the CBT group and 8 hours in the self-help group. There was a small effect between the interventions on self-rated symptoms of social anxiety disorder at post-treatment that was not statistically significant (SMD = −0.26, 95% CI = −1.32 to 0.79) and at follow-up (SMD = −0.50, 95% CI = −1.77 to 0.77). Similarly, there was a small effect on parent-rated symptoms of social anxiety disorder that was not statistically significant at post-treatment (SMD = 0.20, 95% CI = −0.85 to 1.25) and at follow-up (SMD = −0.07, 95% CI = −1.25 to 1.12).

7.5.3   Self-help and supported self-help

Two studies compared internet self-help interventions for children and young people with any anxiety disorder versus waitlist (MARCH2009, SPENCE2011). Interventions were delivered to children and young people with parental involvement. Participants in one study (MARCH2009) were aged 7 to 12 years and participants in the other were 12 to 18 years (SPENCE2011). A third study used an internet intervention aimed specifically at young people (15 to 21 years) with social anxiety disorder (TILLFORS2011). For studies of children and young people with multiple diagnoses, data for those with primary social anxiety disorder were included in the main analysis. A sensitivity analysis included participants with social anxiety disorder as either their primary or secondary diagnosis (see Appendix 17). Treatment lasted 9 to 10 weeks. Therapists spent approximately 2 hours supporting parents in one study (MARCH2009) and the amount of contact was unclear in SPENCE2011 and TILLFORS2011.

In two (MARCH2009, SPENCE2011), the effect was small and not statistically significant for clinician-rated recovery at post-treatment (RR = 0.85, 95% CI = 0.62 to 1.15), with no significant heterogeneity ($I^2 = 24\%$, Chi^2 = 1.31, p = 0.25). The studies did not report controlled effects at follow-up.

Across all three studies, there was a medium effect for self-rated symptoms of social anxiety disorder at post-treatment that was not statistically significant (SMD = −0.47, 95% CI = −1.71 to 0.78), with considerable heterogeneity between studies ($I^2 = 81\%$, Chi^2 = 10.54, p = 0.005). There was a significant difference between the generic anxiety treatments and the study using an intervention specifically designed for social anxiety disorder ($I^2 = 82\%$, Chi^2 = 5.63, p = 0.02). No controlled effects at follow-up were reported.

In two studies (MARCH2009, SPENCE2011) there was a small effect for parent-rated symptoms at post-treatment that was not statistically significant (SMD = −0.33, 95% CI = −0.94 to 0.27), with no heterogeneity (I^2 = 0%, Chi^2 = 0.00, p = 0.97).

One study compared individual CBT with an internet-delivered self-help intervention supported by a therapist (SPENCE2011) over 10 weeks. Participants were aged 12 to 18 years and received approximately 10 hours of contact in the CBT group and 2 hours in the self-help group. There was no statistical difference between the interventions on self-rated (SMD = 0.13, 95% CI = −0.64 to 0.90) or parent-rated symptoms of social anxiety disorder at post-treatment (SMD = 0.21, 95% CI = −0.57 to 1.00). No controlled effects at follow-up were reported.

7.6   CLINICAL EVIDENCE SUMMARY

7.6.1   Pharmacological interventions

A systematic search identified few studies of pharmacological interventions for children and young people with social anxiety disorder. There was some evidence of a small increase in recovery and a moderate reduction in symptoms of social anxiety disorder with two SSRIs (fluoxetine and paroxetine), but these were from a few relatively small studies; bias and publication bias may have also affected the results. The GDG referred to studies of pharmacological interventions for depression in children and young people (NCCMH, 2005), which demonstrate that pharmacological therapy (in particular the SSRIs, with the possible exception of fluoxetine) may be associated with serious adverse events, including increased suicide.

In the one trial comparing drugs (fluoxetine) and group CBT there was a suggestion that group CBT may be more effective in prompting recovery.

7.6.2   Psychological interventions

There is limited evidence that psychological interventions may be efficacious for children and young people with social anxiety disorder, but small sample sizes require caution to be exercised when coming to any conclusions about which specific interventions are most effective. Psychological interventions that include group CBT, exposure and opportunities to practice and receive feedback may have performed better than others. Group CBT specifically for social anxiety disorder may be more effective than group CBT for all anxiety disorders, but there have been no direct comparisons of outcomes following general anxiety and social anxiety-specific treatments.

For younger children, there is some evidence that CBT delivered by parents who received specific training in the intervention can reduce symptoms of social anxiety disorder and help children recover.

7.6.3   Combined interventions

There were no trials of combined psychological and pharmacological interventions for children and young people with social anxiety disorder.

7.7   HEALTH ECONOMIC EVIDENCE

7.7.1   Systematic literature review

No studies assessing the cost effectiveness of children and young people with social anxiety disorder were identified by the systematic search of the economic literature undertaken for this guideline. Details on the methods used for the systematic search of the economic literature are described in Chapter 3.

7.8   FROM EVIDENCE TO RECOMMENDATIONS

The evidence identified in the review is limited and although generally rated at low risk of bias, the size of the dataset and considerable variation in the nature of the interventions and the different populations included in the trials required caution to be exercised when generating recommendations.

The GDG considered that recovery from social anxiety disorder was the most important clinical outcome and that, for pharmacological interventions, side effects were an especially important concern in children and young people because of the potential increased risk of harm with side effects in this age group. Given the limited dataset, the absence of any licence for the use of drugs in social anxiety disorder, and potential harms, the GDG decided that drugs should not be routinely offered for the treatment of social anxiety disorder in children and young people. Drawing on the evidence for physical interventions reviewed in Chapter 6, the GDG decided also not to recommend the use of such interventions (for example, botulinum toxin) for children and young people.

Although the data for psychological interventions were also limited, there was a relatively more substantial and effective set of interventions that did not carry the same potential harms as drugs. The GDG judged that CBT (individual or group) focused on social anxiety disorder was the most promising intervention for children and young people. The GDG wished to emphasise that for younger children, the therapist should consider involving the parents or carers to help deliver the intervention effectively; some trials suggest there are positive effects when parents are offered training to facilitate this. Although the data were limited, these results were consistent with evidence for adults in that CBT was the most efficacious intervention. The GDG was also of the view that the underlying mechanisms of change were also similar. Given these factors the GDG decided that for older adolescents (this typically could include young people aged 15 years and older but would vary with developmental and emotional maturity), consideration should also be given to offering them psychological interventions recommended for adults (see Chapter 6).

As with the delivery of adult psychological interventions, the GDG was concerned that psychological interventions should be delivered properly and the outcomes effectively monitored and therefore they decided to adopt the same recommendation as was developed for adults, adjusting the outcome measures to be appropriate for children and young people. In addition, the GDG was concerned that children and young people would have less control over the home, social and educational environment and decided on the basis of their expert knowledge that those delivering interventions should take care to ensure that wider environmental concerns were taken into consideration when developing and implementing treatment plans. The GDG also judged that offering interventions for comorbid substance misuse as recommended for adults was relevant to young people.

7.9   RECOMMENDATIONS

7.9.1   Treatment principles

7.9.1.1   All interventions for children and young people with social anxiety disorder should be delivered by competent practitioners. Psychological interventions should be based on the relevant treatment manual(s), which should guide the structure and duration of the intervention. Practitioners should consider using competence frameworks developed from the relevant treatment manual(s) and for all interventions should:
● receive regular high-quality supervision
● use routine sessional outcome measures, for example:
– the LSAS – child version or the SPAI-C, and the SPIN or LSAS for young people
– the MASC, RCADS, SCAS or SCARED for children
● engage in monitoring and evaluation of treatment adherence and practitioner competence – for example, by using video and audio tapes, and external audit and scrutiny if appropriate.

7.9.1.2   Be aware of the impact of the home, school and wider social environments on the maintenance and treatment of social anxiety disorder. Maintain a focus on the child or young person's emotional, educational and social needs and work with parents, teachers, other adults and the child or young person's peers to create an environment that supports the achievement of the agreed goals of treatment.

7.9.1.3   For people (including young people) with social anxiety disorder who misuse substances, be aware that alcohol or drug misuse is often an attempt to reduce anxiety in social situations and should not preclude treatment for social anxiety disorder. Assess the nature of the substance misuse to determine if it is primarily a consequence of social anxiety disorder and:

- offer a brief intervention for hazardous alcohol or drug misuse (see *Alcohol-Use Disorders* [NICE clinical guideline 115][29] or *Drug Misuse* [NICE clinical guideline 51][30])
- for harmful or dependent alcohol or drug misuse consider referral to a specialist alcohol or drug misuse service[31].

7.9.2 Treatment for children and young people with social anxiety disorder

7.9.2.1 Offer individual or group CBT focused on social anxiety (see recommendations 7.9.3.1 and 7.9.3.2) to children and young people with social anxiety disorder. Consider involving parents or carers to ensure the effective delivery of the intervention, particularly in young children.

7.9.3 Delivering psychological interventions for children and young people

7.9.3.1 Individual CBT should consist of the following, taking into account the child or young person's cognitive and emotional maturity:
- 8 – 12 sessions of 45 minutes' duration
- psychoeducation, exposure to feared or avoided social situations, training in social skills and opportunities to rehearse skills in social situations
- psychoeducation and skills training for parents, particularly of young children, to promote and reinforce the child's exposure to feared or avoided social situations and development of skills.

7.9.3.2 Group CBT should consist of the following, taking into account the child or young person's cognitive and emotional maturity:
- 8–12 sessions of 90 minutes' duration with groups of children or young people of the same age range
- psychoeducation, exposure to feared or avoided social situations, training in social skills and opportunities to rehearse skills in social situations
- psychoeducation and skills training for parents, particularly of young children, to promote and reinforce the child's exposure to feared or avoided social situations and development of skills.

7.9.3.3 Consider psychological interventions that were developed for adults (see Section 6.13) for young people (typically aged 15 years and older) who have the cognitive and emotional capacity to undertake a treatment developed for adults.

---

[29]NICE, 2011.
[30]NICE, 2007.
[31] This recommendation also appears in Chapter 6 regarding interventions for adults.

7.9.4   **Interventions that are not recommended**

7.9.4.1   Do not routinely offer pharmacological interventions to treat social anxiety disorder in children and young people.

7.9.5   **Research recommendations**

7.9.5.1   What is the clinical and cost effectiveness of specific CBT for children and young people with social anxiety disorder compared with generic anxiety-focused CBT? (See Appendix 9 for further details.)

7.9.5.2   What is the best way of involving parents in the treatment of children and young people (at different stages of development) with social anxiety disorder? (See Appendix 9 for further details.)

7.9.5.3   What is the clinical and cost effectiveness of individual and group CBT for children and young people with social anxiety disorder? (See Appendix 9 for further details.)

8 COMPUTERISED COGNITIVE BEHAVIOURAL THERAPY FOR SPECIFIC PHOBIAS IN ADULTS

8.1 INTRODUCTION

The purpose of this chapter is to review the evidence to update the section of NICE Technology Appraisal *Computerised Cognitive Behaviour Therapy for Depression and Anxiety* (TA97; NICE, 2006), that deals with specific phobias. The *Generalised Anxiety Disorder and Panic Disorder (with or without Agoraphobia) in Adults* guideline (NICE, 2011c) updated the part of TA97 that covered panic disorder and Chapter 6 of this current guideline updates TA97 for 'social phobia'.

Specific phobias are characterised by marked and persistent fear of particular (well-defined) objects or situations. Phobic situations are avoided or endured with extreme distress, which interferes with normal functioning. Specific phobias differ from other anxiety disorders in the central role of fear response rather than anticipation (Craske et al., 2009).

Specific phobias are the most common mental disorders with a median 12-month prevalence in 27 European countries of 6.4% (Wittchen & Jacobi, 2005) and a lifetime risk of approximately 13.2% (Kessler et al., 2005a). Of people with a specific phobia, half have a fear of animals or heights (Stinson et al., 2007). Prevalence of animal phobias is 3 to 7% (Becker et al., 2007; Stinson et al., 2007), and fear of heights is the most common natural environment fear, but other environmental fears (for example, flying and enclosed spaces) are also common (Becker et al., 2007).

Specific phobias typically begin in childhood, with 50% beginning by 7 years and 75% by 12 years (Kessler et al., 2005a). Animal phobias normally begin in early childhood (Becker et al., 2007; Beesdo et al., 2009), while other phobias may begin later in life; notably, situational phobias (for example, flying) may occur in adolescence or early adulthood (Beesdo et al., 2009). They are more common in women than men (Beesdo et al., 2009; Curtis et al., 1998). Children of parents with a specific phobia are at increased risk of developing the same fear (Fyer et al., 1995). Phobias often occur with other disorders, and the other disorder is typically the focus of clinical attention. Like other anxiety disorders, comorbidity is associated with greater impairment (Magee et al., 1996). Of those with one lifetime diagnosis of specific phobia, 75.8% will have a second phobia (Curtis et al., 1998; Wittchen et al., 2007).

The aetiology of phobias has been debated for decades (Mowrer, 1947; Mowrer, 1960), but complete explanatory theories are not required for successful treatment (Marks, 1981). Different forms of exposure therapy have been used successfully for at least 40 years (Wolpe, 1968). Relaxation and other behavioural techniques may be taught as coping methods for use in stress-provoking situations, but these are probably not as beneficial as live exposure, which can be efficacious in a single prolonged session (Hellstrom & Ost, 1995; Ost et al., 2001; Ost et al., 1997). Therapist-delivered CBT is the preferred treatment for most anxiety disorders, but may not be necessary for the successful treatment of specific phobias, and access to therapists may be limited.

To increase access to care and to reduce therapists' caseload, CBT can be delivered using computers and the internet. Evidence from previous reviews of self-help for anxiety and depression is encouraging; however, reviews and meta-analyses are difficult to interpret because of inconsistent methods and conclusions, and it is not clear that results from other disorders apply to specific phobias. Lewis and colleagues provide a useful overview of the older reviews (Lewis et al., 2003), and NICE previously considered CCBT for anxiety and depression through the TA process (NICE, 2006).

TA97 found some support for CCBT in general and recommended one program, FearFighter™, for the treatment of 'phobias'. However, the appraisal did not distinguish specific phobias from other disorders, such as social anxiety disorder (previously called 'social phobia') and agoraphobia. This guideline completes the update of the TA97 and has undertaken a separate analysis of CCBT for social anxiety disorder and for specific phobias, which were grouped under a general heading of 'phobias' in TA97.

8.2   REVIEW PROTOCOL

A systematic review was undertaken using standard NCCMH procedures as described in Chapter 3 (further information about the search strategy can be found in Appendix 6). The review protocol, including the review questions, information about the databases searched, and the eligibility criteria used for this section of the guideline, is presented in Table 23. Where appropriate, meta-analysis was used to synthesise the evidence using a random effects model. For comparison, the review protocol for TA97 is also included in Table 24.

8.3   CLINICAL EVIDENCE

8.3.1   Studies considered[32]

A broad search was conducted to identify studies using a computerised intervention based on cognitive behavioural techniques for the treatment of specific phobias in

---

[32]Here and elsewhere in the guideline, each study considered for review is referred to by a study ID in capital letters (primary author and date of study publication, except where a study is in press or only submitted for publication, then a date is not used).

Table 23: Review protocol for the review of CCBT for specific phobias

Topic	CCBT for specific phobias
Review question(s) (RQs)	**RQ 4.1**: For adults with specific phobias, what are the relative benefits and harms of CCBT?
Topic group	Psychosocial interventions
Objectives	To estimate the efficacy and cost effectiveness of CCBT for specific phobias
Criteria for considering studies for the review	
• *Intervention*	CCBT
• *Comparator*	Attention control No treatment Waitlist Behavioural relaxation intervention Face-to-face CBT Exposure *in vivo*
• *Types of participants*	Adults with a specific phobia.
• *Outcomes*	• Recovery (no longer meet criteria for diagnosis) • Symptoms of specific phobia • Behavioural approach test
• *Time points*	• The main analysis will include outcomes at the end of treatment. • Additional analyses will be conducted for follow-up data.
• *Study design*	• RCTs. • Quasi-RCTs, such as trials in which allocation is determined by alternation or date of birth, will be excluded.
• *Include unpublished data?*	Unpublished research may be included, but specific searches for grey literature will not be conducted.
• *Restriction by date?*	No limit.
• *Dosage*	For psychological interventions, all credible interventions will be included; single session treatments will be excluded.
• *Minimum sample size*	No minimum
• *Study setting*	Primary, secondary, tertiary health and social care

Continued

Table 23: (*Continued*)

Topic	CCBT for specific phobias
Search strategy	**General outline**: Focused search for RCTs **Databases searched**: Core databases: Embase, MEDLINE, PreMEDLINE, PsycINFO Topic specific databases: CENTRAL, CINAHL, IBSS, Sociological Abstracts, SSA, SSCI **Date restrictions**: RCTs – 2004 onwards
Study design filter/limit used	Core databases/topic specific databases: RCT
Question specific search strategy	No
Amendments to search strategy/study design filter	None
Searching other resources	None
• *Updated*	*Depression and Anxiety – Computerised Cognitive Behavioural Therapy (CCBT) (TA97)*

Table 24: Review protocol from TA97

Inclusion criteria	
Subjects	Adults with depression or anxiety with or without depression as defined by individual studies. To include generalised anxiety, panic disorders, agoraphobia, social phobia and specific phobias and OCD.
Intervention	CBT delivered alone or as part of a package of care either via a computer interface (personal computer or internet) or over the telephone with a computer response including the following software packages: Beating the Blues, Overcoming Depression, FearFighter, Cope and BT Steps.

Continued

Table 24: (*Continued*)

Inclusion criteria	
Comparators	Current standard treatments including therapist-led CBT, non-directive counselling, primary care counselling, routine management (including drug treatment) and alternative methods of CBT delivery (such as bibliotherapy and group CBT).
Outcomes	Improvement in psychological symptoms, interpersonal and social functioning, quality of life, preference, satisfaction, acceptability of treatment, site of delivery.
Study type	Papers will be assessed according to the accepted hierarchy of evidence, whereby systematic reviews of RCTs are taken to be the most authoritative forms of evidence, with uncontrolled observational studies to be the least authoritative.
	Unpublished studies will be included. Non-RCT evidence will only be included in this review in the absence of RCT evidence.
Studies from the previous review	Studies from the previous review of the included software packages will be included if they are RCTs. Previous non-RCT evidence of the software packages will only be included in this review in the absence of RCT evidence.
Exclusion criteria	
	The following disorders did not fall within the remit of this review: • post-traumatic stress disorder • post-natal depression • manic depression • depression with psychotic symptoms • past Tourette's syndrome • schizophrenia • bipolar disorder • psychosis • psychosurgery • current comorbid major depression • serious suicidal thoughts or unstable medical conditions in the past 6 months • alcohol or substance abuse.

adults. Because exposure may be the most active ingredient in the treatment of specific phobias, interventions that were mainly behavioural were not excluded.

The search identified 13 RCTs. Of these, seven were included in at least one analysis: ANDERSSON2009 (Andersson et al., 2009), GILROY2000 (Gilroy et al., 2000), GRANADO2007 (Granado et al., 2007), HASSAN1992 (Hassan, 1992), HEADING2001 (Heading *et al.*, 2001), MÜLLER2011 (Müller et al., 2011), SMITH1997 (Smith et al., 1997). Two trials (Marks et al., 2004; Schneider et al., 2005) included in TA97 (NICE, 2006) could not be included in this review because they did not report results for people with specific phobias and the authors were unable to provide disaggregated data for people with agoraphobia, social phobia and specific phobias; one author reported that, in his view, 'group sizes had insufficient power to detect a significant improvement for the different phobia types' (Mark Kenwright, 13 March 2013). Four trials (Fraser et al., 2001; Johnston et al., 2011; Matthews et al., 2011; Tortella-Feliu et al., 2011) were excluded because they did not include an appropriate control (that is, they compared a computerised intervention with another computerised intervention rather than a non-computerised control).

Trials were published from 1992 to 2009 and included a total of 302 participants at baseline (range 25 to 45). Participants were on average (median of means) 32 years old, all white, and mostly (93%) female. All participants had a specific phobia of spiders. See for Table 25 further details about the characteristics of interventions.

8.3.2   Risk of bias

All included trials were assessed for risk of bias (see Figure 13). None were at low risk for sequence generation, and four were at high risk of bias for allocation concealment. Trials were considered at high risk of bias for participant and provider blinding *per se*, but assessor blinding was considered separately for all trials, and five were at high risk of bias. For incomplete outcome data, three trials were at high risk (for example, those that reported per protocol or completer analyses and those with very high amounts of

Figure 13: Risk of bias summary

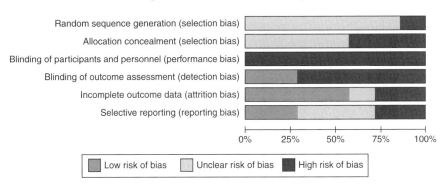

225

Table 25: Characteristics of interventions

Group (N)	Age	% Female	% White	Description	Duration	Available in the UK
ANDERSSON2009						
CCBT (15)	26	85%	N/R	Five text modules presented on web pages. Each participant had a therapist who was responsible for the whole treatment. Emails were used and an instructional videotape was sent by post.	4 weeks	No
Exposure *in vivo* (15)				One brief orientation session and a 3-hour exposure session, following Ost and colleagues' (1997) guidelines. Follow-up relapse prevention programme.	1 week	
GILROY2000						
CCBT (15)	33	100%	100%	Each participant received three 45-minute sessions of computer-aided vicarious exposure.	6 weeks	No
Exposure *in vivo* (15)				Three 45-minute sessions of therapist-delivered live exposure, which did *not* include relaxation exercises, modelling or exposure homework instructions.	6 weeks	
Relaxation (15)				Jacobson's complete deep muscle relaxation was repeated twice to fill the 45-minute treatment sessions.	6 weeks	

Continued

GRANADO2007						
CCBT (13)	31	N/R	N/R	Participants were instructed to run the presentation twice a day at home, consisting of a presentation of images that had a subset of spiders' characteristics.	4 weeks	No
Attention control (12)				The placebo group presentation mirrored the duration of the active condition but consisted of a sequence of images unrelated to spiders.	4 weeks	
HASSAN1992						
CCBT (10)	29	79%	N/A	Two 40-minute sessions per week of computer-based symbolic modelling consisting of still and motion pictures presented in a graduated sequence, showing a human approaching spiders.	Until BAT completion	No
Exposure *in vivo* (9)				Two 40-minute sessions of live graduated exposure per week.	Until BAT completion	
Exposure *in vivo* with modelling (11)				Two 40-minute sessions per week. The condition differed from the exposure *in vivo* procedure in that the participants first observed the therapist before repeating it themselves.	Until BAT completion	
Waitlist (8)				Waitlist control receiving no treatment	To match active conditions	

Table 25: *(Continued)*

Group (N)	Age	% Female	% White	Description	Duration	Available in the UK
HEADING2001						
CCBT (15)	35	95	100	Single-session computer-aided vicarious exposure. The program was reset by the therapist every 45 minutes to total 3 hours.	3 hours	No
Exposure *in vivo* (14)				Therapist-assisted live exposure designed to mirror the length of the computer-aided condition.	3 hours	
Waitlist (16)				Waitlist control receiving no treatment	3 hours	
MÜLLER2011						
CCBT (18)	23	100%	N/R	One 27-minute session of standardised exposure to nine fear-eliciting spider pictures.	27 minutes	No
Attention control (18)				Control participants exposed to nine neutral pictures over the 27-minute session.	27 minutes	

SMITH1997

						No
CCBT (15)	35	98%	N/R	One 45-minute session every 2 weeks. Relevant exposure with feedback gave subjects the choice of systematically exposing the screen figure to a variety of anxiety-evoking situations, ranging from mild to severe. The score rewards exposure behaviour.	6 weeks	
CCBT without feedback (15)				Relevant exposure with no feedback was delivered as above but the feedback score rewarded only neutral behaviours and avoidant behaviours.	6 weeks	
Attention control (15)				Exposure is irrelevant to spider phobia. The anxiety thermometer is operating and the score system rewards exposure to mirror the active conditions.	6 weeks	

Note. BAT = behavioural approach test.

missing data) and one was unclear. None of the trials were registered in advance and there is risk of publication bias.

8.3.3   Quantitative synthesis

Meta-analyses were conducted for all critical outcomes (recovery, symptoms of specific phobia, behavioural approach test [a test commonly used in the evaluation of treatments for a broad range of specific phobias]) for each comparison at each time point (see Table 26 for a summary of trial results). As in previous chapters, the number of participants below is the number in the treatment group represented in the analysis. For all analyses of symptoms, negative SMDs favour CCBT. Similarly, an RR of greater than 1 favours CCBT. For behavioural approach tests, positive values favour CCBT and are noted with a superscript (that is, SMD⁺). GRADE profiles are included in Tables 27 to 30.

Compared with waitlist
Two trials (HASSAN1992, HEADING2001) compared CCBT (23 participants) with waitlist. Neither reported recovery, but there was a large effect with wide CIs for symptoms of specific phobia at post-treatment (SMD = −1.38, 95% CI = −3.72 to 0.97) and in one trial (HEADING2001) at follow-up (SMD = −0.41, 95% CI = −1.19 to 0.37). There was a large effect with wide confidence intervals in one trial (HEADING2001) for a behavioural approach at post-treatment (SMD⁺ = 2.98, 95% CI = −2.71 to 8.66), which was not present at follow-up (SMD⁺ = 0.00, 95% CI = −0.77 to 0.77).

Compared with attention control
Three trials (GRANADO2007, MÜLLER2011, SMITH1997) compared CCBT (61 participants) with an attention control. One study (GRANADO2007) reported little difference in recovery at follow-up (RR = 1.15, 95% CI = 0.40 to 3.31). Combining all trials, there was evidence of a medium-sized effect for symptoms of specific phobia at post-treatment (SMD = −0.58, 95% CI = −0.94 to −0.21) and in one trial (GRANADO2007) evidence of a large effect for a behavioural approach (SMD = −0.83, 95% CI = −1.65 to 0.00). One trial (SMITH1997) reported a small effect at follow-up (SMD = −0.21, 95% CI = −0.77 to 0.35).

Compared with relaxation
One trial (GILROY2000) compared CCBT (15 participants) with a behavioural relaxation intervention. Recovery was not reported. There was evidence of a large effect with wide CIs on symptoms at post-treatment (SMD = −1.19, 95% CI = −1.97 to −0.41), but which decreased at follow-up (SMD = −0.65, 95% CI = −1.39 to 0.08). There was evidence of large effects on a behavioural approach at post-treatment (SMD⁺ = 0.93, 95% CI = 0.17 to 1.69) and at follow-up (SMD⁺ = 1.23, 95% CI = 0.44 to 2.02).

Table 26: Summary of results

Outcome	N	Effect	Heterogeneity	Study ID(s)
Versus waitlist				
Phobia symptoms at post-treatment	44	SMD = −1.38 [−3.72, 0.97]	$I^2 = 89$, Chi^2 = 9.33, p = 0.002	HASSAN1992, HEADING2001
BAT at post-treatment	44	SMD$^+$ = 2.98 [−2.71, 8.66]	$I^2 = 95$, Chi^2 = 20.35, p = 0.00001	HASSAN1992, HEADING2001
Phobia symptoms at follow-up (<1 year)	26	SMD = −0.41 [−1.19, 0.37]	N/A	HEADING2001
BAT at follow-up (<1 year)	26	SMD = 0.00 [−0.77, 0.77]	N/A	HEADING2001
Versus attention control				
Recovery at post-treatment	25	RR = 1.15 [0.40, 3.31]	N/A	GRANADO2007
Phobia symptoms at post-treatment	106	SMD = −0.58 [−0.94, 0.21]	$I^2 = 0$, Chi^2 = 2.12, p = 0.55	GRANADO2007, MÜLLER2011, SMITH1997 (two groups)
BAT at post-treatment	25	SMD = −0.83 [−1.65, 0.00]	N/A	GRANADO2007
Phobia symptoms at follow-up (<1 year)	50	SMD = −0.21 [−0.77, 0.35]	$I^2 = 0$, Chi^2 = 0.21, p = 0.64	SMITH1997 (two groups)

Continued

231

Table 26: *(Continued)*

Outcome	N	Effect	Heterogeneity	Study ID(s)
Versus relaxation				
Phobia symptoms at post-treatment	30	SMD = −1.19 [−1.97, 0.41]	N/A	GILROY2000
BAT at post-treatment	30	SMD$^+$ = 0.93 [0.17, 1.69]	N/A	GILROY2000
Phobia symptoms at follow-up (<1 year)	30	SMD = −0.65 [−1.39, 0.08]	N/A	GILROY2000
BAT at follow-up (<1 year)	30	SMD$^+$ = 1.23 [0.44, 2.02]	N/A	GILROY2000
Versus exposure in vivo				
Phobia symptoms at post-treatment	114	SMD = 0.34 [−0.04, 0.71]	$I^2 = 0$, Chi$^2 = 2.62$, p = 0.62	ANDERSSON2009, GILROY2000, HASSAN1992 (two groups), HEADING2001
BAT at post-treatment	87	SMD$^+$ = −0.63 [−1.09, 0.18]	$I^2 = 4$, Chi$^2 = 3.13$, p = 0.37	GILROY2000, HASSAN1992 (two groups), HEADING2001
Phobia symptoms at follow-up (<1 year)	110	SMD = 0.33 [−0.04, 0.70]	$I^2 = 0$, Chi$^2 = 2.36$, p = 0.67	ANDERSSON2009, GILROY2000, HASSAN1992 (two groups) HEADING2001
BAT at follow-up (<1 year)	86	SMD$^+$ = −0.29 [−0.84, 0.27]	$I^2 = 33$, Chi$^2 = 4.47$, p = 0.22	GILROY2000, HASSAN1992 (two groups), HEADING2001

Note. BAT = behavioural approach test.

Table 27: GRADE profile – CCBT versus waitlist for specific phobias

| No. of studies | Quality assessment | | | | | | No. of participants | | Effect | Quality |
	Design	Risk of bias	Inconsistency	Indirectness	Imprecision	Other considerations	CCBT	Waitlist		
2	Randomised trials	Serious[1]	Serious[2]	No serious indirectness	Serious[3]	Reporting bias[4]	23	21	SMD 1.38 lower (3.72 lower to 0.97 higher)	⊕OOO VERY LOW
2	Randomised trials	Serious[1]	Serious[5]	No serious indirectness	Serious[3]	Reporting bias[4]	23	21	SMD 2.98 higher (2.71 lower to 8.66 higher)	⊕OOO VERY LOW
1	Randomised trials	Serious[1]	No serious inconsistency[5]	No serious indirectness	Serious[3]	Reporting bias[4]	13	13	SMD 0.41 lower (1.19 lower to 0.37 higher)	⊕OOO VERY LOW
1	Randomised trials	Serious[3]	No serious inconsistency	No serious indirectness	Serious[5]	Reporting bias[4]	13	13	SMD 0 higher (0.77 lower to 0.77 higher)	⊕OOO VERY LOW

233

Table 28: GRADE profile – CCBT versus attention control for specific phobias

No. of studies	Design	Risk of bias	Inconsistency	Indirectness	Imprecision	Other considerations	No. of participants		Effect		Quality
							CCBT	Attention control	Relative (95% CI)	Absolute	
1	Randomised trials	Serious[1]	No serious inconsistency	No serious indirectness	Serious[2]	Reporting bias[3]	5/13 (38.5%)	4/12 (33.3%)	RR 1.15 (0.4 to 3.31)	50 more per 1000 (from 200 fewer to 770 more)	⊕OOO VERY LOW
								33.3%		50 more per 1000 (from 200 fewer to 769 more)	
3	Randomised trials	Serious[1]	No serious inconsistency	No serious indirectness	Serious[2]	Reporting bias[3]	61	45	–	SMD 0.58 lower (0.94 to 0.21 lower)	⊕OOO VERY LOW
1	Randomised trials	Serious[1]	No serious inconsistency	No serious indirectness	Serious[2]	Reporting bias[3]	13	12	–	SMD 0.83 lower (1.65 lower to 0 higher)	⊕OOO VERY LOW
1	Randomised trials	Serious[1]	No serious inconsistency	No serious indirectness	Serious[2]	Reporting bias[3]	26	24	–	SMD 0.21 lower (0.77 lower to 0.35 higher)	⊕OOO VERY LOW

Table 29: GRADE profile – CCBT versus relaxation for specific phobias

| No. of studies | Design | Quality assessment | | | | | No. of participants | | Effect | | Quality |
		Risk of bias	Inconsistency	Indirectness	Imprecision	Other considerations	CCBT	Relaxation	Relative (95% CI)	Absolute	
1	Randomised trials	Serious[1]	No serious inconsistency	No serious indirectness	Very serious[2]	Reporting bias[3]	15	15	–	SMD 1.19 lower (1.97 to 0.41 lower)	⊕OOO VERY LOW
1	Randomised trials	Serious[1]	No serious inconsistency	No serious indirectness	Very serious[2]	Reporting bias[3]	15	15	–	SMD 0.93 higher (0.17 to 1.69 higher)	⊕OOO VERY LOW
1	Randomised trials	Serious[1]	No serious inconsistency	No serious indirectness	Very serious[2]	Reporting bias[3]	15	15	–	SMD 0.65 lower (1.39 lower to 0.08 higher)	⊕OOO VERY LOW
1	Randomised trials	Serious[1]	No serious inconsistency	No serious indirectness	Serious[2]	Reporting bias[3]	15	15	–	SMD 1.23 higher (0.44 to 2.02 higher)	⊕OOO VERY LOW

Table 30: GRADE profile – CCBT versus exposure *in vivo* for specific phobias

No. of studies	Quality assessment						No. of participants		Effect	Quality
	Design	Risk of bias	Inconsistency	Indirectness	Imprecision	Other considerations	CCBT	Exposure *in vivo*		
4	Randomised trials	Serious[1]	No serious inconsistency	No serious indirectness	Serious[2]	Reporting bias[3]	52	62	SMD 0.34 higher (0.04 lower to 0.71 higher)	⊕◯◯◯ VERY LOW
3	Randomised trials	Serious[1]	no serious inconsistency	No serious indirectness	Serious[2]	Reporting bias[3]	38	49	SMD 0.63 lower (1.09 to 0.18 lower)	⊕◯◯◯ VERY LOW
4	Randomised trials	Serious[1]	No serious inconsistency	No serious indirectness	Serious[2]	Reporting bias[3]	50	60	SMD 0.33 higher (0.04 lower to 0.7 higher)	⊕◯◯◯ VERY LOW
3	Randomised trials	Serious[1]	No serious inconsistency	No serious indirectness	Serious[2]	Reporting bias[3]	38	48	SMD 0.29 lower (0.84 lower to 0.27 higher)	⊕◯◯◯ VERY LOW

Compared with exposure in vivo

Four trials (ANDERSSON2009, GILROY2000, HASSAN1992, HEADING2001) compared CCBT with exposure *in vivo*. Combining all trials, the effect favoured exposure *in vivo* (SMD = 0.34, 95% CI = −0.04 to 0.71), and was maintained at follow-up (SMD = 0.35, 95% CI = −0.42 to 1.11). There was evidence of a medium-sized effect in three trials (GILROY2000, HASSAN1992, HEADING2001) for a behavioural approach at post-treatment, favouring exposure *in vivo* (SMD$^+$ = −0.63, 95% CI = −1.09 to −0.18) with no important heterogeneity, but the effect was smaller at follow-up (SMD$^+$ = −0.29, 95% CI = −0.84 to 0.27).

8.4 CLINICAL EVIDENCE SUMMARY

Systematic searches identified seven trials of computerised interventions for specific phobia, compared with no treatment or exposure. The review for CCBT for specific phobias identified interventions for spider phobias only. No evaluations of interventions for any other specific phobia were suitable for inclusion in the review. Trials were generally assessed as being of low quality and at high risk of bias, including selective outcome reporting and publication bias, and the numbers of participants in the trials were small. Comparisons with a waitlist or an attentional control produced medium to large effects on symptoms and on the behavioural approach test. In contrast when compared with the results of therapist-delivered exposure treatment, CCBT did not appear to be efficacious, with the direction of the effect favouring exposure *in vivo* on both symptoms and the behavioural approach test.

8.5 FROM EVIDENCE TO RECOMMENDATIONS

In developing recommendations the GDG was mindful of the low quality of the evidence and the high risk of bias. Trials also focused only on one specific phobia (there are a significant number of other common phobias including snakes, heights, flying and needles). The GDG considered that therapist-delivered single session exposure therapy (Davis et al., 2012) is an efficacious treatment for specific phobias and the four trials included in this chapter suggest that it is probably superior to CCBT. The GDG also noted that none of the interventions evaluated is available in the UK. Given the very low quality of the evidence and the narrow focus of the interventions (spider phobia only), the GDG felt that the available data do not provide sufficient evidence to suggest that CCBT is an efficacious treatment for specific phobias. The GDG was aware that other efficacious treatments are available (but not the subject of this review) and in these circumstances decided not to recommend CCBT for the treatment of specific phobias.

8.6 RECOMMENDATIONS

8.6.1.1 Do not routinely offer computerised CBT to treat specific phobias in adults.

9   SUMMARY OF RECOMMENDATIONS

9.1   GENERAL PRINCIPLES OF CARE IN MENTAL HEALTH AND GENERAL MEDICAL SETTINGS

9.1.1   Improving access to services

9.1.1.1   Be aware that people with social anxiety disorder may:
- not know that social anxiety disorder is a recognised condition and can be effectively treated
- perceive their social anxiety as a personal flaw or failing
- be vulnerable to stigma and embarrassment
- avoid contact with and find it difficult or distressing to interact with healthcare professionals, staff and other service users
- avoid disclosing information, asking and answering questions and making complaints
- have difficulty concentrating when information is explained to them.

9.1.1.2   Primary and secondary care clinicians, managers and commissioners should consider arranging services flexibly to promote access and avoid exacerbating social anxiety disorder symptoms by offering:
- appointments at times when the service is least crowded or busy
- appointments before or after normal hours, or at home initially
- self-check-in and other ways to reduce distress on arrival
- opportunities to complete forms or paperwork before or after an appointment in a private space
- support with concerns related to social anxiety (for example, using public transport)
- a choice of professional if possible.

9.1.1.3   When a person with social anxiety disorder is first offered an appointment, in particular in specialist services, provide clear information in a letter about:
- where to go on arrival and where they can wait (offer the use of a private waiting area or the option to wait elsewhere, for example outside the service's premises)
- location of facilities available at the service (for example, the car park and toilets)
- what will happen and what will not happen during assessment and treatment.

When the person arrives for the appointment, offer to meet or alert them (for example, by text message) when their appointment is about to begin.

9.1.1.4   Be aware that changing healthcare professionals or services may be particularly stressful for people with social anxiety disorder. Minimise such disruptions, discuss concerns beforehand and provide detailed information about any changes, especially those that were not requested by the service user.

9.1.1.5 For people with social anxiety disorder using inpatient mental health or medical services, arrange meals, activities and accommodation by:

- regularly discussing how such provisions fit into their treatment plan and their preferences
- providing the opportunity for them to eat on their own if they find eating with others too distressing
- providing a choice of activities they can do on their own or with others.

9.1.1.6 Offer to provide treatment in settings where children and young people with social anxiety disorder and their parents or carers feel most comfortable, for example, at home or in schools or community centres.

9.1.1.7 Consider providing childcare (for example, for siblings) to support parent and carer involvement.

9.1.1.8 If possible, organise appointments in a way that does not interfere with school or other peer and social activities.

9.1.2 Communication

9.1.2.1 When assessing a person with social anxiety disorder:

- suggest that they communicate with you in the manner they find most comfortable, including writing (for example, in a letter or questionnaire)
- offer to communicate with them by phone call, text and email
- make sure they have opportunities to ask any questions and encourage them to do so
- provide opportunities for them to make and change appointments by various means, including text, email or phone.

9.1.2.2 When communicating with children and young people and their parents or carers:

- take into account the child or young person's developmental level, emotional maturity and cognitive capacity, including any learning disabilities, sight or hearing problems and delays in language development
- be aware that children who are socially anxious may be reluctant to speak to an unfamiliar person, and that children with a potential diagnosis of selective mutism may be unable to speak at all during assessment or treatment; accept information from parents or carers, but ensure that the child or young person is given the opportunity to answer for themselves, through writing, drawing or speaking through a parent or carer if necessary
- use plain language if possible and clearly explain any clinical terms
- check that the child or young person and their parents or carers understand what is being said
- use communication aids (such as pictures, symbols, large print, braille, different languages or sign language) if needed.

9.1.3   Competence

9.1.3.1   Healthcare, social care and educational professionals working with children and young people should be trained and skilled in:
- negotiating and working with parents and carers, including helping parents with relationship difficulties find support
- managing issues related to information sharing and confidentiality as these apply to children and young people
- referring children with possible social anxiety disorder to appropriate services.

9.1.4   Consent and confidentiality

9.1.4.1   If the young person is 'Gillick competent' seek their consent before speaking to their parents or carers.

9.1.4.2   When working with children and young people and their parents or carers:
- make sure that discussions take place in settings in which confidentiality, privacy and dignity are respected
- be clear with the child or young person and their parents or carers about limits of confidentiality (that is, which health and social care professionals have access to information about their diagnosis and its treatment and in what circumstances this may be shared with others)[33].

9.1.4.3   Ensure that children and young people and their parents or carers understand the purpose of any meetings and the reasons for sharing information. Respect their rights to confidentiality throughout the process and adapt the content and duration of meetings to take into account the impact of the social anxiety disorder on the child or young person's participation.

9.1.5   Working with parents and carers

9.1.5.1   If a parent or carer cannot attend meetings for assessment or treatment, ensure that written information is provided and shared with them.

9.1.5.2   If parents or carers are involved in the assessment or treatment of a young person with social anxiety disorder, discuss with the young person (taking into account their developmental level, emotional maturity and cognitive capacity) what form they would like this involvement to take. Such discussions should take place at intervals to take account of any changes in circumstances, including developmental level, and should not happen only once. As the involvement of parents and carers can be quite complex, staff should receive training in the skills needed to negotiate and work with

---

[33]This recommendation is adapted from *Service User Experience in Adult Mental Health* (NICE, 2011c).

parents and carers, and also in managing issues relating to information sharing and confidentiality[34].

9.1.5.3   Offer parents and carers an assessment of their own needs including:
● personal, social and emotional support
● support in their caring role, including emergency plans
● advice on and help with obtaining practical support.

9.1.5.4   Maintain links with adult mental health services so that referrals for any mental health needs of parents or carers can be made quickly and smoothly.

9.2   IDENTIFICATION AND ASSESSMENT OF ADULTS

9.2.1   Identification of adults with possible social anxiety disorder

9.2.1.1   Ask the identification questions for anxiety disorders in line with recommendation 1.3.1.2 in *Common Mental Health Disorders* (NICE clinical guideline 123)[35], and if social anxiety disorder is suspected:
● use the 3-item Mini-Social Phobia Inventory (Mini-SPIN) **or**
● consider asking the following two questions:
– Do you find yourself avoiding social situations or activities?
– Are you fearful or embarrassed in social situations?
If the person scores 6 or more on the Mini-SPIN, or answers yes to either of the two questions above, refer for or conduct a comprehensive assessment for social anxiety disorder (see recommendations 9.2.2.2–9.2.2.6).

9.2.1.2   If the identification questions (see recommendation 9.2.1.1) indicate possible social anxiety disorder, but the practitioner is not competent to perform a mental health assessment, refer the person to an appropriate healthcare professional. If this professional is not the person's GP, inform the GP of the referral.

9.2.1.3   If the identification questions (see recommendation 9.2.1.1) indicate possible social anxiety disorder, a practitioner who is competent to perform a mental health assessment should review the person's mental state and associated functional, interpersonal and social difficulties.

9.2.2   Assessment of adults with possible social anxiety disorder

9.2.2.1   If an adult with possible social anxiety disorder finds it difficult or distressing to attend an initial appointment in person, consider making the first contact by phone or internet, but aim to see the person face to face for subsequent assessments and treatment.

---

[34]This recommendation is adapted from *Service User Experience in Adult Mental Health* (NICE, 2011c).
[35]NICE, 2011a.

9.2.2.2   When assessing an adult with possible social anxiety disorder:
- conduct an assessment that considers fear, avoidance, distress and functional impairment
- be aware of comorbid disorders, including avoidant personality disorder, alcohol and substance misuse, mood disorders, other anxiety disorders, psychosis and autism.

9.2.2.3   Follow the recommendations in *Common Mental Health Disorders* (NICE clinical guideline 123)[36] for the structure and content of the assessment and adjust them to take into account the need to obtain a more detailed description of the social anxiety disorder (see recommendation 9.2.2.5 in this guideline).

9.2.2.4   Consider using the following to inform the assessment and support the evaluation of any intervention:
- a diagnostic or problem identification tool as recommended in recommendation 1.3.2.3 in *Common Mental Health Disorders* (NICE clinical guideline 123[37]
- a validated measure for social anxiety, for example, the Social Phobia Inventory (SPIN) or the Liebowitz Social Anxiety Scale (LSAS).

9.2.2.5   Obtain a detailed description of the person's current social anxiety and associated problems and circumstances including:
- feared and avoided social situations
- what they are afraid might happen in social situations (for example, looking anxious, blushing, sweating, trembling or appearing boring)
- anxiety symptoms
- view of self
- content of self-image
- safety-seeking behaviours
- focus of attention in social situations
- anticipatory and post-event processing
- occupational, educational, financial and social circumstances
- medication, alcohol and recreational drug use.

9.2.2.6   If a person with possible social anxiety disorder does not return after an initial assessment, contact them (using their preferred method of communication) to discuss the reason for not returning. Remove any obstacles to further assessment or treatment that the person identifies.

9.2.3   Planning treatment for adults diagnosed with social anxiety disorder

9.2.3.1   After diagnosis of social anxiety disorder in an adult, identify the goals for treatment and provide information about the disorder and its treatment including:
- the nature and course of the disorder and commonly occurring comorbidities

---

[36]NICE, 2011a.
[37]NICE, 2011a.

242

- the impact on social and personal functioning
- commonly held beliefs about the cause of the disorder
- beliefs about what can be changed or treated
- choice and nature of evidence-based treatments.

9.2.3.2 If the person also has symptoms of depression, assess their nature and extent and determine their functional link with the social anxiety disorder by asking them which existed first.

- If the person has only experienced significant social anxiety since the start of a depressive episode, treat the depression in line with *Depression* (NICE clinical guideline 90)[38].
- If the social anxiety disorder preceded the onset of depression, ask: 'if I gave you a treatment that ensured you were no longer anxious in social situations, would you still be depressed?'
  - If the person answers 'no', treat the social anxiety (unless the severity of the depression prevents this, then offer initial treatment for the depression).
  - If the person answers 'yes', consider treating both the social anxiety disorder and the depression, taking into account their preference when deciding which to treat first.
- If the depression is treated first, treat the social anxiety disorder when improvement in the depression allows.

9.2.3.3 For people (including young people) with social anxiety disorder who misuse substances, be aware that alcohol or drug misuse is often an attempt to reduce anxiety in social situations and should not preclude treatment for social anxiety disorder. Assess the nature of the substance misuse to determine if it is primarily a consequence of social anxiety disorder and:

- offer a brief intervention for hazardous alcohol or drug misuse (see *Alcohol-Use Disorders* [NICE clinical guideline 115][39] or *Drug Misuse* [NICE clinical guideline 51][40])
- for harmful or dependent alcohol or drug misuse consider referral to a specialist alcohol or drug misuse service.

9.3 INTERVENTIONS FOR ADULTS WITH SOCIAL ANXIETY DISORDER

9.3.1 Treatment principles

9.3.1.1 All interventions for adults with social anxiety disorder should be delivered by competent practitioners. Psychological interventions should be based

---

[38]NICE, 2009a.
[39]NICE, 2011.
[40]NICE, 2007.

on the relevant treatment manual(s), which should guide the structure and duration of the intervention. Practitioners should consider using competence frameworks developed from the relevant treatment manual(s) and for all interventions should:

- receive regular, high-quality outcome-informed supervision
- use routine sessional outcome measures (for example, the SPIN or LSAS) and ensure that the person with social anxiety is involved in reviewing the efficacy of the treatment
- engage in monitoring and evaluation of treatment adherence and practitioner competence – for example, by using video and audio tapes, and external audit and scrutiny if appropriate.

9.3.2   Initial treatment options for adults with social anxiety disorder

9.3.2.1   Offer adults with social anxiety disorder individual cognitive behavioural therapy (CBT) that has been specifically developed to treat social anxiety disorder (based on the Clark and Wells model or the Heimberg model; see recommendations 9.3.4.1 and 9.3.4.2).

9.3.2.2   Do not routinely offer group CBT in preference to individual CBT. Although there is evidence that group CBT is more effective than most other interventions, it is less clinically and cost effective than individual CBT.

9.3.2.3   For adults who decline CBT and wish to consider another psychological intervention, offer CBT-based supported self-help (see recommendation 9.3.4.3).

9.3.2.4   For adults who decline cognitive behavioural interventions and express a preference for a pharmacological intervention, discuss their reasons for declining cognitive behavioural interventions and address any concerns.

9.3.2.5   If the person wishes to proceed with a pharmacological intervention, offer a selective serotonin reuptake inhibitor (SSRI) (escitalopram or sertraline). Monitor the person carefully for adverse reactions (see recommendations 9.3.5.1–9.3.5.7).

9.3.2.6   For adults who decline cognitive behavioural and pharmacological interventions, consider short-term psychodynamic psychotherapy that has been specifically developed to treat social anxiety disorder (see recommendation 9.3.4.4). Be aware of the more limited clinical effectiveness and lower cost effectiveness of this intervention compared with CBT, self-help and pharmacological interventions.

9.3.3   Options for adults with no or a partial response to initial treatment

9.3.3.1   For adults whose symptoms of social anxiety disorder have only partially responded to individual CBT after an adequate course of treatment, consider a pharmacological intervention (see recommendation 9.3.2.5) in combination with individual CBT.

9.3.3.2   For adults whose symptoms have only partially responded to an SSRI (escitalopram or sertraline) after 10 to 12 weeks of treatment, offer individual CBT in addition to the SSRI.

9.3.3.3   For adults whose symptoms have not responded to an SSRI (escitalopram or sertraline) or who cannot tolerate the side effects, offer an alternative SSRI (fluvoxamine[41] or paroxetine) or a serotonin noradrenaline reuptake inhibitor (SNRI) (venlafaxine), taking into account:
● the tendency of paroxetine and venlafaxine to produce a discontinuation syndrome (which may be reduced by extended-release preparations)
● the risk of suicide and likelihood of toxicity in overdose.

9.3.3.4   For adults whose symptoms have not responded to an alternative SSRI or an SNRI, offer a monoamine oxidase inhibitor (phenelzine[42] or moclobemide).

9.3.3.5   Discuss the option of individual CBT with adults whose symptoms have not responded to pharmacological interventions.

9.3.4   Delivering psychological interventions for adults

9.3.4.1   Individual CBT (the Clark and Wells model) for social anxiety disorder should consist of up to 14 sessions of 90 minutes' duration over approximately 4 months and include the following:
● education about social anxiety
● experiential exercises to demonstrate the adverse effects of self-focused attention and safety-seeking behaviours
● video feedback to correct distorted negative self-imagery
● systematic training in externally focused attention
● within-session behavioural experiments to test negative beliefs with linked homework assignments
● discrimination training or rescripting to deal with problematic memories of social trauma
● examination and modification of core beliefs
● modification of problematic pre- and post-event processing
● relapse prevention.

---

[41]At the time of publication, fluvoxamine did not have a UK marketing authorisation for use in adults with social anxiety disorder. The prescriber should follow relevant professional guidance, taking full responsibility for the decision. Informed consent should be obtained and documented. See the General Medical Council's *Good Practice in Prescribing and Managing Medicines and Devices* (2013) for further information.

[42]At the time of publication, phenelzine did not have a UK marketing authorisation for use in adults with social anxiety disorder. The prescriber should follow relevant professional guidance, taking full responsibility for the decision. Informed consent should be obtained and documented. See the General Medical Council's *Good Practice in Prescribing and Managing Medicines and Devices* (2013) for further information.

9.3.4.2   Individual CBT (the Heimberg model) for social anxiety disorder should consist of 15 sessions of 60 minutes' duration, and one session of 90 minutes for exposure, over approximately 4 months, and include the following:
- education about social anxiety
- cognitive restructuring
- graduated exposure to feared social situations, both within treatment sessions and as homework
- examination and modification of core beliefs
- relapse prevention.

9.3.4.3   Supported self-help for social anxiety disorder should consist of:
- typically up to nine sessions of supported use of a CBT-based self-help book over 3–4 months
- support to use the materials, either face to face or by telephone, for a total of 3 hours over the course of the treatment.

9.3.4.4   Short-term psychodynamic psychotherapy for social anxiety disorder should consist of typically up to 25–30 sessions of 50 minutes' duration over 6–8 months and include the following:
- education about social anxiety disorder
- establishing a secure positive therapeutic alliance to modify insecure attachments
- a focus on a core conflictual relationship theme associated with social anxiety symptoms
- a focus on shame
- encouraging exposure to feared social situations outside therapy sessions
- support to establish a self-affirming inner dialogue
- help to improve social skills.

9.3.5   Prescribing and monitoring pharmacological interventions in adults

9.3.5.1   Before prescribing a pharmacological intervention for social anxiety disorder, discuss the treatment options and any concerns the person has about taking medication. Explain fully the reasons for prescribing and provide written and verbal information on:
- the likely benefits of different drugs
- the different propensities of each drug for side effects, discontinuation syndromes and drug interactions
- the risk of early activation symptoms with SSRIs and SNRIs, such as increased anxiety, agitation, jitteriness and problems sleeping
- the gradual development, over 2 weeks or more, of the full anxiolytic effect
- the importance of taking medication as prescribed, reporting side effects and discussing any concerns about stopping medication with the

prescriber, and the need to continue treatment after remission to avoid relapse.

9.3.5.2   Arrange to see people aged 30 years and older who are not assessed to be at risk of suicide within 1 to 2 weeks of first prescribing SSRIs or SNRIs to:
- discuss any possible side effects and potential interaction with symptoms of social anxiety disorder (for example, increased restlessness or agitation)
- advise and support them to engage in graduated exposure to feared or avoided social situations.

9.3.5.3   After the initial meeting (see recommendation 9.3.5.2), arrange to see the person every 2–4 weeks during the first 3 months of treatment and every month thereafter. Continue to support them to engage in graduated exposure to feared or avoided social situations.

9.3.5.4   For people aged under 30 years who are offered an SSRI or SNRI:
- warn them that these drugs are associated with an increased risk of suicidal thinking and self-harm in a minority of people under 30 **and**
- see them within 1 week of first prescribing **and**
- monitor the risk of suicidal thinking and self-harm weekly for the first month[43].

9.3.5.5   Arrange to see people who are assessed to be at risk of suicide weekly until there is no indication of increased suicide risk, then every 2–4 weeks during the first 3 months of treatment and every month thereafter. Continue to support them to engage in graduated exposure to feared or avoided social situations.

9.3.5.6   Advise people taking a monoamine oxidase inhibitor of the dietary and pharmacological restrictions concerning the use of these drugs as set out in the *British National Formulary*[44].

9.3.5.7   For people who develop side effects soon after starting a pharmacological intervention, provide information and consider one of the following strategies:
- monitoring the person's symptoms closely (if the side effects are mild and acceptable to the person)
- reducing the dose of the drug
- stopping the drug and offering either an alternative drug or individual CBT, according to the person's preference[45].

9.3.5.8   If the person's symptoms of social anxiety disorder have responded well to a pharmacological intervention in the first 3 months, continue it for at least a further 6 months.

9.3.5.9   When stopping a pharmacological intervention, reduce the dose of the drug gradually. If symptoms reappear after the dose is lowered or the drug is

---

[43]This recommendation is adapted from *Generalised Anxiety Disorder and Panic Disorder (With or Without Agoraphobia) in Adults* (NICE clinical guideline 113; NICE, 2011b).
[44]Joint Formulary Committee, 2013.
[45]This recommendation is adapted from *Generalised Anxiety Disorder and Panic Disorder (With or Without Agoraphobia) in Adults* (NICE clinical guideline 113; NICE, 2011b).

stopped, consider increasing the dose, reintroducing the drug or offering individual CBT.

9.4 IDENTIFICATION AND ASSESSMENT OF CHILDREN AND YOUNG PEOPLE

9.4.1 Identification of children and young people with possible social anxiety disorder

9.4.1.1 Health and social care professionals in primary care and education and community settings should be alert to possible anxiety disorders in children and young people, particularly those who avoid school, social or group activities or talking in social situations, or are irritable, excessively shy or overly reliant on parents or carers. Consider asking the child or young person about their feelings of anxiety, fear, avoidance, distress and associated behaviours (or a parent or carer) to help establish if social anxiety disorder is present, using these questions:
- 'Sometimes people get very scared when they have to do things with other people, especially people they don't know. They might worry about doing things with other people watching. They might get scared that they will do something silly or that people will make fun of them. They might not want to do these things or, if they have to do them, they might get very upset or cross.'
  - 'Do you/does your child get scared about doing things with other people, like talking, eating, going to parties, or other things at school or with friends?'
  - 'Do you/does your child find it difficult to do things when other people are watching, like playing sport, being in plays or concerts, asking or answering questions, reading aloud, or giving talks in class?'
  - 'Do you/does your child ever feel that you/your child can't do these things or try to get out of them?'

9.4.1.2 If the child or young person (or a parent or carer) answers 'yes' to one or more of the questions in recommendation 9.4.1.1 consider a comprehensive assessment for social anxiety disorder (see recommendations 9.4.2.1–9.4.2.7).

9.4.1.3 If the identification questions (see recommendation 9.4.1.1) indicate possible social anxiety disorder, but the practitioner is not competent to perform a mental health assessment, refer the child or young person to an appropriate healthcare professional. If this professional is not the child or young person's GP, inform the GP of the referral.

9.4.1.4 If the identification questions (see recommendation 9.4.1.1) indicate possible social anxiety disorder, a practitioner who is competent to perform a mental health assessment should review the child or young person's mental state and associated functional, interpersonal and social difficulties.

9.4.2   **Assessment of children and young people with possible social anxiety disorder**

9.4.2.1   A comprehensive assessment of a child or young person with possible social anxiety disorder should:
● provide an opportunity for the child or young person to be interviewed alone at some point during the assessment
● if possible involve a parent, carer or other adult known to the child or young person who can provide information about current and past behaviour
● if necessary involve more than one professional to ensure a comprehensive assessment can be undertaken.

9.4.2.2   When assessing a child or young person obtain a detailed description of their current social anxiety and associated problems including:
● feared and avoided social situations
● what they are afraid might happen in social situations (for example, looking anxious, blushing, sweating, trembling or appearing boring)
● anxiety symptoms
● view of self
● content of self-image
● safety-seeking behaviours
● focus of attention in social situations
● anticipatory and post-event processing, particularly for older children
● family circumstances and support
● friendships and peer groups, educational and social circumstances
● medication, alcohol and recreational drug use.

9.4.2.3   As part of a comprehensive assessment, assess for causal and maintaining factors for social anxiety disorder in the child or young person's home, school and social environment, in particular:
● parenting behaviours that promote and support anxious behaviours or do not support positive behaviours
● peer victimisation in school or other settings.

9.4.2.4   As part of a comprehensive assessment, assess for possible coexisting conditions such as:
● other mental health problems (for example, other anxiety disorders and depression)
● neurodevelopmental conditions such as attention deficit hyperactivity disorder, autism and learning disabilities
● drug and alcohol misuse (see recommendation 9.2.3.3)
● speech and language problems.

9.4.2.5   To aid the assessment of social anxiety disorder and other common mental health problems consider using formal instruments (both the child and parent versions if available and indicated), such as:
● the LSAS – child version or the Social Phobia and Anxiety Inventory for Children (SPAI-C) for children, or the SPIN or the LSAS for young people

- the Multidimensional Anxiety Scale for Children (MASC), the Revised Child Anxiety and Depression Scale (RCADS) for children and young people who may have comorbid depression or other anxiety disorders, the Spence Children's Anxiety Scale (SCAS) or the Screen for Child Anxiety Related Emotional Disorders (SCARED) for children.

9.4.2.6 Use formal assessment instruments to aid the diagnosis of other problems, such as:

- a validated measure of cognitive ability for a child or young person with a suspected learning disability
- the Strengths and Difficulties Questionnaire for all children and young people.

9.4.2.7 Assess the risks and harm faced by the child or young person and if needed develop a risk management plan for risk of self-neglect, familial abuse or neglect, exploitation by others, self-harm or harm to others.

9.4.2.8 Develop a profile of the child or young person to identify their needs and any further assessments that may be needed, including the extent and nature of:

- the social anxiety disorder and any associated difficulties (for example, selective mutism)
- any coexisting mental health problems
- neurodevelopmental conditions such as attention deficit hyperactivity disorder, autism and learning disabilities
- experience of bullying or social ostracism
- friendships with peers
- speech, language and communication skills
- physical health problems
- personal and social functioning to indicate any needs (personal, social, housing, educational and occupational)
- educational and occupational goals
- parent or carer needs, including mental health needs.

9.5 INTERVENTIONS FOR CHILDREN AND YOUNG PEOPLE WITH SOCIAL ANXIETY DISORDER

9.5.1 Treatment principles

9.5.1.1 All interventions for children and young people with social anxiety disorder should be delivered by competent practitioners. Psychological interventions should be based on the relevant treatment manual(s), which should guide the structure and duration of the intervention. Practitioners should consider using competence frameworks developed from the relevant treatment manual(s) and for all interventions should:

- receive regular high-quality supervision
- use routine sessional outcome measures, for example:

         – the LSAS – child version or the SPAI-C, and the SPIN or LSAS for young people

         – the MASC, RCADS, SCAS or SCARED for children

- engage in monitoring and evaluation of treatment adherence and practitioner competence – for example, by using video and audio tapes, and external audit and scrutiny if appropriate.

9.5.1.2   Be aware of the impact of the home, school and wider social environments on the maintenance and treatment of social anxiety disorder. Maintain a focus on the child or young person's emotional, educational and social needs and work with parents, teachers, other adults and the child or young person's peers to create an environment that supports the achievement of the agreed goals of treatment.

9.5.2   Treatment for children and young people with social anxiety disorder

9.5.2.1   Offer individual or group CBT focused on social anxiety (see recommendations 9.5.3.1 and 9.5.3.2) to children and young people with social anxiety disorder. Consider involving parents or carers to ensure the effective delivery of the intervention, particularly in young children.

9.5.3   Delivering psychological interventions for children and young people

9.5.3.1   Individual CBT should consist of the following, taking into account the child or young person's cognitive and emotional maturity:
- 8–12 sessions of 45 minutes' duration
- psychoeducation, exposure to feared or avoided social situations, training in social skills and opportunities to rehearse skills in social situations
- psychoeducation and skills training for parents, particularly of young children, to promote and reinforce the child's exposure to feared or avoided social situations and development of skills.

9.5.3.2   Group CBT should consist of the following, taking into account the child or young person's cognitive and emotional maturity:
- 8–12 sessions of 90 minutes' duration with groups of children or young people of the same age range
- psychoeducation, exposure to feared or avoided social situations, training in social skills and opportunities to rehearse skills in social situations
- psychoeducation and skills training for parents, particularly of young children, to promote and reinforce the child's exposure to feared or avoided social situations and development of skills.

9.5.3.3   Consider psychological interventions that were developed for adults (see Section 9.3) for young people (typically aged 15 years and older) who have the cognitive and emotional capacity to undertake a treatment developed for adults.

9.6 INTERVENTIONS THAT ARE NOT RECOMMENDED TO TREAT SOCIAL ANXIETY DISORDER

9.6.1.1　Do not routinely offer pharmacological interventions to treat social anxiety disorder in children and young people.

9.6.1.2　Do not routinely offer anticonvulsants, tricyclic antidepressants, benzodiazepines or antipsychotic medication to treat social anxiety disorder in adults.

9.6.1.3　Do not routinely offer mindfulness-based interventions[46] or supportive therapy to treat social anxiety disorder.

9.6.1.4　Do not offer St John's wort or other over-the-counter medications and preparations for anxiety to treat social anxiety disorder. Explain the potential interactions with other prescribed and over-the-counter medications and the lack of evidence to support their safe use.

9.6.1.5　Do not offer botulinum toxin to treat hyperhidrosis (excessive sweating) in people with social anxiety disorder. This is because there is no good-quality evidence showing benefit from botulinum toxin in the treatment of social anxiety disorder and it may be harmful.

9.6.1.6　Do not offer endoscopic thoracic sympathectomy to treat hyperhidrosis or facial blushing in people with social anxiety disorder. This is because there is no good-quality evidence showing benefit from endoscopic thoracic sympathectomy in the treatment of social anxiety disorder and it may be harmful.

9.7 SPECIFIC PHOBIAS

9.7.1 Interventions that are not recommended

9.7.1.1　Do not routinely offer computerised CBT to treat specific phobias in adults.

---

[46]This includes mindfulness-based stress reduction and mindfulness-based cognitive therapy.

10 APPENDICES

APPENDIX 1:
SCOPE FOR THE DEVELOPMENT OF THE CLINICAL GUIDELINE

GUIDELINE TITLE

Social anxiety disorder: recognition, assessment and treatment of social anxiety disorder[47].

SHORT TITLE

Social anxiety disorder.

THE REMIT

The Department of Health has asked NICE: 'to produce a clinical guideline on the diagnosis and treatment of social phobia (social anxiety disorder)'.

CLINICAL NEED FOR THE GUIDELINE

Epidemiology

a) Social anxiety disorder is one of the most common anxiety disorders. Estimates of lifetime prevalence vary but have been as high as 12%, compared with estimates for other anxiety disorders of around 6% for generalised anxiety disorder, 5% for panic disorder, 7% for post-traumatic stress disorder (PTSD) and 2% for obsessive-compulsive disorder.

b) There is a significant degree of comorbidity between social anxiety disorder and other psychiatric disorders. Social anxiety disorder often occurs alongside depression (19%), substance-use disorder (17%), generalised anxiety disorder (5%), panic disorder (6%) and PTSD (3%).

---

[47]The guideline title was shortened during development to *Social Anxiety Disorder: Recognition, Assessment and Treatment.*

c) Social anxiety disorder is common in both men and women, but tends to have a higher prevalence in women. Black and minority ethnic groups have a higher incidence of common mental health disorders but may be under-represented in treatment services.

d) People with social anxiety disorder may use alcohol or other drugs to try to reduce their anxiety and alleviate depression. This can lead to substance abuse. A significant proportion of service users attending mental health services for conditions including anxiety disorders, such as panic disorder or social anxiety disorder, attend as a result of alcohol or benzodiazepine misuse.

e) Social anxiety disorder has an early median age of onset (13 years) and is the most persistent of the anxiety disorders. Despite the extent of suffering and impairment only about half of those with the disorder ever seek treatment, and those that do generally seek treatment only after 15–20 years of symptoms.

f) Social anxiety disorder may have a great impact on a person's functioning, disrupt normal life, interfere with their social relationships and quality of life, and impair performance at work or school.

Current practice

a) Recognition of social anxiety disorder in adults, children and young people by GPs is often poor. The problem of under-recognition for anxiety disorders in general has recently been highlighted by evidence that the prevalence of PTSD is under-recognised in primary care. In part this may stem from GPs not recognising the disorder, and the lack of clearly defined care pathways. But from a patient's perspective, stigma and avoidance may also contribute to under-recognition. Pessimism about possible treatment outcomes on the part of clinicians and those with anxiety disorders may further contribute to this, despite the existence of effective treatments.

b) The early age of onset means that recognition of social anxiety disorder in educational settings is also an issue. Social anxiety disorder is associated with poor school performance, bullying and leaving school early. Teachers and other educational professionals may have limited knowledge of how to recognise and oversee the management of this disorder.

c) In primary care many service users are misdiagnosed as suffering from depression only. For many people depressive symptoms are present, but they may have developed as a consequence of having a social anxiety disorder. Misdiagnosis may also occur in secondary care if an adequate history has not been taken.

d) No national clinical guidelines are currently available for the treatment of social anxiety disorder, although the British Association for Psychopharmacology produced guidance on psychological and pharmacological interventions in 2005. Effective psychological and pharmacological interventions for social anxiety disorder exist but may not be accessed because of poor recognition, inadequate assessment, and limited awareness or availability of treatments.

THE GUIDELINE

The guideline development process is described in detail on the NICE website (see 'Further information').

This scope defines what the guideline will (and will not) examine, and what the guideline developers will consider. The scope is based on the referral from the Department of Health.

The areas that will be addressed by the guideline are described in the following sections.

Population

Groups that will be covered
a) Adults (aged 18 and older) with social anxiety disorder.
b) Children and young people (from school age to 17 years) with social anxiety disorder.
c) Consideration will be given to the particular needs of black and minority ethnic groups (with possible poor access and uptake of treatments).
d) Consideration will be given to the particular needs of people with the following subclassifications of social anxiety disorder:
- generalised social anxiety (for example, those whose fears relate to a wide range of situations, such as meeting new people, talking to authority figures, eating or drinking in public, working while being observed, small groups, parties, and performance situations); a subset of these people also meet diagnostic criteria for avoidant personality disorder
- performance social anxiety (for example, those whose fears are largely restricted to performance situations such as public speaking, music, acting and dance performances)
- selective mutism arising as a consequence of a social anxiety disorder.

Groups that will not be covered
a) Children from birth up to school age.
b) Children and adults with:
- autism spectrum conditions (this will be covered in the autism spectrum conditions guidelines).
- body dysmorphic disorder (this is covered in the obsessive-compulsive disorder guideline).

Healthcare setting

a) Care provided by primary, community and secondary healthcare professionals who have direct contact with, and make decisions concerning, the care of children, young people and adults with social anxiety disorder.

b) Improving access to psychological therapies (IAPT) services.
c) Educational and other settings where healthcare or related interventions may be delivered.

Clinical management

Key clinical issues that will be covered
a) Impediments to access for diagnosis and treatment.
b) Identification and recognition of social anxiety disorder.
c) Content and structure of an assessment.
d) Psychological interventions (for example, individual and group cognitive behaviour therapy [CBT], facilitated and non-facilitated self-help, computerised cognitive behaviour therapy, social skills training, exposure therapy, anxiety management, interpersonal psychotherapy and psychodynamic psychotherapy).
e) Pharmacological interventions (for example, selective serotonin reuptake inhibitors [SSRIs], monoamine oxidase inhibitors [MAOIs], reversible MAOIs, tricyclics, other antidepressants, beta-blockers and benzodiazepines). Note that guideline recommendations will normally fall within licensed indications; exceptionally, and only if clearly supported by evidence, use outside a licensed indication may be recommended. The guideline will assume that prescribers will use a drug's summary of product characteristics to inform decisions made with individual patients.
f) Combined pharmacological and psychological interventions (including the use of cognitive enhancers).
g) Family-based/parenting interventions (for example, the FRIENDS programme, which is a family-based group CBT intervention involving cognitive restructuring for parents and assistance in building social support).
h) Modifying treatment to take account of comorbid conditions.
i) Surgical interventions (for example, surgery for facial blushing and treatment of hyperhidrosis with botulinum toxin A).
j) Pathways into and through care.
k) Monitoring of clinical and other outcomes.

Clinical issues that will not be covered
a) Treatment of comorbid conditions (however, see point 'h' above).
b) Interventions aimed at the primary prevention of social anxiety disorders in children and young people in educational and social care settings.

Main outcomes

a) Accuracy of recognition tools (considering sensitivity, specificity, positive predictive value, negative predictive value and area under the curve).
b) Percentage of people receiving appropriate treatment.

c) Symptom improvement (short and long term).
d) Educational, occupational and social performance/functioning.
e) Health economic outcomes (for example, quality-adjusted life year [QALY]).
f) Health related quality of life.
g) Treatment acceptability.

Economic aspects

Developers will take into account both clinical and cost effectiveness when making recommendations involving a choice between alternative interventions. A review of the economic evidence will be conducted and analyses will be carried out as appropriate. The preferred unit of effectiveness is the quality-adjusted life year (QALY), and the costs considered will usually be only from an NHS and personal social services (PSS) perspective. Further detail on the methods can be found in 'The guidelines manual' (see 'Further information').

STATUS

Scope
This is the final scope.

Timing
The development of the guideline recommendations will begin in July 2011.

RELATED NICE GUIDANCE

Published guidance

NICE guidance to be updated
This guideline will update the section of the following NICE guidance that deals with phobia, subject to stakeholder agreement following a technology appraisal review proposal:

● *Computerised Cognitive Behaviour Therapy for Depression and Anxiety* (review). NICE technology appraisal guidance 97 (2006). Available from www.nice.org.uk/guidance/TA97

Other related NICE guidance
● *Common Mental Health Disorders*. NICE clinical guideline 123 (2011). Available from www.nice.org.uk/guidance/CG123
● *Alcohol-use Disorders: Diagnosis, Assessment and Management of Harmful Drinking and Alcohol Dependence*. NICE clinical guideline 115 (2011). Available from www.nice.org.uk/guidance/CG115

- *Generalised Anxiety Disorder and Panic Disorder (With or Without Agoraphobia) in Adults.* NICE clinical guideline 113 (2011). Available from www.nice.org.uk/guidance/CG113
- *Looked-after Children and Young People.* NICE public health guidance 28 (2010). Available from www.nice.org.uk/guidance/PH28
- *Depression.* NICE clinical guideline 90 (2009). Available from www.nice.org.uk/guidance/CG90
- *Social and Emotional Wellbeing in Secondary Education.* NICE public health guidance 20 (2009). Available from www.nice.org.uk/guidance/PH20
- *Social and Emotional Wellbeing in Primary Education.* NICE public health guidance 12 (2008). Available from www.nice.org.uk/guidance/PH12
- *Obsessive-compulsive Disorder and Body Dysmorphic Disorder.* NICE clinical guideline 31 (2005). Available from www.nice.org.uk/CG31
- *Depression in Children and Young People.* NICE clinical guideline 28 (2005). Available from www.nice.org.uk/guidance/CG28
- *Post-traumatic Stress Disorder.* NICE clinical guideline 26 (2005). Available from www.nice.org.uk/guidance/CG26

GUIDANCE UNDER DEVELOPMENT

NICE is currently developing the following related guidance (details available from the NICE website):

- Autism spectrum disorders in children and young people. NICE clinical guideline. Publication expected September 2011[48].
- Service user experience in adult mental health. NICE clinical guideline and quality standard. Publication expected October 2011[49].
- Autism spectrum conditions in adults. NICE clinical guideline. Publication expected June 2012[50].
- Management of autism in children and young people. NICE clinical guideline. Publication TBC[51].

FURTHER INFORMATION

Information on the guideline development process is provided in:

---

[48]This has since been published (in September 2011) as *Autism Diagnosis in Children and Young People* (NICE clinical guideline 128).

[49]This has since been published (in December 2011) as *Service User Experience in Adult Mental Health* (NICE clinical guideline 136).

[50]This has since been published (in June 2012) as *Autism: Recognition, Referral, Diagnosis and Management of Adults on the Autism Spectrum* (NICE clinical guideline 142).

[51]This has since been published (in August 2013) as *Autism: the Management and Support of Children and Young People on the Autism Spectrum* (NICE clinical guideline 170).

● 'How NICE clinical guidelines are developed: an overview for stakeholders the public and the NHS'
● 'The guidelines manual'.

These are available from the NICE website (www.nice.org.uk/GuidelinesManual). Information on the progress of the guideline will also be available from the NICE website (www.nice.org.uk).

APPENDIX 2:
DECLARATIONS OF INTERESTS BY GUIDELINE DEVELOPMENT GROUP MEMBERS

With a range of practical experience relevant to social anxiety disorder in the GDG, members were appointed because of their understanding and expertise in healthcare for people with social anxiety disorder and support for their families and carers, including: scientific issues; health research; the delivery and receipt of healthcare, along with the work of the healthcare industry; and the role of professional organisations and organisations for people with social anxiety disorder and their families and carers.

To minimise and manage any potential conflicts of interest, and to avoid any public concern that commercial or other financial interests have affected the work of the GDG and influenced guidance, members of the GDG must declare as a matter of public record any interests held by themselves or their families which fall under specified categories (see below). These categories include any relationships they have with the healthcare industries, professional organisations and organisations for people with social anxiety disorder and their families and carers.

Individuals invited to join the GDG were asked to declare their interests before being appointed. To allow the management of any potential conflicts of interest that might arise during the development of the guideline, GDG members were also asked to declare their interests at each GDG meeting throughout the guideline development process. The interests of all the members of the GDG are listed below, including interests declared prior to appointment and during the guideline development process.

CATEGORIES OF INTEREST TO BE WRITTEN IN THIRD PERSON

Paid employment

Personal pecuniary interest: financial payments or other benefits from either the manufacturer or the owner of the product or service under consideration in this guideline, or the industry or sector from which the product or service comes. This includes holding a directorship or other paid position; carrying out consultancy or fee paid work; having shareholdings or other beneficial interests; receiving expenses and hospitality over and above what would be reasonably expected to attend meetings and conferences.

Personal family interest: financial payments or other benefits from the healthcare industry that were received by a family member.

Non-personal pecuniary interest: financial payments or other benefits received by the GDG member's organisation or department, but where the GDG member has not personally received payment, including fellowships and other support provided by the healthcare industry. This includes a grant or fellowship or other payment to sponsor a post, or contribute to the running costs of the department; commissioning of research or other work; contracts with, or grants from, NICE.

Personal non-pecuniary interest: these include, but are not limited to, clear opinions or public statements made about individuals with social anxiety disorder, holding office in a professional organisation or advocacy group with a direct interest in social anxiety disorder, other reputational risks relevant to social anxiety disorder.

Guideline Development Group – Declarations of interest	
Professor David Clark (Chair)	
Employment	Professor of Experimental Psychology, University of Oxford.
Personal pecuniary interest	National Clinical Adviser to the Department of Health's Increasing Access to Psychological Therapies (IAPT) Programme.
Personal family interest	None
Non-personal pecuniary interest	Co-applicant of grant from South London and Maudsley NHS Foundation Trust and King's College London NIHR Biomedical Research Centre in Mental Health. £25,000,000.
	Joint holder of Wellcome Trust Programme Grant entitled 'Cognitive processes in the maintenance and treatment of social phobia and post-traumatic stress disorder'. £2,599,970.
	Developer of one of the models for individual CBT under consideration in the guideline.
Personal non-pecuniary interest	None
Action taken	Recommendations relating to individual CBT for adults were discussed by the GDG on 4 October 2012. It was decided that it was not appropriate for Professor Clark to be present and he left the room for this discussion. All members of the GDG were asked if they felt this approach was acceptable and all agreed.

Dr Safi Afghan	
Employment	Consultant Psychiatrist, Dorothy Pattison Hospital, Dudley and Walsall Mental Health Partnership NHS Trust.
Personal pecuniary interest	Conducted speaker sessions and received fee from Lundbeck Ltd and Astra Zeneca. Also intending to carry out speaker sessions for Pfizer on the topic of generalised anxiety disorder in the next 12 months.
Personal family interest	None
Non-personal pecuniary interest	None
Personal non-pecuniary interest	None
Action taken	None
Mr Peter Armstrong	
Employment	Director of Training, Newcastle Cognitive and Behavioural Therapies Centre, Northumberland, Tyne and Wear NHS Foundation Trust.
Personal pecuniary interest	None
Personal family interest	None
Non-personal pecuniary interest	Employment is within an NHS service that provides CBT treatment, supervision, consultancy and education in relation to social anxiety.
Personal non-pecuniary interest	A member of BABCP and was a board member some years ago. As a CBT practitioner and teacher, Mr Armstrong's approach to understanding and treating social anxiety is largely framed within cognitive-behavioural terms.
Action taken	None
Dr Madeleine Bennett	
Employment	GP, NSPCR Fellow, Department of Primary Care and Population Health, University College London.

Personal pecuniary interest	None
Personal family interest	None
Non-personal pecuniary interest	None
Personal non-pecuniary interest	None
Action taken	None
Dr Sam Cartwright-Hatton	
Employment	Clinical Psychologist, NIHR Career Development Fellow, University of Sussex.
Personal pecuniary interest	None
Personal family interest	None
Non-personal pecuniary interest	None
Personal non-pecuniary interest	Published academic papers on the use/ applicability of CBT for social anxiety in children. Principal investigator for 'A new parenting-based group intervention for young anxious children: randomised trial'.
Action taken	Recommendations relating to group-based interventions for children and young people were discussed by the GDG on 5 October 2012. It was decided that it was not appropriate for Dr Cartwright-Hatton to be present and she left the room for this discussion. All members of the GDG were asked if they felt this approach was acceptable and all agreed.
Dr Cathy Creswell	
Employment	Principal Research Fellow, School of Psychology and Clinical Language Sciences, University of Reading; Honorary Consultant Clinical Psychologist, Berkshire Child Anxiety Clinic, Berkshire Healthcare NHS Foundation Trust.

Personal pecuniary interest	Co-author of book *Overcoming Your Child's Fears and Worries: A Self-help Guide Using Cognitive Behavioural Techniques.*
Personal family interest	None
Non-personal pecuniary interest	None
Personal non-pecuniary interest	Named supervisor for the 'Overcoming your child's fears and worries: a randomised controlled trial of guided self-help for childhood anxiety disorders' trial (ISRCTN92977593).
Action taken	Recommendations relating to guided self-help for children and young people were discussed by the GDG on 5 October 2012. It was decided that it was not appropriate for Dr Creswell to be present and she left the room for this discussion. All members of the GDG were asked if they felt this approach was acceptable and all agreed.
Dr Melanie Dix	
Employment	Consultant Child and Adolescent Psychiatrist, Cumbria Partnership Foundation Trust.
Personal pecuniary interest	None
Personal family interest	None
Non-personal pecuniary interest	None
Personal non-pecuniary interest	None
Action taken	None
Mr Nick Hanlon	
Employment	Service User Representative and Chairman, Social Anxiety West, Bristol.
Personal pecuniary interest	None
Personal family interest	None
Non-personal pecuniary interest	None

Personal non-pecuniary interest	None
Action taken	None

Dr Andrea Malizia

Employment	Consultant Psychiatrist and Clinical Psychopharmacologist, Clinical Partners and North Bristol NHS Trust
Personal pecuniary interest	None
Personal family interest	None
Non-personal pecuniary interest	Occasionally gives talks for pharmaceutical industry, mostly at regional level. The fees for these talks are put in a university account where they support PhD students, research, small expenditure on pilot research projects and conference attendance for members of the team. There are potential projects that may be funded by industry over the next year. None of the above are in the field of social anxiety disorder or with companies that have a current licence or to Dr Malizia's knowledge are currently planning to apply for a licence in social anxiety disorder.
Personal non-pecuniary interest	A member of the British Association for Psychopharmacology and of the Royal College of Psychiatrists – both organisations have a professional interest in the recognition and management of social anxiety disorder.
Action taken	None

Dr Jane Roberts

Employment	Clinical Senior Lecturer in General Practice, University of Sunderland and GP.
Personal pecuniary interest	None
Personal family interest	None
Non-personal pecuniary interest	None

Personal non-pecuniary interest	None
Action taken	None

Mr Gareth Stephens	
Employment	Service User Representative.
Personal pecuniary interest	None
Personal family interest	None
Non-personal pecuniary interest	None
Personal non-pecuniary interest	None
Action taken	None

Dr Lusia Stopa	
Employment	Director of CBT Programmes and Senior Lecturer, Psychology Academic Unit, University of Southampton and Honorary Consultant Clinical Psychologist, Southern Health NHS Foundation Trust.
Personal pecuniary interest	None
Personal family interest	None
Non-personal pecuniary interest	None
Personal non-pecuniary interest	None
Action taken	None

National Collaborating Centre for Mental Health – Declarations of interest	
Professor Steve Pilling (Facilitator)	
Employment	Director, NCCMH; Professor of Clinical Psychology and Clinical Effectiveness; Director, Centre for Outcomes Research and Effectiveness, University College London.

Personal pecuniary interest	Grant holder for £1,440,000 per year (approximately) from NICE for guideline development. Work with NICE International. Undertaken some research into mental health, and the mental health workforce for Department of Health, Royal College of Psychiatrists and the Academy of Medical Royal Colleges.
Personal family interest	None
Non-personal pecuniary interest	None
Personal non-pecuniary interest	None
Action taken	None
Dr Evan Mayo-Wilson	
Employment	Senior Systematic Reviewer and Senior Research Associate, NCCMH.
Personal pecuniary interest	None
Personal family interest	None
Non-personal pecuniary interest	None
Personal non-pecuniary interest	None
Dr Ifigeneia Mavranezouli	
Employment	Senior Health Economist, NCCMH.
Personal pecuniary interest	None
Personal family interest	None
Non-personal pecuniary interest	None
Personal non-pecuniary interest	None
Action taken	None
Mr Benedict Anigbogu	
Employment	Health Economist, NCCMH.

Personal pecuniary interest	None
Personal family interest	None
Non-personal pecuniary interest	None
Personal non-pecuniary interest	None
Action taken	None
Ms Kayleigh Kew	
Employment	Research Assistant, NCCMH.
Personal pecuniary interest	None
Personal family interest	None
Non-personal pecuniary interest	None
Personal non-pecuniary interest	None
Action taken	None
Ms Katherine Leggett	
Employment	Senior Project Manager (from October 2012).
Personal pecuniary interest	None
Personal family interest	None
Non-personal pecuniary interest	None
Personal non-pecuniary interest	None
Action taken	None
Mrs Kate Satrettin	
Employment	Project Manager (until October 2012).
Personal pecuniary interest	None
Personal family interest	None
Non-personal pecuniary interest	None

Personal non-pecuniary interest	None
Action taken	None

Ms Melinda Smith

Employment	Research Assistant, NCCMH.
Personal pecuniary interest	None
Personal family interest	None
Non-personal pecuniary interest	None
Personal non-pecuniary interest	None
Action taken	None

Ms Sarah Stockton

Employment	Senior Information Scientist, NCCMH.
Personal pecuniary interest	None
Personal family interest	None
Non-personal pecuniary interest	None
Personal non-pecuniary interest	None
Action taken	None

Dr Clare Taylor

Employment	Senior Editor, NCCMH.
Personal pecuniary interest	None
Personal family interest	None
Non-personal pecuniary interest	None
Personal non-pecuniary interest	None
Action taken	None

Dr Craig Whittington	
Employment	Associate Director (Clinical Effectiveness), NCCMH
Personal pecuniary interest	None
Personal family interest	None
Non-personal pecuniary interest	None
Personal non-pecuniary interest	None
Action taken	None

APPENDIX 3:
SPECIAL ADVISERS TO THE GUIDELINE
DEVELOPMENT GROUP

Professor Tony Ades (PhD)
Professor of Public Health Science, University of Bristol

Dr Sofia Dias (PhD)
Research Fellow (Statistician), University of Bristol

APPENDIX 4:
STAKEHOLDERS AND EXPERTS WHO SUBMITTED COMMENTS IN RESPONSE TO THE CONSULTATION DRAFT OF THE GUIDELINE

Stakeholders

Anxiety UK
British Association for Behavioural and Cognitive Psychotherapies
British Association for Counselling and Psychotherapy
British Association for Performing Arts Medicine
British Medical Association
British Psychological Society
CCBT Ltd
College of Mental Health Pharmacy
Department of Health
Lilly UK/Eli Lilly and Co Ltd
National Autistic Society
Nottinghamshire NHS Trust
Royal College of Nursing
Royal College of Paediatrics and Child Health (RCPCH)
Selective Mutism Information and Research Association (SMIRA)
Social Anxiety West (SA West)
South London and Maudsley NHS Foundation Trust
TOP UK Triumph Over Phobia

Experts

Andrea Cipriani
Richard G. Heimberg
Ron Rapee
Franklin Schneier
Susan H. Spence

APPENDIX 5:
RESEARCHERS CONTACTED TO REQUEST
FURTHER DATA

Abbott UK
Dr J. Abramowitz
Professor Eliane Albuisson
Dr Lynn Alden
Professor Christer Allgulander
Dr Nader Amir
Dr Page Anderson
Professor Gerhard Andersson
Dr Gavin D. Andrews
Dr A. G. Angelosante
Severine Arthaud
Dr Satoshi T. Asakura
Dr M. K. Atmaca
Dr Terry Kit-fong Au
Professor Susan G. Baer
Professor David Baldwin
Dr Paula M. Barrett
Professor Courtney Beard
Dr Deborah Beidel
Dr Thomas Berger
Dr G. A. Bernstein
Professor Boris A. Birmaher
Professor Carlos Blanco
Dr Denise H. M. Bodden
Dr Sarah W. T. Book
Dr Finn-Magnus H. Borge
Dr François S. Borgeat
Dr Cristina Botella
Dr Jerry Bruns
Dr Kathryn M. Connor
Dr Jean Cottraux
Dr Michelle G. S. Craske
Professor Jonathan Davidson
Dr J. C. V. De Groot
Dr Karen Dineen-Wagner
Dr Ebrahim Dogaheh

Dr Todd Durell
Dr Enrique Echeburua
Deborah Edwards
Eli Lilly
Dr Paul M. G. Emmelkamp
Dr David H. J. Erickson
Dr Douglas Feltner
Laura Fischer
Professor Edna B. Foa
Dr Tomas Furmark
Dr Heather M. R. Gallagher
Dr Raja Ghosh
GlaxoSmithKline
Dr Philippe Goldin
Dr John H. Greist
Dr Karin Gruber
Dr Adam Guastella
Professor Chris V. Hayward
Dr Erik Hedman
Professor Richard G. Heimberg
Dr James Herbert
Dr Dina R. Hirshfeld-Becker
Hoffman-La Roche
Professor Stefan Hofmann
Dr Jazaieri Hooria
Dr Debra A. Hope
Jennie Hudson
Professor Isabelle Jalenques
Professor Derek Johnston
Professor Siegfried Kasper
Dr David J. K. Katzelnick
Professor Philip Kendall
Dr Neil J. Kitchiner
Dr Daniela Zippin B. Knijnik
Dr Kenneth A. Kobak
Dr D Kosycki

Professor Malcolm S. Lader
Dr W. Y. Lau
Dr Deborah Roth Ledley
Dr Falk Leichsenring
Dr U. B. Lepola
Dr Johnson Li
Dr Juliette M. Liber
Dr Michael. R. Liebowitz
Dr J. D. Lipsitz
Jamie Longwell
Lundbeck
Gavin Lyndon
Dr Heidi Lyneham
Dr Malhi
Dr Katharina Manassis
Dr John S. E. March
Professor Isaac M. Marks
Dr Carrie Masia-Warner
Dr Richard P. Mattick
Dr Brett McDermot
Dr Peter M. McEvoy
Meda
Dafna Merom
Dr Siebke Melfsen
Dr Stuart A. Montgomery
Dr Moritz N. Muehlbacher
Dr S. Mulkens
Professor Marko Munjiza
Dr Michelle G. Newman
Professor Hans M. Nordahl
Dr Russell Noyes Jr
Dr D. B. Oosterbaan
Dr Michael W. Otto
Dr Atul C. Pande
Pfizer
Dr Philayrath Phongsavan
Dr Jacob Piet
Dr Daniel S. Pine
Dr Ján Praško
Dr Matthew Price
Professor Ron Rapee
Dr Renner

Dr Karl M. Rickels
Dr Genevieve Robillard
Walton Roth
Dr Peter Roy-Byrn
Mr Lee Ruggiero
Lissette Saavedra
Dr Brad Schmidt
Dr A. J. Schneider
Professor Franklin R. G. Schneier
Dr Sara I. Schutters
Dr Soraya Seedat
Dr Wike Seekles
Dr Phyllis Shaw
Professor M. Katherine B. Shear
Dr Wendy K. Silverman
Professor Naomi M. Simon
Dr Jasper A. J. Smits
Professor Susan Hilary Spence
Dr Uli H. Stangier
Dr Dan J. Stein
Professor Murray B. Stein
Dr Ariel Stravynski
Barr Taylor
Dr Charles T. Taylor
Dr Steven Taylor
Dr Nikolai Titov
Professor Philip Treffers
Professor Peter Tyrer
Dr Elisabeth Utens
Dr Sandeep A. Vaishnavi
Miriam Valentine
Dr M. A. Van Ameringen
Dr Anton van Balkom
Professor Ferdinand Verhulst
Dr Marcio N. Versiani
Dr Benedetto Vitiello
Dr John R. Walker
Dr Steve Watt
Risa Weisberg
Dr Daniel F. K. Wong
Dr W. C. Zhang

APPENDIX 6:
SEARCH STRATEGIES FOR THE IDENTIFICATION
OF CLINICAL EVIDENCE

Search strategies can be found on the CD-ROM.

APPENDIX 7:
SEARCH STRATEGIES FOR THE IDENTIFICATION OF HEALTH ECONOMICS STUDIES

Search strategies can be found on the CD-ROM.

APPENDIX 8:

ECONOMIC EVIDENCE: METHODOLOGY

CHECKLIST TEMPLATE

The applicability and methodological quality of each economic evaluation was evaluated using a checklist constructed by NICE, reproduced below. For information about how to complete the checklist, see *The Guidelines Manual* (NICE, 2011a).

Study identification *Including author, title, reference, year of publication*		
Guideline topic:		
Section 1: Applicability (relevance to specific guideline review question(s) and the NICE reference case). This checklist should be used first to filter out irrelevant studies.	**Yes/ Partly/ No/Unclear/NA**	**Comments**
1.1	Is the study population appropriate for the guideline?		
1.2	Are the interventions appropriate for the guideline?		
1.3	Is the healthcare system in which the study was conducted sufficiently similar to the current UK NHS context?		
1.4	Are costs measured from the NHS and personal social services (PSS) perspective?		
1.5	Are all direct health effects on individuals included?		
1.6	Are both costs and health effects discounted at an annual rate of 3.5%?		
1.7	Is the value of health effects expressed in terms of quality-adjusted life years (QALYs)?		

1.8	Are changes in health-related quality of life (HRQoL) reported directly from patients and/or carers?		
1.9	Is the valuation of changes in HRQoL (utilities) obtained from a representative sample of the general public?		
1.10	Overall judgement: Directly applicable/ Partially applicable/Not applicable There is no need to use Section 2 of the checklist if the study is considered 'not applicable'.		
Other comments:			

Section 2: Study limitations (the level of methodological quality) This checklist should be used once it has been decided that the study is sufficiently applicable to the context of the clinical guideline.	**Yes/ Partly/ No/Unclear/NA**	**Comments**
2.1	Does the model structure adequately reflect the nature of the health condition under evaluation?		
2.2	Is the time horizon sufficiently long to reflect all important differences in costs and outcomes?		
2.3	Are all important and relevant health outcomes included?		
2.4	Are the estimates of baseline health outcomes from the best available source?		
2.5	Are the estimates of relative treatment effects from the best available source?		
2.6	Are all important and relevant costs included?		
2.7	Are the estimates of resource use from the best available source?		

2.8	Are the unit costs of resources from the best available source?		
2.9	Is an appropriate incremental analysis presented or can it be calculated from the data?		
2.10	Are all important parameters whose values are uncertain subjected to appropriate sensitivity analysis?		
2.11	Is there no potential conflict of interest?		
2.12	Overall assessment: Minor limitations/ Potentially serious limitations/Very serious limitations		
Other comments:			

APPENDIX 9:
HIGH-PRIORITY RESEARCH
RECOMMENDATIONS

The GDG has made the following recommendations for research, based on its review of evidence, to improve NICE guidance and patient care in the future.

ADULTS' UPTAKE OF AND ENGAGEMENT WITH INTERVENTIONS FOR SOCIAL ANXIETY DISORDER

What methods are effective in improving uptake of and engagement with interventions for adults with social anxiety disorder?

Why this is important

Effective interventions exist for social anxiety disorder but access to and uptake of services is limited and over 50% of people with social anxiety disorder never receive treatment; of those who do receive treatment many wait 10 years or more for it.

This question should be addressed by a programme of work that tests a number of strategies to improve uptake and engagement, including:

● Development and evaluation of improved pathways into care, in collaboration with low users of services, through a series of cohort studies with the outcomes including increased uptake of and retention in services.
● Adapting the delivery of existing interventions for social anxiety disorder in collaboration with service users. Adaptations could include changes to the settings for, methods of delivery of, or staff delivering the interventions. These interventions should be tested in a randomised controlled trial (RCT) design that reports short- and medium-term outcomes (including cost effectiveness) of at least 18 months' duration.

SPECIFIC VERSUS GENERIC CBT FOR CHILDREN AND YOUNG PEOPLE WITH SOCIAL ANXIETY DISORDER

What is the clinical and cost effectiveness of specific CBT for children and young people with social anxiety disorder compared with generic anxiety-focused CBT?

Why this is important

Children and young people with social anxiety disorder have commonly been treated with psychological interventions that cover a broad range of anxiety disorders, rather than interventions specifically focused on social anxiety disorder. This approach may be considered to be easier and cheaper to deliver, but emerging evidence suggests that children and young people with social anxiety disorder may do less well with these generic treatments than those with other anxiety disorders. There have, however, been no direct comparisons of treatment outcomes using generic compared with social anxiety-specific treatment programmes.

This question should be answered using an RCT design, reporting short- and medium-term outcomes (including cost effectiveness) with a follow-up of at least 12 months. The outcomes should be assessed by structured clinical interviews, parent- and self-reports using validated questionnaires and objective measures of behaviour. The study needs to be large enough to determine the presence of clinically important effects, and mediators and moderators (in particular the child or young person's age) should be investigated.

THE ROLE OF PARENTS IN THE TREATMENT OF CHILDREN AND YOUNG PEOPLE WITH SOCIAL ANXIETY DISORDER

What is the best way of involving parents in the treatment of children and young people (at different stages of development) with social anxiety disorder?

Why this is important

There is very little evidence to guide the treatment of social anxiety disorder in children aged under 7 years. It is likely that treatment will be most effectively delivered either wholly or partly by parents. Parenting interventions have been effective in treating other psychological difficulties in this age group, and this guideline found emerging evidence that these approaches might be useful for the treatment of young socially anxious children.

Furthermore, when considering all age groups, parental mental health difficulties and parenting practices have been linked with the development and maintenance of social anxiety disorder in children and young people. This suggests that interventions targeting these parental factors may improve treatment outcomes. However, interventions for children and young people with social anxiety disorder have varied widely in the extent and manner in which parents are involved in treatment and the benefit of including parents in interventions has not been established.

This question should be addressed in two stages.

● Parent-focused interventions should be developed based on a systematic review of the literature and in collaboration with service users.

- The clinical and cost effectiveness of these interventions at different stages of development should be tested using an RCT design with standard care (for example, group CBT) as the comparison. It should report short- and medium-term outcomes (including cost effectiveness) with a follow-up of at least 12 months. The outcomes should be assessed by structured clinical interviews, parent- and self-reports using validated questionnaires and objective measures of behaviour. The study needs to be large enough to determine the presence of clinically important effects, and mediators and moderators (in particular the child or young person's age) should be investigated.

INDIVIDUAL VERSUS GROUP CBT FOR CHILDREN AND YOUNG PEOPLE WITH SOCIAL ANXIETY DISORDER

What is the clinical and cost effectiveness of individual and group CBT for children and young people with social anxiety disorder?

Why this is important

The majority of systematic evaluations of interventions for social anxiety disorder in children and young people have taken a group approach. Studies with adult populations, however, indicate that individually-delivered treatments are associated with better treatment outcomes and are more cost effective.

This question should be addressed using an RCT design comparing the clinical and cost effectiveness of individual and group-based treatments for children and young people with social anxiety disorder. It should report short- and medium-term outcomes (including cost effectiveness) with a follow-up of at least 12 months. The outcomes should be assessed by structured clinical interviews, parent- and self-reports using validated questionnaires and objective measures of behaviour. The study needs to be large enough to determine the presence of clinically important effects, and mediators and moderators (in particular the child or young person's age and familial and social context) should be investigated.

COMBINED INTERVENTIONS FOR ADULTS WITH SOCIAL ANXIETY DISORDER

What is the clinical and cost effectiveness of combined psychological and pharmacological interventions compared with either intervention alone in the treatment of adults with social anxiety disorder?

Why this is important

There is evidence for the effectiveness of both CBT and medication, in particular SSRIs, in the treatment of social anxiety disorder. However, little is known about the effects of combined pharmacological and psychological interventions despite their widespread use. Understanding the costs and benefits of combined treatment could lead to more effective and targeted combinations if they prove to be more effective than single treatments. The study will also provide important information on the long-term benefits of medication.

This question should be addressed in a large-scale three-arm RCT comparing the clinical and cost effectiveness of combined individual CBT and SSRI treatment with individual CBT or an SSRI alone. Trial participants receiving medication should be offered it for 1 year. The study should report short- and medium-term outcomes (including cost effectiveness) with a follow-up of at least 24 months. The primary outcome should be recovery, with important secondary outcomes being retention in treatment, experience and side effects of medication, and social and personal functioning. The study needs to be large enough to determine the presence of clinically important effects, and mediators and moderators should be investigated.

11   REFERENCES

[Redacted]. Results of investigation of 'all adverse events and verbatim terms that might possibly refer to an event that could be part of suicidal thinking and/or suicide attempt' henceforth referred to as 'possibly suicide-related' from review of Pediatric Studies: Biomedical Data Sciences, GlaxoSmithKline; 15 May 2003 [unpublished].

Abramowitz JS, Moore EL, Braddock AE, Harrington DL. Self-help cognitive-behavioral therapy with minimal therapist contact for social phobia: a controlled trial. Journal of Behavior Therapy and Experimental Psychiatry. 2009;40:98–105.

Acarturk C, de Graaf R, van Straten A, Have MT, Cuijpers P. Social phobia and number of social fears, and their association with comorbidity, health-related quality of life and help seeking: a population-based study. Social Psychiatry and Psychiatric Epidemiology. 2008;43:273–9.

Acarturk C, Smit F, de Graaf R, van Straten A, Ten Have M, Cuijpers P. Economic costs of social phobia: a population-based study. Journal of Affective Disorders. 2009;115:421–9.

Adler LA, Liebowitz M, Kronenberger W, Qiao M, Rubin R, Hollandbeck M, et al. Atomoxetine treatment in adults with attention-deficit/hyperactivity disorder and comorbid social anxiety disorder. Depression and Anxiety. 2009;26:212–21.

AGREE Collaboration. Development and validation of an international appraisal instrument for assessing the quality of clinical practice guidelines: the AGREE project. Quality and Safety in Health Care. 2003;12:18–23.

Albano AM, Mallick R, Tourian K, Zhang HF, Kearney C. Children and adolescents with social anxiety disorder: school refusal and improvement with venlafaxine ER relative to placebo. European Neuropsychopharmacology. 2004;14:S307–S08.

Alden LE. Short-term structured treatment for avoidant personality disorder. Journal of Consulting and Clinical Psychology. 1989;57:756–64.

Alden LE, Taylor CT. Relational treatment strategies increase social approach behaviors in patients with Generalized Social Anxiety Disorder. Journal of Anxiety Disorders. 2011;25:309–18.

Allgulander C, editor. Efficacy of paroxetine in social phobia – a single-center double-blind study of 96 symptomatic volunteers randomized to treatment with paroxetine 20–50 mg or placebo for 3 months. 11th European College of Neuropsychopharmacology Congress; 1998 31 October – 4 November; Paris, France.

Allgulander C. Paroxetine in social anxiety disorder: a randomized placebo-controlled study. Acta Psychiatrica Scandinavica. 1999;100:193–98.

Allgulander CN. A prospective study of 86 new patients with social anxiety disorder. Acta Psychiatrica Scandinavica. 2001;103:447–52.

Allgulander C, Mangano R, Zhang J, Dahl A, Lepola U, Sjodin I, et al. Efficacy of venlafaxine ER in patients with social anxiety disorder: a double-blind, placebo-controlled, parallel-group comparison with paroxetine. Human Psychopharmacology. 2004;19:387–96.

Allgulander C, Jorgensen T, Wade A, Francois C, Despiegel N, Auquier P, et al. Health-related quality of life (HRQOL) among patients with generalised anxiety Disorder: evaluation conducted alongside an escitalopram relapse prevention trial. Current Medical Research and Opinion. 2007;23:2543–9.

Almlöv J, Carlbring P, Källqvist K, Paxling B, Cuijpers P, Andersson G. Therapist effects in guided internet-delivered CBT for anxiety disorders. Behavioural and Cognitive Psychotherapy. 2011;39:311–22.

Alonso J, Angermeyer MC, Bernert S, Bruffaerts R, Brugha TS, Bryson H, et al. Disability and quality of life impact of mental disorders in Europe: results from the European Study of the Epidemiology of Mental Disorders (ESEMeD) project. Acta Psychiatrica Scandinavica Supplementum. 2004:38–46.

Altman DG, Bland JM. Diagnostic tests. 1: sensitivity and specificity. BMJ. 1994a;308:1552.

Altman DG, Bland JM. Statistics notes: diagnostic tests 2: predictive values. BMJ. 1994b;309:102.

American Autoimmune Related Diseases Association. The Cost Burden of Autoimmune Disease: The Latest Front in the War on Healthcare Spending. Eastpoint, MI: American Autoimmune Related Diseases Association; 2011. Available from: www.aarda.org/pdf/cbad.pdf.

American Psychiatric Association. Diagnostic and Statistical Manual of Mental Disorders – Text Revision (DSM-IV-TR). Washington, DC: American Psychiatric Association; 2000.

Amir N, Beard C, Taylor C, Klumpp H, Elias J, Burns M, et al. Attention training in individuals with generalized social phobia: a randomized controlled trial. Journal of Consulting and Clinical Psychology. 2009;77:961–73.

Amir N, Taylor C. Interpretation training in individuals with generalized social anxiety disorder: a randomized controlled trial. Journal of Consulting and Clinical Psychology. 2012;80:497–511.

Andersson G, Carlbring P. Commentary on Berger, Hohl, and Caspar's (2009) internet-based treatment for social phobia: a randomized controlled trial. Journal of Clinical Psychology. 2009;65:1036–38.

Andersson G, Carlbring P, Furmark T. Therapist experience and knowledge acquisition in internet-delivered CBT for social anxiety disorder: a randomized controlled trial. PLoS ONE. 2012;7:e37411.

Andersson G, Carlbring P, Holmström A, Sparthan E, Furmark T, Nilsson-Ihrfelt E, et al. Internet-based self-help with therapist feedback and in vivo group exposure for social phobia: a randomized controlled trial. Journal of Consulting and Clinical Psychology. 2006;74:677–86.

Andersson G, Waara J, Jonsson U, Malmaeus F, Carlbring P, Ost L. Internet-based self-help versus one-session exposure in the treatment of spider phobia: a randomized controlled trial. Cognitive Behaviour Therapy. 2009;38:114–20.

Andrews G, Davies M, Titov N. Effectiveness randomized controlled trial of face to face versus internet cognitive behaviour therapy for social phobia. Australian and New Zealand Journal of Psychiatry. 2011;45:337–40.

Asakura S, Tajima O, Koyama T. Fluvoxamine treatment of generalized social anxiety disorder in Japan: a randomized double-blind, placebo-controlled study. International Journal of Neuropsychopharmacology. 2007;10:263–74.

Atkins D, Best D, Briss PA, Eccles M, Falck-Ytter Y, Flottorp S, et al. Grading quality of evidence and strength of recommendations. BMJ. 2004;328:1490.

Atmaca M, Kuloglu M, Tezcan E, Unal A. Efficacy of citalopram and moclobemide in patients with social phobia: some preliminary findings. Human Psychopharmacology. 2002;17:401–05.

Aune T, Stiles TC, Svarva K, Aune T, Stiles TC, Svarva K. Psychometric properties of the Social Phobia and Anxiety Inventory for Children using a non-American population-based sample. Journal of Anxiety Disorders. 2008;22:1075–86.

Baer S, Garland E. Pilot study of community-based cognitive behavioral group therapy for adolescents with social phobia. Journal of the American Academy of Child and Adolescent Psychiatry. 2005;44:258–64.

Baker SL, Heinrichs N, Kim HJ, Hofmann SG. The Liebowitz Social Anxiety Scale as a self-report instrument: a preliminary psychometric analysis. Behaviour Research and Therapy. 2002;40:701–15.

Baldwin DS, Bobes J, Stein DJ, Scharwächter I, Faure M. Paroxetine in social phobia/social anxiety disorder. Randomised, double-blind, placebo-controlled study. Paroxetine Study Group. The British Journal of Psychiatry. 1999;175:120–26.

Baldwin DS, Cooper JA, Huusom AK, Hindmarch I. A double-blind, randomized, parallel-group, flexible-dose study to evaluate the tolerability, efficacy and effects of treatment discontinuation with escitalopram and paroxetine in patients with major depressive disorder. International Clinical Psychopharmacology. 2006;21:159–69.

Baldwin JS, Dadds MR. Reliability and validity of parent and child versions of the Multidimensional Anxiety Scale for children in community samples. Journal of the American Academy of Child and Adolescent Psychiatry. 2007;46:252–60.

Barbui C, Esposito E, Cipriani A. Selective serotonin reuptake inhibitors and risk of suicide: a systematic review of observational studies. Canadian Medical Association Journal. 2009;180:291–7.

Barnett S, Kramer M, Casat C, Connor K, Davidson J. Efficacy of olanzapine in social anxiety disorder: a pilot study. Journal of Psychopharmacology. 2002;16:365–68.

Beard C, Weisberg RB, Amir N. Combined cognitive bias modification treatment for social anxiety disorder: a pilot trial. Depression and Anxiety. 2011;28:981–8.

Beasley CM, Jr., Koke SC, Nilsson ME, Gonzales JS. Adverse events and treatment discontinuations in clinical trials of fluoxetine in major depressive disorder: an updated meta-analysis. Clinical Therapeutics. 2000;22:1319–30.

Becker ES, Rinck M, Turke V, Kause P, Goodwin R, Neumer S, et al. Epidemiology of specific phobia subtypes: findings from the Dresden Mental Health Study. European Psychiatry. 2007;22:69–74.

Beesdo K, Knappe S, Pine DS. Anxiety and anxiety disorders in children and adolescents: developmental issues and implications for DSM-V. The Psychiatric Clinics of North America. 2009;32:483–524.

Beidel DC, Turner SM, Morris TL. Psychopathology of childhood social phobia. Journal of the American Academy of Child and Adolescent Psychiatry. 1999;38:643–50.

Beidel DC, Turner SM, Morris TL. Behavioral treatment of childhood social phobia. Journal of Consulting and Clinical Psychology. 2000;68:1072–80.

Beidel DC, Turner SM, Sallee FR, Ammerman RT, Crosby LA, Pathak S. SET-C versus fluoxetine in the treatment of childhood social phobia. Journal of the American Academy of Child and Adolescent Psychiatry. 2007;46:1622–32.

Berger T, Hohl E, Caspar F. Internet-based treatment for social phobia: a randomized controlled trial. Journal of Clinical Psychology. 2009;65:1021–35.

Berger T, Hohl E, Caspar F. [Internet-based treatment for social phobia: a 6-month follow-up]. Zeitschrift fur Klinische Psychologie und Psychotherapie: Forschung und Praxis. 2010;39:217–21.

Berlin JA. Does blinding of readers affect the results of meta-analyses? University of Pennsylvania Meta-analysis Blinding Study Group. Lancet. 1997;350:185–6.

Birmaher BB. Psychometric properties of the screen for child anxiety related emotional disorders (SCARED): a replication study. Journal of the American Academy of Child and Adolescent Psychiatry. 1999;38:1230–36.

Bjornsson AS, Bidwell LC, Brosse AL, Carey G, Hauser M, Mackiewicz Seghete KL, et al. Cognitive-behavioral group therapy versus group psychotherapy for social anxiety disorder among college students: a randomized controlled trial. Depression and Anxiety. 2011;28:1034–42.

Black B, Uhde T. Treatment of elective mutism with fluoxetine: a double-blind, placebo-controlled study. Journal of the American Academy of Child and Adolescent Psychiatry. 1994;33:1000–06.

Blanco C, Heimberg RG, Schneier FR, Fresco DM, Chen HN, Turk CL, et al. A placebo-controlled trial of phenelzine, cognitive behavioral group therapy, and their combination for social anxiety disorder. Archives of General Psychiatry. 2010;67:286–95.

Blanco C, Bragdon LB, Schneier FR, Liebowitz MR. The evidence-based pharmacotherapy of social anxiety disorder. International Journal of Neuropsychopharmacology. 2012;6:427–42.

Blomhoff S, Haug TT, Hellstrom K, Holme I, Humble M, Madsbu HP, et al. Randomised controlled general practice trial of sertraline, exposure therapy and combined treatment in generalised social phobia. British Journal of Psychiatry. 2001;179:23–30.

Boettcher J, Berger T, Renneberg B. Internet-based attention training for social anxiety: a randomized controlled trial. Cognitive Therapy and Research. 2011;36:522–36.

Bögels SM. Task concentration training versus applied relaxation, in combination with cognitive therapy, for social phobia patients with fear of blushing, trembling, and sweating. Behaviour Research and Therapy. 2006;44:1199–210.

Bögels SM, Voncken MJ. Social skills training versus cognitive therapy for social anxiety disorder characterized by fear of blushing, trembling, or sweating. International Journal of Cognitive Therapy. 2008;1:138–50.

Bogetto F, Bellino S, Revello RB, Patria L. Discontinuation syndrome in dysthymic patients treated with selective serotonin reuptake inhibitors: a clinical investigation. CNS Drugs. 2002;16:273–83.

Boley TM, Belangee KN, Markwell S, Hazelrigg SR. The effect of thoracoscopic sympathectomy on quality of life and symptom management of hyperhidrosis. Journal of the American College of Surgeons. 2007;204:435–8.

Book SW, Thomas SE, Randall PK, Randall CL. Paroxetine reduces social anxiety in individuals with a co-occurring alcohol use disorder. Journal of Anxiety Disorders. 2008;22:310–18.

Borge FM, Hoffart A, Sexton H, Clark D, Markowitz J, McManus F. Residential cognitive therapy versus residential interpersonal therapy for social phobia: a randomized clinical trial. Journal of Anxiety Disorders. 2008;22:991–1010.

Borge FM, Hoffart A, Sexton H, Martinsen E, Gude T, Hedley LM, et al. Pre-treatment predictors and in-treatment factors associated with change in avoidant and dependent personality disorder traits among patients with social phobia. Clinical Psychology and Psychotherapy. 2010;17:87–99.

Borgeat F, Stankovic M, Khazaal Y, Rouget B, Baumann M, Riquier F, et al. Does the form or the amount of exposure make a difference in the cognitive-behavioral therapy treatment of social phobia? The Journal of Nervous and Mental Disease. 2009;197:507–13.

Botella C, Gallego MJ, Garcia PA, Guillen V, Baños RM, Quero S, et al. An internet-based self-help treatment for fear of public speaking: a controlled trial. Cyberpsychology, Behavior and Social Networking. 2010;13:407–21.

Brambilla P, Cipriani A, Hotopf M, Barbui C. Side-effect profile of fluoxetine in comparison with other SSRIs, tricyclic and newer antidepressants: a meta-analysis of clinical trial data. Pharmacopsychiatry. 2005;38:69–77.

Brazier J, Roberts J, Deverill M. The estimation of a preference-based measure of health from the SF-36. Journal of Health Economics. 2002;21:271–92.

Briggs A, Sculpher M, Claxton K. Decision Modelling for Health Economic Evaluation. Oxford: Oxford University Press; 2006.

Brooks R. Quality of life measures. Critical Care Medicine. 1996;24:1769.

Bruce SE, Yonkers KA, Otto MW, Eisen JL, Weisberg RB, Pagano M, et al. Influence of psychiatric comorbidity on recovery and recurrence in generalized anxiety disorder, social phobia, and panic disorder: a 12-year prospective study. The American Journal of Psychiatry. 2005;162:1179–87.

Buckley NA, McManus PR. Fatal toxicity of serotoninergic and other antidepressant drugs: analysis of United Kingdom mortality data. BMJ. 2002;325:1332–3.

Bunevicius A, Peceliuniene J, Mickuviene N, Valius L, Bunevicius R, Bunevicius A, et al. Screening for depression and anxiety disorders in primary care patients. Depression and Anxiety. 2007;24:455–60.

Burlingame GM, Lambert MJ, Reisinger CW, Neff WM, Mosier J. Pragmatics of tracking mental health outcomes in a managed care setting. The Journal of Behavioral Health Services and Research. 1995;22:226–36.

Burrows GE. Moclobemide in social phobia. A double-blind, placebo-controlled clinical study. European Archives of Psychiatry and Clinical Neuroscience. 1997;247:71–80.

Cabrera J, Emir B, Dills D, Murphy K, Whalen E, Clair A. Characterizing and understanding body weight patterns in patients treated with pregabalin. Current Medical Research and Opinion. 2012;28:1027–37.

Caldwell DM, Ades AE, Higgins JP. Simultaneous comparison of multiple treatments: combining direct and indirect evidence. BMJ. 2005;331:897–900.

Carlbring P, Gunnarsdóttir M, Hedensjö L, Andersson G, Ekselius L, Furmark T. Treatment of social phobia: randomised trial of internet-delivered cognitive-behavioural therapy with telephone support. British Journal of Psychiatry. 2007;190:123–28.

Carlbring P, Nordgren, L.B., Furmark, T. Andersson, G. Long-term outcome of internet-delivered cognitive-behavioural therapy for social phobia: a 30-month follow-up. Behaviour Research and Therapy. 2009;47:848–50.

Carlbring P, Apelstrand M, Sehlin H, Amir N, Rousseau A, Hofmann SG, et al. Internet-delivered attention bias modification training in individuals with social anxiety disorder – a double blind randomized controlled trial. BMC Psychiatry. 2012;12:66.

Cartwright-Hatton S, McNally D, Field AP, Rust S, Laskey B, Dixon C, et al. A new parenting-based group intervention for young anxious children: results of a randomized controlled trial. Journal of the American Academy of Child and Adolescent Psychiatry. 2011;50:242–51.

Chartier MJ, Walker JR, Stein MB. Considering comorbidity in social phobia. Social psychiatry and psychiatric epidemiology. 2003;38:728–34.

Chavira DA, Stein MB, Bailey K, Stein MT. Comorbidity of generalized social anxiety disorder and depression in a pediatric primary care sample. Journal of Affective Disorders. 2004;80:163–71.

Chinn S. A simple method for converting an odds ratio to effect size for use in meta-analysis. Statistics in Medicine. 2000;19:3127–31.

Chung YS, Kwon JH. The efficacy of bibliotherapy for social phobia. Brief Treatment and Crisis Intervention. 2008;8.

Clark DM. A controlled trial of cognitive therapy and pharmacotherapy in the treatment of social phobia. National Research Register; 1998.

Clark DM. Implementing NICE guidelines for the psychological treatment of depression and anxiety disorders: the IAPT experience. International review of psychiatry. 2011;23:318–27.

Clark DM, Wells A. A cognitive model of social phobia. In: Heimberg RG, Liebowitz M, Hope DA, Schneier FR, eds. Social Phobia: Diagnosis, Assessment and Treatment. New York: Guildford Press; 1995. p. 69–93.

Clark DM, Salkovskis PM, Hackmann A, Middleton H, Anastasiades P, Gelder M. A comparison of cognitive therapy, applied relaxation and imipramine in the treatment of panic disorder. The British Journal of Psychiatry. 1994;164:759–69.

Clark DM, Ehlers A, McManus F, Hackmann A, Fennell M, Campbell H, et al. Cognitive therapy versus fluoxetine in generalized social phobia: A randomized placebo-controlled trial. Journal of Consulting and Clinical Psychology. 2003;71:1058–67.

Clark DM, Ehlers A, Hackmann A, McManus F, Fennell M, Grey N, et al. Cognitive therapy versus exposure and applied relaxation in social phobia: A randomized controlled trial. Journal of Consulting and Clinical Psychology. 2006;74:568–78.

Clark DM, Layard R, Smithies R, Richards DA, Suckling R, Wright B. Improving access to psychological therapy: Initial evaluation of two UK demonstration sites. Behaviour Research and Therapy. 2009;47:910–20.

Clark DM, Wild J, Grey N, Stott R, Liness S, Deale A, et al. Self-Study Enhances the Effects of Cognitive Therapy for Social Anxiety Disorder: A Randomized Controlled Trial. 2012.

Cochrane Collaboration. Review Manager (RevMan) Version 5.1 [Computer programme]. Copenhagen: The Nordic Cochrane Centre, The Cochrane Collaboration; 2011.

Coles ME, Gibb BE, Heimberg RG. Psychometric evaluation of the Beck Depression Inventory in adults with social anxiety disorder. Depression and Anxiety. 2001;14:145–8.

Connor KMC. Botulinum toxin treatment of social anxiety disorder with hyperhidrosis: a placebo-controlled double-blind trial. Journal of Clinical Psychiatry. 2006;67:30–36.

Connor KM, Davidson JR, Churchill LE, Sherwood A, Foa E, Weisler RH. Psychometric properties of the Social Phobia Inventory (SPIN). New self-rating scale. The British Journal of Psychiatry. 2000;176:379–86.

Connor KM, Kobak KA, Churchill LE, Katzelnick D, Davidson JR. Mini-SPIN: a brief screening assessment for generalized social anxiety disorder. Depression and Anxiety. 2001;14:137–40.

Connor KM, Cook JL, Davidson JR. Botulinum toxin treatment of social anxiety disorder with hyperhidrosis: a double-blind placebo-controlled trial. Neuropsychopharmacology. 2004;29 Suppl 1:S96.

Connor KM, Davidson JR, Chung H, Yang R, Clary CM. Multidimensional effects of sertraline in social anxiety disorder. Depression and Anxiety. 2006;23:6–10.

Costello EJ, Mustillo S, Erkanli A, Keeler G, Angold A. Prevalence and development of psychiatric disorders in childhood and adolescence. Archives of General Psychiatry. 2003;60:837–44.

Cottraux J, Note I, Albuisson E, Yao SN, Note B, Mollard E, et al. Cognitive behavior therapy versus supportive therapy in social phobia: a randomized controlled trial. Psychotherapy and Psychosomatics. 2000;69:137–46.

Craske MG, Rauch SL, Ursano R, Prenoveau J, Pine DS, Zinbarg RE. What is an anxiety disorder? Depression and Anxiety. 2009;26:1066–85.

Craske MG, Stein MB, Sullivan G, Sherbourne C, Bystritsky A, Rose RD, et al. Disorder-specific impact of coordinated anxiety learning and management treatment for anxiety disorders in primary care. Archives of General Psychiatry. 2011;68:378–88.

Crosby J, Cooper PJ, Creswell C. Characteristics of social anxiety disorder in middle childhood. in preparation.

Curtis GC, Magee WJ, Eaton WW, Wittchen HU, Kessler RC. Specific fears and phobias. Epidemiology and classification. The British Journal of Psychiatry. 1998;173:212–7.

Curtis L. Unit Costs of Health and Social Care 2010. Canterbury: Personal Social Services Research Unit, University of Kent; 2010.

Curtis L. Unit Costs of Health and Social Care 2012. Canterbury: Personal Social Services Research Unit, University of Kent; 2012.

Dalrymple KL, Zimmerman M. Screening for social fears and social anxiety disorder in psychiatric outpatients. Comprehensive Psychiatry. 2008;49:399–406.

Davidson J, Yaryura-Tobias J, DuPont R, Stallings L, Barbato L, van der Hoop R, et al. Fluvoxamine-controlled release formulation for the treatment of generalized social anxiety disorder. Journal of Clinical Psychopharmacology. 2004a;24:118–25.

Davidson JR, Foa EB, Huppert JD, Keefe FJ, Franklin ME, Compton JS, et al. Fluoxetine, comprehensive cognitive behavioral therapy, and placebo in generalized social phobia. Archives of General Psychiatry. 2004b;61:1005–13.

Davidson JR, Hemby LW, Barbato L, van der Hoop RG. Fluvoxamine controlled release for the treatment of generalized social anxiety disorder. 39th Annual Meeting of the American College of Neuropsychopharmacology 2000; Dec 10 14; San Juan; Puerto Rico. 2000:161.

Davidson JR, Hughes DL, George LK, Blazer DG. The epidemiology of social phobia: findings from the Duke Epidemiological Catchment Area Study. Psychological Medicine. 1993a;23:709–18.

Davidson JR, Miner CM, De Veaugh-Geiss J, Tupler LA, Colket JT, Potts NL. The Brief Social Phobia Scale: a psychometric evaluation. Psychological Medicine. 1997;27:161–6.

Davidson JR, Potts N, Richichi E, Krishnan R, Ford S, Smith R, et al. Treatment of social phobia with clonazepam and placebo. Journal of Clinical Psychopharmacology. 1993b;13:423–28.

Davis TE, Jenkins WS, Rudy BM. Empirical status of one-session treatment. In: Davis TE, Ollendick TH, Öst L-G, eds. Intensive One-Session Treatment of Specific Phobias. New York: Springer; 2012.

De Los Reyes A, Alfano CA, Beidel DC. The relations among measurements of informant discrepancies within a multisite trial of treatments for childhood social phobia. Journal of Abnormal Child Psychology. 2010;38:395–404.

Delgado PL. Monoamine depletion studies: implications for antidepressant discontinuation syndrome. Journal of Clinical Psychiatry. 2006;67 (Suppl. 4):22–6.

den Boer JA, van Vliet, IM, Westenberg HG. A double-blind placebo controlled study of fluvoxamine in social phobia. Clinical Neuropharmacology. 1992;15:615.

den Boer JA. Social phobia: epidemiology, recognition, and treatment. BMJ. 1997;315:796–800.

Department of Health. National Service Framework for Mental Health. London: Department of Health; 1999.

Depping AM, Komossa K, Kissling W, Leucht S. Second-generation antipsychotics for anxiety disorders. Cochrane Database of Systematic Reviews. 2010;12:CD008120.

Dias S, Welton NJ, Sutton AJ, Ades A. NICE DSU technical support document 2: a generalised linear modelling framework for pairwise and network meta-analysis of randomised controlled trials. Available at: http://www nicedsu org uk (accessed January 2011). 2011.

Dias S, Sutton AJ, Ades AE, Welton NJ. Evidence synthesis for decison making 2: a generalized linear modeling framework for pairwise and network meta-analysis of randomized controlled trials. Medical Decision Making. 2012;33:607–17.

Dineen-Wagner KDB. A multicenter, randomized, double-blind, placebo-controlled trial of paroxetine in children and adolescents with social anxiety disorder. Archives of General Psychiatry. 2004;61:1153–62.

Dolan P. Modeling valuations for EuroQol health states. Medical Care. 1997;35:1095–108.

Dolan P, Gudex C, Kind P, Williams A. The time trade-off method: results from a general population study. Health Economics. 1996;5:141–54.

Dugan SE, Fuller MA. Duloxetine: a dual reuptake inhibitor. The Annals of Pharmacotherapy. 2004;38:2078–85.

Eccles M, Freemantle N, Mason J. North of England evidence based guidelines development project: methods of developing guidelines for efficient drug use in primary care. BMJ. 1998;316:1232–35.

Ehlers A, Gene-Cos N, Perrin S. Low recognition of post-traumatic stress disorder in primary care. London Journal of Primary Care. 2009;2:36–42.

Emmelkamp PM, Benner A, Kuipers A, Feiertag GA, Koster HC, van Apeldoorn FJ. Comparison of brief dynamic and cognitive-behavioural therapies in avoidant personality disorder. British Journal of Psychiatry. 2006;189:60–64.

Erwin BA, Heimberg RG, Marx BP, Franklin ME. Traumatic and socially stressful life events among persons with social anxiety disorder. Journal of Anxiety Disorders. 2006;20:896–914.

Fahlen T. Personality traits in social phobia, II: Changes during drug treatment. Journal of Clinical Psychiatry. 1995;56:569–73.

Fava M, Mulroy R, Alpert J, Nierenberg AA, Rosenbaum JF. Emergence of adverse events following discontinuation of treatment with extended-release venlafaxine. The American Journal of Psychiatry. 1997;154:1760–2.

Fava M, Rush AJ, Alpert JE, Balasubramani GK, Wisniewski SR, Carmin CN, et al. Difference in treatment outcome in outpatients with anxious versus nonanxious depression: a STAR*D report. The American Journal of Psychiatry. 2008;165:342–51.

Feehan M, McGee R, Raja SN, Williams SM. DSM-III-R disorders in New Zealand 18–year-olds. The Australian and New Zealand Journal of Psychiatry. 1994;28:87–99.

Fehm L, Beesdo K, Jacobi F, Fiedler A. Social anxiety disorder above and below the diagnostic threshold: prevalence, comorbidity and impairment in the general population. Social Psychiatry and Psychiatric Epidemiology. 2008;43:257–65.

Feltner DE, Davidson JR, Pollack MH, Stein MB, Futterer R, Jefferson JW, et al. A placebo-controlled, double-blind study of pregabalin treatment of social anxiety disorder: outcome and predictors of response. 39th Annual Meeting of the American College of Neuropsychopharmacology. San Juan, Puerto Rico. 10–14 Dec, 2000.

Feltner DE, Liu-Dumaw M, Schweizer E, Bielski R. Efficacy of pregabalin in generalized social anxiety disorder: results of a double-blind, placebo-controlled, fixed-dose study. International Clinical Psychopharmacology. 2011;26:213–20.

Fenwick E, Claxton K, Sculpher M. Representing uncertainty: the role of cost-effectiveness acceptability curves. Health Economics. 2001;10:779–87.

Fergusson D, Doucette S, Glass KC, Shapiro S, Healy D, Hebert P, et al. Association between suicide attempts and selective serotonin reuptake inhibitors: systematic review of randomised controlled trials. BMJ. 2005;330:396.

Fischer JE, Bachmann LM, Jaeschke R. A readers' guide to the interpretation of diagnostic test properties: clinical example of sepsis. Intensive Care Medicine. 2003;29:1043–51.

Ford T, Goodman R, Meltzer H. The British Child and Adolescent Mental Health Survey 1999: the prevalence of DSM-IV disorders. Journal of the American Academy of Child and Adolescent Psychiatry. 2003;42:1203–11.

Franchini AJ, Dias S, Ades AE, Jansen JP, Welton NJ. Accounting for correlation in network meta-analysis with multi-arm trials. Research Synthesis Methods. 2012;3:142–60.

François C, Montgomery SA, Despiegel N, Aballéa S, Roïz J, Auquier P. Analysis of health-related quality of life and costs based on a randomised clinical trial of escitalopram for relapse prevention in patients with generalised social anxiety disorder. International Journal of Clinical Practice. 2008;62:1693–702.

François C, Despiegel N, Maman K, Saragoussi D, Auquier P. Anxiety disorders, major depressive disorder and the dynamic relationship between these conditions: treatment patterns and cost analysis. Journal of Medical Economics. 2010;13:99–109.

Fraser J, Kirkby KC, Daniels B, Gilroy L, Montgomery IM. Three versus six sessions of computer-aided vicarious exposure treatment for spider phobia. Behaviour Change. 2001;18:213–23.

Fresco DM, Coles ME, Heimberg RG, Liebowitz MR, Hami S, Stein MB, et al. The Liebowitz Social Anxiety Scale: a comparison of the psychometric properties of self-report and clinician-administered formats. Psychological Medicine. 2001;31:1025–35.

Furmark TT. Common changes in cerebral blood flow in patients with social phobia treated with citalopram or cognitive-behavioral therapy. Archives of General Psychiatry. 2002;59:425–33.

Furmark T, Appel L, Michelgård A, Wahlstedt K, Ahs F, Zancan S, et al. Cerebral blood flow changes after treatment of social phobia with the neurokinin-1 antagonist GR205171, citalopram, or placebo. Biological Psychiatry. 2005;58:132–42.

Furmark T, Carlbring P, Hedman E, Sonnenstein A, Clevberger P, Bohman B, et al. Guided and unguided self-help for social anxiety disorder: randomised controlled trial. British Journal of Psychiatry. 2009;195:440–47.

Fyer AJ, Mannuzza S, Chapman TF, Martin LY, Klein DF. Specificity in familial aggregation of phobic disorders. Archives of General Psychiatry. 1995;52:564–73.

Gallagher HM, Rabian BA, McCloskey MS. A brief group cognitive-behavioral intervention for social phobia in childhood. Journal of Anxiety Disorders. 2004;18:459–79.

Gelernter CS. A comparison of cognitive-behavioral and pharmacological treatments for social phobia. Dissertation Abstracts International. 1990;50:3156.

Gelernter CS, Uhde TW, Cimbolic P, Arnkoff DB, Vittone BJ, Tancer ME, et al. Cognitive-behavioral and pharmacological treatments of social phobia: a controlled study. Archives of General Psychiatry. 1991;48:938–45.

General Medical Council. Good Practice in Prescribing and Managing Medicines and Devices. London: General Medical Council; 2013.

Gilroy LJ, Kirkby KC, Daniels BA, Menzies RG, Montgomery IM. Controlled comparison of computer-aided vicarious exposure versus live exposure in the treatment of spider phobia. Behavior Therapy. 2000;31:733–44.

GlaxoSmithKline. A randomized, double-blind, fixed dose comparison of 20, 40, and 60 mg daily of paroxetine and placebo in the treatment of generalized social phobia. GSK Clinical Study Register; 1997.

GlaxoSmithKline. A randomized, double-blind, parallel-group, placebo-controlled, forced-dose titration study evaluating the efficacy and safety of a new chemical entity (NCE) and paroxetine in subjects with social anxiety disorder. GSK Clinical Study Register; 2006.

Goldin PR, Ziv M, Jazaieri H, Werner K, Kraemer H, Heimberg RG, et al. Cognitive reappraisal self-efficacy mediates the effects of individual cognitive-behavioral therapy for social anxiety disorder. Journal of Clinical and Consulting Psychology. 2012; in press.

Gould R, Buckminster S, Pollack M, Otto M, Yap L. Cognitive-behavioral and pharmacological treatment for social phobia: a meta-analysis. Clinical Psychology Science and Practice. 1997;4:291–306.

Granado LC, Ranvaud R, Pelaez JR. A spiderless arachnophobia therapy: comparison between placebo and treatment groups and six-month follow-up study. Neural Plasticity. 2007;2007:10241.

Grant B, Hasin D, Blanco C, Stinson F, Chou S, Goldstein RB. The epidemiology of social anxiety disorder in the United States: results from the National Epidemiologic Survey on Alcohol and Related Conditions. Journal of Clinical Psychiatry. 2005a;11:1351–61.

Grant BF, Stinson FS, Hasin DS, Dawson DA, Chou SP, Ruan WJ, et al. Prevalence, correlates, and comorbidity of bipolar I disorder and axis I and II disorders: results from the National Epidemiologic Survey on Alcohol and Related Conditions. Journal of Clinical Psychiatry. 2005b;66:1205–15.

Greenhill LL. A multisite treatment of anxiety disorders. 152nd Annual Meeting of the American Psychiatric Association; Washington, DC, 15–20 May, 1999.

Gregorian RS, Golden KA, Bahce A, Goodman C, Kwong WJ, Khan ZM. Antidepressant-induced sexual dysfunction. The Annals of Pharmacotherapy. 2002;36:1577–89.

Greist JH, Liu-Dumaw M, Schweizer E, Feltner D. Efficacy of pregabalin in preventing relapse in patients with generalized social anxiety disorder: results of a double-blind, placebo-controlled 26–week study. International Clinical Psychopharmacology. 2011;26:243–51.

Gruber K, Moran PJ, Roth WT, Taylor CB. Computer-assisted cognitive behavioral group therapy for social phobia. Behavior Therapy. 2001;32:155–65.

Guastella AJ, Richardson R, Lovibond PF, Rapee RM, Gaston JE, Mitchell P, et al. A randomized controlled trial of D-cycloserine enhancement of exposure therapy for social anxiety disorder. Biological Psychiatry. 2008;63:544–49.

Guastella AJ, Howard AL, Dadds MR, Mitchell P, Carson DS. A randomized controlled trial of intranasal oxytocin as an adjunct to exposure therapy for social anxiety disorder. Psychoneuroendocrinology. 2009;34:917–23.

Gunnell D, Saperia J, Ashby D. Selective serotonin reuptake inhibitors (SSRIs) and suicide in adults: meta-analysis of drug company data from placebo controlled, randomised controlled trials submitted to the MHRA's safety review. BMJ. 2005;330:385.

Haddad PM. Antidepressant discontinuation syndromes: clinical relevance, prevention and management. Drug Safety. 2001;24:183–97.

Hassan A. A comparison of computer-based symbolic modelling and conventional methods in the treatment of spider phobia. Doctoral dissertation, University of Leeds; 1992.

Haug TTB. Exposure therapy and sertraline in social phobia: 1-year follow-up of a randomised controlled trial. British Journal of Psychiatry. 2003;182:312–18.

Hayes BB. Comparing the effectiveness of cognitive-behavioral group therapy with and without motivational interviewing at reducing the social anxiety, alcohol consumption, and negative consequences of socially anxious college students. Dissertation Abstracts International: Section B: The Sciences and Engineering. 2006;67.

Heading K, Kirkby KC, Martin F, Daniels BA, Gilroy LJ, Menzies RG. Controlled comparison of single-session treatments for spider phobia: live graded exposure alone versus computer-aided vicarious exposure. Behaviour Change. 2001;18:103–13.

Healey D. The emergence of antidepressant induced suicidality. Primary Care Psychiatry. 2003;6:23–28.

Hedman E, Andersson E, Ljotsson B, Andersson G, Ruck C, Lindefors N. Cost-effectiveness of internet-based cognitive behavior therapy vs. cognitive behavioral group therapy for social anxiety disorder: results from a randomized controlled trial. Behaviour Research and Therapy. 2011a;49:729–36.

Hedman E, Andersson G, Ljotsson B, Andersson E, Ruck C, Mortberg E, et al. Internet-based cognitive behavior therapy vs. cognitive behavioral group therapy for social anxiety disorder: a randomized controlled non-inferiority trial. PLoS ONE. 2011b;6:e18001.

Hedman E, Furmark T, Carlbring P, Ljotsson B, Ruck C, Lindefors N, et al. A 5–year follow-up of internet-based cognitive behavior therapy for social anxiety disorder. Journal of Medical Internet Research. 2011c;13.

Heeren A, Reese HE, McNally RJ, Philippot P. Attention training toward and away from threat in social phobia: effects on subjective, behavioral, and physiological measures of anxiety. Behaviour Research and Therapy. 2012;50:30–9.

Heideman PW. Combining cognitive behavioral therapy with an alcohol intervention to reduce alcohol problems among socially anxious college students. Dissertation Abstracts International: Section B: The Sciences and Engineering. 2008;69.

Heimberg RG. Final Progress Report – NIMH Grant R01MH064481 CBT Augmentation of Paroxetine for Social Anxiety. 2012; in press.

Heimberg RG, Dodge CS, Hope DA, Kennedy CR, Zollo LJ, Becker RE. Cognitive behavioral group treatment for social phobia: comparison with a credible placebo control. Cognitive Therapy and Research. 1990;14:1–23.

Heimberg RG, Horner KJ, Juster HR, Safren SA, Brown EJ, Schneier FR, et al. Psychometric properties of the Liebowitz Social Anxiety Scale. Psychological Medicine. 1999;29:199–212.

Heimberg RG, Juster HR, Hope DA, Mattia JI. Cognitive behavioral group treatment for social phobia: description, case presentation and empirical support. In: Stein MB, ed. Social Phobia: Clinical and Research Perspectives. Washington, DC: American Psychiatric Press; 1995. p. 293–321.

Heimberg RG, Liebowitz MR, Hope DA, Schneier FR, Holt CS, Welkowitz LA, et al. Cognitive behavioral group therapy vs phenelzine therapy for social phobia 12–week outcome. Archives of General Psychiatry. 1998;55:1133–41.

Heimberg RG, Salzman DG, Holt CS, Blendell KA. Cognitive-behavioral group treatment for social phobia: effectiveness at five-year followup. Cognitive Therapy and Research. 1993;17:325–39.

Hellstrom K, Ost LG. One-session therapist directed exposure vs two forms of manual directed self-exposure in the treatment of spider phobia. Behaviour Research and Therapy. 1995;33:959–65.

Herbert JD, Gaudiano BA, Rheingold AA, Moitra E, Myers VH, Dalrymple KL, et al. Cognitive behavior therapy for generalized social anxiety disorder in adolescents: a randomized controlled trial. Journal of Anxiety Disorders. 2009;23:167–77.

Herbert JD, Gaudiano BA, Rheingold AA, Myers VH, Dalrymple K, Nolan EM. Social skills training augments the effectiveness of cognitive behavioral group therapy for social anxiety disorder. Behavior Therapy. 2005;36:125–38.

Herbert JD, Rheingold AA, Gaudiano BA, Myers VH. Standard versus extended cognitive behavior therapy for social anxiety disorder: a randomized-controlled trial. Behavioural and Cognitive Psychotherapy. 2004;32:131–47.

Higgins JP, Green S. Cochrane Handbook for Systematic Reviews of Interventions. Version 5.1.0 [updated March 2011]. The Cochrane Collaboration; 2011.

Higgins JP, Thompson SG, Deeks JJ, Altman DG. Measuring inconsistency in meta-analyses. BMJ. 2003;327:557–60.

Hindmarch I, Kimber S, Cockle SM. Abrupt and brief discontinuation of antidepressant treatment: effects on cognitive function and psychomotor performance. International Clinical Psychopharmacology. 2000;15:305–18.

Hoffart A, F.-M. Borge. Psychotherapy for social phobia: how do alliance and cognitive process interact to produce outcome? Psychotherapy Research. 2012;22.

Hoffart AB. Change processes in residential cognitive and interpersonal psychotherapy for social phobia: a process-outcome study. Behavior Therapy. 2009a;40:10–22.

Hoffart AB. The role of common factors in residential cognitive and interpersonal therapy for social phobia: a process-outcome study. Psychotherapy Research. 2009b;19:54–67.

Hofmann SG, Meuret AE, Smits JAJ, Simon NM, Pollack MH, Eisenmenger K, et al. Augmentation of exposure therapy with D-cycloserine for social anxiety disorder. Archives of General Psychiatry. 2006;63:298–304.

Hofmann SG, Smits JAJ, Rosenfield D, Simon N, Otto M, Meuret A, et al. D-cycloserine as an augmentation strategy for cognitive behavioral therapy for anxiety disorders. American Journal of Psychiatry. 2013;170:751–58.

Hope DA, Heimberg RG, Bruch MA. Dismantling cognitive-behavioral group therapy for social phobia. Behaviour Research and Therapy. 1995;33:637–50.

Hope DA, Heimberg RG, Turk CL. Therapist guide for managing social anxiety: a cognitive-behavioral therapy approach. New York: Oxford University Press; 2006.

Hudson JL, Rapee RM, Deveney C, Schniering CA, Lyneham HJ, Bovopoulos N. Cognitive-behavioral treatment versus an active control for children and adolescents with anxiety disorders: a randomized trial. Journal of the American Academy of Child and Adolescent Psychiatry. 2009;48:533–44.

Hudson JL, Rapee RM, Lyneham H, Wuthrich V, Schneiring CA. Treatment outcome for children with social phobia. World Congress of Behavioural and Cognitive Therapies 2010; Boston, MA.

Hudson JL, Newall C, Rapee RM, Lyneham HJ, Schniering CA, Wuthrich VM, et al. The impact of brief parental anxiety management on child anxiety treatment outcomes: a controlled trial. Journal of Clinical Child and Adolescent Psychology. 2013; Published online: 11 July.

Issakidis C, Sanderson K, Corry J, Andrews G, Lapsley H. Modelling the population cost-effectiveness of current and evidence-based optimal treatment for anxiety disorders. Psychological Medicine. 2004;34:19–35.

Jackson SW. The listening healer in the history of psychological healing. The American Journal of Psychiatry. 1992;149:1623–32.

Jacobson NS, Truax P. Clinical significance: a statistical approach to defining meaningful change in psychotherapy research. Journal of Consulting and Clinical Psychology. 1991;59:12–19.

Jadad AR, Moore RA, Carroll D, Jenkinson C, Reynolds DJM, Gavaghan DJ, et al. Assessing the quality of reports of randomized clinical trials: is blinding necessary? Controlled Clinical Trials. 1996;17:1–12.

James A, James G, Cowdrey F, Soler A, Choke A. Cognitive behavioural therapy for anxiety disorders in children and adolescents. Cochrane Database of Systematic Reviews. 2013;6:CD004690.

Jazaieri H, Goldin P, Werner K, Ziv M, Gross J. A randomized trial of MBSR versus aerobic exercise for social anxiety disorder. Journal of Clinical Psychology. 2012;68:715–31.

Johnston L, Titov N, Andrews G, Spence J, Dear BF. A RCT of a transdiagnostic internet-delivered treatment for three anxiety disorders: examination of support roles and disorder-specific outcomes. PLoS ONE. 2011;6:e28079.

Joint Formulary Committee. British National Formulary. 65th edn. London: BMJ Group and Pharmaceutical Press; 2013.

Judge R, Parry MG, Quail D, Jacobson JG. Discontinuation symptoms: comparison of brief interruption in fluoxetine and paroxetine treatment. International Clinical Psychopharmacology. 2002;17:217–25.

Kaltenthaler E, Brazier J, De Nigris E, Tumur I, Ferriter M, Beverley C, et al. Computerised cognitive behaviour therapy for depression and anxiety update: a systematic review and economic evaluation. Health Technology Assessment. 2006;10:1–168.

Kasper S, Loft H, Smith JR. Escitalopram is efficacious and well tolerated in the treatment of social anxiety disorder. 155th Annual Meeting of the American Psychiatric Association; Philadelphia, PA, 18–23 May, 2002.

Kasper S, Stein DJ, Loft H, Nil R. Escitalopram in the treatment of social anxiety disorder: randomised, placebo-controlled, flexible-dosage study. British Journal of Psychiatry. 2005;186:222–26.

Katon WR-B. Anxiety disorders: efficient screening is the first step in improving outcomes. Annals of Internal Medicine. 2007;146:390–91.

Katzelnick DJ, Kobak KA, DeLeire T, Henk HJ, Greist JH, Davidson JR, et al. Impact of generalized social anxiety disorder in managed care. The American Journal of Psychiatry. 2001;158:1999–2007.

Keller MB. Citalopram therapy for depression: a review of 10 years of European experience and data from U.S. clinical trials. Journal of Clinical Psychiatry. 2000;61:896–908.

Kendler KS, Neale MC, Kessler RC, Heath AC, Eaves LJ. The genetic epidemiology of phobias in women. The interrelationship of agoraphobia, social phobia, situational phobia, and simple phobia. Archives of General Psychiatry. 1992;49:273–81.

Kendler KS, Karkowski LM, Prescott CA. Fears and phobias: reliability and heritability. Psychological Medicine. 1999;29:539–53.

Kerns CM, Klugman J, Kendall PC. Cognitive behavioral therapy for youth with social phobia: differential short and long-term treatment outcomes. Under review. 2012.

Kessler RC, Stein MB, Berglund P. Social phobia subtypes in the National Comorbidity Survey. American Journal of Psychiatry. 1998;155:613–19.

Kessler RC, Berglund P, Demler O, Jin R, Merikangas KR, Walters EE. Lifetime prevalence and age-of-onset distributions of DSM-IV disorders in the National Comorbidity Survey Replication. Archives of General Psychiatry. 2005a;62:593–602.

Kessler RC, Chiu WT, Demler O, Merikangas KR, Walters EE. Prevalence, severity, and comorbidity of 12–month DSM-IV disorders in the National Comorbidity Survey Replication. Archives of General Psychiatry. 2005b;62:617–27.

Knijnik DZ, Kapczinski F, Chachamovich E, Margis R, Eizirik CL. Psychodynamic group treatment for generalized social phobia. Revista Brasileira de Psiquiatria. 2004;26:77–81.

Knijnik DZ, Blanco C, Salum GA, Moraes CU, Mombach C, Almeida E, et al. A pilot study of clonazepam versus psychodynamic group therapy plus clonazepam in the treatment of generalized social anxiety disorder. European Psychiatry. 2008;23:567–74.

Kobak KA, Greist JH, Jefferson JW, Katzelnick DJ. Fluoxetine in social phobia: a double-blind, placebo-controlled pilot study. Journal of Clinical Psychopharmacology. 2002;22:257–62.

Kobak KA, Taylor LV, Warner G, Futterer R. St. John's wort versus placebo in social phobia: results from a placebo-controlled pilot study. Journal of Clinical Psychopharmacology. 2005;25:51–58.

Konnopka A, Leichsenring F, Leibing E, Konig HH. Cost-of-illness studies and cost-effectiveness analyses in anxiety disorders: a systematic review. Journal of Affective Disorders. 2009;114:14–31.

Koszycki D, Benger M, Shlik J, Bradwejn J. Randomized trial of a meditation-based stress reduction program and cognitive behavior therapy in generalized social anxiety disorder. Behaviour Research and Therapy. 2007;45:2518–26.

Kroenke KS. The Patient Health Questionnaire Somatic, Anxiety, and Depressive Symptom Scales: a systematic review. General Hospital Psychiatry. 2010;32:345–59.

Kroenke K, Spitzer RL, Williams JB, Monahan PO, Lowe B. Anxiety disorders in primary care: prevalence, impairment, comorbidity, and detection. Annals of Internal Medicine. 2007;146:317–25.

Kumar R, Pitts C, Carpenter D. Response to paroxetine is maintained during continued treatment in patients with social anxiety disorder. European Neuropsychopharmacology. 1999;9:S312.

Kupper N, Denollet J, Kupper N, Denollet J. Social anxiety in the general population: introducing abbreviated versions of SIAS and SPS. Journal of Affective Disorders. 2012;136:90–98.

Lader M, Stender K, Bürger V, Nil R. Efficacy and tolerability of escitalopram in 12– and 24–week treatment of social anxiety disorder: Randomised, double-blind, placebo-controlled, fixed-dose study. Depression and Anxiety. 2004;19:241–48.

Lambert MJ, Whipple JL, Hawkins EJ, Vermeersch DA, Nielsen SL, Smart DW. Is it time for clinicians to routinely track patient outcome? A meta-analysis. Clinical Psychology: Science and Practice. 2003;10:288–301.

Lau WY, Chan CK, Li JC, Au TK. Effectiveness of group cognitive-behavioral treatment for childhood anxiety in community clinics. Behaviour Research and Therapy. 2010;48:1067–77.

Layard R, Bell S, Clark DM, Knapp M, Meacher M, Priebe S. The Depression Report: A New Deal for Depression and Anxiety Disorders. Centre for Economic Performance Report. London. London School of Economics. Available from: http//cep.lse.ac.uk.; 2006.

Lecrubier Y. Comorbidity in social anxiety disorder: impact on disease burden and management. Journal of Clinical Psychiatry. 1998;59 (Suppl. 17):33–8.

Ledley DRH. Impact of depressive symptoms on the treatment of generalized social anxiety disorder. Depression and Anxiety. 2005;22:161–67.

Ledley DR, Heimberg RG, Hope DA, Hayes SA, Zaider TI, Dyke MV, et al. Efficacy of a manualized and workbook-driven individual treatment for social anxiety disorder. Behavior Therapy. 2009;40:414–24.

Leichsenring F, Hoyer J, Beutel M, Herpertz S, Hiller W, Irle E, et al. The social phobia psychotherapy research network - the first multicenter randomized controlled trial of psychotherapy for social phobia: rationale, methods and patient characteristics. Psychotherapy and Psychosomatics. 2009a;78:35–41.

Leichsenring F, Salzer S, Beutel ME, von Consbruch K, Herpertz S, Hiller W, et al. SOPHO-NET - A research network on psychotherapy for social phobia. PPmP - Psychotherapie Psychosomatik Medizinische Psychologie. 2009b;59:117–23.

Lejoyeux M, Ades J. Antidepressant discontinuation: a review of the literature. Journal of Clinical Psychiatry. 1997;58 (Suppl. 7):11–5; discussion 16.

Lejoyeux M, Ades J, Mourad I. Antidepressant withdrawal syndrome: recognition, prevention and management. CNS Drugs. 1996;5:278–92.

Lepola U, Bergtholdt B, St Lambert J, Davy KL, Ruggiero L. Controlled-release paroxetine in the treatment of patients with social anxiety disorder. Journal of Clinical Psychiatry. 2004;65:222–29.

Lewis G, Anderson L, Araya R. Self-help Interventions for Mental Health Problems. Department of Health; 2003.

Lieb R, Wittchen HU, Hofler M, Fuetsch M, Stein MB, Merikangas KR. Parental psychopathology, parenting styles, and the risk of social phobia in offspring: a prospective-longitudinal community study. Archives of General Psychiatry. 2000;57:859–66.

Liebowitz MR. Social phobia. Modern Problems of Pharmacopsychiatry. 1987; 22:141–73.

Liebowitz MRG. Pharmacotherapy of social phobia: an interim report of a placebo-controlled comparison of phenelzine and atenolol. Journal of Clinical Psychiatry. 1988;49:252–57.

Liebowitz MRH. Cognitive-behavioral group therapy versus phenelzine in social phobia: long term outcome. Depression and Anxiety. 1999;10:89–98.

Liebowitz M. Efficacy of venlafaxine XR in generalized social anxiety disorder. International Journal of Neuropsychopharmacology. 2002;5:211.

Liebowitz MR, Schneier F, Campeas R, Gorman J, Fyer A, Hollander E, et al. Phenelzine and atenolol in social phobia. Psychopharmacology Bulletin. 1990;26:123–25.

Liebowitz MR, Schneier F, Campeas R, Hollander E, Hatterer J, Fyer A, et al. Phenelzine vs atenolol in social phobia: a placebo-controlled comparison. Archives of General Psychiatry. 1992;49:290–300.

Liebowitz MR, Heimberg RG, Schneier FR, Hope DA, Davies S, Holt CS, et al. Cognitive-behavioral group therapy versus phenelzine in social phobia: long-term outcome. Depression and Anxiety. 1999;10:89–98.

Liebowitz M, DeMartinis N, Weihs K, Chung H, Clary C. Results from a randomized, double-blind, multicenter trial of sertaline in the treatment of moderate-to-severe social phobia (social anxiety disorder). European Neuropsychopharmacology. 2002a;12:S352.

Liebowitz MR, Stein MB, Tancer M, Carpenter D, Oakes R, Pitts CD. A randomized, double-blind, fixed-dose comparison of paroxetine and placebo in the treatment of generalized social anxiety disorder. Journal of Clinical Psychiatry. 2002b;63:66–74.

Liebowitz MR, DeMartinis NA, Weihs K, Londborg PD, Smith WT, Chung H, et al. Efficacy of sertraline in severe generalized social anxiety disorder: results of a double-blind, placebo-controlled study. Journal of Clinical Psychiatry. 2003;64:785–92.

Liebowitz MR, Gelenberg AJ, Munjack D. Venlafaxine extended release vs placebo and paroxetine in social anxiety disorder. Archives of General Psychiatry. 2005a;62:190–98.

Liebowitz MR, Mangano RM, Bradwejn J, Asnis G. A randomized controlled trial of venlafaxine extended release in generalized social anxiety disorder. Journal of Clinical Psychiatry. 2005b;66:238–47.

Lipsitz JD, Gur M, Vermes D, Petkova E, Cheng J, Miller N, et al. A randomized trial of interpersonal therapy versus supportive therapy for social anxiety disorder. Depression and Anxiety. 2008;25:542 53.

Lipsitz JD, Markowitz JC, Cherry S. Manual for interpersonal psychotherapy of social phobia. New York: Columbia University College of Physicians; 1997.

Lipsitz JD, Schneier FR. Social phobia. Epidemiology and cost of illness. Pharmaco-Economics. 2000;18:23–32.

Lott M, Greist JH, Jefferson JW, Kobak KA, Katzelnick DJ, J. KR, et al. Brofaromine for social phobia: a multicenter, placebo-controlled, double-blind study. Journal of Clinical Psychopharmacology. 1997;17:255–60.

Lu G, Ades AE. Combination of direct and indirect evidence in mixed treatment comparisons. Statistics in Medicine. 2004;23:3105–24.

Lunn DJ, Thomas A, Best N, Spiegelhalter D. WinBUGS – a Bayesian modelling framework: concepts, structure, and extensibility. Statistics and Computing. 2000;10:325–37.

Lyneham HJ, Abbott MJ, Rapee RM, Sburlati ES. Parent group supported bibliotherapy for child anxiety: a randomised controlled trial comparing standard group treatment and waitlist. 2013 (in preparation).

Macaskill P, Gatsonis C, Deeks JJ, Harbord RM, Takwoingi Y. Chapter 10: Analysing and presenting results. In: Deeks JJ, Bossuyt PM, Gatsonis C, eds. Cochrane Handbook for Systematic Reviews of Diagnostic Test Accuracy. Version 1.0. The Cochrane Collaboration; 2010.

Magee WJ, Eaton WW, Wittchen HU, McGonagle KA, Kessler RC. Agoraphobia, simple phobia, and social phobia in the National Comorbidity Survey. Archives of General Psychiatry. 1996;53:159–68.

Mann T. Clinical Guidelines: Using Clinical Guidelines to Improve Patient Care Within the NHS. London: NHS Executive; 1996.

March JS, Parker JD, Sullivan K, Stallings P, Conners CK. The Multidimensional Anxiety Scale for Children (MASC): factor structure, reliability, and validity. Journal of the American Academy of Child and Adolescent Psychiatry. 1997;36:554–65.

March JS, Entusah AR, Rynn M, Albano AM, Tourian KA. A randomized controlled trial of venlafaxine ER versus placebo in pediatric social anxiety disorder. Biological Psychiatry. 2007;62:1149–54.

March S, Spence SH, Donovan CL. The efficacy of an internet-based cognitive-behavioral therapy intervention for child anxiety disorders. Journal of Pediatric Psychology. 2009;34:474–87.

Marks IM. Fears and Phobias. London: Heinemann; 1975.

Marks IM. Behavioral concepts and treatments of neuroses. Behavioral Psychotherapy. 1981;9:137–54.

Marks IM, Gelder MG. A controlled retrospective study of behaviour therapy in phobic patients. The British Journal of Psychiatry. 1965;111:561–73.

Marks IM, Mathews AM. Brief standard self-rating for phobic patients. Behaviour Research and Therapy. 1979;17:263–67.

Marks IM, Kenwright M, McDonough M, Whittaker M, Mataix-Cols D. Saving clinicians' time by delegating routine aspects of therapy to a computer: a randomized controlled trial in phobia/panic disorder. Psychological Medicine. 2004;34:9–17.

Marques L, Porter E, Keshaviah A, Pollack MH, Van Ameringen M, Stein MB, et al. Avoidant personality disorder in individuals with generalized social anxiety disorder: what does it add? Journal of Anxiety Disorders. 2012;26:665–72.

Martinez C, Rietbrock S, Wise L, Ashby D, Chick J, Moseley J, et al. Antidepressant treatment and the risk of fatal and non-fatal self harm in first episode depression: nested case-control study. BMJ. 2005;330:389.

Masia-Warner CK. School-based intervention for adolescents with social anxiety disorder: results of a controlled study. Journal of Abnormal Child Psychology. 2005;33:707–22.

Masia-Warner C, Fisher PH, Shrout PE, Rathor S, Klein RG. Treating adolescents with social anxiety disorder in school: an attention control trial. Journal of Child Psychology and Psychiatry. 2007;48:676–86.

Matthews AJ, Wong ZH, Scanlan JD, Kirkby KC. Online exposure for spider phobia: continuous versus intermittent exposure. Behaviour Change. 2011;28:143.

Mattick RP, Clarke JC. Development and validation of measures of social phobia scrutiny fear and social interaction anxiety. Behaviour Research and Therapy. 1998;36:455–70.

Mattick RP, Peters L. Treatment of severe social phobia: effects of guided exposure with and without cognitive restructuring. Journal of Consulting and Clinical Psychology. 1988;56:251–60.

Mattick RP, Peters L, Clarke JC. Exposure and cognitive restructuring for social phobia: a controlled study. Behavior Therapy. 1989;20:3–23.

McEvoy PM, Perini SJ, McEvoy PM, Perini SJ. Cognitive behavioral group therapy for social phobia with or without attention training: a controlled trial. Journal of Anxiety Disorders. 2009;23:519–28.

McManus F, Clark DM, Grey N, Wild J, Hirsch C, Fennell M, et al. A demonstration of the efficacy of two of the components of cognitive therapy for social phobia. Journal of Anxiety Disorders. 2009a;23:496–503.

McManus S, Meltzer H, Brugha T, Bebbington P, Jenkins R. Adult Psychiatric Morbidity in England, 2007: Results of a Household Survey. Leeds: NHS Information Centre; 2009b.

McQuaid JR, Stein MB, McCahill M, Laffaye C, Ramel W. Use of brief psychiatric screening measures in a primary care sample. Depression and Anxiety. 2000;12:21–9.

Means-Christensen AJ, Sherbourne CD, Roy-Byrne PP, Craske MG, Stein MB. Using five questions to screen for five common mental disorders in primary care: diagnostic accuracy of the Anxiety and Depression Detector. General Hospital Psychiatry. 2006;28:108–18.

Meijer WE, Bouvy ML, Heerdink ER, Urquhart J, Leufkens HG. Spontaneous lapses in dosing during chronic treatment with selective serotonin reuptake inhibitors. The British Journal of Psychiatry. 2001;179:519–22.

Melfsen S, Kühnemund M, Schwieger J, Warnke A, Stadler C, Poustka F, et al. Cognitive behavioral therapy of socially phobic children focusing on cognition: a randomised wait-list control study. Child and Adolescent Psychiatry and Mental Health. 2011;5:5.

Meltzer H, Gill B, Petticrew M, Hinds K. OPCS Surveys of Psychiatric Morbidity in Great Britain, Report 2: Physical Complaints, Service Use and Treatment of Adults with Psychiatric Disorders. London: HMSO; 1995.

MHRA. Report of the CSM Expert Working Group on the Safety of Selective Serotonin Reuptake Inhibitor Antidepressants. Available at: http://www.mhra.gov.uk/home/groups/pl-p/documents/drugsafetymessage/con019472.pdf; 2004.

MHRA. Updated Prescribing Advice for Venlafaxine (Efexor/Efexor XL). Available at http://wwwmhragovuk/. 2006.

MHRA. Citalopram and escitalopram: QT interval prolongation—new maximum daily dose restrictions (including in elderly patients), contraindications, and warnings. Drug Safety Update, 5 December 2011.

Michail M, Birchwood M. Social anxiety disorder in first-episode psychosis: incidence, phenomenology and relationship with paranoia. British Journal of Psychiatry. 2009;195:234–41.

Michelson D, Fava M, Amsterdam J, Apter J, Londborg P, Tamura R, et al. Interruption of selective serotonin reuptake inhibitor treatment. Double-blind, placebo-controlled trial. The British Journal of Psychiatry. 2000;176:363–8.

Montgomery SA, Kennedy SH, Burrows GD, Lejoyeux M, Hindmarch I. Absence of discontinuation symptoms with agomelatine and occurrence of discontinuation symptoms with paroxetine: a randomized, double-blind, placebo-controlled discontinuation study. International Clinical Psychopharmacology. 2004;19:271–80.

Montgomery SA, Nil R, Dürr-Pal N, Loft H, Boulenger JP. A 24-week randomized, double-blind, placebo-controlled study of escitalopram for the prevention of generalized social anxiety disorder. Journal of Clinical Psychiatry. 2005;66:1270–78.

Morgan H, Raffle C. Does reducing safety behaviours improve treatment response in patients with social phobia? The Australian and New Zealand Journal of Psychiatry. 1999;33:503–10.

Morgan O, Griffiths C, Baker A, Majeed A. Fatal toxicity of antidepressants in England and Wales, 1993–2002. Health Statistics Quarterly/Office for National Statistics. 2004:18–24.

Mortberg EB. Temperament and character dimensions in patients with social phobia: Patterns of change following treatments? Psychiatry Research. 2007;152:81–90.

Mortberg E, Clark DM. Intensive group cognitive therapy and individual cognitive therapy for social phobia: sustained improvement at 5-year follow-up. Journal of Anxiety Disorders. 2011;25:994–1000.

Mortberg E, Clark DM, Sundin O, Wistedt AA. Intensive group cognitive treatment and individual cognitive therapy vs. treatment as usual in social phobia: a randomized controlled trial. Acta Psychiatrica Scandinavica. 2007;115:142–54.

Mowrer OH. On the dual nature of learning: a re-interpretation of 'conditioning' and 'problem-solving'. Harvard Educational Review. 1947;17:102–48.

Mowrer OH. Learning Theory and Behavior. Hoboken, NJ: John Wiley & Sons; 1960.

Muehlbacher M, Nickel MK, Nickel C, al. E. Mirtazapine treatment of social phobia in women: a randomized, double-blind, placebo-controlled study. Journal of Clinical Psychopharmacology. 2005;25:580–83.

Müller BH, Kull S, Wilhelm FH, Michael T. One-session computer-based exposure treatment for spider-fearful individuals: efficacy of a minimal self-help intervention in a randomised controlled trial. Journal of Behavior Therapy and Experimental Psychiatry. 2011;42:179–84.

Mulkens S, Bögels SM, de Jong PJ, Louwers J. Fear of blushing: effects of task concentration training versus exposure in vivo on fear and physiology. Journal of Anxiety Disorders. 2001;15:413–32.

Munjack DJ, Baltazar PL, Bohn PB, Cabe DD, Appleton AA. Clonazepam in the treatment of social phobia: a pilot study. Journal of Clinical Psychiatry. 1990;51:35–40.

Muris P, Merckelbach H, Kindt M, Bogels S, Dreessen L, van Dorp C, et al. The utility of Screen for Child Anxiety Related Emotional Disorders (SCARED) as a tool for identifying children at high risk for prevalent anxiety disorders. Anxiety Stress and Coping. 2001;14:265–83.

Mykletun A, Bjerkeset O, Overland S, Prince M, Dewey M, Stewart R. Levels of anxiety and depression as predictors of mortality: the HUNT study. British Journal of Psychiatry. 2009;195:118–25.

Nardi AE, Lopes FL, Valenca AM, Freire RC, Nascimento I, Veras AB, et al. Double-blind comparison of 30 and 60 mg tranylcypromine daily in patients with panic disorder comorbid with social anxiety disorder. Psychiatry Research. 2010;175:260–5.

NCCMH. Depression in Children and Young People: Identification and Management in Primary, Community and Secondary Care. London: The British Psychological Society & The Royal College of Psychiatrists [Full guideline]; 2005.

NCCMH. Depression: The Treatment and Management of Depression in Adults. Updated edition. London & Leicester: The British Psychological Society and the Royal College of Psychiatrists [Full guideline]; 2010.

NCCMH. Common Mental Health Disorders: Identification and Pathways to Care. Leicester & London: The British Psychological Society and the Royal College of Psychiatrists [Full guideline]; 2011a.

NCCMH. Generalised Anxiety Disorder in Adults: Management in Primary, Secondary and Community Care. Leicester & London: The British Psychological Society & the Royal College of Psychiatrists [Full guideline]; 2011b.

NCCMH. Service User Experience in Adult Mental Health: Improving the Experience of Care for People Using Adult NHS Mental Health Services. Leicester & London: The British Psychological Society & the Royal College of Psychiatrists [Full guideline]; 2012.

NCCMH. Antisocial Behaviour and Conduct Disorders in Children and Young People: Recognition, Intervention and Management. London: The British Psychological Society and The Royal College of Psychiatrists; 2013.

Nepon J, Belik SL, Bolton J, Sareen J. The relationship between anxiety disorders and suicide attempts: findings from the National Epidemiologic Survey on Alcohol and Related Conditions. Depression and Anxiety. 2010;27:791–8.

Newman MG, Hofmann SG, Trabert W, Roth WT, Taylor CB. Does behavioral treatment of social phobia lead to cognitive changes? Behavior Therapy. 1994; 25:503–17.

NHS Business Services Authority Prescription Pricing Division. Electronic Drug Tariff for England and Wales, February 2013. Compiled on behalf of the Department of Health 2013.

NICE. Computerised Cognitive Behavioural Therapy for Depression and Anxiety. Review of Technology Appraisal 51. NICE Technology Appraisal Guidance 97. London: NICE; 2006. Available from: http://www.nice.org.uk/ta97.

NICE. Drug Misuse: Psychosocial Interventions. NICE clinical guideline 51. London: NICE; 2007. Available from: http://www.nice.org.uk/CG51. [NICE guideline].

NICE. Social Value Judgements: Principles for the Development of NICE Guidance. 2nd edn. London: NICE; 2008. Available from: http://www.nice.org.uk/aboutnice/ howwework/socialvaluejudgements/socialvaluejudgements.jsp.

NICE. Depression in Adults: The Treatment and Management of Depression in Adults. NICE clinical guideline 90. London: NICE; 2009a. Available from: www. nice.org.uk/CG90. [NICE guideline].

NICE. The Guidelines Manual. London: NICE; 2009b. Available from: http://www. nice.org.uk/guidelinesmanual.

NICE. Alcohol-use Disorders: Diagnosis, Assessment and Management of Harmful Drinking and Alcohol Dependence. NICE clinical guidance 115. London: NICE; 2011a. Available from: http://guidance.nice.org.uk/CG115. [NICE guideline].

NICE. Common Mental Health Disorders: Identification and Pathways to Care. NICE clinical guideline 123. London: NICE; 2011b. Available from: www.nice.org.uk/ CG123. [NICE guideline].

NICE. Generalised Anxiety Disorder and Panic Disorder (With or Without Agoraphobia) in Adults: Management in Primary, Secondary and Community Care. NICE clinical guideline 113. London: NICE; 2011c. Available from: www.nice. org.uk/CG113. [NICE guideline].

NICE. Service User Experience in Adult Mental Health: Improving the Experience of Care for People Using Adult NHS Mental Health Services. NICE clinical guideline 136. London: NICE; 2011d. Available from: www.nice.org.uk/CG136. [NICE guideline].

NICE. Patient Experience in Adult NHS Services: Improving the Experience of Care for People Using Adult NHS Services. NICE clinical guideline 138. London: NICE; 2012. Available from: www.nice.org.uk/CG138. [NICE guideline].

NICE. Guide to the Methods of Technology Appraisal 2013. London: NICE; 2013. Available from: http://www.nice.org.uk/aboutnice/howwework/devnicetech/Guide ToMethodsTechnologyAppraisal2008.jsp.

Nordgreen T, Havik OE, Ost LG, Furmark T, Carlbring P, Andersson G. Outcome predictors in guided and unguided self-help for social anxiety disorder. Behaviour Research and Therapy. 2012;50:13–21.

Norton PJ, Barrera, T. L. Transdiagnostic versus diagnosis-specific CBT for anxiety disorders: a preliminary randomized controlled noninferiority trial. Depression and Anxiety. 2012;29:874–82.

Noyes R Jr, Moroz G, Davidson JR, Liebowitz MR, Davidson A, Siegel J, et al. Moclobemide in social phobia: a controlled dose-response trial. Journal of Clinical Psychopharmacology. 1997;17:247–54.

Nunnally JC. Psychometric Theory. 3rd edn. New York: McGraw-Hill Inc.; 1994.

Oei TP, Moylan A, Evans L. Validity and clinical utility of the Fear Questionnaire for anxiety-disorder patients. Psychological Assessment: A Journal of Consulting and Clinical Psychology. 1991;3:391.

Olivares-Olivares PJ, Rosa-Alcázar AI, Olivares-Rodríguez J. Does individual attention improve the effect of group treatment of adolescents with social phobia? International Journal of Clinical and Health Psychology. 2008;8:465–81.

Oosterbaan DB, van Balkom AJLM, Spinhoven P, van Oppen P, van Dyck R. Cognitive therapy versus moclobemide in social phobia: a controlled study. Journal of Clinical Psychology and Psychotherapy. 2001;35:889–900.

Osman A, Kopper BA, Barrios FX, Osman JR, Wade T. The Beck Anxiety Inventory: Reexamination of factor structure and psychometric properties. Journal of Clinical Psychology. 1998;53:7–14.

Osório F, Crippa JA, Loureiro SR. A study of the discriminative validity of a screening tool (MINI-SPIN) for social anxiety disorder applied to Brazilian university students. European Psychiatry. 2007;22:239–43.

Ost LG, Ferebee I, Furmark T. One-session group therapy of spider phobia: direct versus indirect treatments. Behaviour Research and Therapy. 1997;35:721–32.

Ost LG, Alm T, Brandberg M, Breitholtz E. One vs five sessions of exposure and five sessions of cognitive therapy in the treatment of claustrophobia. Behaviour Research and Therapy. 2001;39:167–83.

Otto MW, Pollack MH, Gould RA, Worthington JJ, McArdle ET, Rosenbaum JF. A comparison of the efficacy of clonazepam and cognitive-behavioral group therapy for the treatment of social phobia. Journal of Anxiety Disorders. 2000;14:345–58.

Owen RT. Controlled-release fluvoxamine in obsessive-compulsive disorder and social phobia. Drugs of Today. 2008;44:887–93.

Paediatric Formulary Committee. BNF for Children. London: BMJ Group, Pharmaceutical Press, and RCPCH Publications; 2012–2013.

Pande AC, Davidson JR, Jefferson JW, Janney CA, Katzelnick DJ, Weisler RH, et al. Treatment of social phobia with gabapentin: a placebo-controlled study. Journal of Clinical Psychopharmacology. 1999;19:341–48.

Pande AC, Feltner DE, Jefferson JW, Davidson JR, Pollack M, Stein MB, et al. Efficacy of the novel anxiolytic pregabalin in social anxiety disorder: a placebo-controlled, multicenter study. Journal of Clinical Psychopharmacology. 2004;24:141–49.

Patel A, Knapp M, Henderson J, Baldwin D. The economic consequences of social phobia. Journal of Affective Disorders. 2002;68:221–33.

Pfizer. A 10-week, randomized, double-blind, placebo-controlled study of paroxetine and pregabalin in patients with social phobia (1008-081 and 1008-153). Web Synopsis Protocol 1008-081/153 - 21 June 2007 - Final. In press.

Piet J, Hougaard E, Hecksher MS, Rosenberg N. A randomized pilot study of mind-fulness-based cognitive therapy and group cognitive-behavioral therapy for young adults with social phobia. Scandinavian Journal of Psychology. 2010;51:403–10.

Pine DS, Cohen P, Gurley D, Brook J, Ma Y. The risk for early-adulthood anxiety and depressive disorders in adolescents with anxiety and depressive disorders. Archives of General Psychiatry. 1998;55:56–64.

Polit DF, Beck CT, Owen SV. Is the CVI an acceptable indicator of content validity? Appraisal and recommendations. Research in Nursing and Health. 2007;30:459–67.

Prasetyo J, Horacek J, Paskova B, Praskova H. Moclobemide and/or CBT in the treatment of social phobia: 6-months study. XII World Congress of Psychiatry, Yokohama, Japan, 9–24 August 2002.

Prasko JK. Pharmacotherapy and/or cognitive-behavioral therapy in the treatment of social phobia: control study with two year follow up. Ceska a Slovenska Psychiatrie. 2003;99:106–08.

Prasko J, Kosova J, Klaschka J, Seifertova D, Paskova H. Pharmacotherapy and psychotherapy in the treatment of social phobia: controlled study. XI World Congress of Psychiatry, Hamburg, 6–11 August 1999; Abstracts Volume II:94.

Prasko J, Horacek J, Paskova B. Moclobemide and/or CBT in the treatment of social phobia. 32nd Congress of the British Association for Behavioural and Cognitive Psychotherapies; Manchester, 7–11 September 2004.

Prasko J, Dockery C, Horacek J, Houbova P, Kosova J, Klaschka J, et al. Moclobemide and cognitive behavioral therapy in the treatment of social phobia. A six-month controlled study and 24 months follow up. Neuro Endocrinology Letters. 2006;27: 473–81.

Randall CL, Johnson MR, Thevos AK, Sonne SC, Thomas SE, Willard SL, et al. Paroxetine for social anxiety and alcohol use in dual-diagnosed patients. Depression and Anxiety. 2001a;14:255–62.

Randall CL, Thomas S, Thevos AK. Concurrent alcoholism and social anxiety disorder: a first step toward developing effective treatments. Alcoholism: Clinical and Experimental Research. 2001b;25:210–20.

Ranta K, Kaltiala-Heino R, Rantanen P, Marttunen M. Social phobia in Finnish general adolescent population: prevalence, comorbidity, individual and family correlates, and service use. Depression and Anxiety. 2009;26:528–36.

Rapee RM. Overcoming Shyness and Social Phobia: A Step by Step Guide. Lanham, MD: Jason Aronson; 1998.

Rapee RM, Abbott MJ, Lyneham HJ. Bibliotherapy for children with anxiety disorders using written materials for parents: a randomized controlled trial. Journal of Consulting and Clinical Psychology. 2006;74:436–44.

Rapee RM, Abbott MJ, Baillie AJ, Gaston JE. Treatment of social phobia through pure self-help and therapist-augmented self-help. British Journal of Psychiatry. 2007;191:246–52.

Rapee RM, Gaston JE, Abbott MJ. Testing the efficacy of theoretically derived improvements in the treatment of social phobia. Journal of Consulting and Clinical Psychology. 2009;77:317–27.

Ravindran LN, Kim DS, Letamendi AM, Stein MB. A randomized controlled trial of atomoxetine in generalized social anxiety disorder. Journal of Clinical Psychopharmacology. 2009;29:561–64.

Reich J, Goldenberg I, Goisman R, Vasile R, Keller M. A prospective, follow-along study of the course of social phobia: II. Testing for basic predictors of course. The Journal of Nervous and Mental Disease. 1994a;182:297–301.

Reich J, Goldenberg I, Vasile R, Goisman R, Keller M. A prospective follow-along study of the course of social phobia. Psychiatry Research. 1994b;54:249–58.

Renner KA. Overall effectiveness and cognitive mediators of a brief intensive treatment for social anxiety. Dissertation Abstracts International: Section B: The Sciences and Engineering. 2008;69.

Revicki DA, Wood M. Patient-assigned health state utilities for depression-related outcomes: differences by depression severity and antidepressant medications. Journal of Affective Disorders. 1998;48:25–36.

Rickels K, Mangano R, Khan A. A double-blind, placebo-controlled study of a flexible dose of venlafaxine ER in adult outpatients with generalized social anxiety disorder. Journal of Clinical Psychopharmacology. 2004;24:488–96.

Roberson-Nay R, Strong DR, Nay WT, Beidel DC, Turner SM, Roberson-Nay R, et al. Development of an abbreviated Social Phobia and Anxiety Inventory (SPAI) using item response theory: the SPAI-23. Psychological Assessment. 2007;19:133–45.

Robillard G, Bouchard S, Dumoulin S, Guitard T, Klinger E. Using virtual humans to alleviate social anxiety: preliminary report from a comparative outcome study. Studies in Health Technology and Informatics. 2010;154:2010.

Rodebaugh TL, Chambless DL, Terrill DR, Floyd M, Uhde T. Convergent, discriminant, and criterion-related validity of the Social Phobia and Anxiety Inventory. Depression and Anxiety. 2000;11:10–14.

Rosenbaum JF, Fava M, Hoog SL, Ascroft RC, Krebs WB. Selective serotonin reuptake inhibitor discontinuation syndrome: a randomized clinical trial. Biological Psychiatry. 1998;44:77–87.

Ross J. Social phobia: the Anxiety Disorders Associated of America helps raise the veil of ignorance. Journal of Clinical Psychiatry. 1991;52 (Suppl.):43–7.

Rytwinski NK, Fresco DM, Heimberg RG, Coles ME, Liebowitz MR, Cissell S, et al. Screening for social anxiety disorder with the self-report version of the Liebowitz Social Anxiety Scale. Depression and Anxiety. 2009;26:34–38.

Saarni SI, Suvisaari J, Sintonen H, Pirkola S, Koskinen S, Aromaa A, et al. Impact of psychiatric disorders on health-related quality of life: general population survey. The British Journal of Psychiatry. 2007;190:326–32.

Salaberria K, Echeburua E. Long-term outcome of cognitive therapy's contribution to self-exposure in vivo to the treatment of generalized social phobia. Behavior Modification. 1998;22:262–84.

Sanderson WC, Wetzler S, Beck AT, Betz F. Prevalence of personality disorders among patients with anxiety disorders. Psychiatry Research. 1994;51:167–74.

Sattler JM. Assessment of Children: Cognitive Applications (4th ed.). San Diego: Jerome M. Sattler Publisher Inc; 2001.

Scharfstein L, Beidel D, Finnell LR, Distler A, Carter N. Do pharmacological and behavioral interventions differentially affect treatment outcome for children with social phobia? Behavior Modification. 2011;35:451–67.

Schmidt NB, Richey JA, Buckner JD, Timpano KR. Attention training for generalized social anxiety disorder. Journal of Abnormal Psychology. 2009;118:5–14.

Schneider AJ, Mataix-Cols D, Marks IM, Bachofen M, Schneider AJ, Mataix-Cols D, et al. Internet-guided self-help with or without exposure therapy for phobic and panic disorders. Psychotherapy and Psychosomatics. 2005;74:154–64.

Schneier FR, Goetz D, Campeas R, Fallon B, Marshall R, Liebowitz MR. Placebo-controlled trial of moclobemide in social phobia. British Journal of Psychiatry. 1998;172:70–77.

Schutters SI, Van Megen HJ, Van Veen JF, Denys DA, Westenberg HG. Mirtazapine in generalized social anxiety disorder: a randomized, double-blind, placebo-controlled study. International Clinical Psychopharmacology. 2010;25:302–04.

Schwartz RH, Freedy AS, Sheridan MJ, Schwartz RH, Freedy AS, Sheridan MJ. Selective mutism: are primary care physicians missing the silence? Clinical Pediatrics. 2006;45:43–48.

Seedat S, Stein MB. Double-blind, placebo-controlled assessment of combined clonazepam with paroxetine compared with paroxetine monotherapy for generalized social anxiety disorder. Journal of Clinical Psychiatry. 2004;65:244–48.

Seeley-Wait E, Abbott MJ, Rapee RM. Psychometric properties of the Mini-SPIN. The Primary Care Companion to the Journal of Clinical Psychiatry. 2009;11: 231–36.

Servant D, Montgomery SA, Francois C, Despiegel N. Cost-effectiveness of escitalopram versus placebo in relapse prevention in patients with social anxiety disorder. Value in Health. 2003;6:351–51.

Shaw P. A comparison of three behaviour therapies in the treatment of social phobia. British Journal of Psychiatry. 1979;134:620–23.

Silverman WK, Albano AM. Anxiety Disorders Interview Schedule (ADIS-IV) Child and Parent Interview Schedules. Oxford: Oxford University Press; 1996.

Simon NM, Otto MW, Wisniewski SR, Fossey M, Sagduyu K, Frank E, et al. Anxiety disorder comorbidity in bipolar disorder patients: data from the first 500 participants in the Systematic Treatment Enhancement Program for Bipolar Disorder (STEP-BD). The American Journal of Psychiatry. 2004;161:2222–9.

Simon NM, Worthington JJ, Moshier SJ, Marks EH, Hoge EA, Brandes M, et al. Duloxetine for the treatment of generalized social anxiety disorder: a preliminary randomized trial of increased dose to optimize response. CNS Spectrums. 2010;15: 367–73.

Simonoff E, Pickles A, Charman T, Chandler S, Loucas T, Baird G. Psychiatric disorders in children with autism spectrum disorders: prevalence, comorbidity, and associated factors in a population-derived sample. Journal of the American Academy of Child and Adolescent Psychiatry. 2008;47:921–9.

Simpson HB, Fallon BA. Obsessive-compulsive disorder: an overview. Journal of Psychiatric Practice. 2000;6:3–17.

Singleton N, Bumpstead R, O'Brien M, Lee A, Meltzer H. Psychiatric morbidity among adults living in private households. London: The Stationery Office; 2001.

Sir A, D'Souza RF, Uguz S, George T, Vahip S, Hopwood M, et al. Randomized trial of sertraline versus venlafaxine XR in major depression: efficacy and discontinuation symptoms. Journal of Clinical Psychiatry. 2005;66:1312–20.

Smith KL, Kirkby KC, Montgomery IM, Daniels BA. Computer-delivered modeling of exposure for spider phobia: relevant versus irrelevant exposure. Journal of Anxiety Disorders. 1997;11:489–97.

Smits JA, Powers MB, Buxkamper R, Telch MJ. The efficacy of videotape feedback for enhancing the effects of exposure-based treatment for social anxiety disorder: a controlled investigation. Behaviour Research and Therapy. 2006;44:1773–85.

Sonntag H, Wittchen HU, Hofler M, Kessler RC, Stein MB. Are social fears and DSM-IV social anxiety disorder associated with smoking and nicotine dependence in adolescents and young adults? European Psychiatry. 2000;15:67–74.

Spence SH, Donovan C, Brechman-Toussaint M. The treatment of childhood social phobia: the effectiveness of a social skills training-based, cognitive-behavioural intervention, with and without parental involvement. Journal of Child Psychology and Psychiatry and Allied Disciplines. 2000;41:713–26.

Spence SH, Barrett PM, Turner CM. Psychometric properties of the Spence Children's Anxiety Scale with young adolescents. Journal of Anxiety Disorders. 2003;17:605–25.

Spence SH, Donovan CL, March S, Gamble A, Anderson RE, Prosser S, et al. A randomized controlled trial of online versus clinic-based CBT for adolescent anxiety. Journal of Consulting and Clinical Psychology. 2011;79:629–42.

Spiegelhalter DJ. Bayesian methods for cluster randomized trials with continuous responses. Statistics in Medicine. 2001;20:435–52.

Stangier U, Heidenreich T, Peitz M, Lauterbach W, Clark DM. Cognitive therapy for social phobia: individual versus group treatment. Behaviour Research and Therapy. 2003;41:991–1007.

Stangier U, Schramm E, Heidenreich T, Berger M, Clark DM. Cognitive therapy vs interpersonal psychotherapy in social anxiety disorder: A randomized controlled trial. Archives of General Psychiatry. 2011;68:692–700.

Stein DJ, Berk M, Els C, Emsley RA, Gittelson L, Wilson D, et al. A double-blind placebo-controlled trial of paroxetine in the management of social phobia (social anxiety disorder) in South Africa. South African Medical Journal. 1999;89:402–06.

Stein D, Ipser J, van Balkom A. Pharmacotherapy for social anxiety disorder. Cochrane Database of Systematic Reviews. 2000:CD001206.

Stein DJ, Stein MB, Goodwin W, Kumar R, Hunter B. The selective serotonin reuptake inhibitor paroxetine is effective in more generalized and in less generalized social anxiety disorder. Psychopharmacology. 2001;158:267–72.

Stein DJ, Cameron A, Amrein R, Montgomery SA. Moclobemide is effective and well tolerated in the long-term pharmacotherapy of social anxiety disorder with or without comorbid anxiety disorder. International Clinical Psychopharmacology. 2002a;17:161–70.

Stein DJ, Versiani M, Hair T, Kumar R. Efficacy of paroxetine for relapse prevention in social anxiety disorder: a 24–week study. Archives of General Psychiatry. 2002b;59:1111–18.

Stein DJ, Westenberg HG, Yang H, Li D, Barbato LM. Fluvoxamine CR in the long-term treatment of social anxiety disorder: the 12- to 24-week extension phase of a multicentre, randomized, placebo-controlled trial. International Journal of Neuropsychopharmacology. 2003;6:317–23.

Stein DJ, Andersen EW, Lader M. Escitalopram versus paroxetine for social anxiety disorder: an analysis of efficacy for different symptom dimensions. European Neuropsychopharmacology. 2006;16:33–38.

Stein MB, Chartier MJ, Hazen AL, Kozak MV, Tancer ME, Lander S, et al. A direct-interview family study of generalized social phobia. The American Journal of Psychiatry. 1998a;155:90–7.

Stein MB, Liebowitz MR, Lydiard RB, Pitts CD, Bushnell W, Gergel I. Paroxetine treatment of generalized social phobia (social anxiety disorder): a randomized controlled trial. Journal of the American Medical Association. 1998b;280:708–13.

Stein MB, Fyer AJ, Davidson JR, Pollack MH, Wiita B. Fluvoxamine treatment of social phobia (social anxiety disorder): a double-blind, placebo-controlled study. American Journal of Psychiatry. 1999a;156:756–60.

Stein MB, McQuaid JR, Laffaye C, McCahill ME. Social phobia in the primary care medical setting. The Journal of Family Practice. 1999b;48:514–9.

Stein MB, Pollack MH, Bystritsky A, Kelsey JE, Mangano RM. Efficacy of low and higher dose extended-release venlafaxine in generalized social anxiety disorder: a 6-month randomized controlled trial. Psychopharmacology. 2005; 177:280–88.

Stinson FS, Dawson DA, Patricia Chou S, Smith S, Goldstein RB, June Ruan W, et al. The epidemiology of DSM-IV specific phobia in the USA: results from the National Epidemiologic Survey on Alcohol and Related Conditions. Psychological Medicine. 2007;37:1047–59.

Stone M, Laughren T, Jones ML, Levenson M, Holland PC, Hughes A, et al. Risk of suicidality in clinical trials of antidepressants in adults: analysis of proprietary data submitted to US Food and Drug Administration. BMJ. 2009;339:b2880.

Stravynski A, Arbel N, Bounader J, Gaudette G, Lachance L, Borgeat F, et al. Social phobia treated as a problem in social functioning: a controlled comparison of two behavioural group approaches. Acta Psychiatrica Scandinavica. 2000;102:188–98.

Sutherland SM, Tupler LA, Colket JT, Davidson JR. A 2–year follow-up of social phobia. Status after a brief medication trial. Journal of Nervous and Mental Disease. 1996;184:731–38.

Swenson JR, Doucette S, Fergusson D. Adverse cardiovascular events in antidepressant trials involving high-risk patients: a systematic review of randomized trials. Canadian Journal of Psychiatry Revue Canadienne de Psychiatrie. 2006;51:923–9.

Taylor D. Antidepressant drugs and cardiovascular pathology: a clinical overview of effectiveness and safety. Acta Psychiatrica Scandinavica. 2008;118:434–42.

Taylor D, Stewart S, Connolly A. Antidepressant withdrawal symptoms: telephone calls to a national medication helpline. Journal of Affective Disorders. 2006;95:129–33.

Thirlwall K, Cooper P, Karalus J, Voysey M, Willetts L, Creswell C. The treatment of child anxiety disorders via guided CBT self-help: randomised controlled trial. Under review. 2012.

Thyer BA. Cognitive behavioral group therapy and phenelzine both effective in social phobia. Western Journal of Medicine. 1999;171:240.

Tillfors M. Why do some individuals develop social phobia? A review with emphasis on the neurobiological influences. Nordic Journal of Psychiatry. 2004;58:267–76.

Tillfors M, Carlbring P, Furmark T, Lewenhaupt S, Spak M, Eriksson A, et al. Treating university students with social phobia and public speaking fears: internet delivered self-help with or without live group exposure sessions. Depression and Anxiety. 2008;25:708–17.

Tillfors M, Andersson G, Ekselius L, Furmark T, Lewenhaupt S, Karlsson A, et al. A randomized trial of internet-delivered treatment for social anxiety disorder in high school students. Cognitive Behaviour Therapy. 2011;40:147–57.

Tint A, Haddad PM, Anderson IM. The effect of rate of antidepressant tapering on the incidence of discontinuation symptoms: a randomised study. Journal of Psychopharmacology. 2008;22:330–2.

Titov N, Andrews G, Choi I, Schwencke G, Mahoney A. Shyness 3: randomized controlled trial of guided versus unguided internet-based CBT for social phobia. Australian and New Zealand Journal of Psychiatry. 2008a;42:1030–40.

Titov N, Andrews G, Schwencke G. Shyness 2: treating social phobia online: replication and extension. Australian and New Zealand Journal of Psychiatry. 2008b; 42:595–605.

Titov N, Andrews G, Schwencke G, Drobny J, Einstein D. Shyness 1: distance treatment of social phobia over the internet. Australian and New Zealand Journal of Psychiatry. 2008c;42:585–94.

Titov N, Andrews G, Choi I, Schwencke G, Johnston L. Randomized controlled trial of web-based treatment of social phobia without clinician guidance. Australian and New Zealand Journal of Psychiatry. 2009a;43:913–19.

Titov N, Andrews G, Johnston L, Schwencke G, Choi I. Shyness programme: longer term benefits, cost-effectiveness, and acceptability. (Provisional abstract). Australian and New Zealand Journal of Psychiatry. 2009b;43:36–44.

Titov N, Andrews G, Schwencke G, Solley K, Johnston L, Robinson E. An RCT comparing effect of two types of support on severity of symptoms for people completing internet-based cognitive behaviour therapy for social phobia. Australian and New Zealand Journal of Psychiatry. 2009c;43:920–26.

Titov N, Gibson M, Andrews G, McEvoy P. Internet treatment for social phobia reduces comorbidity. Australian and New Zealand Journal of Psychiatry. 2009d;43:754–9.

Titov N, Andrews G, Schwencke G, Robinson E, Peters L, Spence J. Randomized controlled trial of internet cognitive behavioural treatment for social phobia with and without motivational enhancement strategies. Australian and New Zealand Journal of Psychiatry. 2010;44:938–45.

Tortella-Feliu M, Botella C, Llabrés J, Bretón-López JM, del Amo AR, Baños RM, et al. Virtual reality versus computer-aided exposure treatments for fear of flying. Behavior Modification. 2011;35:3–30.

Turk CL, Heimberg RG, Orsillo SM, Holt CS, Gitow A, Street LL, et al. An investigation of gender differences in social phobia. Journal of Anxiety Disorders. 1998;12:209–23.

Turner SM, Beidel DC, Dancu CV. Social Phobia and Anxiety Inventory: Manual. Toronto: Multi-Health Systems Inc.; 1996.

Vaishnavi S, Alamy S, Zhang W, Connor KM, Davidson JR. Quetiapine as monotherapy for social anxiety disorder: a placebo-controlled study. Progress in Neuro-Psychopharmacology and Biological Psychiatry. 2007;31:1464–69.

Van Ameringen M, Swinson R, Walker JR, Lane RM. A placebo-controlled study of sertraline in generalized social phobia. Journal of the European College of Neuropsychopharmacology. 1999;9:S235.

Van Ameringen MA, Lane RM, Walker JR, Bowen RC, Chokka PR, Goldner EM, et al. Sertraline treatment of generalized social phobia: a 20–week, double-blind, placebo-controlled study. American Journal of Psychiatry. 2001;158:275–81.

Van Ameringen M, Mancini C, Farvolden P. The impact of anxiety disorders on educational achievement. Journal of Anxiety Disorders. 2003;17:561–71.

Van Ameringen M, Oakman J, Mancini C, Pipe B, Chung H. Predictors of response in generalized social phobia: effect of age of onset. Journal of Clinical Psychopharmacology. 2004;24:42–48.

Van Gastel WF. Screening capacity of the Multidimensional Anxiety Scale for Children (MASC) for DSM-IV anxiety disorders. Depression and Anxiety. 2008;25: 1046–52.

Van Vliet IM, den Boer JA, Westenberg HG. Psychopharmacological treatment of social phobia: clinical and biochemical effects of brofaromine, a selective MAO-A inhibitor. European Neuropsychopharmacology. 1992;2:21–29.

Van Vliet IM, Boer JA, Westenberg HGM. Psychopharmacological treatment of social phobia; a double blind placebo controlled study with fluvoxamine. Psychopharmacology. 1994;115:128–34.

Versiani M, Nardi AE, Mundim FD, Alves AB, Liebowitz MR, Amrein R. Pharmacotherapy of social phobia. A controlled study with moclobemide and phenelzine. British Journal of Psychiatry. 1992;161:353–60.

Viana AG, Beidel DC, Rabian B. Selective mutism: a review and integration of the last 15 years. Clinical Psychology Review. 2009;29:57–67.

Walker JRV. Prevention of relapse in generalized social phobia: results of a 24-week study in responders to 20 weeks of sertraline treatment. Journal of Clinical Psychopharmacology. 2000;20:636–44.

Walker JR, Ameringen MAV, Swinson RP, Lane RM, eds. A 24-week prevention of relapse of generalized social phobia study in responders to 20 weeks of sertraline treatment. 155th Annual Meeting of the American Psychiatric Association, Philadelphia, PA, 18–23 May 2002.

Wang PS, Lane M, Olfson M, Pincus HA, Wells KB, Kessler RC. Twelve-month use of mental health services in the United States: results from the National Comorbidity Survey Replication. Archives of General Psychiatry. 2005;62:629–40.

Watson D, Friend R. Measurement of social-evaluative anxiety. Journal of Consulting and Clinical Psychology. 1969;33:448–57.

Weeks JW, Spokas ME, Heimberg RG. Psychometric evaluation of the mini-social phobia inventory (Mini-SPIN) in a treatment-seeking sample. Depression and Anxiety. 2007;24:382–91.

Wei Y, Higgins JPT. Estimating within-study covariances in multivariate meta-analysis with multiple outcomes. Statistics in Medicine. 2013;32:1191–205.

Weinrieb RM, Auriacombe M, Lynch KG, Chang KM, Lewis JD. A critical review of selective serotonin reuptake inhibitor-associated bleeding: balancing the risk of treating hepatitis C-infected patients. Journal of Clinical Psychiatry. 2003;64:1502–10.

Werneke U, Northey S, Bhugra D. Antidepressants and sexual dysfunction. Acta Psychiatrica Scandinavica. 2006;114:384–97.

Wernicke J, Lledo A, Raskin J, Kajdasz DK, Wang F. An evaluation of the cardiovascular safety profile of duloxetine: findings from 42 placebo-controlled studies. Drug Safety. 2007;30:437–55.

Westenberg HG, Stein DJ, Yang H, Li D, Barbato LM. A double-blind placebo-controlled study of controlled release fluvoxamine for the treatment of generalized social anxiety disorder. Journal of Clinical Psychopharmacology. 2004;24:49–55.

Whisman MA, Sheldon CT, Goering P. Psychiatric disorders and dissatisfaction with social relationships: does type of relationship matter? Journal of Abnormal Psychology. 2000;109:803–8.

Wiltink J, Ruckes C, Haselbacher A, Canterino M, Leichsenring F, Joraschky P, et al. Transfer of manualized short term psychodynamic psychotherapy (STPP) for social phobia into clinical practice: study protocol for a cluster-randomised controlled trial. Trials. 2011;12:142.

Wittchen HU, Fehm L. Epidemiology and natural course of social fears and social phobia. Acta Psychiatrica Scandinavica Supplementum. 2003:4–18.

Wittchen HU, Jacobi F. Size and burden of mental disorders in Europe: a critical review and appraisal of 27 studies. European Neuropsychopharmacology. 2005; 15:357–76.

Wittchen HU, Fuetsch M, Sonntag H, Muller N, Liebowitz M. Disability and quality of life in pure and comorbid social phobia: findings from a controlled study. European Psychiatry. 1999a;14:118–31.

Wittchen HU, Stein MB, Kessler RC. Social fears and social phobia in a community sample of adolescents and young adults: prevalence, risk factors and co-morbidity. Psychological Medicine. 1999b;29:309–23.

Wittchen H-U, Lecrubier Y, Beesdo K, Nocon A. Relationships among anxiety disorders: patterns and implications. In: Nutt DJ, Ballenger JC, eds. Anxiety Disorders. Malden, MA: Blackwell; 2007. p. 23–37.

Wolpe J. Psychotherapy by reciprocal inhibition. Conditional Reflex. 1968;3:234–40.

Wong DFK, Sun SYK. A preliminary study of the efficacy of group cognitive-behavioural therapy for people with social anxiety in Hong Kong. Hong Kong Journal of Psychiatry. 2007;16:50–56.

World Health Organization. The ICD-10 Classification of Mental and Behavioural Disorders: Clinical Description and Diagnostic Guidelines. Geneva: World Health Organization; 1992.

Wren FJ, Berg EA, Heiden LA, Kinnamon CJ, Ohlson LA, Bridge JA, et al. Childhood anxiety in a diverse primary care population: parent-child reports, ethnicity and SCARED factor structure. Journal of the American Academy of Child and Adolescent Psychiatry. 2007;46:332–40.

Young BJ, Beidel DC, Turner SM, Ammerman RT, McGraw K, Coaston SC. Pretreatment attrition and childhood social phobia: parental concerns about medication. Journal of Anxiety Disorders. 2006;20:1133–47.

Yuan Y, Tsoi K, Hunt RH. Selective serotonin reuptake inhibitors and risk of upper GI bleeding: confusion or confounding? The American Journal of Medicine. 2006;119:719–27.

Zamora J, Abraira V, Muriel A, Khan K, Coomarasamy A. Meta-DiSc: a software for meta-analysis of test accuracy data. BMC Medical Research Methodology. 2006;6:31.

Zhang W, Connor KM, Davidson JR. Levetiracetam in social phobia: a placebo controlled pilot study. Journal of Psychopharmacology. 2005;19:551–53.

12 ABBREVIATIONS

ADHD	attention deficit hyperactivity disorder
AEI	Australian Education Index
AGREE	Appraisal of Guidelines for Research and Evaluation
AMED	Allied and Complementary Medicine Database
APD	avoidant personality disorder
ASSIA	Applied Social Services Index and Abstracts
AUC	area under the curve
BAT	behavioural approach test
BEI	British Education Index
BNF	*British National Formulary*
CAMHS	child and adolescent mental health service
CBT	cognitive behavioural therapy
CCBT	computerised CBT
CDSR	Cochrane Database of Systematic Reviews
CENTRAL	Cochrane database of RCTs and other controlled trials
CI	confidence interval
CINAHL	Cumulative Index to Nursing and Allied Health Literature
CrI	credible interval
CRD	Centre for Reviews and Dissemination
CT	cognitive therapy
DARE	Cochrane Database of Abstracts of Reviews of Effects
df	degrees of freedom
DSM-IV-TR	*Diagnostic and Statistical Manual of Mental Disorders,* 4th Edition Text Revision
Embase	Excerpta Medica Database
EQ-5D	European Quality of Life – 5 Dimensions
ERIC	Education Resources in Curriculum
GAD(-2)	Generalised Anxiety Disorder scale (two-item)
GDG	Guideline Development Group
GP	general practitioner
GRADE	Grading of Recommendations Assessment, Development and Evaluation
GSK	GlaxoSmithKline

HMIC	Health Management Information Consortium
HRQoL	health-related quality of life
HTA	health technology assessment
IAPT	Improving Access to Psychological Therapies
IBSS	International Bibliography of Social Science
ICD-10	*International Classification of Diseases*, 10th Revision
ICER	incremental cost-effectiveness ratio
IPT	interpersonal psychotherapy
K	number of studies
LOR	log-odds ratio
LR–	negative likelihood ratio
LR+	positive likelihood ratio
LSAS(-SR)	Liebowitz Social Anxiety Scale (-Self-Report)
MAO	monoamine oxidase
MAOI	monoamine oxidase inhibitors
MASC	Multidimensional Anxiety Scale for Children
MEDLINE	Medical Literature Analysis and Retrieval System Online
Mini-SPIN	Mini Social Phobia Inventory
MHRA	Medicines and Healthcare products Regulatory Agency
NA	not applicable
NCCMH	National Collaborating Centre for Mental Health
NHS	National Health Service
NICE	National Institute of Health and Care Excellence
NMA	network meta-analysis
NMB	net monetary benefit
N/R	not reported
NSPCR	NIHR School for Primary Care Research
OCD	obsessive-compulsive disorder
OIS	optimal information size
PC	personal computer
PICO	population, intervention, comparison and outcome
PreMEDLINE	National Library of Medicine's in-process database for MEDLINE
PSS	personal social services

PsycBOOKS	A full-text database of books and chapters in the American Psychological Association's electronic databases
PsycEXTRA	A grey literature database, which is a companion to PsycINFO
PsycINFO	Psychological Information Database
PTSD	post-traumatic stress disorder
QALY	quality of life year
QTc	corrected QT interval
RCT	randomised controlled trial
ROC	receiver operator characteristics
RQ	review question
RR	relative risk
SCARED	Screen for Child Anxiety Related Emotional Disorders
SCAS	Spence Children's Anxiety Scale
SCID-SP(-entry)	Social Phobia module of the Structured Clinical Interview for DSM Disorders (entry question)
SD	standard deviation
SE	standard error
SF(-36, -6D)	Short Form Questionnaire (36 items, Six Dimensional Health State Classification)
SG	standard gamble
SIAS	Social Interaction Anxiety Scale
SMD	standardised mean difference
SMD^N	SMD from the NMA
SNRI	serotonin and noradrenaline reuptake inhibitor
SPAI-C	Social Phobia Anxiety Inventory (for Children)
SPIN	Social Phobia Inventory
SPQ(-Anx)	Social Phobia Questionnaire (Anxiety subscale)
SSA	Social Services Abstracts
SSCI	Social Sciences Citation Index – Web of Science
SSRI	selective serotonin reuptake inhibitor
TA	Technology Appraisal
TCA	tricyclic antidepressant
T/F	true/false
TTO	time trade-off technique
WTP	willingness to pay
YLD	years lived with disability